Science, Not Sorcery:

Behavioral Economics for Marketers

Rebecca L. Sullivan

Copyright © 2026 Rebecca L. Sullivan

ISBN: 979-8-9944091-0-7

All rights reserved

Published in 2026 by Olive, Ember & Ink Press
Lansing, Michigan.

For information or permission to reproduce selections from this book, find contact information at
www.oliveemberandinkpress.com.

To

Sean and Kate,
who make everything worthwhile.

Contents

Introduction 13
Storytelling 19
    Why Stories Matter 20
    Better Brand Storytelling 21
        The Halo Effect and First Impressions 22
        Making Stories Memorable 23
        Relevance, Specificity, and Focus 32
        Authenticity and Credibility 34
        Clarity of Message 36
        Cohesive Narrative and Personality 38
        Tension, Resolution, Engagement 48
        On The Villain 52
        Relatability 56
        Happily Ever After & Peak-End 64
    Becoming a Better Brand Storyteller 69
Emotional Engagement 71
    Brands as Somatic Markers 72
        Backstory: The Heart vs. the Head 73
        The Somatic Marker Hypothesis 78
        Leveraging Somatic Markers to Build Brand Equity 83
    Brands as People 99
        Building Brand Equity through Anthropomorphism 101
    Appealing to Emotions Across Marketing Work 120

    Promotional Messaging.. 121
    Generating Word-of-Mouth 123
    Usability 123
    Appealing to the Senses.. 124
    Omnichannel Support 128
    CSR, Causes, and Politics... 131
Final Thoughts on Emotion and Marketing.................................... 137

Beating the Competition 141

Systematic Nudging 142
    Identify the Desired Behavior 142
    Evaluate Incentives and Deterrents 143
    The Good Old CBA 144
    Refining the Choice Architecture 145
Combatting Choice Overload... 146
    Options Can Be Damaging for Businesses and Consumers. 149
    Finding the Goldilocks Choice Set... 152
The Art of Framing.. 157
    Risk, Framing, and Choice 158
    Attribute Framing and Promotional Strategy 160
    Goal Framing.. 164
Positioning and The Great Homogenization 170
    Be the Tiger Tail.. 171
    Framing vs. Positioning 173
Anchoring 174
    Implications for Pricing 177
The Default Effect.. 181

- Becoming the Default 182
- Priming 184
  - Implications for the Marketing Mix 186
  - Context Effects 188
- Balancing Cost, Risk, Complexity, and Attention 193
  - Risky Decisions 193
  - Costly Decisions 195
  - Complex Decisions 195
  - Attention 196
- Projection Bias 197
  - Marketing Implications Depend on the Time Frame 199
- Personalization and Messaging 202
  - Buzzfeed and The Forer Effect 204
- Relatable Marketing & Base Rate Neglect 207
- Leveraging Loss Aversion to Incentivize Switching 211
- The Halo and Horns Effects 212
- Adaptation Effects, The Hedonic Treadmill, and Marketing Messages 215
  - What does your audience want from you? 216
- Go Forth and Slay the Competition 219

Loyalty and Retention 221
- Changes, Expectations, and Retention 222
  - Framing Changes 223
- Fairness 227
  - The Ultimatum Game 228
  - What is Fair? 231

- Pricing Implications 234
- Retention and Intent 235
- Bottom Line on Retention and Fairness 236

Loyalty 237
- Identity or Reality? 237
- Identity and Loyalty 240
- Growth *versus* Loyalty or Growth *is* Loyalty? 246
- A Final Word on Loyalty Campaigns 251

Cognitive Biases That Influence Retention 251
- Status Quo Bias and Mere Exposure 252
- Endowment Effect 254
- Loss Aversion and Anticipated Regret 256
- Loss Aversion & Retention 258
- LinkedIn Emphasizes Losses to Improve Retention 259
- Gilt Balances Urgency and Credibility 260
- Sonos: A Cautionary Tale 262
- Best Practices 268

Customers Want to Like You 270

Increase Engagement with Ziegarnik 271

Temporal Discounting and Subscription Design 273
- Temporal Discounting and Consumer Behavior 274
- Implications for Delayed Gratification Brands 275
- Implications for Immediate Gratification Brands 277
- Planning for Temporal Discounting 278

Mental Accounting and Customer Growth 278
- Mental Accounting and Your Brand 280

Final Notes on Loyalty and Retention 282
Research and Planning **285**
   Consumers Don't Know Why: Should we ask? 286
      Love & Branding 287
      The Inherent Problems with Asking Why 290
      Research Implications of Inaccurate Introspection 291
   Profiling Customers 294
      Writing Better Personas 296
      Types of Personas 297
      Context Is Everything 301
      Profiling Advice Potpourri 303
      Researching Identity 307
   Case Studies Are Not Evidence 309
      First, The Caveats 309
      We See Patterns That Aren't There 310
      It's Hard to Separate Fact from Fiction 311
      Success is Somewhat Random 315
      Let's Get Smarter 316
   You Can't Overestimate the Impact of Culture 316
      Can You See Blue? 317
      Multicultural Research 318
      Applying Cross-Cultural Insights 319
      A Brief Survey of Cross-Cultural Research Methods 320
      Quantifying Cultural Differences 327
      Using Customer Journey Research to Refine Messages 331
      Don't Underestimate Cross-Cultural Insights 333

Better Brainstorming 334
    Preserving Diversity of Thought 335
    Thinking Inside the Box 336
    Considering the Group Makeup 337
    Spurring Innovation with Dissent 338
Knowing When to Start Planning 339
    Zero-Sum Bias in Planning 341
No, We Didn't Already Know This: Hindsight Bias in Research and Planning 346
    Experiments 347
    Application: Improving Insights Operations 349
Anticipating the Future: Why We're Just Awful at It. 354
    Projection Bias and New Year's Resolutions 354
    Projection Bias: Not Only for the Small Stuff 355
    Adding Optimism Bias to the Mix 356
    Application: Making Better Plans 357
Framing for Internal Decision-Making 362
    Reframing and the Challenger Launch 363
    Planning Opportunity: Form a Red Team 365
    Management Imperative: Align Incentives by Reframing ... 366
Cutting Your Losses 371
    The Sunk Cost Effect 371
    Adding Loss Aversion, Endowment Effect, and Ziegarnik Effect 373
    Overcoming Bias and Leaving the Past Behind 374
Focus on What You Can Change 377

In Closing	379
References	383
Endnotes	419
Acknowledgments	451
Index	453

Introduction

Marketing isn't sorcery; it's science.

Presentations at elementary school assemblies can be a bit of a mixed bag: Sometimes you get ice cream, and sometimes you get a dentist telling you to floss more often. The best presentation of my elementary school years was delivered by wizards. Dressed in lab coats and goggles, they combined ingredients with exotic-sounding names I didn't understand to create a ball of fire. They blew up a bottle of soda using only magic and Mentos, which I had previously considered the most boring candy. They also used magical potions to make a foam that exploded from beakers and splattered all over the gym floor—and didn't get in trouble. We were mesmerized: These people were only a few years older than us and had already mastered sorcery!

The group presenting was called The Science Wizards. When they weren't blowing the minds of children, they were just high school chemistry students who understood that the razzle-dazzle wasn't wizardry, but simple chemical reactions.

In this way, marketers are like The Science Wizards. The handiwork of smart practitioners can look like magic to those that don't understand the science underpinning their work.

In our globalized, connected world, competition is fierce for businesses of all kinds. Faced with a global marketplace with endless competition and infinite substitutes, the only chance for businesses to succeed is to outsmart the competition. Doing so requires a scientific approach to marketing.

This brings us to the problem: Too many marketers understand the art of the profession—the razzle-dazzle—but they neglect the science. As a marketing professional, you have probably worked with people who have successfully relied on an intuitive understanding of what is popular or attractive; however, they have rarely if ever bothered to study the science behind what works.

As competition mounts and margins tighten, marketers will increasingly need to prove their worth. By investing time and effort into understanding the science behind marketing, professionals in this field can develop smarter strategies that give their businesses a competitive edge. This begins with a deeper understanding of why people make the choices they do.

Enter Behavioral Economics

We live in a world of scarcity. We have finite time and limited resources, and because of this, we must make choices. Economists study these choices. Traditionally, economists have built theories and models around the idea that people take the information at their disposal, rationally weigh the costs and benefits of each alternative, and then make the choice that maximizes utility.

Sure, people are theoretically capable of behaving rationally, but we don't usually take such a meticulous approach to weighing costs and benefits, which leads to irrational choices. Most often, we're satisficing, settling for an option that's good enough, rather than exhaustively analyzing each option. It's not that we're making random or intentionally irrational choices. We just don't have the time or mental resources to analyze each decision we face exhaustively. So, we make decisions with a sort of bounded rationality in which we depend on heuristics (mental shortcuts), cognitive biases, and gut feelings to make quick, good-enough decisions. Then we move on with our days.

Scientists have long observed the decision-making quirks that lead to seemingly illogical choices. People will pay more for one product than another of equal quality. They might rely on irrelevant information due to emotional appeal. They sometimes participate in behaviors known to be harmful to themselves or others. Consumers fail to take advantage of better technologies because they prefer traditional methods. The list goes on. These seemingly irrational choices are the basis of study for economists, neuroscientists, psychologists, and others contributing to the field of behavioral economics.

A core idea behind the study of behavioral economics is that most decisions are made in what Daniel Kahneman called System 1, or fast-thinking, mode. This type of decision-making is based on instincts and initial impressions, not slow and methodical consideration. For marketers, this means that the target audience is not *homo economicus*, the perfectly logical decision-maker. Rather, we're attempting to reach intuitive thinkers whose decisions are subject to many influences, many of which are subconscious.

To write this book, I mined the vast body of research on behavioral economics. My goal was to find insights on consumer behavior that can improve the effectiveness of marketing work. Many of the cognitive biases and heuristics covered in this book could fill even more books; indeed, many top-notch academics have written tomes on the psychology of choice and the cognitive biases herein. My goal, however, is not to offer a comprehensive overview of every cognitive bias that could impact a person's decisions, but to give you a better understanding of how customers think so that you can create smarter marketing strategies. I describe the primary quirks that affect human decision-making, offer examples of how they manifest, and review steps that marketers can take to leverage them.

The book is organized according to key marketing use cases: storytelling, emotional engagement, beating the competition, loyalty, and research and planning. This design allows you to read at your leisure, target a specific problem, or flip to a section that is most relevant to your daily needs. Many concepts explored in this book could be applied across the marketing lifecycle. I hope that my ideas will inspire you to extend the knowledge presented in this book to your own unique applications.

Importantly, I do not believe that marketers should attempt to exploit cognitive biases at the expense of customers. Not ever. There are myriad ethical concerns when businesses attempt to leverage biases to manipulate consumer choices. (I'm looking at you, merchants of miracle weight-loss products and purveyors of pyramid schemes.). Not only is such manipulation unethical, but it's also bad for companies. In our always-on digital age, marketers who attempt to harmfully manipulate consumers usually suffer a well-deserved backlash.

There is a better approach. I offer ideas for how you can leverage the latest behavioral science insights to improve your marketing strategy and communicate more effectively with your customers. The goal is to help you build long-term value for both the consumer and the brand.

Storytelling

Marketing professionals have often heard the line that "people have always loved stories, and [insert new channel/site/device] is the new campfire." Personally, I think this prosaicism is nearly as overdone as speeches that feature dictionary definitions. Still, the campfire chestnut may be around for a while because it's built on an important insight: Our brains are wired for stories.

Stories are more memorable than other forms of communication because they're more engaging and relatable. As people consume information, they subconsciously filter and file it according to how it fits into their personal narratives. This means that we *think* in stories.

Marketers have long understood that a great story can help people connect with a brand, but it takes more than the "About Us" trope of a heroic founder who bootstrapped through hard times to drive meaningful engagement. There is a science to storytelling, and there are reasons why a well-constructed story is more memorable than the sum of its parts.

> "The sizzle has sold more steaks than the cow ever has, although the cow is, of course, mighty important." -Elmer Wheeler[1]

Decades ago, when sales guru Elmer Wheeler talked about "sizzle," he referred to the tang in the cheese, the whiff in the coffee, and the bubbles in the wine. In other words, he showed us that what sells is the inspiration people feel when watching, for example, a Nike commercial or the smell of chocolate and the warm glow in a Godiva shop. It is the emotional connection with a brand that grows engagement and strengthens loyalty, and a compelling story is the best way to build that connection.

Why Stories Matter

The 2012 book *Wild* tells the story of a woman who seeks peace hiking the Pacific Crest Trail after a series of personal tragedies and a struggle with drug addiction. The book was released as a movie starring Reese Witherspoon in 2014. After the book was published, the number of people who attempted to hike the long trail increased by 30 percent. After the movie's release, traffic on the PCT website rose 300 percent.[2] Hiking aficionados credited the subsequent surge in their sport's popularity to "The *Wild* Effect."

Perhaps you know someone who watched *Invincible* and then talked about becoming a better athlete. Or you might know someone who started to rap a little after watching *8 Mile*. If you have a friend who watches *Grey's Anatomy*, you've probably heard an emotional discourse after one of the show's many deaths, departures, or breakups. Your friends who have watched *Game of Thrones* have probably shared passionate opinions about the program.

These common reactions to films and books reflect the fact that stories stimulate the brain. Neuroscientists have confirmed what fiction lovers have said for centuries: people *feel* stories. Words associated with scent—lavender, coffee—stimulate the olfactory area. Metaphors that evoke a sense of touch, such as "leathery hands," excite the sensory cortex. Reading about physical activity ignites the parts of the brain that handle corresponding motor movements.[3] This is why most of us have cried over a book or talked about TV characters as if they were real people in our lives, even though we were aware that the story's fictional.

Great stories are so engrossing that we feel like we are part of them. The advertising agency Droga5 did fantastic work for Amazon's streaming service by using the power of story. In one spot, an office worker who has been watching the *Vikings* TV series becomes increasingly aggressive in the face of day-to-day disrespect. At the end of the commercial, she responds to a coworker using her coffee mug by pounding the counter and screaming until the coworker hands it over. In another ad, a bored married couple who has watched *Outlander* begin to passionately make out in places like a bus stop and public bathroom. The line at the end hits it on the nose: "Great shows stay with you."

Better Brand Storytelling

Stories matter because they feel real. Great storytellers engage us and make us care about the tale's outcome. But could a mere brand have a story that people would genuinely care about? Is there a way to tell the story without it becoming trite? Yes, and yes.

The key is to apply a few crucial aspects of storytelling correctly and to leverage cognitive science to help us better tell stories in ways that will resonate with customers.

The Halo Effect and First Impressions

Research has shown that when people know one positive thing about an otherwise unknown product or company, they tend to place a figurative halo around it. They fill in the blanks with the best assumptions. This is known as the "Halo Effect" or "exaggerated emotional coherence." Nobel Laureate Daniel Kahneman illustrates this tendency by asking us to imagine meeting someone at a party and finding her personable. Later that evening, someone brings up the idea of asking the woman to contribute to a charity. Although you know nothing about her, you assume she would be generous based on your favorable first impression. Moreover, this creates a virtuous cycle: Once you imbue the woman with this generous quality, you end up liking her even more.[4]

Classic psychological research, according to Kahneman, demonstrates the importance of first impressions. Consider the character descriptions of two people:

> Alan: Intelligent, industrious, impulsive, critical, stubborn, envious.
>
> Ben: Envious, stubborn, critical, impulsive, industrious, intelligent.

Who would you like more? In experiments, most people report that they would like Alan more than Ben because, as Kahneman points out, the initial traits change what the final traits mean. That is, Alan may have become intelligent by being stubborn, but Ben's intelligence might seem like an afterthought compared to how envious and stubborn he is. On first impression, he seems like a guy who would take credit for your work or undermine you in front of your boss.[5]

First impressions have outsized influence, including for companies. In this constantly connected age, any single brand communication will be someone's first impression of the company. So, it's critical for all messaging to tell the story you want people to remember.

Making Stories Memorable

If people do not remember the brand story, they will not remember your brand. Fortunately, though the mechanics behind memory aren't always rational, they are rather predictable, so we know a fair amount about how to get people to remember a story.

Memory and Availability Bias

Availability bias results from our reliance on whatever information is most readily available. This bias is influenced by other factors, such as the recency of exposure to the information, how the information was presented, and subjective interpretations of the information. Fundamentally, availability bias is impacted by resonance; that is, whether the information "strikes a chord" with the consumers. When that happens, people will be more likely to remember the story.

We can't remember everything but, if we could depend on our brains to retain unbiased recollections of the most important information, we could logically expect that the stuff we remember is also the most important. Much to the detriment of educators the world over, however, we can't depend on our brains to accurately record memories in descending order of importance. Think of an important literary book that you read in high school and then think of a song that was popular at that time. If you are like most people, you can probably recite more lines from the pop song than the book, even though the song was educationally less important than the book. I, for one, can remember more lines of "Genie in a Bottle" than *The Odyssey*. (Thanks, Brain.)

Availability bias causes us to behave illogically even in high-stakes scenarios, like evaluating mortal risk. People worry about accidental deaths, so we buy insurance, track tornadoes on our phones, prepare emergency kits, buckle our seatbelts, and buy bear spray. These are all prudent choices but, in the US, we are about four times more likely to die of heart disease than an accident. Logically, we should focus at least four times the resources on preventing heart disease that we dedicate to accident prevention. And yet people are often more afraid of encountering a downed power line, armed mugger, dangerous animal, or tornado than they are of fatty foods and sedentary jobs. The more probable deaths aren't as front-of-mind because they're less memorable than the stories of rare diseases, freak accidents, and weather catastrophes that we encounter through the media or friends. And, because the stories we've heard of uncommon accidents are more memorable, they have an outsized influence on our subsequent decisions.

Availability bias works against you as a learner or insurance purchaser, but it can work in a marketer's favor. If you can create a resonant story, people will be more likely to remember your brand and, because of this, they'll be more likely to assume that it's relevant to their needs.

Connecting with the Customer's Narrative

In the third season of AMC's *Mad Men*, Joan is preparing to depart the ad agency. In one scene, her colleague, Peggy, told her, "I don't want you to think I never listened to you. It's just, we can't all be you." Joan accepted the compliment and replied, "Be that as it may, I do take some credit for your success here."

This scene is interesting, because fans of the show may recall that the relationship between Joan and Peggy was contentious from the outset. Viewers who were more sympathetic to Peggy's plight might have viewed Joan as a vindictive workplace bully who never missed a chance to lob an insult. But Joan viewed herself as a pragmatist and mentor who did what was necessary to protect the business.

I like that scene because it demonstrates an important human truth: Memory is less about helping us accurately recall past experiences than about helping us function as we move forward with our lives. Essentially, psychologists propose, memory isn't a tool for recollection, it's a narrative: a story we invent to help us understand our current state and guide our future actions.[6]

Many secretaries in the *Mad Men* series had formed a narrative about Joan. They did this to explain her bullying and insults while also protecting their own sense of self-worth in the face of Joan's insults. For instance, Peggy developed a personal narrative of perseverance in the face of Joan's bullying, which became an important aspect of her identity. By comparison, Joan's internal narrative was that she was being tough on people as a form of mentorship, not cruelty. She saw herself as an experienced leader who could help the secretaries avoid problems in the corporate "boys' club" and keep them focused on their work. This narrative supported her identity as a person who was essential for running the business.

On *Mad Men*, as beyond the fictional realm, behavior is not driven by objective reality, but personal narratives and identities. The narratives we form in our minds affect how we perceive, interpret, and remember information. Likewise, we interpret the world around us so that it fits into our broader personal narratives. And our personal narratives form our sense of identity. Joan's narrative about herself is that she is cruel to be kind. But others do not see her behavior in the same light and react negatively to what they perceive as bullying. Upon seeing these responses, Joan feels that other employees take her efforts for granted, leading her to be even more forceful in mentoring younger workers.

We're all at the center of our own stories. Therefore, a meaningful brand story should have the customer at the center—as the hero of your story. Accordingly, your brand can only fit into the customer's narrative if you're effective in proving that you empathize with his situation and needs.

We gain understanding and empathy by actively listening to our customers and learning about what they need, so we can identify the most compelling connection between our brand and the customer's story. Caveat: We're talking about the real, deep, human truth here not just ticking the box on an immediate need. Only the brand that truly connects with the customer can cut through the clutter to be front-of-mind at the moment of choice.

Consider the vacation and tourism vertical. Vacations are expensive, so usually, tourism brands target customers with higher levels of disposable income or cash. But let's imagine that your company also wants to invest in building loyalty with younger generations. Most of the young and affluent are working. So, you research the reasons why those people would be interested in taking a vacation. You quickly (and unsurprisingly) discover that they want to take a break from work. You could stop your research there, in which case you might write copy about the standard stuff: an exciting destination with unique entertainment options—anything to help them break free from work. But this would only be writing a "nutrition label," connecting a list of expressed needs with a checklist of brand offerings.

If you were to keep laddering down to find their deeper reasons for wanting a vacation, you might find that your customers aren't just tired, but burned out. They might see themselves as slaves to their careers, that work has become so all-encompassing that their relationships are suffering. Maybe they are so bored with their routines that they worry about becoming boring people. Your research reveals that this population has been living for work and now they long to *really live*. They believe that they *deserve* a vacation.

To cut through the clutter and really engage with the customer, you need to connect your brand story with these deeper personal narratives. You want to promise that your vacation brand will do more than just get your customers out of the house; you will take them to a place where they will reconnect with their true selves, develop themselves as interesting people, and become amazing spouses. You will help them see that their lives are about more than giving all their energy to "The Man."

A couple of short case studies will further illustrate the importance of developing a memorable brand story.

Case: It's Different Out Here
The brilliant Norwegian Cruise Lines campaign from the 1990s was a bit racy. One TV spot encouraged viewers to "form a more perfect union" while a scantily clad couple kissed. In another, a bare-shouldered woman waded in the water while the copy beckoned, "There is no law that says you can't make love at four in the afternoon on a Tuesday." But Goodby Silverstein & Partners wasn't just selling sex. The soothing music over gorgeous black and white imagery of beaches and hammocks, the assurance that couples could reconnect, the promise that "it's different out here"—collectively, these messages conveyed that an escape from the hustle would help people remember their true selves and remind couples why they

love each other. The campaign paid off: Bookings went up by 20 percent in the first year, despite heavy industry competition.[7]

The campaign worked so well because it connected with the customer's deeper story—that people do not just want a vacation; they need a reset to feel whole again. The 1990s Norwegian campaign transcends that time and target audience. It feels just as relevant today because the brand story resonates with the customer's story. This is the kind of connection that leads consumers to remember a brand at the point of decision.

Case: Lockheed Martin Keeps the Hero at the Center
Lockheed Martin is a massive aerospace and defense contractor with a fascinating history. The US government—the Department of Defense, the Department of Energy, and NASA—spent nearly $49 billion at Lockheed Martin in 2019 alone.[8] The company, first called the Lockheed Aircraft Company, dates to the 1920s. One of its clients was Amelia Earhart.[9] The Martin Marietta corporation, after it built the first floating nuclear power station and the monorail at Disneyland, merged with Lockheed. The Sikorsky company, purchased by Lockheed in 2015, was founded by Igor Sikorsky, the man who designed the helicopter as we know it. Now, the company builds aircraft, missiles, and spacecraft.

Lockheed Martin could credibly claim, "We basically invented all of the stuff you need, and we build stuff for NASA, so we can help your company too." But, instead, Lockheed puts its customer at the center of its brand story.

Current creative builds on a simple idea: "Lockheed Martin. Your Mission is Ours." Video work on the site and YouTube shows military personnel, pilots, and first responders while the voiceover explains how the company works to innovate on behalf of end users. "Our mission is to build the integrated solutions you can depend on

… because the world is depending on you."[10] The company's vision statement also places the hero at the center: "Be the global leader in supporting our customers' missions, strengthening security, and advancing scientific discovery." And the values build on the message: "Do what's right. Respect others. Perform with excellence."

Lockheed Martin's website also demonstrates its authority. There is content about the company's experience and competence, much of it easily sharable. The site has an extensive capabilities section. Product pages cover specific features and include in-depth information about each of the company's innovations. But, even when Lockheed Martin talks about itself, the customer is at the center of the story, as the brand focuses on how its accomplishments benefit the customer. Consider the content from the Black Hawk page:[11]

The Black Hawk multirole helicopter serves with the U.S. military and the armed forces of twenty-eight other countries worldwide as a tough, reliable utility helicopter.

During the last forty years, this remarkable aircraft has fought its way in and out of countless combat zones to deliver and extract troops, save lives as a medevac or casualty evacuation platform, provide critical supplies to troops, deliver emergency supplies during natural disasters, and perform as an aerial firefighter and border patroller.

Now the modern variant of this utility aircraft is taking on a new mission set—as an armed helicopter to provide fire suppression when supporting ground troops, as well as armed escort. With digital avionics, powerful GE engines, high strength airframe structures and composite wide chord rotor blades, today's Black

Hawk platform has better survivability and situational awareness, and can fly higher and carry more than its predecessors ever did.

Lockheed Martin could've emphasized its history of dominance in this category, or it could've focused on how its company culture and smart engineers developed such strong rotor blades. Instead, the company focused on how the aircraft benefits the end users: medevac, providing supplies, better survivability, higher load capacity, etc. Lockheed Martin excels at keeping the customer at the center of its story, which is one reason why its content is so engaging.

There's a pervasive myth that brand storytelling is less important for B2Bs than for B2C companies. This is problematic because, after work, the B2B client is just a regular consumer who is accustomed to the compelling, polished storytelling produced by major consumer brands. She doesn't simply forget that baseline when she clocks in.

If a defense contractor that caters mainly to the government can prioritize the development of a compelling brand story, what excuse does any other company have for not doing the same?

Emotional Engagement and Memory

Even if it has been a while since you have seen a version of *Beauty and the Beast*, you can probably still recall the main storyline. There has been a constant barrage of information coming at your brain since you last encountered *Beauty and the Beast*. So why would you remember this story, but not all that other information?

Neuroscientists have concluded that stories are more memorable than statistics and facts because stories simultaneously engage multiple parts of the brain as you take in information, empathize with characters, and experience complex emotions. In the case of

Beauty and the Beast, you may have felt that it was unfair for the woman to be imprisoned in her father's stead and considered if he could ever truly enjoy his freedom, given the circumstances. Perhaps you sympathized with the beast because you felt that being turned into a monster was an outsized punishment for the crime of selfishness and imagined yourself as Beauty/Belle, in love with a monster, living in a palace.

Stories resonate with our minds and hearts as we read, listen, or watch, helping us to *feel the* character's experiences. When multiple senses are engaged in this manner, the story is cemented in our memories. Perhaps that is why ancient stories like *Beauty and the Beast* have even outlived the languages in which they were originally told.

In the marketing world, John Lewis and Nike are excellent examples of how to emotionally engage with consumers. British retailer John Lewis' annual tearjerkers tell moving stories that connect with the sentimental importance of the holiday season. Classic rock fans loved the 2018 spot featuring Elton John that moved backwards through his life and career, ending with the childhood Christmas morning when his mom and grandmother gave him a piano. Then, the copy, "Some gifts are more than just a gift."

Nike consistently tells timely, relevant, emotionally engaging stories that emphasize that sports are more than mere entertainment or exercise. As the coronavirus pandemic forced schools and professional leagues to cancel or postpone sports, Nike ran ads showing elite athletes overcoming setbacks. The athletes promised, "We're never too far down come back." When Kobe Bryant died, Nike commercials emphasized how he inspired fans and athletes in sports and beyond. Nike ads never focus on new sneaker technology or flashy designs; rather, the brand's work across channels is always about the emotional experience of being an athlete.

Relevance, Specificity, and Focus

The modern consumer is pummeled with thousands of advertising messages each week. As a result, if your story is not relevant to your customers' lives and stories, you cannot expect them to even *notice* it, let alone remember your brand at the point of decision.

In a fascinating study of just how "blind" our brains can be, one experiment asked subjects to watch a video in which people—some dressed in white, some in black—passed basketballs. Test subjects were tasked with counting how many times players in white passed the ball. As they focused on counting only the passes, most of the viewers totally missed the person in the gorilla suit who walked across the scene. When the researchers told the subjects about the gorilla, they were certain they couldn't have possibly missed something so obvious. Some even asked to rewatch the video, because they didn't believe they could've missed it.[12]

Customers will not connect with your narrative unless it's immediately clear that your brand is relevant to their needs. And that means that you need to focus on a specific need, even—especially—if it's not everyone's need.

The Louis Vuitton Customer

Consumers often cite quality as a principal reason for buying luxury brands, and the quality of Louis Vuitton handbags is certainly among the best. That said, other brands charge less for similar quality. If quality and price were the only factors in the handbag purchasing decision, then the logical consumer would choose one of the many less-expensive options. The fact that the company has persisted since 1854 indicates that price and quality aren't the only considerations.

We know the Vuitton customer's true need isn't a coated canvas tote. She wants to feel like a woman who can afford the brand, who has earned a certain status, and she wants to signal this status to herself or others. In her book, *Girl, Wash Your Face*, internet influencer Rachel Hollis recalled how she had dreamed of buying a Louis Vuitton bag because it represented the woman she had longed to become. After earning her first large consulting check, she immediately drove to the nearest store and purchased one. The bag assured Hollis and her followers that she had earned and achieved the Louis Vuitton lifestyle.

Of course, not everyone wants to buy a Vuitton bag. Not everyone recognizes Vuitton ownership as a milestone in life, as Hollis did. Some can't afford to spend thousands on a bag. Some of those who can afford the bags might find the idea of such lavish spending to be selfish or gauche. All these consumers would prefer a lower-priced alternative.

It follows that if Vuitton created a more affordable line, the company could sell more handbags. Yet so far, the brand has not made this move. Why not? If Louis Vuitton tried to appease people who oppose such conspicuous consumption, or if it developed less-expensive products for customers who can't afford to spend more than $200 on a handbag, the company would alienate its core customers and gut its brand equity.

Instead of trying to please everyone, Vuitton focuses on adding value on behalf of its core customer by protecting the scarcity of its bags and retaining its unique aesthetics—so that the bags remain recognizable signals of luxury. The company's brand managers know that any attempt to please everyone will please no one.

Take a page from their book and focus on the story that's relevant to your target even—especially—when that comes at the expense of broad appeal.

Authenticity and Credibility

In *Mrs. Doubtfire, The Parent Trap, Sister Act,* and many other movies, protagonists pretend to be someone they're not and hilarity ensues. When they're exposed, the other characters—and the audience—forgive the protagonists, and we all enjoy a heartwarming ending.

This type of moral consequentialism seems to play well in family movies, but the outcome can be decidedly less heartwarming when brand stories are inauthentic. In 2018, McDonald's flipped some of its signs, turning the golden arches into golden Ws. McDonald's intended to honor International Women's Day. Detractors, however, were quick to point out that the company had been resistant to raising wages for its lowest earners—who were disproportionately women—and that it had ignored numerous sexual harassment complaints.

Whatever the brand's true intentions, the perception of hypocrisy left consumers with the impression that flipping the signs was a half-baked attempt to win attention on social media sites, not a credible signal of the brand's priorities. The perception that the brand was "woke-washing" made McDonald's a target of social media backlash and critical memes. Perhaps the posts were made and approved by people who knew more about social media tools than they knew about the McDonald's brand or managers so deeply entrenched in the brand that they were out of touch with public perception. Either case would've led employees to think of boosting vanity metrics before considering how the scheme might backfire.

That episode was particularly cringe-inducing because Pepsi had a similar gaffe the summer before. One ad showed model and influencer Kendall Jenner walking through a crowd as people protested an indistinguishable issue. Jenner arrived on the scene and offered a Pepsi to a police officer. Suddenly, the crowd cheered, apparently satisfied that the problem had been solved. Pepsi pulled the ad amid accusations that it was piggybacking on the Black Lives Matter movement, which protested police killings of black people, to sell soda.

More recently, as Covid-19 spread, airlines tried to stem losses with constant messages about their commitment to customers' health, comfort, and general well-being. But numerous social media posts pointed out that most airlines aren't exactly known for caring about customer well-being. These are, after all, companies that have leveled fees for bags that are five pounds overweight, that have intentionally overbooked flights and then dragged passengers off planes when they refused to vacate, and that have made it difficult for even the most loyal customers to use rewards points. In response, airlines have constantly reminded us that delayed flights and missed connections aren't their fault (even when they are). Surely, airlines must have expected their ads about prioritizing consumers' well-being to be met with suspicion.

Consumers are aware that when brands speak to them, it's because they're selling something. Consumers don't have a problem with marketing messages per se, but people usually will not stand for green-washing, woke-washing, or truth-stretching. As marketers, we're often asked to participate in trending conversations. As you do this, rather than trying to mislead the consumer, shift the conversation to one that *credibly and authentically* paints your brand in a positive light. When the conversation does not reference something your brand can be proud of, better to keep quiet.

Clarity of Message

A muddled message is worse than no message. If you say nothing, there will be no risk of misinterpretation. By contrast, a complicated, confusing message will be problematic. This is why planning by committee doesn't work: You can't achieve every stakeholder's objective in the same campaign. If your message is unclear, there's no telling what consumers will take away—and no reason to assume that it will benefit your brand. Above all, your messages must communicate, with absolute clarity, who you are, what purpose you serve, and why customers should choose you.

You should also avoid excessively grandiose messaging. For example, a glass company could use elevated wording, such as "Our glaziers facilitate connections with the world while protecting you from its harshest elements." That story might be authentic, credible, and relevant to your customer's needs, but the fact is, glaziers install glass windows and doors. To use wording that is excessively grandiose will come across as esoteric and pretentious. That type of language will also kill SEO efforts.

Clarity Fail: Burger King's #EatLikeAndy Spot

Lest you question whether experienced marketers could fail to create a clear message, consider Burger King's forty-five-second spot during the 2019 Super Bowl. The nearly silent commercial featured a white-haired man in a suit removing a plain burger from a Burger King bag, unwrapping it, struggling to pour ketchup from a Heinz bottle, mumbling something, dipping the burger in ketchup, and then taking a bite. The hashtag #EatLikeAndy flashed at the end.

Savvy viewers might have realized that the actor looked like Andy Warhol. Very savvy viewers might have recognized the actor *actually was* Andy Warhol. The art or film school graduates in the room may have even recognized that the footage was from the 1982 Danish documentary titled *66 Scenes from America*. And the particularly erudite may have appreciated the original filmmaker's take on the hamburger as a socioeconomic equalizer, enjoyed by people across social strata.[13]

This ad is a classic example of a muddled message. I suspect that the number of people who watch both antique Danish docufilms and Super Bowl commercials is extremely small—and I bet nearly all work at ad agencies. About half of today's US population had not yet been born when Warhol died in 1987, and many Americans would not recognize him. To further confuse the audience, the Burger King bag and Heinz bottle were both front-and-center during the entire spot. Thus, audiences could not determine which brand was being promoted. In addition, the plain burger was squashed and did not look appetizing. All of this begged the question: Was this a Burger King ad or the work of a competitor hoping to mock the company's food? So much ambiguity in such a short ad!

Brands often use Super Bowl spots to generate buzz, but there's not much branding value when the buzz is generated by confused people asking what they just saw. Theoretically, there exists a brand that could find value in making obtuse art references that make viewers feel unsophisticated, but that brand would not target customers who buy burgers and fries at drive-through windows.

Some bloggers and insiders celebrated the artistic brilliance of the Burger King spot, but most consumers didn't know what was going on. It is possible that the marketers and art directors wanted to show off their talents by pushing conventions in ways that would challenge the audience. The use of high-concept ads with many artistic layers might be interesting to dissect in books and academia, but they can leave consumers befuddled. Telling a story that nobody understands is just bad branding. We usually can't ask audiences to give us much cognitive space when reading our websites or watching our commercials. They should not have to work to understand what we're saying.

When tempted to sacrifice clarity for an ego-boosting rush of pretension, we should return to our grandfather's advice:

> *"I do not regard advertising as entertainment or an art form, but as a medium of information. When I write an advertisement, I don't want you to tell me that you find it 'creative.' I want you to find it so interesting that you buy the product."*
> -David Ogilvy[14]

There is no shortage of creative talent in marketing. Many people I have known during my marketing career have been aspiring artists and writers who sought a consistent paycheck while working in a field adjacent to their interests. Because there are so many talented people in the field, even small marketing firms can produce work with panache—without sacrificing clarity. One of my favorite examples of marketing work that offers both is *The Washington Post* slogan, which tells a powerful story in only four words: "Democracy Dies in Darkness."

Cohesive Narrative and Personality

Stories have lasting power because they work the way our brains do, weaving people, problems, and details together into a coherent message.

The electronic memory game called Simon plays a string of notes that correspond to lights behind four colored buttons. When the string of notes is done, the player's job is to reproduce them in the same order. Each time the player succeeds the sequence gets longer by one note. So, by the time the player gets up to ten notes, he or she has heard the first note ten times, the first two notes nine times, and so on. Some people narrate "red, blue, red, green" while they play; others will try to sing the sequence to trigger their memories.

If you were asked to sing a random ten-note sequence from a Simon game a few minutes later, you probably wouldn't be successful. But you could probably sing along with the chorus of ABBA's "Dancing Queen" or The Jackson 5's "ABC" before you finished hearing the song for the first time. That's because the chord progressions and lyrics are organized and make sense in the context of the songs. Similarly, you could probably remember the first lines from *A Tale of Two Cities* or *The Night Before Christmas* after hearing them once. By contrast, you wouldn't do as well with a string of random words.

To ensure that your story is effective, you've got to create a cohesive personality, narrative, and message and then stick to it. Creative across channels needs to look and feel the same and there needs to be a clear, logical connection back to the single narrative that unites all your brand messages.

The Red Thread

Chinese mythology gives us the concept of the red thread of fate. This is the idea that you're connected to the person westerners would call your soulmate via an invisible red thread. Circumstances can complicate your lives and the thread can become tangled, but it can never be cut and will always connect you with your one, true love.

The idea of the red thread has been taken much more literally in film and television. Hollywood would have us believe that most murders (and some medical mysteries) are solved by meticulous detectives who painstakingly pin evidence to corkboards and then run string from one item to the next to visualize the connections. In a harrowing scene in *A Beautiful Mind*, we see John Nash's office, where every wall is covered in clippings with a web of red thread showing the links conjured by his ailing mind.

We can also think of the red thread as the Swedes do: the idea or theme that binds a narrative together. If this "through line" is lost, then the story has lost coherence. (By the way, when a Swede has lost his train of thought, he says, "I lost the thread.")[15]

In Roald Dahl's *Matilda*, the red thread is the idea that the virtuous triumph. The sweet Miss Honey ultimately triumphs over the mean Miss Trunchbull and the good-natured Matilda ultimately finds a way out of her cruel family. In Jane Austen's *Pride and Prejudice*, the key theme is right there in the title. The book is a satirical commentary about the roles of class and bias in Regency-era England in which the protagonists struggle to overcome their pride and prejudice. In both books, the events and dialogues throughout connect with the central themes.

If you understand your customer—his central problem—and how your brand can solve it, you have the central theme of your story. The red thread. But reaching today's omnichannel consumers requires you to run the red thread from one channel to the next while adapting to each channel's features and audience, without losing the connection to your brand story. This means staying on message and limiting yourself to information that supports the central message in your brand story wherever possible. The challenge is in doing this without becoming repetitive. You can't simply slap the slogan on an image, print it in a magazine, and then copy it to X. You've got to leverage the benefits of each channel to extend your story in a relevant manner. The good news is that a consistently presented story will resonate with consumers' brains, predisposing them to remember your brand.

Case Study: P&G's Connected Brand Narrative
Procter & Gamble provides a fantastic example of a best practice here because of the elegance with which the brand connects its many lines of business. If a huge company like Proctor & Gamble can connect this many sub-brands around a cohesive narrative, then smaller, simpler businesses can too.

In its 181 years, P&G has become a massive house of personal care brands, including Bounce, Pampers, Tide, Tampax, Gillette, Old Spice, and Pepto Bismol. The company, which is also the world's largest advertiser,[16] faces a conundrum when attempting to tell a story: For the individual brand stories to be meaningful, they must be unique and differentiated ... but for the parent brand to tell a story, it must somehow unite the brands.

At the time of this writing, P&G's red thread is "making every day more than ordinary." The company makes various claims throughout its digital presences, but they all build on that simple theme.

- o We believe in finding small but meaningful ways to improve lives—now and for generations to come.[17]
- o P&G products have made a name for themselves by combining "what's needed" with "what's possible"—making laundry rooms, living rooms, bedrooms, kitchens, nurseries, and bathrooms a little more enjoyable for over 181 years.[18]

- All day, every day, P&G people are #SteppingUp and serving others as a #ForceForGood. Improving everyday life since 1837. #proctergamble #ItsOurHome[19]

Case: The Cohesive Personality of Orange Theory Fitness
From the website and X feed to the interior designs and coaching staff, Orange Theory Fitness offers a consistent, differentiated brand experience.

In addition to the obvious color choice, the look and feel across channels exude energy and expertise, and all content supports the narrative that the company offers a smarter path to fitness. Even messages from corporate retain the energetic, expert personality. During the pandemic, many businesses printed messages about local mask ordinances and displayed clip art of spray bottles alongside promises to disinfect surfaces. By comparison, Orange Theory posted signs with messages like, "Resist the urge to high five." They showed a video that promised they would implement "new health and safety protocols that would make the CDC proud."

Confirmation Bias: Your Customers Will Find Evidence to Support Your Story

The logical thing to do when analyzing a situation is to review all the information you've encountered, carefully consider each alternative, and then form an opinion. Of course, that's not how our brains work. What actually happens is that we internalize information that confirms our pre-existing beliefs and we exclude, forget, or ignore information that conflicts with those beliefs. This is called "confirmation bias." It leads us to seek and remember information that conforms to our pre-existing narratives, and it can even impact how we interpret ambiguous information.

In one experiment, subjects who identified as strong Democrats and strong Republicans were hooked up to MRI machines while listening to a debate between George W. Bush and John Kerry. The researchers found that parts of the brain associated with reasoning were dark, while parts associated with emotions and moral judgments lit up. In other words, the subjects' brains responded more to emotional appeals than reasonable arguments. And for those hoping this tendency is a result of modern political polarization, I regret to report that a lower-tech study conducted in 1940 led to ostensibly the same observation: People are more emotionally engaged with evidence that confirms their previously held beliefs.[20] This means that people are processing information from a place of emotional cognition, not cool rationality. And, as we've established, emotional engagement supports memory, so we should expect that these people also remembered the information they agreed with more reliably than the other points of the debate.

If you have acquaintances who use Facebook as a platform to share their political opinions, you've seen confirmation bias in action. This can test your respect for vocal people who express beliefs you don't share because their perception of information will seem ridiculous to you. Some of this is conscious: Sometimes, people intentionally collect information that they can use to support an argument. Often, though, confirmation bias is unconscious. As we process information, we naturally seek and remember information that supports our identities and beliefs. It's much easier to process the warm comfort of identity-supportive information than the disquieting feeling of cognitive dissonance that arises when we're faced with information that challenges our personal narratives.

Though confirmation bias can be annoying in political discussions, this cognitive bias will help with your effort to tell a connected brand story. Faced with a constant stream of information from numerous sources, our brains take special note of evidence that supports our pre-existing beliefs. We remember information that is relevant to and supports our narratives, even when the issue is relatively unimportant. For instance, a senior citizen who isn't financially strained may still lament rising prices. Even though rising prices are not important to him, he might talk endlessly about the five-cent movie tickets of his childhood and, correctly, state that movie tickets are more expensive now, even when the price is adjusted for inflation. But he might neglect to mention that TVs and ready-to-wear clothing have become less expensive or that, in real terms, eggs cost less than a quarter of what they did in 1950. This isn't because he's consciously furthering an agenda; rather, at some point he became interested in the story of rising prices and now he focuses on information that supports that story.

This man, and the people that use Facebook as a political platform to the annoyance of friends, are examples of how we elevate information that supports what we already believe to be true and diminish information that doesn't support our beliefs. We also interpret ambiguous information in a way that favors our preconceived notions.

The American Library Association publishes a list of its most frequently challenged books each year. These are books that have been restricted, removed, or banned from libraries and schools. *Twilight*, a novel about a teenage girl falling in love with a vampire, was on the list in 2009 and 2010. Some people were offended by the occult themes and sexually explicit passages, which they felt undermined their Christian values. At the same time, others criticized the book for its overtly Christian themes. People on both sides of the debate cited specific passages in the book to support their view.

Another modern example of confirmation bias is seen in debates on parenting blogs about children's behavioral issues. No matter which behavior is in question—from relatively mild obstinance to behaviors more characteristic of ADHD or autism spectrum disorders—someone who opposes child vaccination will, without fail, speculate that the MMR vaccine caused the problem. Even though the medical community disagrees, people that oppose vaccinating children view every article about behavioral problems in young children as evidence that vaccines are damaging.

How Confirmation Bias Can Help Brands
Though confirmation bias can make it hard to love social media connections who don't share your beliefs, the tendency to see what we already believe—what fits the narrative we've already constructed—is great for brands because it predisposes people to loyalty and builds brand equity. For example, Tide's commercials promise superior cleaning capability. People who, after seeing the ad, purchase Tide and successfully clean their laundry will be more likely to remember subsequent successful experiences with the detergent than the times when it couldn't get the stain out.

Likewise, people who think SUVs are cooler than minivans will think that every ad showing an SUV's off-road capabilities, towing capacity, or superior handling on ice is further support for their preference for SUVs. When an SUV fan gets to a dealership and hears a salesperson talk about towing capacity and torque, the added information confirms that he is making a smart choice. His bias will lead him to justify the SUV's poor gas mileage and higher cost with the fact that the car will have more power and possibly more safety. By contrast, SUV aficionados will be unimpressed by minivan commercials that show storage space for juice boxes and seating for an entire soccer team. That information will not resonate with the narratives of SUV drivers, even if they are more likely to take kids to soccer practice than to tow a boat up a mountain.

This bias also makes us susceptible to suggestions. For example, if you ask a person, "Do you buy organics?" or say something like, "You buy organics, right?", that person will be more likely to express a preference for organics than if you simply asked, "How do you choose produce?" Infomercials often use the strategy of making suggestions to sell products. They will describe a problem in a way that causes otherwise happy viewers to think, *Wait. That is a problem that's been bugging me!* Then, the infomercial suggests some uses for the product, leading the viewer to think of even more.

Once something is suggested to us, we're more likely to notice it. You've probably experienced this with your friends, as TV friends have. There's an episode of *How I Met Your Mother*, "Spoiler Alert," in which the characters point out annoying aspects of each other's personalities. (A tendency to be pedantic, using the word "literally" incorrectly, loud chewing, etc.) The characters hadn't noticed these quirks before but, once the minor annoyances were mentioned, they suddenly remembered numerous instances when they experienced their friends' idiosyncrasies and couldn't help noticing them throughout the rest of the episode. During a *Friends* episode, Rachel sets Chandler up on a date with her boss. Later, he mentions that the boss always has mascara goop at the corners of her eyes. Rachel hadn't noticed this before but couldn't ignore it after Chandler brought it to her attention.

When it comes to brand storytelling, confirmation bias is your best friend. Once you introduce a credible story, your customers will be primed to register evidence that supports your story and agree. Maybe you've thought about how coffee *is* the best part of waking up since you first heard the Folger's jingle. Perhaps you've noticed the relationship between hunger and irritability more often since you first heard the word "hangry" during Snickers ads. Or, maybe you now think about the Farmers Insurance campaign when you read about freak accidents.

Retailers that compete on price don't need to have the lowest prices on everything. They only need to run ads reminding us that their stores offer great values and point out great deals on key products. Customers who are engaged with the "great value" story won't notice that some of the products are actually slightly more expensive than at a competing shop.

Clustering Illusion: Customers Will Connect the Dots

Another big helper in your quest to tell a connected, cohesive story is your customer's natural tendency to try to connect the dots. As we internalize data points—or observe our surroundings—our brains try to create order from chaos. That leads us to believe that we're seeing patterns where there are none. Known as the "clustering illusion," this leads us to overlook obvious variances and to irrationally assume that an imagined pattern applies to a wider data set.

The clustering illusion is helpful when you're trying to tell a consistent story without being patronizing or redundant, but it can work against you if the company is facing a scandal. That's because customers can be prone to see negative patterns after a scandal or negative press thereby multiplying the negative effects of the situation. In those scenarios, you have to fight the bad press with a powerful explanation that ties back into the positive story customers once loved.

When, in 2018, nearly a thousand Kentucky Fried Chicken restaurants in the UK and Ireland ran out of chicken because of a distribution problem, the brand reacted quickly by apologizing, explaining the issue, describing how it was resolving the problem, promising to compensate employees, and updating its website every fifteen minutes to help customers find fried chicken. In social media posts and a couple of newspaper ads, the company rearranged its KFC logo as FCK as a way of apologizing for the "FCK up." The humorous move worked because of the brand's honest, transparent approach. The casual voice was true to the brand's personality, so it felt authentic.[21] As a result, the company managed to redirect consumers away from the scandal and back to the positive narrative.

By touting a cluster of recent successes in your newsletter or on your X feed, you give followers an irrationally positive impression of your brand. If you share a series of consumer choice awards, unveil a remarkable innovation, mention how many people have chosen your brand, or publish testimonials, people will connect those dots and see a complete picture of your brand's success.

Tension, Resolution, Engagement

You want to tell an engaging brand story. By *engaging* I don't mean a story designed to create buzz on social media, but a persuasive story that truly resonates with your audience. Great stories keep us engaged by adhering to a logical progression, and by creating tension and then releasing it. Thus, to create an effective story, you should consider the structural arc that you learned in English class.

Structuring the Story

Many great stories could be distilled into bland descriptions. More than one of Agatha Christie's books are basically: someone got murdered and the protagonist will now ask a bunch of people a bunch of questions to figure out who did it. The first *Star Wars* movie (chronologically, by release date) essentially portrayed an intergalactic conflict that can only be resolved if the good team destroys an important weapon. The plot points and theme do not make a story great. A story is great because of how it is told.

Back in 335 BCE, Aristotle noted that a well-constructed plot should represent a complete action and, therefore, have a beginning, middle, and end. Freytag's model—or dramatic arc—has five parts: introduction, rising action, climax, falling action, and resolution. (Freytag's structure was about theatrical plays, but it can be applied to all manner of storytelling.)

For example, we can apply the Freytag method of analysis to two of the twentieth century's greatest philosophical works: *The Great Gatsby* by F. Scott Fitzgerald and *A Boy Named Sue*, which was written by Shel Silverstein and popularized by Johnny Cash.

	A BOY NAMED SUE	THE GREAT GATSBY
INTRODUCTION	A boy's father names his son Sue, then abandons his family without providing for the boy.	We meet Nick and learn he has an enigmatic neighbor, Gatsby, who throws frequent parties at his large house.
RISE	The boy grows up "quick" and "mean" and searches for his father to murder him.	Driving home after a day of drinking in the city, Daisy hits Tom's mistress, killing her, but doesn't stop the car.
CLIMAX	The boy finds his father in Gatlinburg, and they have a violent fight.	A scared Daisy returns to Tom and Gatsby is shot.
FALL	The father explains that he named his son Sue so that he would either "get tough or die" in this rough world.	The parties end, the people disappear, and Nick finds himself alone in mourning Gatsby.
RESOLUTION	Sue drops his weapon and grows to appreciate his father's logic but concludes that he'll name his son Bill or George.	Nick considers how, like Gatsby, we're all locked in a futile struggle to transcend our pasts.

This model of storytelling essentially emphasizes creating tension and then releasing it. The same is true of songwriting: A good bridge creates tension that's subsequently released in the chorus, through words and sound. The tension and climax keep us engaged until the resolution makes us feel satisfied.

The narrative arc must be further abbreviated for brand messages, which are delivered in shorter forms than songs. The message must be: We understand you and we know what you want, but there's a problem, and our brand can help you solve it by [insert reason to believe here]. For this story to work, you need to provide enough variance to keep things interesting, and you need to be right about the problem.

Moving the Story Forward

The challenge for brands is that we can't tell the story only once. It must be presented consistently across channels and throughout the life of the brand—without boring the customers.

Songwriting provides some inspiration here. If you listen to an old U2 album, you might notice how the engineers have made the music sound like the guitars are on one side, the vocals are on the other, and the kick drums are out front. The goal is to hold your attention by separating and shifting the sounds. If the Black Keys are more your style, think about the song "Sister." The guitars come through the left speaker, the bass is on the right, and the drums and vocals sound like they're in the rear center, where drummers usually sit. Vocals are often centered because songwriters tend to believe that the lyrics are the heart of the story. These placements lend the feeling of being at a live show, which creates interest.

As you present your brand story, take a page from musicians. The best ones keep the musical story or experience moving to keep the audience engaged. In the same way, you need to keep the customer at the center while constantly varying the creative and considering unique approaches to keep things interesting.

The Olay brand leverages influencers on Instagram, engages with current events on X, and offers a skin advisor tool on its website.

The brand constantly offers a stream of new, unique content to keep things fresh and interesting. It adjusts its tactics by location, but it always keeps the customer at the center of the story.

Humans naturally relate to stories, and millennia of storytelling have led us to expect this simple, logical structure. This means that sticking with a classic, predictable story structure helps your customers wrap their heads around your message. To wit: Researchers have confirmed that ads that offer fully-developed storylines outperform others, regardless of other content.[22]

On The Villain

The customer should be the hero at the center of your brand story, which means the tension in your story should be rooted in a customer problem that's best solved by your brand. This comes with a warning: As you articulate the problem your brand can solve, ensure that you're focused on the right problem and remember that the customer's problem is different from yours.

The marketer's villain is the competitor. It follows that you should tell a story about the reasons you're better than the competition, so the customer will understand why a switch to your brand is the only resolution to the problem. But a customer hearing this story, trusting the conclusion that your product is better, and then buying from you is the story *you* want to hear. That's not our hero's story.

For your customer, the villain isn't your competitor; the villain is her problem. Your job is to figure out what that problem is. If your customer is looking for life insurance, her stated problem will probably be the challenge of comparing coverage details to pick the best company. But her deeper problem—the problem she really needs to solve—is that she might die and leave her family unable to pay the mortgage. Understanding that, your conversation with her shouldn't focus on the types of death your competitor might not cover. That would only add stress and complexity to a process that's already dreadful. Instead, your story should assure your customer that you want to help her protect her family. The coverage specifics can be addressed later, after she's already chosen your brand.

This logic isn't only for high-consideration purchases. In the case of a customer choosing a spa, her most profound problem is that she's pulled in too many directions and feeling stressed out. She needs to relax to be her best. You won't connect with this customer if you open with price lists and details about the technology that makes your massage tables marginally better than your competitor's. Instead, she'll be swayed by pictures of serene rooms and an easy booking experience, all of which demonstrate your commitment to her well-being.

Energizer vs. GMC on Knowing the Villain

You care more about your competitors than your customer does. While your top competitors are on your mind every day, your customer has his own problems. It follows that ads that focus on specific downfalls of competitors run the risk of coming off as dull and petty. Still, you might experience internal pressure to address your competition directly. This can be done effectively, without seeming petty, as long as you focus on the customer's true obstacle.

Energizer has been running ads featuring the pink bunny and his drum for decades. The premise is always that Energizer batteries outlast the competition. The customers' problem is that there is never a good time for batteries to die. Energizer batteries solve the problem by lasting longer, which makes them less likely to die at a bad time. For years, the brand's ads have built on that simple theme: Christmas for children would be ruined without batteries for their toys, and a kid's birthday party would be disappointing if the batteries for her new toy died. The folks over at Energizer have been able to run successful ads on this theme without worrying about diminishing returns because they understand their customer's fundamental fear that batteries could die at the worst possible moment. These ads resonate with consumers because Energizer knows—and promises to slay—the customer's villain.

In contrast, consider recent work from GMC. The brand introduced a new tailgate design for the 2019 Sierra. In the commercial, Steam's "Na Na Hey Hey Kiss Him Goodbye" plays while a parade of people carry tailgates from the trucks made by competing brands. Atop a hill, the GMC Sierra owner presses a button on his tailgate and, after the steps appear, climbs up into his truck's bed to watch the spectacle. "The tailgate to end all tailgates" appears as the camera zooms out to reveal the long line of people disposing of their outmoded tailgates. GMC probably hoped to portray itself as an innovative brand by emphasizing a newly designed tailgate. But the ad demonstrated only one of the tailgate's purported six functions: its step feature. Other features whizzed by so swiftly at the end of the ad that casual viewers couldn't possibly internalize them.

As a result, the ad felt mildly petty. Truck owners tend to be brand loyal, so GMC owners might've snickered at the not-so-subtle dig at the competition. But when GMC decided to focus on throwing punches at the competition, it diminished the quality of its brand storytelling. Because the ad was more inside baseball than brand storytelling, it probably resonated more with people that work on the GMC brand than with prospective customers. The ad's story would have had more impact if it had focused on its customer's problems, not GMC's.

Case: Hewlett-Packard Carries the Story Down the Funnel

The sales process for enterprise technology companies has become increasingly complex, in part because the number of employees involved has exploded at many organizations. Technology decisions that were once the domain of a top manager are now influenced by stakeholders across the organizations, including C-suite leaders, developers, and ancillary influencers from marketing, sales, and other departments. This is true of decision-making in many industries beyond tech, as well.

The democratization of the decision-making process has implications for the architecture of your brand story because each influencer has a different problem to solve. The CEO is looking out for shareholders and the board, the COO is concerned with cost efficiencies, and the CTO is thinking about impacts on the technical organization now and in the future. Individual developers are concerned about the pain of changing technologies and, more than likely, about which other organizations are using the technology (so that their resumes will be appealing when they apply for jobs in the future). Marketers may be concerned with SEO implications or the ease with which changes can be made to public-facing content as campaigns rotate. The lawyers are thinking about security and service level agreements. With all these people influencing decisions, it's a challenge to identify the right villain and put the customer at the center of the story to connect with his narrative.

HP provides an example worth emulating. Its story is that it "create[s] technology that makes life better for everyone, everywhere" and "with our technology, you'll reinvent your world." The red thread of "making life better" extends throughout the site, even though the wording and formats change in relation to the preferences of various stakeholders. Operations executives concerned with cost efficiencies can find easy-to-share videos with high-level solutions, and tacticians can dive into specific technical details and find case studies about how similar businesses leverage HP technology.

Offering the story's broad strokes on the homepage, then offering more specific substantiation progressively as the customer travels down the funnel, ensures that customers can follow the red thread to experience a connected story that's relevant to their needs.

HP's model can help you if you need to appease a large and diverse group of decision-makers. You can present the overarching brand story and then offer some personalization to ensure that the story stays relevant to various audiences. This is crucial, as a connected, relevant story is one that customers will remember beyond the research phase, when it's time to make a purchasing decision.

Relatability

Amazon is the largest book retailer in the world with millions of titles available. A TechCrunch analysis way back in 2014 estimated that a new title was added every five minutes. On its 2019 bestsellers list, social influencer Rachel Hollis snagged slots five and eleven. How can one writer win that much attention? Research findings on social categorization and ingroup bias can offer some insights.

The Role of Affiliation Motivation and Ingroup Bias

Consider how you would describe yourself in a couple of sentences. Then, think about how you would describe the last person you spoke with. If you're like most people, you probably included salient group memberships in your self-description—perhaps a company you work at, your profession, an educational institution you attended, the place where you were born, or your religion. You would also describe others according to their groups: Packers fan, government employee, Californian, Harvard alum, etc.

Humans are fundamentally social creatures with a strong instinct to affiliate with groups or, in the modern parlance, "find our tribes." This instinct leads us to seek acceptance in groups and define ourselves by groups we're part of. And it has a huge influence on our decisions and behaviors.

Social identity theory posits that we each define ourselves by the unique combination of social groups or categories to which we belong. Academic research has demonstrated that when people join a group, they become more like the members of that group, and they come to view themselves as the prototypical member of the group. Subsequently, they define themselves by the similarities they have with the "ingroup" and the contrasts they have with the "outgroup."[23] [24] [25]

Once people identify with a group, they feel more committed to it and want to stick with it, even when it's a relatively low-status group.[26] We also tend to adopt the group's social stereotypes (of both ingroup and outgroup members)[27] and participate in the group's culture and behaviors.[28]

This primal desire to belong can strengthen our feelings of connection to the workplace[29] or to a favorite sports team,[30] and it helps keep our local drug dealers in business.[31] While it's tempting to write off cult members as fundamentally gullible or broken, psychologists have long argued that they're just average people who follow what religious scholars call "new religious movements" in a quest for acceptance and a sense of belonging.[32] "No one ever joins a 'cult,'" psychologist Philip Zimbardo noted. "People join interesting groups that promise to fulfill their pressing needs."[33]

Social categorization also helps us make sense of the data points our brains collect about other people. Think about how many people you interact with in a week, how many things there are to notice about them, and how many choices you make about your conversations and interactions based on your diverse relationships. Social interaction is complex and requires a lot of our brains—we have to remember names, faces, relationships, and personal details. Social categorization helps our brains handle that immense amount of information. It also leads us to—consciously and unconsciously—make assumptions about people based on shared characteristics.

We assume certain things about individuals when we hear them described in terms of group membership, even though we know the group isn't homogenous. Consider what assumptions come to mind if someone is described as a stay-at-home mother, drummer, Yankees fan, physics major, Yale alumnus, kindergarten teacher, Mormon, LARPer, Texan, recovering addict, runner, or "cat person." You probably think about stereotypes related to each group, even though you know those stereotypes are not true for all members of each group. And, if any of these categories described what is for you an outgroup, those stereotypes would likely be unflattering. For instance, cat lovers would conjure a much more flattering profile of someone described as a "cat person" than would someone who dislikes cats.

I used to live in Oregon where, by law, gas is generally pumped by employees at the gas station, not by customers. Someone once posted to a local Facebook group asking if there were any self-service gas stations in our small city. Within minutes after the post, there were dozens of heated replies. One said, "No, this is Oregon, not California. Sorry ... Stop trying to make one place like the other." This response had nothing to do with the original question and it wasn't about responsibility for a task that people in other states consider a part of driving (if they consider it at all). Rather, the commenter felt that people who suggest that Oregonians pump their own gas are trying to take away a key identifier of his ingroup. He implied that, without gas station attendants, Oregonians could become indistinguishable from Californians—the outgroup.

Our bias towards people like us—ingroup bias—leads us to prefer people like ourselves to people in other groups, even when we don't know other members of our group personally, and even if the commonality just isn't that important (like whether or not you've ever used a gas pump). The classic example here is sports fans, but fMRI studies have demonstrated intergroup biases between people of different religious affiliations and political parties as well.[34]

Pop Culture & Ingroup Bias
In 2006, a friend told me that he had rejected a woman even though he thought she was probably "out of his league." She was beautiful, and they had a good time on their first date, but he decided not to call her back because her favorite musician was Britney Spears. He didn't like Spears' music and, more importantly, he felt that an affinity for vapid pop music revealed something fundamentally unsavory about the woman's character.

Years later, in what some might consider a karmic smack, the same friend was unceremoniously dumped an hour into a weekend away. What would lead a woman to dump someone, knowing she'd have to sit through the remainder of the drive *and a return journey* with a now-ex? When she opened a conversation about literature, presumably expecting a deep discussion about the characters and ideas that excite her, my friend declared, "I don't read fiction." She was so appalled by his denunciation of the entire genre that she knew the relationship stood no chance.

You might accuse anyone in this story of being uncommonly judgmental, but I submit that they were simply more willing to admit to their own ingroup biases and their low levels of interest in relationships with outgroup members than most.

Ingroup bias is a central theme in Nick Hornby's *High Fidelity*. The central questions: Is it what you like or what you *are* like that's important? And, is there even a difference? When the novel opens, Hornby's protagonist is locked in a state of arrested adolescence. He spends most of his time at his record shop with his employees, Dick and Barry, who spend most of their time making top-five lists and mocking customers.

> *"A while back, when Dick & Barry & I agreed that what really matters is what you like, not what you *are* like, Barry proposed the idea of a questionnaire for potential partners, a 2 or 3 page multiple-choice document that covered all the music/film/TV/book bases. It was intended: a) to dispense with awkward conversation, and b) to prevent a chap from leaping into bed with someone who might, at a later date, turn out to have every Julio Iglesias record ever made. It amused us at the time... But there was an important & essential truth contained in the idea, and the truth was that these things matter, and it's no good pretending that any relationship has a future if your record collections disagree violently, or if your favorite films wouldn't even speak to each other if they met at a party."*
> -Nick Hornby, High Fidelity

Many of us like to think that we're more evolved than these immature characters who judge people so openly—and harshly—on musical taste. Still, perhaps you're willing to admit that there's a 'certain type of person' that likes death metal, bro-country, or Justin Bieber? Can you see yourself with that type of person?

Inspired by my friend's dating story, I surveyed undergraduate students and found that about a third were willing to admit that they would be less likely to go on a second date with someone if, on the first date, they learned the person loved music that they hated. About the same percentage of them agreed that there are songs or bands they secretly like, but they wouldn't admit it to their friends. In a classroom discussion about my survey, one student pointed out that she was open-minded and had friends with all sorts of musical tastes. Another said that he didn't object to people with music tastes different than his, but he couldn't imagine having much in common "with the sort of person who enjoyed listening to Justin Bieber." This was met with chuckles, nods of approval, and my growing suspicion that the survey results dramatically underestimated the impact of ingroup bias and pop culture on mate selection.

A 2021 study showed that we tend to prefer music from musicians with personalities similar to our own. The researchers also found that personality is as good of a predictor of musical taste as demographic factors like age and gender.[35] It seems that my friend and the minority of students willing to admit to similar views have intuited something that the research supports: What you like is a pretty good predictor of what you are like. Or, more precisely, what you're willing to admit you like is a signal of your identity, which is a pretty good predictor of your behavior and, by extension, a reasonably good predictor of your romantic compatibility.

We can infer that if you're the intellectual sort who reads heady books about behavioral psychology, is not interested in trends, and hasn't once posted a selfie on Instagram, it's logical to expect that you would not be compatible with someone who has paid to see Justin Bieber on multiple occasions.

Just Another Unconscious Bias

Some people, like my friend and a third of my students, have observed that musical taste is such a good indicator of a person's character that they're willing to make judgment calls about possible dates based on that information. Dating costs time and energy, so they avoid second dates with people who identify with certain groups. They base this decision on the assumption that things probably would not work out, so the benefits won't justify the costs. These people also won't admit to listening to some music for fear they will be perceived as a member of an outgroup, thereby deterring the right kind of date. (That is, they won't date death metal fans and they won't admit to liking that one death metal song, for fear of being perceived as the sort of person that enjoys that sort of music.)

But there's broad neuroscientific evidence that ingroup bias isn't entirely conscious. For example, hardcore soccer fans might see a player on the opposing team fall and complain that "he's flopping," but defend a player on their team who does the same thing. What's interesting isn't the fan's loyalty to the team, but the fact that he honestly believes that his team's player is innocent. Our brains process information related to members of our ingroup and the outgroup differently, and our biases toward outgroup members affect our perceptions, attitudes, and behaviors toward people who aren't in our ingroups. Researchers have even shown that we empathize less with outgroup members' physical pain than people we perceive to be more like us.[36] Think about this for a moment: We see people that "aren't like us" so differently that we're less concerned about their physical pain than we would be if they were more like us. This type of reaction is usually not intentional or even conscious; it's just how we're wired.

Implications for Marketers

There are clear implications here for the entire organization, including taking conscious steps to build diverse teams and relationships with people who aren't "like" you. When it comes to marketing, the data bears out the importance of ingroup bias: Nielsen data shows that 92 percent of global consumers trust recommendations from people they know, compared with only 58 percent that trust editorial content like newspaper articles. [37] Marketers need to convince customers that they understand them and that their brands will benefit them.

This can mean adopting spokespeople and models who reflect the diversity of the customer base as Dove, American Eagle, and ThirdLove have done. And it means ensuring that we understand the customer's problem with such depth that the brand's claims of empathy are credible.

The best ways to establish that you're an expert in the customer's problem are basic and intuitive:

1. Ensure you fully understand the customer's problem.
2. Tell your story in a way that's relatable for the customer.
3. Take a painfully honest assessment of whether your brand can credibly offer a solution.

This brings us back to Rachel Hollis. The internet influencer wrote two books that each outsold nearly every other book in 2019. *Girl, Wash Your Face* and *Girl, Stop Apologizing* have been denounced as deeply problematic prosperity gospel for the privileged and white, among other critiques. So why did they do so well? Because Hollis was deeply relatable and, by extension, trustworthy to her audience. Members of Hollis' audience identified her as part of their ingroup—Christian, mom, white, suburban, hustlers—and thus imbued her with outsized credibility to solve their problems.

Hollis' first viral post was a picture of her stretchmarks beside which she wrote, "I wear a bikini because I'm proud of this body and every mark on it. Those marks prove that I was blessed enough to carry my babies and that flabby tummy means I worked hard to lose what weight I could." She offers her followers a painstakingly curated highlight reel of perfectly imperfect photos and Insta-friendly tidbits that tell a clear story. She's not perfect, her sometimes-messy hair and squinty smiles imply, she's just like the people in her audience. (Or at least she used to be, before she made it big.) The message is that her followers can become like her if they follow her counsel. Her plainspoken aphorisms are relevant to her followers' daily struggles, and because she's a member of their ingroup, she's the most qualified guide to get them to where they want to be. Criticisms from people in outgroups just aren't relevant, regardless of their validity, because the opinions of outgroups aren't important.

As you tell your brand story, take a page from this influencer and focus on demonstrating that you fit with the target's ingroup. Establishing your relevance to the target's social identity is far more important than any product, feature, or service.

Happily Ever After & Peak-End

In an episode of *Seinfeld*, "The Burning," George comes up with a plan to end every conversation on a "high note" to "leave them wanting more." While spending time with friends and in a business meeting, he waits until he strikes a chord, bids them adieu, and leaves everyone laughing.

George was keyed into what psychologists have deemed the peak-end rule. Experiments on colonoscopy patients, test takers, and people dipping their hands in ice water have all demonstrated that our memories of how pleasant (or painful) an experience was do not accurately reflect the sum of that experience; instead, we remember the climax—the peak of pleasure or pain—and the end of the experience.

In Kahneman's classic experiment, people exposed to a thirty-second stretch of 14° ice water reported the experience was more painful than did people exposed to sixty seconds of 14° ice water, followed by thirty seconds of 15° ice water.[38] The second group objectively experienced more pain, but it didn't seem like it, because it ended less painfully than it began.

Perhaps this is a case of science catching up with Shakespeare. As the Bard's 1623 play is titled, *All's Well That Ends Well*.

In telling the brand story, you first need to understand your hero and then highlight the problem that vexes her, building tension to build emotional engagement. Next comes your brand's best moment: the resolution, in which you illuminate how your brand is the solution. (Although your relationship with your customer won't end at purchase, that's usually a nice place to end the story in marketing messages, because it provides the neat resolution our brains crave.) To get your customer to this ever after, you first have to get him to visualize the post-purchase state.

The Vision and Anecdotal Fallacy

The classic challenge for advertisers is getting the prospective customer to understand how great the resolution will feel before he buys. The human tendency to commit anecdotal fallacies gives storytellers an advantage.

Many expectant parents are reticent to share the baby names they're considering because they imagine a friend saying, "I had a boyfriend named Ethan, and I'm pretty sure he wound up in jail!" Clearly, not *every* person named Ethan is prison-bound. Implying as much is an anecdotal fallacy, much like the person who questions the surgeon general because "Grandpa lived to be a hundred and he smoked every day!" Stories are easier to recall than hard facts, which is why anecdotes readily pop to mind and supplant logic. But we commit an anecdotal fallacy when we cherry-pick a story to support a point that's not reflected in the data.

It's clearly unethical to leverage this tendency to nudge people into behaviors like smoking or away from their preferred baby names, but you can improve brand perceptions by providing testimonials from happy customers. A relatable customer from the target's ingroup who explains how she suffered from a problem and found a resolution through your brand will have far more impact than a simple product demonstration.

Consider Amazon Web Services. AWS is the branch of Amazon that controls nearly half of the cloud market, including powering Netflix and Pinterest.[39] The website offers a robust collection of case studies that can be filtered by location, industry, customer segment, product, and use case. AWS is leveraging both the power of anecdotes and the benefits of ingroup bias. You can search for a client exactly like you who works at a company just like yours and see how they're using Amazon's tech. Amazon is effectively offering up ingroup bias and anecdotal fallacies on a platter to let its customers sell AWS to themselves.

Another strategy for leveraging anecdotal thinking to engage customers with your story is to emphasize the feeling of fulfillment that comes with buying into your brand.

Cases in Point: Aspiration & Anecdotes for the Less-Glamorous Brand

CPG companies and household appliance manufacturers are selling products that help us with day-to-day housecleaning, a decidedly unglamorous aspect of life. For this reason, these companies make ideal case studies for how marketers can "sell the dream" about any product by telling an engaging story. Some advertisers emphasize functional benefits (e.g., no water spots on the dishes, a washing machine that uses less water, etc.). Water usage and spotty wine glasses are real problems that will come up in focus groups, but the most effective messages are those that connect with the deeper value of the products.

Redecoration and changes in life stages are important drivers for appliance purchases. It follows that if you're a high-end dishwasher brand, you don't want to lean on the glassware cycle or the ability to leave dishes clean. Those are baseline expectations. Even the middle-of-the-line dishwasher my mom had in the 1980s had a gentle cycle. Rather, you need to convince the baby boomer who is redecorating that you share her attention to detail and can help her turn a humdrum kitchen into the one she's always dreamed of. You need to reach her through the designers and other influencers who she considers to be credible experts on dream kitchens. Anecdotes from the Pioneer Woman and sponsorships that lead to recommendations from the local design center are solid bets in this example.

Similarly, the affluent couple who are expecting their first child expects a high-end washer to be able to clean clothes, but even dated models in apartment complexes can do that, at least to some extent. These consumers need to know that your washer will handle the laundry so that they can focus on creating the family life they've imagined for their new child. To win these consumers, you need to show them people who are living the life they also want, but with the help of *your* washer. Fashion bloggers, Pinterest, and Houzz have all been applied to great effect here. People who can see your product in a dream home can visualize it in their homes. For example, Samsung has done some great brand work with Kristen Bell and Dax Shepard. Bell and Shepard are influencers with a lifestyle that reflects the aspirations of Samsung's target demographic and a fun, comedic energy that makes them a fit for the family-friendly humor of an appliance ad. But they're also accessible enough that we might believe they've done their own laundry, and therefore know a thing or two about washing machines.

Featuring influencers with aspirational lifestyles has been a staple strategy from the beginning of advertising—brands have long leveraged celebrities, social media influencers, or people who reflect the audience's aspirations. In recent years, another strategy has gained more traction: Brands have been demonstrating that they can help their customers feel fulfilled just as they are. ThirdLove has built its bra brand on the idea that each body is distinct. Because ThirdLove's designers understand this, they can create underwear that fits more comfortably. American Eagle has shown products on models of varying sizes, including 000 through 24, to demonstrate its rejection of impossible standards for its young customers' bodies. Dove has employed models of a range of sizes and skin tones in its long-running Real Beauty campaign. The goal is to demonstrate its commitment to making women feel beautiful. In its current iteration, the campaign claims, "Beauty is not defined by shape, size or color—it's feeling like the best version of yourself. Authentic. Unique. Real. Which is why we've made sure our site reflects that. Every image you see here features women cast from real life. A real-life version of beauty."[40]

Becoming a Better Brand Storyteller

People retain information from stories better than from other formats because we relate better to stories. For marketers, this means that better stories, told more effectively, build connections that drive conversions.

A compelling story will connect the brand with the customer's personal narrative. That connection will transcend the moment and follow the customer to the moment of choice. The best stories will speak authentically and credibly to your customer. So, every message you send should align with the customer's story in a relevant way.

Remember not to give in to the temptation to put art or pretension ahead of clarity. Also be aware that the brand story is your chance to connect with your customer, not your brand's autobiography. Don't fall into the ego trap of focusing on yourself; focus on developing a deep understanding of the customer and how your brand can be the solution he needs to make his life what he wants. Once you've made these deep connections, customers will believe the story of how your brand will help them find fulfillment.

Finally, you need to take a position to forge an authentic human connection. In doing so, you might say something that is unappealing to some people. That's OK. The sound of a steak sizzling on a grill will probably nauseate vegetarians, but it will drive a steak house's audience to change their dinner plans.

Emotional Engagement

Introductory economics textbooks usually present the basic assumption that people behave rationally. Similarly, marketing textbooks emphasize the importance of price, product, place, and promotion because, like economists, marketers expect consumers to compare options to make the rational choice. If only life—or even marketing—were so simple.

The assumption of rationality is valuable because it helps economists model some behaviors and analyze complex situations. Likewise, the four Ps are still critical to good marketing. And, sure, people are capable of being rational and they can logically compare products based on facts and data, at least to some extent. But the latest research on the brain indicates that our default is not to think, but to feel.

Naturally, this truth extends to the realm of marketing. Thanks to advances in neuroscience and behavioral economics, we now know that a customer's relationship with a brand is fundamentally emotional. The propensity to recall a brand, the way people perceive a brand, and the willingness of customers to pay a premium for the brand—these are all founded on emotion and social cognition, not on cool rationality.

It follows that marketers must shift the way that we think about brand and brand management. We must face the reality that we can't control a brand through rigorous attention to the four Ps alone. Brand isn't a neat little box that encompasses a business; it's an *idea* that's viewed differently by each individual consumer. To effectively build and manage a brand, we must shift our focus to understanding the emotional processes behind consumer perceptions.

Brands as Somatic Markers

For years, Steve Jobs promised, "it just works." He vowed that Apple technology did what it was supposed to do without a bunch of hassle. If you were an elite designer, you could appreciate the superior graphics card and solid-state drive that wouldn't freeze up while you were editing high-res images in Photoshop. If your mom sat in front of your machine, you could trust that she wouldn't accidentally destroy it with a virus by installing a corrupted coupon toolbar. If you wanted to listen to music on your run, you could just plug your iPod into your computer and the playlists on iTunes would easily sync. All this was radically unfussy compared with the alternatives at the time.

The tech would "just work." The brand provided a respite from the cognitive demands of complicated comparisons in crowded competitive sets. You could pay a little bit more and know that you were getting a state-of-the-art device that would work as expected. After years of hearing this promise—and seeing Apple devices live up to it—brand users developed a loyalty so fierce that they lined up to buy new Apple products on release day, before even testing them. Other brands weren't even in the decision set for Apple loyalists. The emotional connection that Apple had made with its customers was so strong that the idea of buying phones or laptops from another brand felt risky and scary.

You may view quality, performance, service, aesthetics, or value as your core offering but, no matter what you're selling, you're selling your brand. And your brand lives and dies on how it makes your customer feel. Information lacks meaning without personal, emotional context. And that emotional context—the way the brand makes the customer feel—is of paramount importance, because emotional processes drive purchase decisions, whether you're selling paper plates or cars.

Backstory: The Heart vs. the Head

René Descartes proposed an abyssal separation of mind and body back in the seventeenth century. His idea was that there's a duality to human nature: The thinking brain and the mechanical body, with the latter being the source of emotions. The two entities operate separately and, Descartes concluded, the most rational decisions are made when we employ logic without emotion.

Descartes' scientific approach to distinguishing reason from emotion and his commitment to rationality heavily influenced Western thinking. Thus, since the French Enlightenment, many fields of study have been building on the idea that the thinking self is separate from the feeling self. We assume that calm rationality should drive behavior, not wild, unpredictable emotions. As a result, we've been conditioned to think of ourselves as logical decision-makers who are unaffected by emotions. Confirmation bias bolsters this belief by leading us to recall the logic behind our choices, not the emotion.

If you earned a poor grade on an exam, your parents probably didn't open the conversation by asking you to tell them about the environmental and psychological influences that impacted your performance. If the vice principal of your school called you to her office to discuss a disciplinary problem, she probably didn't ask you about how the other kid made you feel, or whether hunger, an oncoming virus, or other stresses impacted your behavior. Instead, parents and educators probably asked, "What were you *thinking?*" These adults were training you to defend the logic behind your actions, which requires you to assume that all actions are logical.

Of course, this post hoc examination of motives isn't limited to kids. A week and a half after the Los Angeles police picked up Hugh Grant for "an act of lewd conduct" with a sex worker, Jay Leno opened his interview with, "What the hell were you thinking?" Leno echoed the question in many viewers' minds, even though, surely, no one *really* thought Grant had carefully weighed costs and benefits and concluded that this course of action was for the best. (To his credit, Mr. Grant owned his actions, waved off excuses, and said, "I think you know in life pretty much what's a good thing to do and what's a bad thing and I did a bad thing.")

The idea that thinking is somewhat separate from feeling has also permeated academia. Social scientists have long recognized that emotions play some role in human decision-making, but they've generally fallen short in routinely considering and measuring the impact of emotions on behaviors. Economists have tended to begin with the assumption that rational self-interest will drive decisions.

They believe that reasonable people will follow incentives to make rational decisions, so predictions can be made by carefully considering incentives.

Marketers, similarly, employ researchers to predict purchase intentions by asking consumers what they would do, hypothetically, given a specific set of choices. If consumers don't choose their brand over the others, the marketers conclude that the other brand must've made a more compelling argument or enjoyed more prominent shelf space.

An awareness of our conditioning to explain what we were thinking—not how we were feeling—might give you a new frame of reference for understanding consumer research. If you've read much consumer research, you might have noticed that people tend to justify choices with logical arguments about superior quality, availability, or investment value, and rarely reference emotional drivers when asked about purchase decisions. Consumers usually don't say that they bought the Burberry trench because it aligns them with a group they perceive to have superior social status, allows them to signal their success to others, or makes them feel confident and proud. Rare is the research subject who will say that she's biased towards Burberry because she associates it with the hopeful final scene of *Breakfast at Tiffany's*. On the contrary, research subjects are far more likely to say that the $2,000 raincoat was a practical investment, partly because researchers likely asked some version of, "What were you thinking?" The question itself primed them to explain logic, not emotion. Questions about purchase drivers will lead to responses that imply reasoning over feeling.

Consumers tend to report that they care primarily about quality and investment value, but these responses are post hoc justifications for a heavily emotional process. Much as we'd like to think otherwise, the body often leads the brain. People frequently do things that *feel* right without pausing to weigh the costs and benefits. As marketers, we need to stop ignoring this reality. If we embrace the role that emotion plays in the consumer's relationship with the brand, we can leverage it to build equity and drive revenue.

The American Crowbar Case and the Ventromedial Prefrontal Cortex

The idea that we employ our logical minds to make decisions and that emotions follow is pervasive. But modern neurologists have proven that this couldn't be further from the case. Some of the most interesting research on the topic has roots in an antebellum industrial accident.

September 13, 1848 was just another day at work for railroad foreman Phineas Gage, until an explosion sent a tamping iron—a forty-three-inch-long, thirteen-pound metal rod—careening through his skull. The tamping iron went in through his cheek, traveled through the frontal lobe of his brain, and exited out the top of his skull before it landed yards away. Amazingly, Gage was conscious and talking within minutes. He lived for more than a decade after the injury. But he reportedly suffered extreme changes in personality. The historical record of the matter is somewhat incomplete, but the consensus is that Gage, who had been a responsible foreman, lost some critical judgment and planning skills and became undependable. Gage's case is a fixture in introductory psychology textbooks and lives on in the annals of medical history as early evidence that brain trauma can lead to personality change.[41]

To dig into the connection between emotion, judgment, and the brain, neuroscientist Antonio Damasio studied modern patients who also experienced ventromedial prefrontal cortex injuries. He found that, like Gage, the patients were generally functional after injuries, able to make calculations, remember situationally relevant knowledge, and employ logic skills. But their personalities changed. As a result, their personal and professional lives suffered, they didn't experience emotions the way they once had, and they suffered severe problems with practical reasoning.

One of Damasio's patients was a successful executive before experiencing brain trauma. After the injury, he still did fine on IQ and memory tests, but he could no longer complete reports on time. Earlier in his career, he excelled at preparing and presenting information effectively but after the injury, he obsessed over tangential details to the point that he couldn't complete projects. His ability to process facts and logic remained intact, but he lost practical rationality skills, which compromised his ability to evaluate the potential outcomes of various actions and left him unable to make good choices. He ultimately lost his job and his marriage.[42]

Conventional wisdom passed down from the time of Descartes holds that, without emotions getting in the way, we would make better, logical decisions. But Damasio's patients made poor decisions, even though their emotions had been stifled. Damasio's revolutionary conclusion was that the neural processes that drive emotion play a critical role in decision-making. Through these processes, emotions influence our decisions all the time, often subconsciously.

Enter the "somatic marker hypothesis."

The Somatic Marker Hypothesis

Our bodies and brains constantly work together to help us make decisions. When you're exhausted, your body is sluggish and your mind starts thinking about sleep and trying to ignore stimuli that could delay rest. As another example, people who are creeped out by a stranger's behavior will feel physically chilled.[43] If you see a predator, your body will release adrenaline. That will make you feel hyperalert as your mind plans a fight or flight. In these circumstances, your body and its feelings heavily influence your thoughts and decisions.

Emotions are essentially bodily feelings that manifest in the brain. Over time, physiological responses and the resulting emotions become linked in our minds. For example, your brain might associate a rapid heartbeat with fear, nausea with disgust, clenched teeth with anger, or hyperventilation with anxiety. When our ventromedial prefrontal cortex draws a connection between a perception of something we are presently experiencing and something we've experienced in the past, that part of our brain will trigger the same emotional-physical response. Damasio referred to these reflexive physiological manifestations of our emotions as somatic markers.[44]

Over the course of your life, your unique experiences and the resulting emotions and physiological responses to those experiences—the somatic markers—have become connected in your mind. Your brain uses these somatic markers and emotions consciously and unconsciously as you make decisions.

One of my friends had a kind and loving grandmother who was great at listening without judgment and building others up. When my friend was feeling down, her grandmother would serve brownies and offer wise perspectives and kind words, leaving my friend feeling calm, happy, and loved. As a result, my friend's brain connected brownies with comfort and love. Now, she reflexively opts for brownies when things are stressful at work, and brownies are her go-to when she wants to comfort others.

Somatic markers also lead us to avoid things that caused negative experiences in the past. For example, if you became ill from a ride at an amusement park, your brain recorded all of the emotions and physical sensations surrounding the incident. If you returned to a similar park, saw a similar ride, tasted that same nacho cheese, or caught a whiff of funnel cake today, your brain might 'pull that file,' and you would be hit with that same nauseous, panicked feeling that preceded your illness the last time. Your brain has that somatic marker in place to help you avoid a situation that has proven harmful to your well-being in the past.

In line with the theme of this text, the brain doesn't limit itself to somatic markers that are rational or beneficial. If you've ever become ill and regurgitated after eating a specific dish, the mere smell of a signature ingredient in that dish may trigger nausea, even if the dish itself was not to blame for the illness. Maybe seeing a calico cat triggers feelings of joy and nostalgia as you recall a beloved pet, even though you know there's no reason to believe that each calico cat will be as loving. Perhaps you've grown to hate a song you once loved because you associate it with a relationship that ended with a painful breakup. If your mother made you pie when you were a kid, the feelings of warmth and nostalgia may lead to an urge to order pie every time you're in a café, even though you know that salad is the more rational choice.

Somatic markers can also *evolve* throughout your lifetime. The county fair may have delighted you as a child. But now, even the sight of the eggbeater ride you once loved might trigger nausea and an elevated heart rate as your brain dredges up feelings associated with a more recent experience or a news article about a tragic carnival accident. Similarly, you could overcome negative feelings about athletics that stem from a cruel P.E. teacher and learn to love running.

Typically, if we're weighing choices and imagining outcomes, and a somatic marker associated with something that makes us happy is triggered, it leads us to favor that choice, consciously or unconsciously. Imagine that it's Saturday morning and, as you finish your coffee, you unlock your phone and see that there are a couple hundred unread emails. You don't have time to read every email at that moment, but you'd like to see if there are any worth reading. As you scan senders and subject lines, most don't trigger any feelings at all—coupons you won't use, newsletters you don't care much about, etc.—but you might unconsciously smile and feel your shoulders drop when see a message from the close friend who makes you feel great about yourself. You'll immediately open that message. By contrast, the email from the repugnant coworker who always criticizes your work and undermines you in meetings will wait until Monday.

The decision to open one email and postpone the other would not be a carefully considered choice but an emotionally guided decision made in a fraction of a second. Phineas Gage and others who have suffered damage to the ventromedial prefrontal cortex couldn't come to quick conclusions like this. Without emotional involvement and "gut feelings," trivial decisions like which email to open first become overwhelming.

Damasio's research shows that emotions don't get in the way of rational decision-making; to the contrary, they play a critical role in helping us make decisions efficiently. Emotions help us apply our past experiences to project potential outcomes and filter options so that we can quickly make sound choices and get on with our lives.

Put another way, we cannot expect to separate thinking and feeling, and we shouldn't try. Emotional-physical reactions are a part of our everyday lives, so emotions influence our reasoning and judgments all the time. This should be a critical consideration as you make plans for your brand and customer experience.

Implication: Brand as a Somatic Marker

Traditional theorists reasoned that, when faced with a choice, we weigh costs and benefits, make the rational (utility-maximizing) decision, then experience emotions as a result of that decision. But Damasio's somatic marker hypothesis suggests that these emotional-physical reactions are baked into our everyday experiences and color how we perceive the world around us. When we're faced with a decision, we experience a reflexive emotion based on a somatically marked experience—a gut feeling—that guides us to make our choice. And after this emotionally driven choice, we come up with a reason, consciously or unconsciously, that serves to justify the decision and fits with our preconceived narrative.

This has staggering implications for marketers. If you ask a consumer how he shops for pencils, he might tell you that he considers cost, or maybe that he mostly uses pens. Maybe he'd talk about a preference between mechanical and traditional pencils. The reality is that, for most people, pencils are a low-consideration purchase that isn't planned or researched beforehand. Answering the questions in your survey might be the sum of the time a respondent would spend thinking about pencil purchase considerations in his entire life.

Pencils on their own don't elicit primary emotions. A person with no experience with pencils wouldn't feel excited or afraid the first time they encountered one. But if our consumer loved school as a child, he might see a pencil and experience positive, nostalgic feelings generated in part by the ventromedial prefrontal cortex. He would come across box of pencils in the store and immediately feel happy and nostalgic. Then, he would feel compelled to buy a box of the Dixon Ticonderoga No. 2 pencils even though he rarely used pencils and even though those pencils cost a dollar more than the store brand. All this because he had used a sharpened Dixon Ticonderoga No. 2 pencil to write his name for the first time and had received delighted praise from his sweet kindergarten teacher and his loving mother. His purchasing choice would have been based the emotional connection to the hours he had spent with those green stripes while he sketched Teenage Mutant Ninja Turtles in class when the teacher wasn't watching.

The first time this consumer saw a pencil, it probably meant little to him. But each positive experience strengthened the positive emotional connection with the Dixon brand until he developed strong, positive secondary emotions around it. Maybe he even had a negative experience or two with a cheap, store-brand pencil that wouldn't sharpen properly in the old hand-crank sharpener in his elementary school classroom, further strengthening this positive somatic marker. The point is that the consumer's choice between pencils isn't high stakes, so he's not going to spend hours researching pencils or reviewing marketing materials. He's just going to reach for the pencils that trigger the positive somatic marker, without thinking.

Leveraging Somatic Markers to Build Brand Equity

Somatic markers are as fluid as they are personal. We can learn to reframe negative experiences to view them as foundational to our current identities and parts of our personal journeys, making reliving them less painful. We can learn to love the experiences we hated as children, feeling more self-satisfied than disgusted when we crunch on the limp, bitter blades in a salad at lunchtime. And we can learn to hate brands we once loved.

As marketers, we're constantly eliciting these physiological affective states in customers. If most of the brand experiences are positive and make customers feel good, their relationships with the brand will strengthen over time, increasing loyalty. The goal is for the brand to become somatically marked positively so that it will become the automatic choice, even when it's not the easiest.

Customer Experience is Brand

When I moved to a new city after college, there were numerous coffee shops between my apartment and my office. They all touted fair-trade beans and special blends, but the coffee all tasted roughly the same to me. So, after trying several of the most conveniently located cafes, I began to frequent the shop with the environment I liked best. There was always punk or garage band music playing and flyers advertising concerts on the walls, and the baristas had the sort of piercings, tattoos, and hairstyles that would preclude them from employment at many establishments. After a while, the baristas started greeting me with "mocha, right?" They asked about my day, talked about their dogs or bands, or gave me a free cookie when things were slow. Because they made me feel like I fit in there, it helped me bridge the gap between feeling like a youthful student and a boring adult. My many experiences at the shop helped me feel like I was holding onto my true self and comforted me at a time when everything in my life was new and unfamiliar.

I was a loyal customer for a few months, even when road construction made parking more difficult. Then, there appeared a snarling new barista who, on each of my next two visits, called me "Suit" and messed up my order. Her sneer made clear that I wasn't cool enough to drink coffee there and that I shouldn't dare ask her to correct my order unless I wanted to drink some of her spit with my coffee. I switched to another coffee shop without giving her a third chance. Visiting the place that was once my Cheers now made me feel stressed and insecure.

The employees tasked with interacting with customers are usually the lowest profile at an establishment. These employees are the lowest-earning and may be looked down on by managers that find their lack of experience and professionalism annoying. In turn, these employees are unlikely to be heavily invested in jobs where the managers are condescending and the paychecks won't even cover rent. But front-line employees are the main connection between the brand and the customer, so they're critical to the business' success.

For me, the coffee shops were all initially interchangeable, so I had chosen the one that made me feel best as I prepared for a day at the office or whiled away a Saturday morning. But when a new barista made me feel self-conscious and out of place, the dozens of great experiences I had before at that shop became irrelevant. The thought of going back made me feel panicked. My brain kept calling up the feeling of being mocked for my outfit and intimidated by the snarling barista.

> *"I've learned that people will forget what you said, people will forget what you did, but people will never forget how you made them feel."*
> -Maya Angelou

Maya Angelou's observation that we remember, foremost, how people make us feel is consistent with the somatic marker hypothesis. When it comes to building and reinforcing the customer's associations with your brand, everything matters. Every experience with your brand can serve to strengthen, rebuild, or undermine the experiences before it. If the customer has strong, positive emotions associated with your brand, your relationship can probably weather a storm or two. But your customers will remember if you treat them poorly and make them feel like they don't matter. That could undercut months of positive experiences.

The same is true of the digital customer experience; a buggy, unresponsive website is as frustrating as a rude, unresponsive human.

To accept the somatic marker hypothesis—that our brain uses somatically marked experiences as shortcuts for making decisions—is to accept that anytime you're interacting with the customer, you're creating an experience that could have an outsized impact on his future purchase decisions. Experience is the real source of equity and emotion is the currency. Therefore, you can build brand equity by creating positive feelings about the brand.

How Much Does it Matter?
The degree to which any positive somatic markers associated with your brand can be undermined—and the degree to which that matters—depends on a number of factors. Customers might

consider the nature of your business, the competitive landscape, and whether a bad experience seems like part of a pattern.

The coffee shop market in my city was highly saturated, the products weren't differentiated, and switching shops wasn't difficult. Further, it seemed like the surly new barista was there to stay. So, it was easy for that first shop to lose my business once the new barista undermined the shop's best quality: the environment.

Relationships with brands that involve high-consideration purchases may be even more vulnerable because the consumer is taking on more risk when he makes a choice, and a negative outcome will be more painful for him. I used to fly frequently for work and was loyal to a single airline until a particularly egregious issue occurred. The most remarkable part of that story isn't the tale of the appallingly bad customer service I experienced, but the reactions I got when I shared my experience with others. They listened to me with angry expressions and then shared horror stories of their own, which generally ended with sworn promises that they would never give that brand another cent. These stories are delivered with the venom you'd expect to be reserved for personal matters, not business transactions, because the level of disrespect felt degrading.

Academic research on B2B services suggested that customers consider their cumulative experiences with your brand when deciding whether to switch. The researchers noted that the customer may give you another chance if a negative experience seems like an outlier, underscoring the importance of making every effort to convince the customer that it won't happen again.[45]

Researchers have concluded that the "magic ratio" of positive to negative emotions in successful relationships is about 5:1. Specifically, researchers have found that couples who experience less than five positive interactions for each negative interaction during a conflict were more likely to divorce.[46] This indicates that there's hope for businesses that have messed up or routinely require customers to experience something painful, as long as they can offer sufficient upside.

Aligning with Positive Experiences

The saying "the couple that plays together stays together" has become cliché for a reason. If you have an exciting, fun experience with your spouse, you'll associate your spouse with that invigorating physiological-emotional state. Memories of the experience will ultimately become conflated with your feelings about your spouse, so thinking of her will trigger the heart-pumping feelings of excitement that you experienced on your shared adventure.

You should go out of your way to create memorable, positive experiences for customers for the same reason you should keep date nights or anniversary celebrations with your spouse. You want your spouse to have positive, fulfilled feelings when she thinks of you, and you want your customers to associate your brand with positive, satisfying experiences.

Kodak labeled the irreplaceable, precious moments in life "Kodak moments." It presented ads with imagery of families and love and underscored the brand's unique ability to help you remember the moments that make life worth living. Similarly, Skype's 2014 "Stay Together" campaign told stories of scattered families and friends who stay connected thanks to Skype's technology. A perfume called Vacation—which the makers say smells like "sunscreen and summer" elicits positive feelings in wearers because the scent triggers beach memories. One reviewer said, "I close my eyes and feel like I'm in Florida on the beach again." Another said that she finds people leaning in and smiling when she wears the fragrance.

Kodak, Skype, and the makers of Vacation didn't have to create these positive experiences to reap the benefits—they just had to align their brands with the experiences.

When most people see pictures of the Rocky Mountains, they probably think of cold snow, fresh air, and natural beauty. By prominently featuring the Rockies for years, Coors has benefitted from these positive associations. Seeing images of the Rocky Mountains might trigger somatically marked experiences like feeling the crisp air on your cheeks at a ski resort or the fresh, cool breeze on a stroll through a shady forest. These refreshing sensations are relevant and appealing to people searching for a cold pilsner on a sticky summer afternoon, which can only benefit the brand. By choosing imagery that evokes the sensation that Coors customers want to feel at the moment of consumption, Coors has aligned its product with those positive experiences, thus giving the product an edge. I loved the 2022 extension in which exhausted, sweaty men in mascot costumes share a locker room couch while they enjoy Coors Light. The TV spots, which were in heavy rotation during March Madness, closed by calling the beer "the official beer of being off the clock." After days of make-or-break games, viewers could imagine how drained the mascots must've been—and how great that first taste of cold beer would feel.

Because somatic markers are different for each person, no one signal will evoke the same positive associations for every customer. The key to avoiding missteps is to remain mindful of prominent cultural associations with individual aspects of the brand identity you're creating.

Application: The Power of Nostalgia and Rosy Retrospection
During a recent conversation with a millennial, we discussed the 1990s games Nintendo is releasing on new platforms. He said, "My

eyes hurt just thinking about playing Mario Kart on N64." But as he talked about this pain, he was grinning, chuckling, and moving his hands as though holding an old controller. He said he had downloaded some of these old (painful) games to play with his kid.

In a day and age when there's more gaming content available than anyone could possibly consume, he chose to purchase antiquated games to play with his child. Clearly, this man associates the games (and the eye pain) with the puerile joy of a free Saturday morning. His parents were sleeping in, his homework deadlines weren't yet looming, his cereal was innutritious and delicious, and he was free. When he saw that one of his favorite games from his youth was an option, he reflexively chose it over the thousands of competing titles because his mind connected that choice with nostalgia and joy.

Indeed, tapping the power of nostalgia is one of the best ways to get customers to associate your brands with positive experiences. Advertising research has demonstrated that nostalgic ads measurably increase consumers' connections with brands and their likelihood of choosing the brand.[47] In findings that are notably consistent with the somatic marker hypothesis, one study found that the most effective ads were those that were so engaging that they evoked both positive emotions and physiological reactions, such as goosebumps, laughter/smiles, or memories so intense that subjects said they could taste, smell, or hear things from their pasts.[48]

Your bottom line will benefit if you can induce consumers to associate your brand with a happier time, but this begs the question: What if that time wasn't happier for all your customers? It turns out, it doesn't really matter, because we generally look at the past with rosy retrospection, remembering it as being better than it was.

In a series of studies on rosy retrospection, University of Washington researchers found that people tended to remember vacations as being more fun in retrospect than they had reported during the escapes.[49] There appears to be an enjoyment curve: people tend to look forward to a trip with anticipation, then experience an increase in negative feelings as annoyances accumulate during the vacation, and then they look back with what the researchers called a "rosy view." Think about summer vacations during childhood. If you're like most people, you probably recall happy times on your bike, at the pool, or with friends. We're less apt to remember how feelings of boredom, loneliness, or skinned knees tinged those months. As Proust said, "remembrance of things past is not necessarily the remembrance of things as they were."

There's merit to focusing on the good in your past, but this bias could lead you to unwise choices, such as rekindling a romance you shouldn't or adopting a declinist view about life in general. Think of the fortysomething who complains that all new music is awful and that bands aren't as good as they were in his day. He bases this view on a dislike of some new pop songs, but he forgets that he did not like all the 1990s music he grew up with either. And, importantly, he's associating those songs with fading memories of his teenage years—memories that skew positive. There's no reason to believe that he'd love those same songs as much if they were new and playing on the radio today.

Our tendency to have inaccurately positive views of the past can work well for marketers. Calls to nostalgia are calls to the known and comfortable, which is why they work particularly well on audiences that find themselves in times of turmoil. The BBC found that its G.O.L.D. channel—where it reran archival comedy programming—particularly appealed to those who felt older than their chronological age and wanted to remember happier times. Meanwhile, the segment that felt more "young at heart" found modern programming more appealing.[50]

Rosy retrospection combines with contrast effects to drive otherwise happy people to find the present lacking when they recall positive memories.[51] Thus, you can nudge Gen-X into a nostalgic frame of mind—and prime them to purchase nostalgic products—by reminding them of Saturday morning cartoons, sugary cereal, and "Thriller." But, as we'll discuss in the next chapter, contrast effects can work against you, too. Reminding Gen-X of the worst parts of the past will remind them that the present is better and nudge them to purchase modern products that didn't exist in the 1980s.

We can look to General Mills for a best practice. Each Fall, many millennials and Gen-Xers who navigate cereal aisles are delighted to find Franken Berry and Count Chocula cereals in boxes that still feature the monster characters of our youth. After seeing box after box of granola and bran, the nostalgic characters hearken back to a perceived simpler time when we could enjoy a bowl of sugar with our morning cartoons. There's no logical reason for an adult to buy herself a breakfast cereal with more sugar than a doughnut, with a cartoon character on the box, but many choose to do so anyway. The brand's retention of classic characters isn't an attempt to ensnare today's children; it's General Mills' reminder to adults that its cereal was a part of our happy childhood memories. General Mills hopes we will buy the cereal to relive those memories or to create similar memories with our own children.

If you're seeking a 'worst practice' example of nostalgia in marketing, look no further than Hasbro and its game *Monopoly for Millennials*. Rather than contrasting the past with the present and leveraging nostalgia, Hasbro made the past-present comparison to point out how hard the economy has been on millennials, with a mocking line across the box: "Forget real estate. You can't afford it anyway." A little dark for game night and the millennials of X made clear that they didn't appreciate the big business mocking their relative poverty. You heard it here first: Insulting your audience is rarely a path to success in marketing.

While it may feel like legacy brands and products are a better fit for leveraging the power of association and positive somatic markers via a nostalgic campaign, nostalgia isn't just for older brands. Since our sepia-toned, idealized version of the past never actually happened, a brand need not be a part of the past to forge an authentic connection. In a scene on *Mad Men*, protagonist Don Draper said Kodak's Carousel slide projector enabled people to travel as a child does: "Around and around and back home again, the place where we know we're loved." The pitch centered on him clicking through a series of happy family photos—so happy that a colleague who had recently cheated on his wife left, in tears.

Whatever realities belie Draper's story don't matter. Many marriages have ended in divorce, and everyone has painful childhood memories, but painful memories don't undermine the effectiveness of a nostalgia-oriented marketing strategy. After all, wrapping customers in the warmth of nostalgia isn't about helping them accurately recall their pasts. It's about triggering positive feelings and aligning your brand with them. My millennial coffee companion has painful childhood memories, but the memories triggered by the old Mario Kart game are warm and fuzzy. As marketers, our job is to select past highlights, as Draper did in his Kodak pitch. We need to find the fun songs, the beloved movies, the whacky pop-culture phenomena, and the fun aspects of childhood that people want to remember. Your brand doesn't need to be a part of these memories to invoke them. Recall that Instagram's original product was filters and dimensions that made smartphone photos look like Polaroid photos from the 90s. And Uber Eats ran a Super Bowl commercial featuring the guys from *Wayne's World*—a movie released over 20 years before Uber was founded.

Another key benefit of nostalgic campaigns is that they do the work of personalization for you. A reference to products from the past will conjure unique memories for each person. The smell of cologne that was popular in a specific era might remind people of school dances, a first love, or a friend they've lost touch with. An old song could transport them back to a barbeque with people they haven't thought about in twenty years. By coaxing your audience into a nostalgic frame of mind, you can align your product with each person's unique, deeply personal experiences without creating and managing a complicated, personalized campaign. Pepsi's 2022 campaign offered a chance to win some Crystal Pepsi—a clear soda it manufactured for a couple of years in the 1990s—to customers who shared a picture of themselves from the 1990s and tagged the brand. This made the brand engagement fun, nostalgic, and emotionally engaging—because it was deeply personal.

The key to leveraging nostalgia without seeming passé or irrelevant is to keep the message relatable and appropriate. People enjoy references from their past that they understand, but they won't respond to any random tidbit you dredge up. You can't expect to create an impression if the past references are not relevant to the brand and interesting to the customers.

Creating Positive Experiences

The kind of somatic marker that your customer's mind creates for your brand is critical to ongoing success, but this doesn't mean that you need to make every interaction with every customer spectacular. You only need to consistently meet or exceed their expectations for your brand.

Your brand is your promise to customers, employees, and anyone who interacts with it. These interactions should tell people what they can expect from your company. If you underperform relative to those expectations, you've broken a promise, and customers will feel disappointed. Some will harbor a painful memory about your brand that could undermine any previously positive experiences with your company. By contrast, if your employees consistently endeavor to deliver on brand values, the customer will see that you are at least trying to keep your promise and that they matter to you. Every part of the experience matters: high environmental standards, comfortable bathrooms, mobile-optimized web experiences, and attention to other relevant details will support positive emotional states and demonstrate to the customers that they are valued.

Somatically marked experiences that positively resonate with customers in relevant ways are the best possible differentiators for your brand. Attention to perceptual experiences creates somatic markers that draw people to your brand, bias them in your favor, and make them feel great about purchasing from you. These positive experiences will also build brand equity, which can sustain loyalty through instances when you don't meet expectations.

Case Study: The Abercrombie of Yore

We've established that, for adults, most decisions are driven by emotional processes, with more analytical involvement in higher-consideration purchases. Because the prefrontal cortex, which governs this analytical thinking, doesn't mature until about age twenty-five, nearly all decisions for younger shoppers are reactionary and emotionally driven.

This means that, to engage younger shoppers, your *entire* focus should be on appealing to relevant emotional needs. For example, you might want to offer young people the promise of fitting in, feeling confident, or looking good. You don't need to worry about detailed information on products and features, even if your product is expensive. Carefully staged images of clothing on groups of people who look like friends having fun imply that the clothing can help adolescents fit in and feel good about themselves. This kind of imagery—and the implied emotional promises—are far more important to the purchase decision than details about fabric content or cleaning instructions.

Emotional engagement like this is where Abercrombie & Fitch shined. A&F knew that winning teens' hearts was key to winning their cash, so it went full-throttle on creating emotional engagement and positive somatic markers.

Messaging focused primarily on the insight that teens wanted to be like the cool kids. And responses to hormonal urges also played a role. Stores employed uncommonly attractive, shirtless male models to stand outside of store entrances (in front of the giant, black and white photos of other beautiful, scantily clad twentysomethings). As they walked past the models, teens transitioned from their mom's mall—Hallmark, Ann Taylor, Ross—into the sort of place that was, pop culture told them, more their scene. The stores reeked of cologne, the music was loud, and the lights were so low that parents struggled to read price tags. This wasn't a place for moms to feel comfortable or for the budget-conscious to find deals. This was a place for the cool teenagers—the ones who had sex and cars—and the brand didn't pretend otherwise.

> *"In every school there are the cool and popular kids, and then there are the not-so-cool kids. We go after the cool kids. We go after the attractive all-American kid with a great attitude and a lot of friends. A lot of people don't belong [in our clothes], and they can't belong. Are we exclusionary? Absolutely."* -Mike Jeffries, CEO of Abercrombie & Fitch

The Abercrombie of the 1990s and 2000s knew what was cool—and teens could own the brand and feel cool too if they were willing to splash out three times what the clothes at JC Penney cost. They'd be assisted by gorgeous, young employees that embodied the look of the brand (thin, hot, and usually white), then carry the jeans home in a bag with another shirtless guy on it—the kind of guy who might notice you if *you* had those jeans, the kind of picture that was edgy enough to make parents uncomfortable.

This aspirational world wasn't limited to hedonistic shopping environments and low-rise jeans. In addition to some of the sexiest print ads out there, the brand had a quarterly magazine with articles about pop culture that, like the print ads, essentially served up softcore to elevate desire for the brand and its exclusive, affluent lifestyle. Articles included drinking games and cocktail recipes (in a back-to-school issue) and sex advice (for a Christmastime 'Naughty or Nice' issue).

The obsessive attention to emotional engagement paid off. Entering the twenty-first century, Abercrombie & Fitch was ranked by teens as one of the "coolest" brands of any kind[52], and the rapid expansion seemed unstoppable. The stores sold clothes, but really, they sold the teenage dream of being "the popular kid." The clothing retailer had evolved into a true lifestyle brand that embodied the effortless-cool image every high schooler wanted to project. The brand knew exactly how to harness hormones and aspirations to engage shoppers and turn teenage dreams into sales.

Entering the new millennium, A&F seemed unstoppable. But by 2017, its stock was selling for an eighth as much as it had ten years before. What happened? The recession and the fall of mall shopping hurt. The shift to digital shopping was also hard on Abercrombie's bottom line. A&F stores excelled at creating a hedonistic, emotionally charged environment that drove teens to buy, so the shift to digital meant that it had to sacrifice some control of the environment and the shopper's emotional state. But the true death knell was the shifting zeitgeist.

The sexy ads and flagrantly elitist positioning that had made the brand unbeatable in the 1990s were out of step with the rising emphasis on inclusivity in subsequent decades. Perhaps as a reaction to the anorexic, elite lookbook that excluded most people, the new generation of teens and influencers began to talk more about body positivity, racial inclusivity, and anti-elitism.

The elite, white, exclusive world that Abercrombie had venerated wasn't aspirational anymore. Taking its place in the hearts of teens were inclusive brands like American Eagle, which offered extended sizes, diverse models, and a commitment to demonstrating that they're in line with the new generation's values.

Ever savvy, the marketers over at A&F have tried to keep up with this cultural evolution, peppering the site and social feeds with words like respect, unity, and inclusivity, and promising that they're "embracing diversity."

> "Abercrombie isn't a brand where you need to fit in—it's one where everyone truly belongs. We lead with purpose, and that inclusive and equitable spirit is woven throughout all we do." -Fran Horowitz, CEO A&F Co.

Only time will tell if consumers too young to remember the previous brand identity will find this new positioning credible, whether they care about the brand's past, and whether the 2022 Netflix documentary about A&F will distance younger generations from the brand forever. For those of us old enough to remember the 1990s, the old A&F marketers may have done their jobs too well. The brand that became synonymous with white elitism and exclusivity will have a hard time convincing us that it truly values everyone.

Getting It Right with Young Adults
So, how can your brand engage younger audiences with your message? First, I beseech you to refrain from flagrantly selling sex to children as Abercrombie did. Teens today are savvier about how skeevy that is, and their social-influencer mothers will have your hide faster than you can say "Fitch the Homeless."

Instead, approach them like you would adults by looking for connections that are as authentic as they are aspirational. Influencers who embody your target's best qualities and reflect aspirations they can be proud of, like athletic achievements, persistence, and unique beauty, are great choices. Calls to aspire to something relevant, authentic, and meaningful can be an opportunity to show your customers that you understand them—the best parts of them. This is, essentially, your brand can act as a mirror for them, but a flattering one. A beauty brand, for instance, could demonstrate that it's cutting-edge in reflecting trends, but also that it's accessible. The brand can balance coolness with a sense of self-worth.

The next step is to research, research, research. But remember that asking young adults what they would choose in a hypothetical situation or putting them in a focus group will be of little value. The social dynamics of a focus group will impact the teens' willingness and ability to pinpoint what's trending. Even in interviews, teens are unlikely to provide a meaningful explanation for why they find specific trends appealing. Instead, try ethnographic methods that allow you to study teens' in-the-moment decisions. For example, Abercrombie reportedly hired workers to visit college campuses across the country to observe and predict trends that the brand could leverage. Now, a sophisticated—and surprisingly affordable—crop of research tools can help you do the same from afar. Social listening tools provide insights so robust that they seem almost predictive, and mobile research tools like mFour enable you to be "in the moment" as shoppers make decisions, without worrying (as much) about testing effects.

Brands as People

If you read the reviews of iRobot products, you'll notice that people name their robotic vacuums. Not Roomba #2 or Upstairs Vacuum, but Larry or Mr. Carson. Owners sometimes speak of the robots as though they're people, explaining how "he got stuck on a cable and tried to hang himself" or "I worried Bob would fall down the stairs, but he stopped in time." These customers know the robots aren't people, but they've consciously anthropomorphized their vacuums. It's clear that the reviewers see the vacuums with a sort of metaphoric humanness.

While iRobot hasn't intentionally anthropomorphized its products in marketing communications, many brands in the past have. Think of the Kool-Aid Man or the Cinnamon Toast Crunch cereal characters. We've also seen some more direct approaches to portraying brands as people. The Apple ads that featured Mac and PC as people come to mind. The sharp, youthful Mac in his jeans and hoodie spoke of entertainment apps and contrasted with the stodgy PC in his suit, who said that spreadsheets and pie charts *are* fun. The ads took a lighthearted approach to explain why Apple products were worth the premium. The general message was that PCs are fine for boring work activities like spreadsheets, but that Apple's machines are better for all the fun stuff at home, and that they're safer and easier. Essentially, the play here was to take something that would be a cold, technical decision (deciding whether Apple machines were worth the higher cost) and reframing it as a more human, emotional decision, coaxing people to abandon the more logical analyses typically reserved for pricier products and go with the cool choice.

The decision to infuse a brand with human characteristics is one of the most ridiculed in marketing. Critics argue that consumers are too smart to conflate brands with people and that consumers resent the implication they're not. I submit that this argument is on the order of "advertising doesn't work on me." Consumers naturally imbue nonhuman entities like brands with human characteristics; therefore, building on the consumer's instincts helps create a stronger impression of the brand, which is favorable for marketers. The caveat is the same as any other marketing work: It only works if it's done well. Consumers don't resent quality marketing work; they resent having their days interrupted with crappy ads.

Moms waiting for children at dance practice quickly learn to avoid the mom that's interrupting their applause and photography to sell them something. People trying to follow live commentary on a sporting event on X are just as annoyed by frequent tweets about toothpaste. Even if the voice behind the tweets is funny and on-brand, just like the otherwise friendly mom at dance practice, it's annoying because it's interrupting someone with an unsolicited sales pitch. The issue isn't that the brand was acting like a person, but that it was acting like the type of person you'd rather avoid.

Infusing humanity into your brand will help people understand its role and relevance in their lives, thereby attracting customers. But if you bring your brand to life as an annoying person your customer would not want to be around, you will deter customers. You'd never go to a dinner party and spout random factoids about a store while ignoring what everyone else is saying, so why would you act like that on social media?

Building Brand Equity through Anthropomorphism

As our minds try to parse information, we naturally tend to anthropomorphize and begin to consider attributes of brands and products as if they were people. This anthropomorphic tendency can vary between individuals, but researchers have demonstrated that marketers can benefit from campaigns that build on the consumer's natural tendency to relate to a brand as if it were a person.

A growing body of research has found that people tend to automatically anthropomorphize nonhuman objects, particularly those that are more complex (e.g., cars, laptops),[53] and ads can influence this. Anthropomorphized presentations of products lead people to relate better emotionally to brands which, ultimately, leads people to prefer the brands.[54] Naturally, a stronger emotional connection leads people to relate to brands in social terms rather than as purchasers of utilitarian benefits. And when people approach purchasing decisions from a place of social cognition, they tend to choose brands with likable personalities that express their self-concepts.[55] Who would want to be the stodgy PC Guy when you could be the cool, young Apple Guy?

Emphasizing the humanness of a brand also makes it more trustworthy in the eyes of customers,[56] reduces feelings of risk related to using products,[57] improves consumer evaluations of products,[58] and reduces the likelihood of replacement.[59] Experimental research has demonstrated that anthropomorphized brands can even influence behaviors beyond the purchasing process. For instance, researchers have found that priming consumers with mention of a healthy brand can increase consumers' willingness to choose the stairs over an elevator.[60]

Anthropomorphism leads people to relate to a brand on a less logical, more human, and more emotional level even though they know a brand isn't a person. Building on the customer's natural tendency to endow your brand with some human characteristics will enable you to develop a deeper emotional connection and build brand equity among consumers.

Anthropomorphism: Where to Start

As you try to create and describe your brand-person, the easiest approach is to implement one of the frameworks psychologists use to describe people. If you're starting from an internal vision of a brand, as you do when launching a new business or brand, the Big Five framework is an intuitive fit. With the Big Five framework, you would consider where the brand falls on spectrums of extraversion, agreeableness, openness to experience, conscientiousness, and neuroticism.

This approach is supported by psychologists, who affirm that it offers a relatively comprehensive representation of personalities (as opposed to binary characteristics like introvert and extrovert). It is also extremely easy for teams to understand, so you can develop a clear idea of your brand's personality. Describing a brand in terms of these five scales could result in a description like "reserved, helpful, practical, careful, and confident." This description might come to life as someone like Martin Short's character in *Captain Ron*, who would be a great spokesman for an insurance firm or tax software brand.

Who are your customers? Who are they trying to impress?
Consumers prefer brands that are socially relevant and consistent with their self-concepts. This means that people purchase and surround themselves with specific brands not because the products are necessarily the best or most affordable, but to support their sense of identity. Consumers understand that brands are a social signal. We use brands to mentally categorize each other, and we expect others to infer things about us based on the brands we display.[61][62][63] To wit: Helga Dittmar titled one of her papers on this topic, in part, "To Have is to Be."[64]

You might choose a brand to signal something about yourself, or to avoid signaling something about yourself. A designer at an agency where I once worked told me that she bought an Apple laptop, even though it was more expensive than a PC that met her needs, to avoid being endlessly mocked by coworkers.

Many of us have been guilty of making unconscious judgments about people based on the brands they choose. My favorite examples of this are university rivalries. People from Michigan say that you go to Michigan State University to learn about cows and to the University of Michigan to date them. Just seeing someone in a university sweatshirt might lead you to assume that he is more likely to be more politically conservative, smarter, or more likely to be a history major. These types of superficial judgments can happen with any brand. I once heard a business major quip that when you see someone in a Carhart beanie, you can assume that he is either a construction worker or an art major.

Our preference for brands that support the identities that we'd like to signal to others means that people will prefer your brand over others if its anthropomorphized form represents their self-concepts.[65] If you're working to anthropomorphize an existing brand, the clearest path forward is to consider your existing customers. You should start with an analysis of the people already attracted to your brand and a qualitative evaluation of how relatable or aspirational those customers are for the group you're targeting.

The VALS™ data many agencies buy is a great tool for determining the personalities and values of your customers. Questions about faith, openness to change and new experiences, intellectual curiosity, comfort with technology, values, or character traits will give you an idea of how your customers see themselves and what they pride themselves on.

Aspirations and self-images can vary as widely as other personality characteristics. Saks Fifth Avenue shoppers may see themselves as sophisticated curators of quality. They might work statements like "I got it at Saks'" into their conversations. Walmart's core customers, by contrast, may view themselves as savvy bargain hunters and pride themselves on their ability to stretch their dollars. They might boast, "I got it at Walmart!"

Not everyone will aspire to own your brand simply because it's associated with a group that your internal team believes to have a higher social status. It would be folly to assume that the Walmart shopper wishes she could afford the $98 Diptyque candles at Saks or that the Sak's shopper would brag about how little she paid for a clearance item.

Romcoms would have us believe that opposites attract, but research has demonstrated that people prefer to relate to others like themselves. This is true in hiring, [66] dating, [67] or forming friendships.[68] For this reason, it often makes sense to reflect the existing customers back to themselves as you work to bring the brand to life—as long as you emphasize the characteristics that they are proud of. If self-reported survey data about your customers shows that they tend to have low openness to experience, some may think of them as the killjoy hall monitor type, but they probably see themselves as practical, dependable, and pragmatic. On the opposite end of the spectrum, a person some see as spontaneous to the point of mania may view themselves as an imaginative, creative dreamer. The key to impactful marketing messages isn't understanding how you see your consumer, but how she sees herself.

If you're marketing a bakery brand, the pragmatist wants the ability to order ahead and to know that you'll have the precise item she wants at the appointed time. You need to assure this customer that you offer dependable quality and efficiency. To capture the dreamer's attention, you'll need to signal that your brand is creative and open-minded, like her. This customer would be interested in a unique in-store experience with the opportunity to sample unexpected flavor combinations. She won't mind paying a few cents extra for coffee if it comes in unique cups designed by local artists.

As critical as understanding your customer is considering who the customer is trying to impress or be accepted by. Often, you'll find the customer is trying to impress others like themselves. Some may think the Hermès customer is a materialistic slave to social pressures who wishes to blow money on signals of wealth so that everyone will know how rich she is. This line of thinking would lead a marketer to recommend that Hermès stamp giant logos all over a high-end handbag so that it's a more recognizable signal. But this customer probably views herself not as a frivolous shopper, but as a discerning connoisseur who has earned access to the best products. She's probably not trying to signal her high status to everyone that passes on the street; she's trying to signal it to other women like her in her circle. And those women don't need a conspicuous logo to recognize a five-figure handbag.

Understanding the Nature of the Relationship
In addition to understanding how your customer sees himself and who he's trying to impress, marketing teams need to understand the nature of the relationship between the brand and the customer before they consider anthropomorphism. Consumer response to brand anthropomorphism tends to depend on the role of the brand in the customer's life.

For instance, do customers consider your brand to be a partner or more like an assistant? This subtle difference can have a dramatic impact on the results of anthropomorphism. One study found that well-liked, anthropomorphized brands that people viewed as *partners* primed people to behave in line with the brand's identity. By comparison well-liked, anthropomorphized brands that consumers viewed as a *servant* have the opposite effect.[69]

Selective Search, a matchmaking company, ran a print campaign with ads that included the following copy:

> *You've worked hard to enjoy the finer things in life. But somehow you're still missing the best part, a passionate connection with someone special. Make this summer your summer of love. Contact North America's leading matchmaking firm for a complimentary consultation.*

The brand presents itself as intelligent, sophisticated, and the best in its field, just like the wealthy professionals it's targeting. Selective search understands that people are looking for a partner in a matchmaker, so it has imbued its brand with the characteristics its customers see in themselves.

This contrasts with Mr. Clean's website, which emphasizes functional benefits like durability, scents, effectiveness against soap scum, discounts, and cleaning tips. Mr. Clean's brand managers understand that its customers aren't looking for a brand that they aspire to; they're looking for Mr. Clean to put some competence and elbow grease into that grimy mess so they don't have to.

Both strategies are likely highly effective because the brand managers understand the role of their brands in their customers' lives. Dating service customers want to see the best version of themselves and what they aspire to be in an ad, but cleaning product customers want to see a competent source of help.

Implementation Tactics

You can choose from a variety of approaches to brand anthropomorphism, ranging from releasing with a fully developed character to hinting and building at the humanity of a brand over time. You can begin by simply speaking about the brand in more human terms, referring to it as trustworthy, understanding, wild, or active. Storytelling is also a clear path to bringing your brand to life. Whatever the case, it is vital to start with a clear identity and remain consistent across messages, channels, and tactics. This consistency can be sustained by giving careful thought to the people who represent the brand, as they will have an outsized influence on how customers perceive the brand.

Faces of the Brand

Celebrities, athletes, and other influencers can be incredibly powerful assets as you work to close the gap between the anthropomorphized version of the brand customers are visualizing and the one you're trying to create. Over time, the line between the product's and the person's qualities will blur. The spokesperson can become the personification of the brand, and the brand can subsume the attributes of the spokesperson. But this tactic introduces risk. Humans are human, so reputations can change. If those changes are negative, the brand's reputation can take a hit, but the level of damage depends more on your brand than your spokesperson.

Reality TV stars have traditionally presented themselves as superficial characters who pay their bills by acting on base instincts to entertain others. For a beauty brand, this might not be a bad association. Viewers will probably associate the brand with the star's uncommon beauty more than her life choices, so the risk of damage to the brand if a volatile star says something ridiculous is probably low. But if you're concerned with presenting a practical, intelligent brand, you would be wise to use another approach or find a highly stable spokesperson.

Celebrities and Founders
Tiger Woods suffered a series of public embarrassments when news outlets ran stories of multiple marital infidelities and speculations about the cause of a car accident in 2009. Brands like AT&T, Buick, Accenture, and others distanced themselves in the following months, but Nike and EA didn't sever ties. Why? At the end of the day, his marital woes aside, Woods was still an amazing golfer, which aligned with Nike's mantra of "authentic athletic performance," and EA's quest to immerse gamers in courses that Woods had dominated.

An internal spokesperson can be less risky and more credible, if you have the right one. Consider Gert Boyle, the former president then chairwoman of Columbia Sportswear who became the face of the Portland, Oregon brand. Boyle's family had fled Nazi Germany. After the untimely death of her husband, she and her son realigned and dramatically grew the business. She appeared in various ads over the years as Ma Boyle, the "tough mother" who ensured that products were "tested tough" and able to withstand the harsh elements of the northwest. One campaign showed her using her son as a product tester—putting him through car washes, dropping him on a mountain with only a map, spraying snow onto him as she drove by in a plow—all to prove that the products were up to snuff. Building on that success, later work blurred the lines between the brand and Gert herself. These campaigns featured her stern face and "born to nag" tattoo while emphasizing that the products, too, were "tough mothers." Who could more credibly attest to the rugged durability of products than a stern maternal figure who had, herself, overcome so much?

It's tempting to believe that an objectively attractive and/or popular celebrity could make any product more appealing, but people tend to evaluate options relative to mental categories. So, the persuasive influencer is the most relevant influencer, not the most popular.[70]

In choosing a face for your brand, the top considerations should include the person's relevance to the category and the level of reputational risk you're willing to assume. If you want to be edgy and modern, you'll have to choose popular influencers and be willing to live with a measure of volatility to keep up with the zeitgeist and remain one of the "cool kids." If you're running a heritage brand, like Tag Heuer, or a company that targets a wide audience, like AT&T, or you are a stable, quality-oriented company, like Buick, then you shouldn't take on the risk of a controversial figure to bring your brand to life. (This explains why TAG Heuer, AT&T, and Buick cut ties with Woods in the wake of the scandals.)

Influencers

A celebrity spokesperson can be a valuable part of a portfolio of marketing investments for major brands with multimillion-dollar budgets. Many businesses can leverage their founders to tell compelling stories. But influencer marketing has proven to be incredibly effective for brands of all sizes.

For brands and small businesses considering a foray into social partnerships, partnerships with micro-influencers can be affordable and effective. Micro-influencers have between 2,500 and 100,000 followers, not the millions celebrities boast. You probably follow some yourself: These are the personal trainers with the unique workouts, the bakers with the unbelievably intricate pie crust designs, or the artists with tips for painting miniatures for role-playing games. They probably won't ever command celebrity followings, but their followers are deeply engaged with their highly specific content. So, their recommendations are incredibly influential if your product is relevant to their following.

The major downside of influencer programs is that it can require a lot of effort to find the right influencer, come to an agreement, and create content that works for both the influencer and your brand. In response to this, many influencer agencies have popped up, and this is a place where even the scrappiest company with the smallest marketing budget should consider outsourcing. These agencies maintain rosters of influencers with whom they work regularly, so they can assume the work of identifying the right influencers for your brand and audience, and they can manage the contracts. And the agency will be able to streamline the content creation work, so you won't have to reinvent the wheel each time you want to add to your brand's partnerships.

When engaging an influencer, your main consideration should be the ROI of a potential deal. Consider what you would have to pay to get a similar number of impressions on your own or on another channel. Professional influencers are increasingly offering rate cards with a list of specific services they offer (five "shout outs" in stories, tagging on two posts, a product demonstration, etc.), but many influencers are amateurs who are just looking for free stuff.

Social influencers can offer entries into niche audiences, and they often have deep knowledge of the sorts of posts that their followers respond to. But if you plan to offer people free samples, you'll likely see better returns from a program at a relevant retailer or subscription box program. Instead of offering freebies to influencers, you should consider giving them commissions on the purchases made by followers, as evidenced by a dedicated code.

Employees

Large businesses spend millions of dollars each year trying to influence consumer perceptions of their brands. Media buys, Super Bowl commercials, celebrity influencers, dedicated teams at advertising agencies, pop-up shops, sampling programs, coupons. When it comes to high-dollar campaigns, every detail is considered. Pixels are pushed, photos are tweaked, food stagers place sesame seeds on buns with tweezers. What if, after all that effort, the customer's in-store experience is negative?

When people feel creeped out, they become hyper-vigilant, looking for cues that indicate whether they're in danger.[71] This heightened awareness pulls them out of a relaxed state, thereby reducing the amount they're willing to pay for your products.[72] You could invest millions in media buys and brand managers, only to have the customer experience wholly undermined by a staff member leering at a woman while she shops.

Everyone has a customer experience horror story. You don't want to test out how many of these stories your brand can weather. To whatever extent possible, hire people that are consistent with the brand personality you're trying to convey. Only hire people to work in your bookshop if their faces light up when they talk about literature. If your company promises expertise in a certain area, screen applicants for technical knowledge. If friendliness is central to your brand, you should emphasize approachability in your employee training efforts.

Customers & Ingroup Members

The 1983 classic film *Valley Girl* introduced us to romantic protagonists Randy and Julie, teens from different social strata. When Julie abruptly breaks it off with Nic Cage's Randy, he seems confused. Then it dawns on him: "I know what this is. It's your fing friends, right?" The soundtrack was more inspired than the dialogue, but Randy was correct. Julie's "valley girl" friends were keyed into a social truth that academics have been studying for decades; in seeking belonging, people become tribal. They take on characteristics of the tribe, or ingroup, and favor their ingroups over others. Punk rocker Randy was from a different tribe than valley girl Julie, and Julie's tribe viewed Randy's as inferior. Accordingly, Julie's friends couldn't understand why she would consider trading her tribe for his.

Just as Julie's friends judged Randy by his leather-clad, working-class tribe, perceptions of your brand's personality aren't fully within your control, because they're also impacted by consumers' perceptions of *other brand users*.[73]

You don't want to be associated with someone if you don't like the people around them. Likewise, consumers will make purchase decisions on the basis of how they would feel about being associated with members of the tribe that they associate with your brand. This is why social media nudges that your connections already follow a brand are effective.

Inspiration: Harley Davidson's Continued Evolution

Harley-Davidson is a brand that deeply understands our tribal tendencies. People who love the brand visit Harley stores across the US to buy t-shirts with the shop's name on them, just like other tourists buy postcards or little spoons. They buy branded biker boots and leather jackets and many have tattoos of the logo.

When you picture the typical Harley customer, you probably think of the guys with beards, tattoo sleeves, and cigarettes—the guys who view their bikes as an extension of themselves. But many women are interested in riding motorcycles, and many of the people who can afford the premium price are clean-cut people with white-collar jobs. But women and white collar suburbanites don't fit into the traditional definition of HD's tribe. Thus, the challenge: The company needs access to the broader customer base to sustain and grow its business, which opens the question of whether it needs to alienate its most loyal tribe to do so.

Many companies in this situation have chosen to rebrand or, at least, evolve the brand identity to target larger customer groups. Luxury brands have been particularly amenable to this strategy. As the 2008 recession dragged on and demographics shifted, the market for accessible luxury apparel and accessories suffered. In response, many of these companies leaned on outlets, factory stores, flash-sale sites, and other discounting to get by. These efforts opened brands up to larger markets but only at the expense of brand equity, which had taken decades to build.

By contrast, Harley-Davidson opted to stay true to its tribe while communicating that others were welcome to join. The hope was that new fans would embrace the gritty brand image and that the old fans would welcome new entrants. Harley-Davidson created classes to help people learn how to ride and dealerships encourage people to sit on bikes and start them up under supervision, to help new riders feel confident on their bikes. The company also works to help riders connect and network online, to help new owners find other members of their new group. Offering courses for women and featuring them on the site and in social media messages demonstrates that female riders are welcome, making it less intimidating to join the male-dominated culture.

By retaining the gritty, rebellious attitude and aesthetic while also stressing its openness to new riders, Harley-Davidson is demonstrating its commitment to its core customers while simultaneously welcoming new members to the tribe.

Anthropomorphism and the Marketing Operation

Is your brand the chic, elegant, haute-but-playful French woman, Chanel, that women worldwide want to emulate? Is it Dunkin, the cheerful, supportive coworker that helps you feel better about the day ahead? Maybe it's Monster, the adrenaline junkie teen up the street that lights stuff on fire and then jumps over it on his bike.

If efforts at anthropomorphism are successful, the brand you're marketing will transcend utilitarian needs for completing a task to become viewed as possessing human traits. More specifically, it will be viewed as the type of person your audience wants to be. As you work to bring your brand to life, don't abandon the brand onion and positioning work that mapped your true values, personality, and character—elevate it. Whether you merely hint at human characteristics like trustworthiness or empathy in communications or embrace a spokesperson, the imagery you create will become the face of the brand—and the emotional reaction to that brand-person will become the mental shortcut at the point of decision.

Social Media and Brand Identity

Social channels present a unique opportunity to make personal connections with customers. People can go to the website for product details or location information. They come to social media sites to enjoy a more personal connection. Don't blow this opportunity by letting the siren songs of improved rankings and instantaneous publishing tempt you to prioritize constant communication over emotionally engaging customers with an authentic brand identity.

Live your brand authentically. Don't glom onto the hashtag of the moment if it's not relevant to your brand. Don't blindly follow every account you encounter, or try for "like for like" exchanges. And, above all, don't confuse the quantity of interactions with the quality of the connections. Inexperienced social media managers often measure their success with vanity metrics such as the number of followers or likes on an irrelevant meme. But one hundred engaged followers are likely better for the brand than ten thousand people who followed you in exchange for a free contest entry.

Avoid monotony as you seek to sustain adherence to your brand identity. The nature of social media discussions should depend on the changing context of your customers' lives. You would not communicate with your best friend at her mother's wake the same way you would at her bachelorette party. Likewise, you need to consider the mood of your followers, their relationship with the brand, and the subject at hand. People didn't want to see chipper Applebee's commercials between news segments about the Ukrainians who died during Russia's 2022 invasion.

Think of a social site as if it were a high school cafeteria. This is where people come for an hour of respite from their busy days, and to seek the comfort and care of people like them. People want to know that their friends are interested in what they have to say. But you can't sit at every table simultaneously. You have to choose which table to sit at. In the same way, building authentic emotional connections that drive loyalty requires you to choose a clear and convincing identity, and that means that you can't connect with everyone. If you try to be a chameleon who behaves differently around different people in an attempt to fit into every group, then you'll be exposed as inauthentic or, worse, of appropriation or mocking. To forge authentic connections, you need to accept that you can't connect with everyone, and not everyone will relate to the brand identity.

Consumers who connect with brands on social sites are opting into deeper relationships. Treating this like any other advertising channel would be an egregious waste. Use this channel to bring your brand to life and forge the deep, authentic, emotional connections that drive people to choose your brand automatically, from instinct, the way they gravitate towards friends in a cafeteria.

Compassionate Customer Service
Customers might seem irrationally upset—even betrayed—by a broken product. A consumer that endows a smartphone with human-like characteristics will be extremely upset if it fails, far more upset than he would feel if his toilet kept running or his toaster kept burning bagels. A broken smartphone will feel like a breakup with a partner who took irreplaceable mementos with them. This customer does not need you to patronize him. He needs the same care that anyone needs when their trust has been betrayed. He needs to know that you understand his concerns and care that he's hurt. He needs to know how you'll help him live through the heartbreak and avoid future issues.

If you've effectively anthropomorphized your brand then consumers will assign outsized importance to the way they feel about your communications, regardless of the channel. The stronger the brand identity, the more consistent their expectations will be. This means that the investments in website usability and shopper marketing will create a baseline for expectations. When customers feel a strong connection to your brand, they will feel disappointed or betrayed if the person on the other end of an 800 number blows them off while reading from a script. If you fall short of their expectations, they will take it more personally and even feel deeply wounded.

Sensitive PR
If you successfully endow your brand with human characteristics, then the brand needs to treat people like humans. People will be more likely to trust an anthropomorphized brand, but they'll also be more likely to assign blame when things go wrong. [74] Accordingly, negative publicity can have a larger impact on anthropomorphized brands than their non-anthropomorphized counterparts, [75] and public relations problems can be more damaging.

How to respond? The brand needs to connect with customers like the human it purports to be. We don't forgive people that refuse to own up to the damage they've created. The same applies to brands. You must explain the error, take full responsibility, then explain the steps you're taking to prevent future recurrence.

Incentivizing Upgrades
When people anthropomorphize products, it can lead them to delay replacement purchases,[76] potentially harming sales. This is because they become more connected with these products and are therefore less likely to replace them. [77] Consumers also tend to anthropomorphize complex products more than simpler products, even when they have not seen advertising communications.

How do you convince a man to buy a PC when he talks about his Apple like it's a person (e.g., possessing a mind of its own or being sexy)? Or how do you persuade a woman to upgrade her car when she has named her current car Larry? First, you should approach customers with respect and recognize that people ascribe deep personal value to the things they own. You shouldn't begin your relationship by lowballing on trade-in value or offering unsolicited advice on recycling.

Second, you'll need to offer highly compelling reasons to upgrade anthropomorphized products. Consumers don't need to be persuaded to replace an old toothbrush, but they need to know that the new cellphone has dazzling new features. For this reason, the iPhone 12 advertisements promised "4x better drop performance" and "the fastest chip ever in a smartphone."

Caveat: This Can't Save a Disliked Brand

Endowing your brand with human characteristics is only good if the humanized version of your brand is attractive. Humanizing a brand that people love will help them connect with it even more, but the opposite is also true. The humanization of a brand will only intensify people's disdain if they don't like it. In such a case, you might have more success by presenting it in product-oriented terms.[78] In other words, if you're running a brand that people purchase out of necessity (not joy) while holding their noses (e.g., telecoms, health insurance, etc.), then customers will be harder on you because of your successful anthropomorphism. They might choose a non-anthropomorphized competitor instead. This is harsh punishment for great marketers who apply their skills to the weak brands that need them most!

Aspiring Doctors Frankenstein, take note: you need to know your brand and understand how consumers see it before you make long-term plans. If sentiment is low, you should develop a remedy and ensure that the plan is successful before you attempt to anthropomorphize the brand. Put another way, make sure the brand you bring to life is someone your customers imagine they would like.

Finally, I'd like to emphasize the importance of credibility. Amusing, humanizing creative may elicit emotional responses among internal audiences with skin in the game, but these types of efforts can become fodder for snarky tweets if the brand's claims lack credibility. No ad could've credibly positioned Enron's leadership as trustworthy or Sur La Table as an affordable option. You should pursue anthropomorphism as a strategy for improving emotional engagement or helping consumers understand your brand. This approach should not be used to reinvent a brand or sell a pack of lies.

Appealing to Emotions Across Marketing Work

Emotions don't only *influence* decisions; they're often the primary driver of decisions. Kahneman and Tversky found that most of the choices we face are made quickly, based on automatic, emotionally guided processes and little else. [79] With the somatic marker hypothesis, Damasio and subsequent researchers have demonstrated that emotions always play some role in decisions, even when slower, more objective informational processes come into play. [80]

More recently, neuroimaging studies have confirmed that brands are consistently *felt* as people make choices. [81] In one set of experiments, researchers observed subjects' brains via fMRI and found that strong brands activated the pallidum, an area of the brain associated with positive emotions, whereas weak and unfamiliar brands activated the insula, a region associated with negative emotions. [82] The authors considered their findings to be consistent with the somatic marker hypothesis and theorized that the negative emotions associated with making a decision involving an unknown or weak brand could become permanently associated with that brand. This implies a one-two punch for an under-promoted brand because that unknown brand will feel risky and intimidating to consumers. They will unconsciously retain those negative feelings about the brand—unless the brand can displace those feelings with positive messages.

Research has established that emotional engagement increases retention and the likelihood of a brand becoming familiar. In addition, familiar brands then trigger positive emotions, which makes people more likely to buy them. Therefore, to build brand equity, you should give precedence to emotional engagement tactics over other strategies across all aspects of your marketing work.

Promotional Messaging

Novice marketers tend to take a scientific approach to promotional messaging, trying to squeeze as many product features as possible into each ad and making sure that the value proposition is crystal clear. This is logical. They're responding to the very real pressure to prove the ad's ROI in an age when we have data for everything. Unfortunately, this approach can undermine effectiveness.

When trying to engage a customer before the decision point, the perfect message isn't the one that effectively enumerates the countless reasons that your product is better than the competitor's. That information is more important after the purchase, when the customer rationalizes what was actually an emotional choice. The better pre-purchase strategy is to present an emotionally engaging message that pulls them into the world of the ad, engaging as many senses as possible to help them internalize your brand's narrative. This message will make them feel connected to the brand and, above all, feel good.

Promotional messages should also be repeated frequently. Chaucer's quip that familiarity breeds contempt may apply to roommates and exes, but the opposite is true for ads. You need a clear message, and you need to repeat it until it's familiar to the audience. Familiarity breeds comfort, [83] which puts people at cognitive ease. [84] That will encourage them to choose your brand without thinking because it's the easy, comfortable choice. Also note that messages shouldn't be cognitively challenging, which risks pulling customers out of 'feeling' mode and into the more strenuous thinking/analysis mode, in which they exhaustively research the benefits of opting for another brand.

Authenticity

Nothing can undermine brand trust like being caught in a lie. When we've been lied to, we feel annoyed or betrayed at best. At worst, we feel ashamed as we realize that we were lied to and we weren't savvy enough to see it coming. This sort of feeling is so strong and memorable that it can create an association that your brand almost certainly can't recover from. I worry that the important meaning of the words *authenticity* and *transparency* is becoming degraded by buzz, but these words express what brands must sustain.

For example, many articles on behavioral economics and sales emphasize the importance of creating a sense of scarcity or exclusivity to motivate people to move fast. But these tactics are so widely used that consumers look upon them with skepticism, even when the products or time are indeed scarce. Tactics like that might have worked decades ago but, today, any short-term sales gains will come at the expense of brand equity.

To build trust, be trustworthy.

Generating Word-of-Mouth

Marketers know that word-of-mouth is incredibly influential. Reviews from friends, family, and other product users are more credible than ads, and a series of poor reviews can spell doom for a new product. For this reason, we often beg customers, "please leave us a review" or "tell your friends!" Counterintuitively, experimental research found that asking for reviews is less effective at generating WOM than influencing the customer's emotional state.

Instead of asking for a review, the research suggests that brands should appeal to consumers' arrogant tendencies to generate word-of-mouth. In a series of experiments, researchers found that they could trigger a consumer's arrogance, such as by identifying him as a superior customer and offering an opportunity to brag about purchases. Further, triggering arrogance increased the consumer's likelihood of engaging in both online and offline word-of-mouth. (Of course, this isn't great when consumers have a negative experience, as nudging them into arrogant states also makes them more likely to spread negative WOM.)[85]

Usability

Kahneman put forward the dual process theory. The idea is that when we have cognitive ease, we leverage System 1 thinking, which is our intuitive, emotional pattern of thought that requires less effort, but is more accident-prone. By contrast, System 2 thinking is analytical and driven by objective information. It is more accurate, but it also requires more effort.[86]

Our tendency to default to System 1—the emotional mode—is great for marketers, because we tend to have more control over the brand experience than the product. It's easier if people choose our brand because they recognize and trust us, or because they like the environment we create. Thus, if we can keep people comfortable and happy, the good vibes they associate with our brand will win them over.

If we introduce any sort of cognitive strain, then we require customers to exert careful attention, which pulls people out of System 1 thinking and into System 2 thinking. We force our customers into 'logic mode,' prompting them to consider the costs and benefits of each option. This is where usability optimization comes in. Illegible text, unnecessarily complicated task flows, or otherwise complex situations could lead people away from making a quick, intuitive choice based on positive feelings. This is a problem, unless your brand is the only option.

If you've got a superior product, you would expect that you could drop the marketers and appeal to customers by emphasizing technical specifications, but this could lead your customer to associate your brand with that taxing experience and avoid interacting with your brand in the future. The smallest usability tweaks can improve an experience and drive revenue, which is why major brands ceaselessly use a/b test designs to evaluate even the tiniest differences.

Prioritize usability, pay neutral third parties to conduct usability audits, minimize barriers that could add cognitive strain, and, per the eponymous book by Steve Krug, *Don't make me think!*

Appealing to the Senses

The visual identity should match your brand personality and the emotions that you're trying to elicit.

Pharmaceutical companies tend to choose bright, energetic colors, and to show actors who are happy and free of pain while enjoying their lives. If you wanted to tell a story of how your drug brought relief to people who suffered ongoing pain because of a chronic disease, you might open the commercial with a suffering person who talks about how easy it is to get a prescription from a doctor and take the pills. You could then close the spot with the actor who is now enjoying life without pain. To support the story, you could deploy supportive visuals, such as glum, dull colors as a sad actor holds her back and looks at her dog apologetically. Then you could portray the actor as she listens carefully to a doctor in a bright, hopeful office. Then you could close the spot with the smiling actor walking through a park, enjoying the perfect skies and sunshine with her dog. The energetic activity and a bright, cheerful day in the end would implicitly support your message: your drug provides relief and enables patients to enjoy life again. (Now that you've read this paragraph, confirmation bias may lead you to notice that nearly all pharmaceutical commercials follow this pattern.)

Traditional marketers would encourage you to emphasize product features and value props, but behavioral economics teaches us the opposite. Detailed product images are important, but to emotionally engage consumers, we need to lead with images that emphasize the *brand experience*. Detailed product information can be made available on product labels or deeper on the website; the first appeal must be to the senses.

The December 2019 print ads from Disney comprised photos of young children asleep in cars and holding souvenirs. The only copy was the small Walt Disney World logo in the bottom corner. There was no information about Disney World—no prices, no park images, not even a reference to Orlando. Despite the lack of detailed information, the message was crystal clear: These children were so exhausted from their fun days that they fell asleep on the way home, clutching mementos that would forever remind them of the great memories they had created with their families. These visuals emotionally engaged parents by implicitly promising that the park would offer the opportunity to make lasting memories with their children.

You can take a similar approach to engage the non-visual senses too. By engaging multiple senses, you can lead consumers to process ads as though they're living the experience, subsequently influencing their purchasing decisions.

Level of Emotion

The feelings you evoke should be relevant to the brand and customers' needs, and the level of emotion you elicit should be proportional to the decision you're asking your customers to make.

It is appropriate to discuss death in a life insurance commercial, but not in a yogurt commercial. If you're selling yogurt to moms, you do not need to hammer them with statistics about food insecurity or images of starving children around the world until they cry and change the channel. You could, instead, promise that your nutritious product is something they can feel good about in a world where moms face so much guilt and fear. Or you could leverage nostalgia as you remind her that your sugary yogurt is just as great as it was when her mom put it in her lunch. Alternatively, you could position your yogurt as a luscious treat, a well-deserved indulgence to enjoy after the kids go to bed.

You get the idea. A relatable, humorous ad could be just as engaging and memorable as the one with the starvation statistics, but wouldn't leave the moms feeling conned or emotionally spent over a yogurt commercial.

Which Emotion to Elicit?

The somatic marker hypothesis and dual process theory indicate that we want people to associate our brand with positive feelings, so it's clear that our promotional messaging should, generally, make people feel good. How to pick from the menu of positive emotions when designing a campaign?

Our brains are association machines. They're constantly taking in stimuli, cues, and clues from all our senses and then categorizing them. For this reason, information that fits our previously held beliefs is more memorable. It's why we can more easily remember things about people by putting them into social categories, and it's why ads that feel relevant to our needs are more salient. We should expect, then, that ads that elicit relevant emotions are going to be more memorable and, therefore, more effective in swaying purchase decisions. A company that is trying to sell you an expensive flood insurance policy wants to shift your mindset so that you will plunk down a pile of cash to hedge against losing your possessions to a flood. So, using an ad with physical comedy is probably not the right emotional engagement tactic.

An ad's relevance to each situation and brand can vary, but some good feelings will usually be relevant to many brands. One is the feeling of relaxation. A series of experiments found that people who felt relaxed were willing to pay more for various products than people in equally positive, but less-relaxed states.[87] Synthesizing these findings with those of previous studies, the researchers concluded that relaxed subjects were willing to pay more because they focused on abstractions like the product's "overall desirability," whereas others focused on specifics like cost or features. Assuming you're in the position of marketing something that consumers find desirable, getting the consumer to shift her perspective from specific features to the overall feeling of ownership should result in her assigning more value to your product. Feelings of relaxation will increase as we optimize every aspect of the customer experience, from streamlining the digital user experience to repainting the bathrooms.

Omnichannel Support

To effectively support your brand, you need to establish an identity and then support it relentlessly—live it—in every message and on every channel. The brand needs to feel the same to customers when they visit the website, when they hear the ad on the radio, when they pass the billboard on the way home, when they look at an Instagram feed, and when they're in the store. Consistent, cross-channel support of brand goals seems like an obvious imperative, but it's surprisingly uncommon in practice.

Some of the best brand work I've seen has been from my local taco shop, a business that consists of a restaurant and a trailer. That's because the brand identity is closely guarded by a small group of engaged employees who genuinely understand and advocate for it. The brand identity can fade as companies hand the reins over to larger teams, contractors, and agencies. It often makes sense to engage specialists for content creation or management—I've never met anyone who specializes in both Instagram and radio—but those specialists need to adhere to a larger, omnichannel plan.

A Very Informal Experiment on Brand Identity

Marketers should ensure that they're telling the same story across channels and that, no matter the channel, the creative is clearly identifiable as a part of your brand. You won't see the ROI on a great logo, photo, or audio clip if it's expected to stand alone. The returns are best when every channel is working in concert to support a consistent brand identity.

To explore how effectively major brands are reaching people with their true identities, I conducted an informal experiment with the group that has contributed the most to academic research: undergraduate university students.

Study Design

I began by surreptitiously taking note of major brands that were present in the classroom over the course of a week, brands that were also active marketers. I developed a list of brands that students were exposed to recently and frequently, both in-person and through advertising. The final list of brands was Nike, Android, The North Face, Rockstar, and Gatorade.

I collected samples of creative work from social media, print, and TV, and I was careful to black out logos and slogans as I prepared to present the samples. I also avoided ads that consisted primarily of product images. For example, I blocked out "just do it" from Nike creative and didn't select any samples from Rockstar or Gatorade that had images of beverage packaging.

Next, I presented creative samples and the students' task was to shout out the corresponding brand as soon as they recognized it. I told them that they could guess and that they would be neither rewarded nor penalized for answers. (They received a little extra credit for staying a couple of minutes late to participate.) This study's design was far from being adequate for formal, scientific research, but the results did offer insight into the consistency with which brand imagery conformed to the brand identity.

Outcomes

The most interesting outcome was that students recognized every piece of work from Nike. They quickly identified the brand using creative samples pulled from Instagram, video, and random screenshots from the website, even though I had removed the most recognizable spokespeople from the images. Without fail, many students would see the Nike creative and either shout the brand name simultaneously or nod in decisive agreement after others called it out.

Android creative was almost completely unrecognizable without the little green robot or product images. The North Face, Rockstar, and Gatorade samples were sometimes identified correctly, but they were frequently confused with other brands within and beyond their categories.

Interestingly, when I asked students how they recognized the brands behind the ads, they had a hard time articulating which cues had tipped them off. They struggled to express why most athletic-themed brands lacked distinction, but they knew Nike when they saw it. I think this indicates that Nike had managed to embed itself in subconscious, emotional processes. Some ads just *felt like Nike*.

Implications
These results are anecdotal and shouldn't be given the weight of experimental research. Still, the outcomes raise an important question: Is it problematic if the work isn't recognizable without the logo (or slogan, or audio clip)? Absolutely.

Effective branding requires effective emotional engagement. You need to draw customers into your brand's identity, ensconcing them in the world of the brand, eliciting the relevant feelings. So, if each message has a different look, feel, or story, then you're not supporting that identity. Instead, the customers will experience disparate messages and imagery. They will have a choppy, fragmented impression with no cohesive meaning. As a result, customers will feel like they have been advertised *at*, like you've taken their valuable time and attention to shout some random thought.

CSR, Causes, and Politics

Corporate social responsibility (CSR), cause marketing, and charitable work are often an afterthought for marketers. Some companies might add a blurb to the bottom of the homepage touting a holiday donation or put postcards from a local classroom on the bulletin board for employees to enjoy, but that doesn't add up to a true marketing effort. Many companies stop short of marketing the work because they don't want to leave the impression that they only did it for the press attention. Other companies support a potpourri of causes, but that can convey a lack of commitment to any particular charitable need.

Companies that fail to market their CSR work miss huge opportunities to build their brands. Consumers are interested in CSR work, and involvement with a relevant cause will improve the brand's reputation, particularly among millennials. That group reports that CSR efforts make them more likely to buy, invest, and work at a company.[88]

As with any investment of resources, you should select charities and causes that align with your brand identity. The connection will make your contribution more memorable for consumers, but the most important benefit will be the emotional impact to your customer of selecting a cause that matters to them.

To determine what matters to your customers, consider the Moral Foundations Theory. Social and cultural psychologists that study the foundations of morality in cultures around the world have identified several common pillars of morality: care/harm, fairness/cheating, loyalty/betrayal, authority/subversion, sanctity/degradation and, more recently, liberty/oppression.[89]

Individuals vary in the importance they place on each of these foundations of morality but, in the absence of data on your customers' specific attitudes, political leanings can be predictive of moral attitudes. Researchers who study moral foundations have found that liberals are primarily concerned with the care/harm foundation, which emphasizes kindness and empathy. Their morality is supported, secondarily, by the pillars of fairness and liberty. For this reason, when liberals protest or make political pleas, they tend to focus on people who have been unfairly victimized or oppressed. By contrast, political conservatives place relatively equal value on each pillar. This explains why conservatives aren't as concerned with the victims of harm or unfairness as their liberal counterparts, but they're much more concerned with loyalty, respect for the law and authority, and "sanctity" (in relation to traditional marriage and family, the Bible, etc.).[90]

These political tendencies have significant implications for investments in CSR programs. If your customers tend to be liberal, they'll respect your efforts to make the world fairer and they'll appreciate any support you give to programs that help the victims of cruelty or unjust systems, regardless of whether those institutions have liberal political connections. These consumers care about causes that benefit animals, abused children, and victims of sexual harassment. They'll respond to programs that encourage girls to participate in STEM fields or commitments to increase the hiring of diverse applicants. They'll be sensitive to any history of harassment or harm connected with a charity, and they will be deterred if you support organizations that have been subject to allegations of fraud or bias. Conservatives, on the other hand, will be more responsive to donations that demonstrate that you value authority, loyalty, and sanctity, such as organizations that advocate for law enforcement officers, veterans, restoration of monuments and historical sites, or faith-based charities. They won't be as sensitive to historical missteps on equity issues, but they won't support organizations that focus on flaws in institutions or traditions they hold sacred.

The primary goal in selecting a cause is to demonstrate that your organization is aligned with your audience's values. You should choose a cause that fits with your product and brand goals. If your audience spans the political spectrum, it is best to avoid faith-based organizations or those that defend dubious institutions (to keep the liberals engaged) and avoid organizations that explicitly question law enforcement, the armed services, or churches (to keep the right on board). However, if you've developed a comprehensive brand with deeply engaged users, you may not be able to dodge every political conversation. The moral foundations theory research demonstrates that you can use political leanings to predict consumers' values, but self-reported attitudinal data is the best way to determine what really matters to your customers.

A person's morality is the lens through which they see the world, a determinant of how they behave and, critically, how they believe you should behave. If your company's behavior offends their morality, they'll have a deep-seated, profoundly emotional reaction. If you commit to a cause that's in line with their values, then you will demonstrate your desire to bring the world closer to their ideal.

Demonstrating Shared Values:
Oreo, Chick-fil-A, and Uber

As evidence of the importance of cause selection and shared values in emotional engagement efforts, consider the poignant October 2020 spot from Oreo. The commercial, entitled "Proud Parent," shows two parents accepting their daughter's girlfriend. It closes with, "A loving world starts with a loving home. Show you're a #ProudParent."

The anti-LGBT group One Million Moms issued an impassioned response that accused Oreo of "attempting to normalize the LGBTQ lifestyle" and to "brainwash children and adults alike." The group urged Christians to boycott Mondelez for "supporting the homosexual agenda." Responses on social media, however, provided ample evidence that there were many more positive reactions, which were equally emotional. People talked about crying when they saw the spot, feeling validated, and appreciating the brand's commitment to love and acceptance.

Oreo is working to demonstrate that its old brand is keeping pace with shifting US values, particularly among mothers, because they skew younger and more socially liberal. Through the spot, the company demonstrated a commitment to a cause that's critically important to moms—acceptance and love of all children—in a manner that feels authentic and credible.

At the opposite end of the effectiveness spectrum, in terms of emotional engagement via shared values, is Uber. The company reportedly spent half a billion dollars to mend its image after public-relations setbacks.[91] There have been numerous criticisms lobbed at the company, but the most passionate have been from people who are offended by its apparent hypocrisy. They point out that the company espouses liberal values like diversity and inclusiveness, but they say its actions demonstrate otherwise.[92] This gap between words and behavior could indicate the company has failed to develop a true brand identity to guide it through decisions on how to behave in the face of PR setbacks. This is problematic because mismatches between words and behaviors undermine emotional connections.

Somewhere between Oreo's triumph and Uber's struggle is Chick-fil-A's ongoing battle to retain its owners' values while expanding to geographies where audiences don't share those values. Chick-fil-A has become well-known for its anti-LGBTQ image. Initially, when the privately held company gave donations to groups that discriminate against gays and when its executives expressed strong anti-LGBTQ stances during public interviews, the sales did not appear to decline. But, as the company has attempted to expand north and west in the US and overseas, it has faced friction from consumers that don't share these positions.

In response, Chick-fil-A has publicized support of more widely palatable causes like youth education and homelessness, while stopping short of directly contradicting the previous stances, which are held by its devoutly religious owners.[93] Only time will tell if the chain's new approach to charitable giving will drive increased brand acceptance. The chain hasn't committed to making the changes permanent and it hasn't reversed its anti-gay stances, even though many potential customers in the US and abroad find them repugnant. But shifting to more widely respected charities has generated more favorable press.

A critical challenge for the company is how to control its brand identity. The company is privately held and so its marketers are having trouble drawing a credible distinction between the owners' words and investments and the brand. These identity issues will persist until Chick-fil-A either pulls back from investments in markets that don't share its values or gets the owners to align with brand values that don't offend large groups of potential customers.

Most consumers won't exhaustively research every brand they buy, but values do matter. Brands that demonstrate congruence with customers' values are brands that customers recommend to friends and endorse on social media. This kind of strong loyalty will make the company's reputation less susceptible to an executive's transgression, or to a price increase. Cause marketing—putting your money where your mouth is—is the quickest and most credible way to demonstrate that your values are aligned with your customers' values.

Final Thoughts on Emotion and Marketing

The idea that reason can be separated from emotion to drive purely rational decisions is pervasive in Western culture. People are quick to blame economists for creating the rational being called *homo economicus* to drive analyses, but to be fair, economists have long recognized that emotions couldn't be completely brushed aside. Philosopher and economist David Hume, for example, recognized that human actions follow emotions.

> *"Reason is, and ought only to be the slave of the passions, and can never pretend to any other office than to serve and obey them."*
> -David Hume, *A Treatise of Human Nature*, 1739-40

And economist Adam Smith recognized that cool indifference is fundamentally impossible.

> *"When we are about the act, the eagerness of passion will seldom allow us to consider what we are doing, with the candour of an indifferent person. The violet emotions which at that time agitate us, discolour our view of things..."*
> -Adam Smith, *The Theory of Moral Sentiments*, 1759

More at fault than economists, I think, is pressure from deadlines, managers, and budgets to move quickly, forcing us to over-simplify as we create campaigns. Also at fault is the Big Data revolution, which has lulled people into a complacent belief that quantitative research is sufficient for any decision. Meanwhile, we all like to think that we're logical, rational, and impervious to outside influence.

It's more than a little scary to think of ourselves as fundamentally irrational creatures, meandering through life, depending on feelings to make important decisions, and forming bonds with nonhuman, abstract entities like brands. We want to think of ourselves as architects empowered to create our destinies, not pawns, subject to manipulation by forces we're unaware of. Clearly, we're not mindless fools, following only our feelings, bumbling through life like the early-generation robotic vacuums that wandered until they hit an obstacle then changed direction. But we're also not *homo economicus*, only making decisions on the basis of rational self-interest and logical utility maximization.

The reality is that reason and emotion are deeply intertwined. If we ignore this truth, then we will doom marketing strategies to failure. Emotions heavily influence most of our choices, including our purchase decisions.

Humanizing your brand and emphasizing emotional engagement in brand work will make the work more memorable and desirable, influencing consumer choice, and leading to the kind of loyalty that product-centric campaigns just can't produce. If you choose to anthropomorphize your brand, just remember to ensure that the work authentically signals corporate values and product attributes. Consumers will quickly see through patronizing or misleading brand work, and you'll end up being mocked on social media platforms.

Marketers should design brand and messaging strategies with an understanding that customers' decisions will be influenced by complex amalgamations of social cognition and anthropomorphic reasoning, not simple rationality. This means that we're selling feelings more than products. TAG Heuer is selling the feeling of status, Nike the feeling of athletic accomplishment, country clubs the feeling of belonging to an elite circle.

We must focus on the relationship between the customer and the brand, and we need to consider how the brand is making the customer feel at each point of contact. A relationship-centric approach will sow more loyalty than any punch card or coupon program could ever achieve.

"We must give up the insane illusion that a conscious self, however virtuous and however intelligent, can do its work singlehanded and without assistance."

-Aldous Huxley, The Education of an Amphibian

Beating the Competition

Clients, managers, and financial sorts like to offer up some form of this old gem: "I know that half the money I spend on advertising is wasted; the trouble is knowing which half." (Europeans tend to attribute that quip to the founder of Unilever, while Americans tend to think it was either Henry Ford, J.C. Penney, or retailer John Wanamaker. There's no evidence that any of them ever said it.[94])

Even though marketing is a valid business investment that offers less risk and consistently better returns than other types of investments, managers often cut promotional plans and marketing departments first when revenues are down. And small business owners who would never compromise on the quality of their raw materials or store locations are often content to let unqualified nephews handle digital initiatives to save money.

Consumers share the belief that marketing is inessential. Consumer panel data consistently show that most people don't view themselves as easily influenced by marketing messages but find them a good source of information. This suggests that people believe they can consume marketing content dispassionately, looking past the marketer's narrative to identify objective facts for later use when they make purchasing decisions.

In the previous chapter, we established that emotions influence all decisions: The idea of a purely rational choice is oxymoronic. Consumers are neither mindless drones subject to easy manipulation by marketers nor unfeeling bots that make only rational, utility-maximizing choices. In this chapter, we'll dig deeper into some of the myriad contextual factors that can influence customers to choose your brand over the competitors.

Systematic Nudging

Beating your competitors is, fundamentally, about influencing consumer behavior. There are a variety of reasons you might want to modify existing behaviors: You might want to entice your customers to buy your product over a competitor's, convince them to commit to a subscription, or shift certain tasks to a cheaper channel so you can deliver more value for the price. Any of these behavioral tweaks is well within the capabilities of the smallest marketing department and the process for nudging your customers in a mutually beneficial direction is straightforward.

Identify the Desired Behavior

The first step in behavior modification is to identify the behaviors you want to change. You obviously want people to always choose your brand, but you should break that overarching business goal into specific, individual behaviors. For example, one of Adobe's goals is to encourage people to sign up for Photoshop subscriptions.

Evaluate Incentives and Deterrents

Next, you need to systematically evaluate the elements of your customer experience that incentivize the desired behavior as well as any factors that deter the behavior to evaluate the influences your target is facing. (Matt Wallaert refers to this as "pressure mapping."[95]) Building on our example:

Incentives driving Photoshop signups include the trustworthy brand, the sophisticated features, the wide use of the software in creative professions (which makes Photoshop expertise valuable on a resume), and the affordable price point of $21/month (less for students).

Deterrents that may inhibit Photoshop signups include the work to sign up, the time required to install and set up, and the complexity of the software (which makes it difficult to learn).

Don't forget to focus on your audience when enumerating these influences. For example, imagine that a student who is considering a career in graphic design is excited about the sophisticated features offered by Photoshop. He knows that software sophistication usually means added complexity, which will take him more time to learn, but he is willing to do this work because he knows that mastering the software will help him get his dream job. By comparison, an English literature major who wants to paste an image of Shakespeare's head on a meme for a few laughs would be frustrated by the complexity of the software. For her, learning the software isn't worth the time and effort. Adobe probably shouldn't focus on making the software so easy that the meme-maker can use it because that would mean sacrificing the capabilities that make it valuable to the target audience.

The Good Old CBA

Once you've identified the factors that incentivize or deter the desired behavior, you need to do a little cost-benefit analysis (CBA). There will always be deterrents because the customer has to expend some effort or payment to acquire the product. We don't need to remove all costs; we only need to understand the relative strength of incentives and deterrents *from the target's point of view*. With this insight, we can reduce the strong deterrents and amp up the conversation about the most compelling benefits.

To understand which factors matter most to your customers, you usually need to do some research. The most important thing to remember in conducting that research is that context is everything. You need to get as close as possible to the customer's point of decision and/or observe him using the product to get a sense of how he's feeling in the context of the choice.

For instance, let's say a restaurant were trying to increase food sales to affluent, urban customers who eat out frequently. If you simply surveyed these customers on what matters most when they're selecting a restaurant, they might report "unique flavors" or "a memorable dining experience." But the same customers who order pork belly on special occasions will check calorie counts when they're grabbing snacks on the way out of the gym. These customers might buy Culver's frozen custard when they have a car full of kids after a lacrosse game because it's tasty, affordable, and quick, and because the plastic dishes make it easy to eat in the car. But those very benefits would be deterrents to a member of this group when he's planning a romantic date.

Refining the Choice Architecture

With research in hand, we can trim down the list of incentives and deterrents so that only the most important and addressable remain, and then tackle those. This requires a systematic approach to developing or refining the option set (the "choice architecture") to nudge customers toward the goal.

Adobe has carefully assessed and addressed the points of friction that deter customers during signup and installation. It has done this by continually testing and optimizing forms and installation task flows. The company makes it as easy as possible for people who want to pay for the software to sign up, install it, and get to work. The company has addressed the complexity of its software by offering scads of well-produced tutorials for users at all levels. Training content ranges from quick demos within the software to more complex end-to-end courses with in-depth training on specific features. The company also plays-up incentives like the sophistication of the software in ads that demonstrate the dazzling array of art that its tools can support.

For many modern companies, the optimization of digital user experiences is a great place to begin reducing deterrents. Usability issues are very important for customers, and they can be relatively inexpensive to fix. I once conducted an audit of a one-page recruiting form that resulted in a fifty-two-page report on how the form could be improved, with examples of forms that were more effective at accomplishing similar goals. In addition to other sources, I cited multiple books about website forms. (Yes, there are entire volumes on that topic!) My report was not a page-turner, but the client knew it was important because each candidate who abandons the form forces recruiters to churn through prequalifying questions—a job a computer can do—instead of focusing on deeper engagement with prequalified candidates.

The deterrent for some brands is that they are new and unknown. In these cases, promotional efforts and trials can build trust. If the audience doesn't think the value of your product justifies the price, you can persuade them to anchor to a more relevant comparison. If your product requires long-term thinking at the expense of short-term fun, the language in your messaging can be designed to nudge customers into a long-term mindset. We'll delve into these and other options to refine the choice architecture throughout this chapter.

Combatting Choice Overload

Markets are driven by free choice and competition. Abundant choice in the marketplace forces businesses to compete, leading to improvements in technology and efficiency, driving down costs and prices, thereby leading to economic growth. Competition can also lead competing businesses to increase the quality of their offerings and allows consumers to signal, with their purchases, which goods should be produced. (This is the "invisible hand" stuff that makes economics teachers smile and wave excitedly at graphs.)

With few exceptions, consumers prefer to have more choices.[96] Having many options fulfills our deep-seated psychological needs to feel like we have freedom and control of our environment.[97,98] It increases our likelihood of engaging in tasks and achieving goals,[99,100,101,102] and it improves our general sense of well-being.[103] So it shouldn't surprise you when customers ask for more and more options.[104] Survey respondents will likely offer suggestions for how to expand your line to serve edge cases. Taste testers will suggest new flavor combinations. Feedback from beta testers will lead product teams to gleefully ideate entirely new offerings.

In a year-2000 television spot from Geico, a man in a diner inspects his sandwich and then tells the waitress, "Oh, uh, I didn't want mayo . . ." The waitress grabs the top slice of bread, uses the edge of the table to scrape the mayonnaise off, then replaces it atop the sandwich. She is clearly inconvenienced by the customer's expectation that he should be able to customize his sandwich. The spot promises, "You don't have to sacrifice service to save money." Geico was responding to the insight that consumers tend to conflate customization options and choices with the quality of service.

Offering choices is great, but how many choices do customers actually need to be satisfied with your brand? In many sectors, the number of choices available seems to have gotten out of hand. At the time of this writing, The Cheesecake Factory lists three dozen different types of cheesecake on its menu, as well as other desserts. The Kroger in Dearborn, Michigan has sixty-five peanut butter options from a variety of brands, in a variety of sizes and package types. Zappos stocks *five hundred and sixty-five* black pumps in a women's size eight. The number of choices available to today's consumers can be overwhelming, so marketers should tread carefully when it comes to increasing options, even if doing so is relatively easy and seemingly cost-effective. And even if customers ask.

Paradoxically, experimental research shows that increased choice may reduce sales and satisfaction. Consumers say they prefer broad selections, but their behavior indicates the opposite.

In an experiment back in 2000, psychologists offered shoppers at a grocery store in Menlo Park, California a sample of twenty-four varieties of jam. Anyone who approached the sampling table could try as many jams as they wished, and each sampler received a coupon for $1 off of the jam. Another experiment offered only six jams. This is where things get interesting: The table with twenty-four options attracted far more samplers, but the people at the table with only six options were ten times more likely to purchase jam.[105] It appears that the samplers were dazzled by the array of options at the twenty-four-jam table, but too overwhelmed by the possibilities to make a choice.

In another experiment, psychologists offered students either a single chocolate (control), a choice of six chocolates, or their choice of thirty chocolates. Anticipated satisfaction was the same across both choice groups, and both groups felt sufficiently informed about the chocolates, but the six-option group reported significantly higher satisfaction with their selections than the group that had more options. At the close of the experiment, participants were offered a choice between the $5 they had been promised for participation or a box of Godiva chocolates valued at $5. Participants who had been exposed to fewer choices were four times more likely to choose the chocolate than the group that had been given many choices or the control group.[106] In other words, those who had fewer options were happier all around and more likely to make a purchase.

Elsewhere, in the case of the supermarket—a place where we've learned to expect abundant options—experimental research has shown that reducing the number of options increases sales. One study found that about 40 percent of families who were loyal to a specific brand continued purchasing from the same market even after their preferred brand had been eliminated.[107] The same study found that, though managers risk losing a customer if his favorite option is eliminated, these losses are outweighed by increases in sales to other customers.

Life without any options is choking, but decision paralysis can occur when people face an overabundance of choices. Economists refer to this as "diminishing marginal utility." It means that each additional option adds a little less value than the one before and, after a point, additional options can begin to decrease happiness.

As psychologist Barry Schwartz wrote, people can reach a point when "choice no longer liberates but debilitates. It might even be said to tyrannize."[108] Schwartz has even argued that economists' belief in abundant choices and consumers' ability to make rational choices has led to an "excess of freedom" in modern American society, leading to dissatisfaction and even clinical depression.[109]

Almost no one would want to curtail freedoms afforded by the government, but there is solid evidence that marketers should pull back from attempts to deliver a unique product or service for every possible use case. Given too many options, people are less likely to decide,[110] [111] and they tend to shut down in the face of choice overload. We become more fearful of making a bad decision, we spend too much time with too much information, we have a hard time figuring out which information is important, we poorly predict our own future tastes, and ultimately, we end up feeling less satisfied with the choices we make.[112] [113]

Options Can Be Damaging for Businesses and Consumers

As the number of choices increases, there are more factors to consider. Logically, this means that people should create progressively more complex decision rules to ensure that they're making the best possible choice. Paradoxically, it turns out that as the number of options increases, people tend to consider fewer of them.[114] They also tend to employ progressively simpler rules to make a choice,[115] such as choosing the most expensive option on the assumption that it'll be the highest quality, or simply limiting themselves to the options available at a single store.

People also have a tendency to mix decision-making strategies. For example, to reduce the size of the choice set, people sometimes eliminate all the options that don't meet some basic requirement of dubious relevance. Then they only need to pick the best of the remaining alternatives.[116] In this case, the implication for marketers is that your brand must first understand the customers' criteria for surviving that initial elimination so that you can be among the best of the remaining alternatives. However, consumers use many criteria to make purchasing decisions, including factors as simple as a friend's recommendation. You can't develop a unique strategy for each consumer, so how can you win the consumer's favor if the process isn't clear? To make matters worse, consumers aren't consistent in how they make their choices. People don't reliably make the same choice under the same circumstances.

Here's another concerning quirk of human decision-making: There's evidence that consumers who spend time considering options become deeply attached to *all the options*. Thus, after they make a choice for one, they mourn the loss of the others. This is like a Schrödinger's choice set or, as some researchers call it, a sense that "choosing feels like losing."[117] The risk of regretting a choice is even higher in our digital age. We encounter so much information and so many options that there's a looming risk of seeing a lower price or a superior option soon after making a choice.

Addressing The Maximization Paradox

I once went to lunch with a coworker when she was on a calorie-restrictive diet that allowed her one "cheat day" each week. On that day she could indulge in a treat that put her over her usual calorie allotment. So, on the day we had lunch together, she purposefully selected a table that had a view of the dessert case and, as she ate her salad, she discussed the options in great detail. Some desserts just weren't "worth the calories" and some didn't feel special enough. One was so beautiful that she worried flavor might have been sacrificed for form. We ultimately went to the coffee shop around the corner where she stared down an equally abundant dessert case. She enumerated the pros and cons of the options and eventually selected a Danish. Upon swallowing the first bite, she said it was good but that she should have chosen the cake at the previous place.

If there had only been a couple of dessert options, my friend could've easily eliminated the ones she didn't like and landed on the best choice. She enjoyed the Danish, but because there were more than a dozen dessert choices at each location, the decision-making process was stressful.

Herein lies another paradox of choice: When faced with larger sets of choices, people can be less satisfied with their selection than they would've been with fewer choices. This is particularly true of maximizers like my friend who are willing to put in extra effort to find more options and make the best possible choice.[118] A team of Canadian psychologists who researched this phenomenon referred to it as the "maximization paradox."[119] It is a problem across verticals these days because we live with unprecedented access to instantaneous information. We can use our smartphones to find other nearby options while standing in an aisle. We can easily learn about price changes after our purchases. And we can order nearly anything online. Maximization could easily become a time sink, preventing all sorts of purchases.

As a marketer, you can't control your customer's maximization tendencies, and you can't control how many or the types of choices that will be available to her. But there are a few effective solutions.

1. **Limit the number of options** you're making available to a few very good ones. A café doesn't need to offer chocolate cake, devil's food cake, and Sacher Torte. To a baker, there is a significant difference between the three but, to a chocolate-loving customer in need of a sugar fix, the amount of complexity introduced by a second or third chocolate cake is disproportionate with the amount of value it introduces. You should consider whether the options you offer improve the customer experience or just make his decision more complicated. Remember that you're getting paid to understand the differences, but your customer is not.
2. **Offer a set of recommendations as a default** and let customers tweak as desired. This approach can reduce the cognitive load that would otherwise be required of them.
3. **Reduce the choice** set by being a better marketer. Effective differentiation creates the impression that there aren't many other viable options. If you've effectively framed, positioned, and differentiated the options, then the customer will be less likely to believe that there are other good alternatives. That will reduce the odds that the customer who chooses your product will walk away feeling like she might have been happier with an alternative.

Finding the Goldilocks Choice Set

If you ask, your customers will tell you they want more options or more ability to customize products. People prefer making their own choices. They expect to be happier when they have the freedom to choose, even when the choice is among relatively unattractive alternatives.[120] Still, you and I know that giving the customers an expanded set of choices might come at the expense of sales and customer satisfaction. Thus, the most effective marketers will offer just enough options to meet needs and make customers feel like they have control in relation to the magnitude of the decision.

Many brands are seeing success by offering narrower selections of carefully curated products. Anthropologie is one of many brands that brought this idea to the mall. Their stores offer a selection of clothing, home décor, and beauty products for artistically minded, affluent women with eclectic tastes. The items don't have broad appeal and the store doesn't dependably stock all items; instead, it offers a limited selection of goods that appeal to its specific audience. Booksellers sometimes use the same strategy. They're not trying to sell every book in the Library of Congress, or even every book within a narrow genre; they only offer a curated selection of books that suit their specific audience's tastes.

What if your product is expensive and customers want a lot of control? Even when buying a car or building a house, people usually don't expect infinite options. More often, they have a choice of several packages: granite and porcelain in the kitchen, rearview cameras and in-console phone chargers in the crossover. Customers may complain when they can only have one part of a package, but they don't walk away from the purchase because of that limitation.

For some businesses, it still makes sense to offer a wide selection. In those cases, you need to help consumers wade through the options. You can help them feel like you're saving them time and helping them come to the right choice without making them feel like they're ceding control of the decision-making process.

Trunk Club stylists work with clients remotely to ascertain their style preferences and then the company sends them curated selections of apparel. For instance, a consumer could send the stylist her measurements and a link to a Pinterest board of styles she likes. She could add that she's looking for casual wear and shoes. Then, the next week, a box with a small selection of tops, bottoms, and accessories would arrive. This is a valuable service for those who are uninterested in filtering through the thousands of options Trunk Club's parent company, Nordstrom, has made available. To ensure that customers feel sufficiently in control of their wardrobes, all items can be returned for a full refund.

Coursera, an online education platform, also demonstrates best practices in this regard. The company offers an overwhelming number of courses on dozens of topics. Cutting that number would be detrimental to its business goal of acquiring and retaining subscribers. Instead of reducing selections, Coursera helps customers to find the courses they need by offering specializations, certificates, guided projects, and other course groupings. Site visitors who want to learn about a topic like data science are presented with several options related to specific content and varying time commitments. The company offers a free trial, which quickly moves people into learning without having to read through a full course catalog or speak with a program manager. Learners also have the option of taking any individual course, which gives them a sense of control, but they don't have to wrap their heads around hundreds of options to get started.

It's important to understand your customers' desires, but when it comes to increasing variety, the science tells us that more choice isn't better. So, you should pare down your offerings to a core set of meaningfully differentiated choices. Any decision to add more options should be carefully considered. You will do well to recognize that, for most brands, offering a vast number of options is not a good marketing strategy.

Leveraging the Decoy Effect

Imagine that you're spending a lazy Saturday morning watching a TV show about a couple that's trying to find a house for their growing family. They meet with a real estate agent and outline their needs and budget. Here's what the agent shows them:

1. A house that's not in their preferred neighborhood and doesn't have enough bedrooms, but the price is low—well within their budget.
2. An absolute dream house that's so far above their stated budget that you want to fire the agent on their behalf.
3. A house that meets their needs and is much cheaper than the second option, but still over budget.

Unsurprisingly, the clients are disappointed by the first house and balk at the price of the second house. After some dramatic debates at a coffee shop, the two announce that they've settled on the third house. As they serve cheese and crackers from their new kitchen in the final scene, they affirm that they made the right choice. Even though it was over their budget, the third house was so much more affordable than the second house that it was the obvious choice.

So, how did the real estate agent get them to feel so happy about buying a house that was beyond what they said they could afford? By showing them the second house. She didn't expect them to pick the second house; it was a decoy to nudge them into going over budget to buy the third house. She hoped that their preference for the first house would change when they were presented with a third option. This is called the decoy effect,[121] or the asymmetric dominance effect. Now that you're aware of that strategy, you'll see it a lot in marketplaces. The decoy effect indicates that our preferences aren't always stable or logical; instead, they are heavily influenced by the choices before us.

Behavioral economist Dan Ariely did one experiment in which he showed respondents images of three faces and asked which they would date. Half of the respondents saw images of men called Tom, Jerry, and Ugly Tom. Ugly Tom was created by Photoshopping an image of Tom to create a face that was much like Tom's, but slightly less attractive. The other half of respondents saw pictures of Tom, Jerry, and Ugly Jerry, the latter a slightly less attractive version of Jerry.

We would, logically, expect roughly the same proportion of each group to prefer Tom. If 66% of one group preferred Tom, we would expect the result to be similar in the second group. To expect this would be to think like an economist. A foundational principle of rational choice models, which date back centuries to Adam Smith, is the principle of regularity, which states that the probability that people select any option can't be increased by adding another option.[122]

Here's what happened: Respondents were more likely to choose Jerry than Tom when Ugly Jerry was included. Participants that saw Ugly Tom were more likely to select Tom.[123] The mere presence of Ugly Jerry made Jerry more appealing, winning him potential suitors that, the other group suggests, might've otherwise chosen Tom.

The experiment indicates that our preferences aren't stable, as would be logical, but heavily influenced by the choice set before us. Also, Ariely pointed out, you shouldn't go barhopping with someone who looks like you but is a little more attractive.

Restaurants often offer small, medium, and large drinks. When they offer only a small and a large, customers are torn between the two and tend to prefer the small, thinking the large costs more than they want to spend. Adding a medium option that's closer in price to the large tends to nudge customers to shift their preference to the large because, for only a few cents more than the medium, it seems like a great deal.

Adding a decoy option—a choice that's similar, but obviously inferior, to another—can shift the customer's perspective and, in turn, shift their decision in favor of the option that's best for your business. An additional option can also effectively demonstrate that a more expensive alternative is a good value. Just be sure to consider a choice set that works for your business and the customer: People like choices but don't like feeling manipulated by marketers.

The Art of Framing

We would expect rational people to consistently come to the same conclusion given the same information, but experimental research has demonstrated that the ways that information is presented has a significant impact on the choices people make. We refer to this inconsistency as a framing effect.

The framing effect is related to the prospect theory, which holds that there are essentially two phases in the choice process: editing and evaluation. The decision-maker first defines the problem and options, and then she evaluates the alternatives and chooses. However, people irrationally place nonequivalent values on gains and losses. We tend to put more weight on losses, so a loss is more painful than an equivalent gain is pleasing.[124][125] This means that marketers who carefully frame the riskiness of the decision, the attributes of the product, and the nature of the choice can influence the way the consumer perceives alternatives at each stage of the decision-making process, thereby influencing the choice.

Risk, Framing, and Choice

In their seminal research on framing,[126] Tversky and Kahneman posed a hypothetical situation to university students: a virus outbreak that was expected to kill six hundred people. Two alternative programs are proposed, with the following potential outcomes:

A. Two hundred people will be saved.
B. There's a 33 percent probability that six hundred people will be saved and a 66 percent probability that none will be saved.

Asked to choose between the programs, most students chose the first scenario. They preferred the promise that two hundred lives would be saved to gamble in option B, even though the numerical value of each option is mathematically equivalent.

Another group was given the same backstory, but presented with these potential outcomes:

C. Four hundred people will die.
D. There is a 33 percent probability that nobody will die and a 66 percent probability that six hundred people will die.

Nearly 80 percent of respondents in the second group chose option D even though, again, the expected number of lives saved is mathematically equivalent. We would expect an even split, which begs the questions: Why weren't results split between mathematically equivalent options? And why were people willing to take the gamble in the second scenario but not in the first?

Tversky and Kahneman concluded in this and subsequent studies that people react to prospective gains differently than they react to prospective losses. In the first set of choices, the options were framed as gains—lives saved. And so most people opted for certainty. They preferred the guarantee of knowing that two hundred people would certainly live under option A to the gamble offered in option B. By contrast, the second set of choices framed the options in terms of losses (i.e., the number of people who would die). Thus, the idea of loss became more worrisome than the risk of the gamble. Subjects found it more palatable to gamble and try to save everyone under option D than to select option C, knowing that four hundred people would certainly die.

A 2006 experiment used functional magnetic resonance imaging (fMRI) technology to look at what happens in human brains when faced with a similar scenario.[127] In this study, researchers posed the following questions to subjects while scanning their brains.

1. You receive £50. Consider the following choices.
    a. Keep £20.
    b. Gamble to keep that amount or lose all the money.
2. You receive £50. Consider the following choices:
    c. Lose £30.
    d. Gamble to keep or lose all the money.

In the first scenario of the experiment, the choices were framed in terms of gains whereas in the second scenario the choices were framed as losses. In both scenarios, the options were mathematically equivalent. Once again, the group's preference reversed when the choices were framed as gains rather than losses. As with previous studies, participants were more likely to go the safe route (keep £20) in the first scenario and more likely to gamble in the second.

These researchers noted that the amygdala was activated with the safer option in the first scenario, and it was activated with the gamble option in the second. They interpreted this to indicate emotional involvement in the decision, which supports the idea that the thought of experiencing a loss is so painful that we're willing to gamble to avoid it. In a similar study, other researchers employed fMRI scanning and concluded that people will choose a certain gain because that choice requires less cognitive effort.[128]

Another experiment on the subject looked at cabs in New York City. I like this one, because it gets us out of the theoretical and out of the lab. When demand is higher than usual, perhaps because there's a sporting event or conference, the cab driver can earn his average day's wage faster because he wastes less time searching for his next fare. When demand is low, he wastes time seeking out fares, so he must work more hours to make a given amount of money. If economists drove cabs, they would "make hay while the sun shines." That is, a perfectly rational driver would work longer hours on days with high demand to offset the inevitable low-demand days. This approach would help them smooth their income over the course of the year. Instead, cabbies tend to set daily income goals, which lead them to work extra-long hours when demand is low. This implies that the cabbies are loss averse. The idea of coming in $50 under their daily income goal weighs on them more heavily than the joy of coming in $50 over lightens them.[129]

Applying this information comes down to context. You must consider, from the customer's point of view, the riskiness of the choice. People generally prefer not to gamble when given the choice, but we also tend to weigh losses more heavily than equivalent gains. This means that your customers prefer certainty when it comes to gains, but they hate losses so much that they're willing to gamble to avoid them.

Attribute Framing and Promotional Strategy

The research leads us to expect that customers will respond better when we frame brands in terms of customer gains while minimizing references to risks or costs. This is called "attribute framing." Research demonstrates that the way you label the attributes of your product will impact how people evaluate their options.

Consumers in one study reported that meat tastes better, is higher quality, and is less greasy when it's described as 75 percent lean than when it's labeled 25 percent fat.[130] This comes as little surprise to marketers, who are accustomed to emphasizing the benefits of our wares rather than the downsides. We instinctively advertise that "90 percent of women said their skin looked younger" when they used a lotion, rather than reminding viewers that it costs $30 an ounce, or that there's "only a 10 percent chance it won't help," or that it "only causes zits on one out of every two hundred users." But are we using this approach because that's what we were taught or because it works?

The short answer is that attribute framing works, but not because customers are easily manipulated. Attribute framing works because the positive framing of attributes triggers associations that bias the customer's evaluation in favor of the product.[131] [132] [133] By triggering a positive, gains-oriented mindset,[134] attribute framing makes people more likely to take risks, such as spending money to purchase an unknown product.

Consumers clearly know that advertising messages are biased. No matter how you slice panel data, the results always show that target audiences believe that advertising is designed to manipulate, but that individuals believe themselves impervious to the influence. Yet research has found that consumers who test products after ads tend to internalize the advertisement as a hypothesis. This leads them to look for even weak evidence to confirm the claims in the ad before making a purchase.

Logically, the rational consumer should give each product on the market equal scrutiny, but they're usually just looking for a "good enough" solution that lets them make a selection and move on with their lives.[135] Even consumers who wish to test products more extensively usually can't do that in stores, so the advertised product feels like a more informed, less-risky choice. Thus, the information from the ad, confirmed with the in-store experience (e.g., the meat looks lean, as the ad said; the nutrition label confirms that the juice does contain vitamin C), is enough to drive preference. As a result, advertised products have an edge.[136]

In short, promotional money is a solid investment because consumers that see your ads are unconsciously biased in favor of trying your product and liking it.[137]

When to Temper the Ad Spend

When it comes to costs, a heavy promotional budget will usually give your product an edge, but there are some important caveats.

If your product is measurably superior to competitors, you should give customers a chance to compare products side-by-side. A sampling program of some sort is in order: in-store sampling, sampling with other relevant choices, or subsidizing use in relevant environments. For instance, hair salons that use specific lines of products allow customers to experience high-end products that are too expensive to try on a whim and many technology brands encourage use with free trials. When your product is less-expensive, advertising is a great way to present your product as the one that offers the most value within the competitive set. But if your product is objectively superior, you should spend some of the promotional budget to get the product in front of customers.

Brands that are new or that have a small market share would also benefit from getting their products in the hands of consumers. These low-share brands must contend with consumers' preferences for the status quo; it's easier for them to stick with what they've always bought than to make a change. So, low-share brands will see higher ROI on promotional spend than well-used brands, but they won't realize these gains until they can get products into customers' hands. Thus, new entrants and brands with lower market shares should save some of their promotional budgets for trials.

Timing the Message

Framing appears to be most effective when consumers have no prior impressions of the brand or product, but framing effects are still present for customers who have had little experience with the brand.[138][139]

People who see the ads before they experience the brand tend to spend more time considering the ad claims. They pay attention to evidence that confirms the claims and they land on more positive impressions. Users who had ambiguous experiences with your product can still be open to influence because people tend to use an average of experiences from various sources to form their impressions.[140] As a result, your message could nudge their brand perceptions from neutral to positive. It is clear, though, that positive framing can't balance a poor initial impression of your product,[141] so you'll need more than a feel-good campaign to sway disgruntled customers.

When it comes to determining whether impressions were indistinct enough that customers are still up for grabs, the question is how to diagnose their experiences with the brand. If you're running a food cart and the customer has tasted two of the three things you sell, that implies that their opinion of your food is relatively set. But advertising will certainly work better when the customer has a less distinct impression of the brand.[142]

Here's the bottom line: Developing messages with positive attribute framing will help you to convert the neutral and draw uninitiated consumers to take interest in your products, especially when you can sell ahead of the product experience. That said, this sort of promotional campaign will have a lower ROI in markets where you've already got strong penetration or where you've got a negative reputation.

Goal Framing

Our goals impact what we notice, what we ignore, what information and skills are front-of-mind, and our preferences.[143] Imagine that you went to the grocery store to buy spumoni ice cream. At home, a relative asks you specific questions about the stock. You would probably be able to tell that person about the spumoni options in detail, but you probably wouldn't be able to share information about the price of apples or whether the store had almond milk. Because apples and almond milk weren't relevant to your goal at the time, you wouldn't have noticed them, even if you walked right by them.

Humans are driven by three overarching goals, or goal frames, which comprise many subgoals: the normative, gain, and hedonic. The normative goal frame is about doing the "right" thing. *Normative goals* are related to socially acceptable behaviors and the greater good of the group. Things like recycling for the good of the planet, donating to charity, and trimming your trees so people can jog through your neighborhood comfortably. *Gain goals* encompass subgoals related to preserving or increasing your personal resources, like getting a raise or seeking a promotion for increased status. *Hedonic goals* are those related to changing how you feel right now, like seeking pleasure or excitement or avoiding negative feelings or thoughts.

We're constantly juggling multiple goals and desires, so the goal of a moment will impact your perceptions by making you sensitive to information that is situationally relevant to that goal. For instance, if you're hungry, the hedonic goal of finding something to eat becomes focal. In this state, you'll be hyper-aware of opportunities to satisfy your hunger. If you go to a grocery store hungry, you might buy all sorts of chips, candy, and prepared food because you would be thinking about immediate satisfaction, not overarching nutritional goals or meal plans. In this hungry state, you'll also be sensitive to other things that impact the way you feel, like pain, things going wrong, people being rude, etc.[144] This might lead to you being offended by things that you would usually ignore, or you might become more easily angered by relatively minor irritations. (In the modern parlance, the word is *hangry*.)

The dominant goal frame impacts sensitivity to information, perception, and behavior. The opportunity for marketers is that goals are subject to both conscious and subconscious manipulation, and goals that result from subconscious priming are just as effective as acts of will in driving behavior.[145] Translation: You can nudge people into a frame of mind that makes them more interested in what your brand has to offer.

Goal Framing in Marketing

Cues from people, messages, and our environment can influence which goal frame becomes focal, thereby impacting need, preference, and choice.[146] [147]

Hedonic Framing

Any lover of baked goods that has walked past the gorgeous display case at Panera Bread would be unsurprised to hear that exposure to the treats increases customers' likelihood of ordering them. More surprising is that this sort of exposure doesn't only put you in the mood for a muffin; it moves the hedonic goal frame to the forefront, triggering unrelated hedonic preferences. For instance, one experiment found that when people saw pictures of decadent desserts, their preferences shifted to smaller, more immediate monetary gains instead of larger, delayed rewards. Another experiment found that a cookie-scented candle in the room led to similar shifts in temporal preference.[148] Just thinking about dessert put people in a "gotta have it now" mindset, even though the thing they wanted in the moment wasn't related to dessert.

Environmental cues that trigger the hedonic goal frame can lead to all sorts of short-term, pleasure-seeking behaviors, and this has clear implications for the customer experience. A display of cookies at a car dealership can nudge customers into a more hedonic state, leading them to overspend for a car that's more fun than the beige sedan that meets their needs.

Magnum ice cream ads lean into the sinfulness of their treats. The site calls visitors to "indulge NOW" and spots say the brand is "for pleasure seekers." Sexy ads prompt people to "release the beast" and use words like rich, temptation, and satisfying, framing the ice cream as satisfying a hedonic need. By prompting customers to do something naughty, with ads eliciting other primal behaviors, Magnum is bringing the hedonic goal frame to the forefront, priming them to indulge in ice cream and persuading them that competing options with fewer calories and lower-quality chocolate aren't even an option.

Gain Frames

Just as the use of culinary delights can trigger the hedonic goal frame, marketers can use cues about competition to trigger the gain goal frame, at least in most people.[149] These types of cues could be conveyed with messages that emphasize, for example, business, savings, and profits.

To determine how wording might affect behavior, one study gave two different titles to the same game. Two-thirds of participants demonstrated cooperative behavior when the game was called the Community Game. When the same game was labeled the Wall Street Game, people shifted to a competitive mindset; cooperative behavior shrank to 31 percent.[150] The name of the game was apparently a strong signal of appropriate behavior, so when the name indicated gain orientation, it shifted participants' goals from normative goals to gain goals. In fact, the game's name proved to be a far better predictor of competitive behavior than pre-experimental personality assessments designed to recruit either competitive or cooperative subjects. Let that sink in, marketers: In this experiment, a person's personality was a less-significant driver of behavior than the name of the game.

Normative Framing

When a normative goal frame is focal, people are concerned with behaving appropriately, contributing to group welfare, and otherwise doing what's "right." When marketing effectively emphasizes teamwork, joint goals, or the good of humanity, it can shift people into a normative mindset and reduce their focus on personal gain.[151]

Predictably Irrational offers an example of this. When the AARP asked lawyers if they would provide services to needy seniors at a deeply discounted rate, the lawyers declined. But when the organization asked lawyers to volunteer their time to needy seniors, the lawyers agreed.[152] Surely the lawyers were aware that they would make more money if they charged a reduced fee than if they offered pro bono services, so why would they agree to volunteer rather than charge a reduced fee?

This seemingly irrational behavior can be explained by goal framing. When lawyers were offered a low fee, it prompted them to think about money. That led them to focus on the opportunity cost of their time. Because the AARP's suggested fee was much lower than what lawyers would normally charge, the lawyers focused on the pain of a pay cut. But when the lawyers were asked to volunteer, it led them to approach the decision with a normative frame of mind. They knew that donating their skills to needy seniors would meaningfully contribute to society, which felt like a valuable use of time. This and other research indicate that market-based incentives could deter pro-social behaviors. If you work at a nonprofit or if you want customers to think of the greater good, you should focus on normative signals, not economic incentives.

The AARP nudged the lawyers from a gain frame to a normative frame, nudging them into pro-social behavior. Other experiments have demonstrated the ease with which environmental cues can coax people into *bad* behavior. For example, some research has found that people in environments where others have violated laws and social norms are more likely to do so themselves, leading disorder to spread. (I like to think these experiments were inspired by the scene in *The Breakfast Club* in which Judd Nelson's character sarcastically goads the detention supervisor that he can't allow one student out of his seat because "if he gets up, we'll all get up. It'll be anarchy!") Researchers have found that people were more than twice as likely to litter in front of a graffiti-covered wall compared to a wall without graffiti. Other experiments in the study found that people were twice as likely to steal in an environment that had graffiti or litter.[153] The mere presence of graffiti or litter acted as a signal that everyone else was ignoring social norms thereby shifting their goals away from doing "what's right" and inclining them to pursue selfish goals.

Framing for Competitive Edge
People are incredibly sensitive to labeling, messaging, and environmental cues, which can all subconsciously shift the prioritization of their goals, behaviors, and choices. Therefore, to beat the competition, you should obsessively consider every aspect of the customer experience, from the colors on the website to the employee dress code and the in-store environment. You should also consider how your brand fits into the user's life and ensure that you're eliciting the appropriate goal frame. You may be giving cues that influence behavior in suboptimal ways. A dirty bathroom hints that employees don't care about the location, leading customers to not care either. A decadent dessert indicates that it's OK to focus on doing what feels good in the moment. An uptight corporate environment with a strict dress code will nudge people toward the gains orientation and a feeling that they need to compete for resources.

By carefully framing the problem or goal, you can influence how the customer sees the choice and, therefore, who they view as your competitors and which alternatives are most appealing. It's impossible to overstate the impact that strong goal framing can have on the persuasiveness of a message and the edge it can give you over your competition.

Positioning and The Great Homogenization

A great positioning statement differentiates your brand from competitors, allowing you to capture customers who don't believe there's a substitute for your brand. It can help you define what makes sense for your brand, including your product offerings, messaging strategies, and even website colors. Positioning strategy has long been accepted as foundational to branding. So why has brand work been so forgettable lately?

Picture a perceptual map like you might have seen in business school—the cartesian plane to help visualize brand positioning. Imagine that one axis ranges from fun to function, the other from value to premium. Now, think about a few major brands in a category and where you would put them on that plane. If the points you visualize all hover around the same spot, that's a problem. It would mean that they're poorly differentiated; therefore, they would all be competing for the same space in the customer's mind. Even if you were to change the labels on the axes, you would probably still see clusters of points.

Major brands seem to be drifting away from meaningful differentiation. For example, think about taste and healthfulness for major restaurants, or performance and price for sneaker brands. As Kim and Mauborgne's blue ocean metaphor illustrates,[154] the lack of differentiation means that a lot of brands are sustaining major casualties battling with competitors in bloody waters instead of moving to blue ocean.

This is shockingly bad strategy, especially when we consider how much brainpower is dedicated to any major brand. I think this is occurring because marketers are panicking. They're afraid of betraying one group of customers to appease another and, above all, they're terrified that their brands will trend on social media for the wrong reasons.

So, instead of taking a real position, marketers insist that their customer is "everyone" and then nix messages that feel too specific to have universal appeal. The result? Brands that were once unique have been "optimized" to the point of homogeneity. The tendency to avoid taking any real position and become the "Goldilocks of the category" has led to a glut of indistinguishable, milk-toast brands that are so busy trying to be everything to everyone that they don't stand for anything to anyone. They don't offend anyone, but they're also not memorable, simply because they lack a credible, differentiated position.

Differentiation works because it distinguishes your brand from the rest of the category, making your brand the clear choice. If you want customers to choose you, you need to be meaningfully unique. You need to embrace the idea that your brand is not vanilla and it's not for everyone.

Be the Tiger Tail

Everyone likes vanilla ice cream, but nobody loves it passionately. Nobody writes online reviews about it or brings it up at a book club meeting. Vanilla ice cream is like the nice-enough place in the suburbs you visit while house hunting, the place you can't remember two hours later. It's the restaurant you occasionally visit with friends, but you can't recommend a great dish when someone asks.

Then there's tiger tail ice cream, a Canadian flavor with a swirl of orange and licorice. This is an ice cream flavor that people have strong feelings about. Tiger tail has been the subject of blog posts, articles, and Reddit comments. People post videos of Americans trying it for the first time, and people share photos of it on Instagram. Tiger tail is the cool girl in every high school. She's got a strong personality, and she's intimidating. She might not be the girl to bring home to mom, but she's so magnetic, she's the girl that everyone's trying to impress. This ice cream is like the store you drive across town to visit, even though it's overpriced, or the sportscar that's wildly impractical but so fun to drive.

Sure, tiger tail has fewer fans than vanilla, but its fans are passionate. They will keep the flavor alive. One Canadian ice cream maker told *The New York Times* that the company keeps tiger tail in production, even though it's not a top seller, "largely because loyal tiger tail fans raise an enormous fuss whenever its future appears in jeopardy."[155]

Positioning and Resonance

The mind can't remember everything, so it remembers interesting things that are relevant to your goals and identity. Cutting through the clutter in an age of choice overload therefore means taking a compelling and unique position. You shouldn't try to fit everything about your brand into a message—only what's important to the target customer. Any message designed to please everyone will lack differentiation and, thus, be doomed to fail. You should keep your story focused on the specific needs of your key customer or risk becoming irrelevant to everyone.

Unfortunately, marketers can't expect consumers to believe us if we claim that our products stand out. When we present something new to an audience, people naturally think, "This is like x, only..." or, "This is Uber for y." This is where framing and positioning can work in concert to define your brand.

Framing vs. Positioning

Framing will help your customers think about your brand or product, and positioning will communicate how you compare with the competition. Therefore, marketing efforts should begin with a deep consideration of how to frame your offering. That work could change how you think about your competitive set. Consider the case of DiGiorno frozen pizza.

Premium positioning would have been the obvious strategy for Kraft when they launched DiGiorno. At that time, the frozen pizza marketplace was crowded, and Kraft's new option was considerably more expensive than most. Most marketers asked to work with the high price point would've put appetizing photos on the box and then run campaigns emphasizing the pizza's quality ingredients. They might have encouraged people to question the ingredients in competitors' pizzas. Many would've positioned DiGiorno as "the tastiest pizza for busy families" or "the quality option for true pizza lovers."

But instead of positioning the brand within the frozen pizza category, Kraft shifted the frame of reference from frozen pizza to pizzeria pizza. The message was that DiGiorno is more than a mere frozen pizza; it's restaurant pizza without the expense and hassle. "It's not Delivery. It's DiGiorno." With that slogan, Kraft shifted DiGiorno pizza into a different category reframing the product's reference value. This approach changed the choice set and, in turn, the expected purchase price. The price at launch was steep for frozen pizza, but not for a delivery from a pizzeria.

To replicate this strategy, don't just look at obvious competitors. Step back and consider different definitions of the customer's problem or goal, corresponding choice sets, and which choice set your brand could dominate. If you can reframe the choice set and position your brand as the defining competitor within that set, you will beat competitors even if you charge higher prices.

Anchoring

Our brains naturally make connections and comparisons, which helps us to remember information and make inferences, but that means that irrelevant information can influence our judgments. This is called *anchoring*. It happens when we mentally "anchor" to information that influences subsequent decisions, even if the information is not valid or relevant.

A teenager who supports raising the minimum wage may have a hard time convincing his parents that he should earn no less than $20 per hour when they remember working for $3 an hour as teens. The parents in such a conversation would anchor to the memory of what they earned at his age, even though they worked at different jobs, in a different decade when a dollar had a different value. People will often anchor to a first experience and then compare subsequent experiences with that one. I submit Foreigner's song, "Feels Like the First Time."

To take advantage of anchoring behavior, you can first address the manufacturer suggested retail price (MSRP), which consumers see on everything from cars to sweaters. Marketers offer MSRPs (or "regular prices") as points of reference so that customers will believe that a lower price is a great deal. This can be incredibly effective. Just ask notorious MSRP doubter Ron Johnson, the former CEO of JCPenney. After a successful run leading Apple's retail stores, where there are almost no discounts or sales, Johnson must have thought that JCPenney's endless potpourri of sales and coupons was outrageous. Customers must have known, he reasoned, that businesses inflated MSRPs to compensate for discounts. As a result,

Johnson thought that it would be a wildly inefficient use of employees' time to manage endless sign changes and coupon expirations. So, Johnson made a change: Items were marked with "everyday low prices," and the constant sales and discounts came to an end.

Johnson expected customers to appreciate the transparency, the low prices, and the ease of figuring out what something cost without having to subtract 25 percent from the lowest marked price. That turned out to be a bad call. Revenues dropped and Johnson was fired after less than a year and a half at the helm.

The flaw in Johnson's logic was that he underestimated the importance of anchoring in consumer behavior. Consumers may claim they don't trust MSRPs, but they depend on them to determine whether they're getting a good deal. With no point of reference beyond the "everyday low price," customers didn't trust that they were getting a good deal. At issue isn't the prices, but the fact that people usually don't know what something should cost, even if it's something they purchase regularly.

One study found that less than half of the people in a grocery store could recall the price of items they'd just put in their carts.[156] Another study found that only a third of people in department stores could give accurate estimates of prices for things they regularly purchased. One in seven respondents couldn't even identify prices inflated by 20% as bad deals or prices discounted by 20% as good deals.[157]

Even if you ask people about prices they've just seen or items they frequently buy, most don't have the cognitive power to recall such mundane information with much accuracy. Consumers need a reference price to anchor to. JCPenney removed that reference, forcing shoppers to trust the store's prices, which proved to be a stretch.

Problematically, our brains are so desperate for informational reference points that we can be influenced by totally irrelevant information. In a pioneering study on anchoring, Kahneman and Tversky spun a wheel with values ranging from zero to one hundred in a subject's presence. Once the wheel landed on a number, they asked the subject to complete two tasks:

1. Estimate whether the percentage of UN member states from Africa was higher or lower than the number they'd spun.
2. Estimate the percentage of UN member states from Africa.

Participants who landed on the number sixty-five estimated that 45 percent of UN member countries were from Africa, whereas students who landed on the number ten had an average estimate of 25 percent.[158] Even though everyone presumably knew that the numerical result of the spin wasn't related to UN membership, the number influenced the participants' views of how many African countries are UN members. This anchoring effect did not change even when the researchers offered participants money for accuracy.

To dig into what's going on here, let me first pose a question: Do you know, off the top of your head, the percentage of UN member states that are African countries? Most people don't. (At time of writing, fifty-four of the 193 member states are in Africa. That's 28 percent.) So, to make an estimation, most people start with some initial value—an anchor—and then they adjust it to generate an answer. This anchor could be suggested as part of the question or it could be generated by the subjects themselves, but in either case, the adjustments from the anchor tend to be insufficient.[159]

Our tendency to be heavily influenced by the first information we encounter means that if marketers can persuade consumers to choose their brand once, the customers will be biased in favor of choosing that brand again. If you can influence someone to visit your site first, they'll compare all subsequent products and experiences to yours. If you can convince them to purchase your product, then it will become the standard against which future decisions are measured.

Evidence also shows that marketers can suggest anchors to trigger assimilation and contrast effects, which have interesting implications for pricing.[160]

Implications for Pricing

There are many tomes on the models, math, and science of pricing. For your customer, the question is simply whether the product is worth the cost.

Here's a story from a business technology decision-maker I know, who we'll call Jim. Jim recently considered purchasing a subscription to a technology service for his business. The company website advertises that businesses can license this technology for $99 per user. Business users must, however, submit to a call with the sales team before they can sign up.

During Jim's call, the sales team revealed that the $99 fee was for the first five users. After the fifth user, the price per seat increased to $350. Jim's company could afford the additional cost, and the cost wasn't unreasonable for the service, but this felt high compared with the $99 per seat Jim had expected. When he pointed this out, the sales team offered him a discount rate of $275 per seat—if Jim's company would commit to a year-long contract. Jim had now lost a couple of hours of productivity to meetings and emails with the sales team just to settle on a price well above what he had expected to pay. He chose a competitor.

There are a few things to unpack from this anecdote. First, people who make technology purchasing decisions are accustomed to tiered pricing models. They also expect to face a lack of pricing transparency, drawn-out price negotiations, and inefficient sales calls. Such annoyances, on their own, wouldn't have deterred Jim. And, because Jim was playing with the company's money, so to speak, he was not particularly sensitive to price disparities. He could have justified a few dollars a month for a service or brand he preferred. The issue was that Jim had already anchored to the $99 price because of the company's marketing site. Jim ultimately chose another company that offered an equally good service for about the same amount because of the first company's dismal anchoring strategy. Yikes. That company essentially inverted the logic behind the MSRP by presenting a price for Jim to anchor to, then quoting *above* it.

Using MSRPs and "regular prices" is the easiest way to create an effective anchor for customers. But customers might already have an anchor. Their anchor may be based on your competitor's prices, or on pricing for something that they mentally categorize you with. For instance, if you were launching a new digital service for restaurants, you would want to be aware of the prices that customers are paying for Open Table, Grubhub, and other digital services—even if those companies aren't your direct competitors. In the absence of direct competitors, the restauranteur will mentally anchor to the prices she pays for the most similar services. It's also worth noting that you should be cautious about using freemium models. If you give away your service for free, that will set an anchor in the minds of your customers, an anchor that you will have to compete with for the life of the relationship. A time-bound free trial is a better strategy.

When manufacturing dominated the economy, companies set prices based on the cost to produce a unit. In addition, companies also used pricing models based on how much goods or services had historically cost. But if a business has significant upfront investment and lower per-unit costs, or if it is launching something without direct competitors, as is generally the case with software, then value-based pricing models are usually the most logical. In this scenario, the key is to determine how much the customer values the product.

Unfortunately, pricing research can be spotty, in part because a customer's self-reported willingness to pay isn't necessarily accurate. A better approach would be a careful look at the customer's anchor. You need to figure out which product is most adjacent to yours in the mind of the customer. You should study other competitors working in the space, other services customers in the category use, and other products in your sector that might be of interest to your customer to figure out what the customer might compare you with. Once you understand these competitive forces better, you can better ascertain the value of your brand to the customer and charge accordingly.

Reference Point & Value-Based Pricing

In the first phase of decision-making, when people consider their problem and look at the prospects, they don't look at the *objective value* of products and services in the marketplace as though conducting a SWOT analysis. Instead, they consider gains or losses relative to their current state or some natural reference point.[161] So, to beat the competition, you need to frame the conversation in terms of how your product is superior to the alternatives implied by that reference point. The catch: Often, the customer's alternatives aren't aligned with your definition of the competition.

For inspiration, consider movie streaming. In 2020, Disney released its live-action version of *Mulan* on its Disney Plus streaming service. To watch the film, viewers had to subscribe to the streaming service and then pay an additional $30 to rent the movie. Assessment of whether that was too much to charge requires an understanding of the customer's frame of reference.

Mulan came out as Covid-19 shuttered theaters across the US, so Disney released the movie directly to its streaming service. The company hoped that customers would use the cost of taking a spouse and two children to see the movie at a theater—over $50 (not counting the inflated price of popcorn and candy)—as their price reference. That being the case, customers probably would have framed the $30 streaming fee as being $20 cheaper than going to a theater, and therefore a good deal.

But if another customer had based his pricing reference on the cost of Amazon Prime's live-action *Beauty and the Beast*, which was half the cost of watching *Mulan* on Disney Plus, he might have balked at paying $30 to watch *Mulan*.

Depending on whether she viewed the rental as an alternative to the theater or an alternative to other movies available to stream, the decision-maker could've concluded Disney's charge for the movie was either a great deal or downright predatory. Thus, to properly price your product, you need to understand how the customer is framing the choice and the competition. Ideally, you can reframe your offering to imply it belongs in a pricier category, like how streaming services hope you'll see streaming new movies at home as an alternative to the theater, not an alternative to streaming older movies. Whatever the case, a deep understanding of how the customer views the choice and the alternatives should define your strategy.

The Default Effect

We can face a slew of large and small decisions, even before breakfast. For that reason, we often lighten the mental load by relying on defaults, which help us make choices without using precious cognitive capacity. Sticking with the default—the brand you usually buy—is essentially deciding not to decide, which is an appealing shortcut for modern, overwhelmed consumers.

People don't re-evaluate their laundry needs or run comprehensive cost-per-load comparisons each time they run out of detergent; they rely on their default. So, if your brand has already won a customer's business, she will rely on you as her default, and that means that competitors will struggle to supplant you. If you're not that default, you need to make a compelling case for the customer to switch.

Governments and employers sometimes take a stance of libertarian paternalism in establishing defaults, essentially nudging people toward the choice they think best without compromising the individual's freedom to choose. An analysis of one Fortune 500 company's 401k plan found that participation increased dramatically when employees were automatically enrolled with the option to opt-out, compared with when they were invited to opt-in. The same study found that the default contribution rate and investment allocations significantly influenced employee selections, even though employees had the power to change both. Sixty-one percent of employees hired after the institution of automatic enrollment did nothing to change participation status, contribution rate, or fund allocation.[162] Also worth noting, these employees weren't sticking with the defaults because they were superior or popular choices: The defaults of 3% contribution and full allocation to a money market fund were chosen by less than 1% of the other employees. Saving for retirement is one of the most important financial decisions many Americans can make, but most corporate employees simply rolled with the defaults.

Another example of the power of defaults is in organ donation. Organ donation rates are dramatically higher in European countries like Austria and Hungary, where everyone is a donor by default, compared to countries like Denmark and Germany, where one must opt into organ donation. This is true even though the option to change donor status is always available in all of these countries. The Netherlands is an opt-in country where you must register to become a donor. The country launched a national donor registry in 1998 and, with it, an extensive public education campaign. The government sent twelve million letters (to a population of less than sixteen million) asking people to register but saw no significant change in the consent rate.[163] Even on complicated ethical matters such as organ donation, people are far more likely to stick with the default than to make a change.

Becoming the Default

For marketers, it is not wise to force people into a default purchase of your product or service. That can feel manipulative to consumers, which will cause them to look upon you with scorn. If that happens, any short-term improvements in quarterly revenues could come at the expense of long-term brand health. Instead of engineering a program that leans on questionable ethics like auto-renewals and difficult opt-out processes, you should look for opportunities in digital experience planning and positioning to establish your brand as the default.

This underscores the importance of strong branding and memorable ads. Promotional work can go far to paint your brand as the pioneer, the value, or the quality option, effectively positioning it as the brand to beat. This also highlights the importance of winning the user the first time he makes a choice in the category. If you can get him to select your brand the first time he chooses, and he doesn't have a problem with your performance, you'll become the default against which all other products must compete.

One word of caution: Procrastinators who rely on default options are more likely to feel dissatisfied with their selections later.[164] You can reduce this problem by reassuring customers that they can easily shift away from the default option. That approach will protect your brand from the damage of dissatisfied users down the road. A subscription-based service, for instance, can drive signups by offering a narrow selection of plans, presenting a default level of service, and then informing customers that they can upgrade or cancel at any time.

Your digital user experience should be designed so that it is extremely simple for customers to choose the most beneficial plan for the brand. That choice should feel to them almost like a default. The most prominent items on any page should be those that guide the user forward through the purchase process. You can use appealing imagery to introduce a product, a "buy now" button, or a form on the purchase page that lets the user quickly complete the purchase process. The most prominent items on any Amazon product page are the product image and the "Buy Now" and "Add to Cart" buttons, which are intuitively positioned at the top right where even the least digitally savvy users will look. If your business is one where offering a wide variety of options or customizations is necessary, featuring "popular choices" and noting a particular option as the default will reduce the cognitive load on the customer.

Priming

Picture this: it's Saturday morning and you're sipping coffee and looking out the window at the cloudless blue sky. You grab a muffin and offer one to your roommate, but she declines, saying that she's going out for pancakes. Now, what's the first fruit that comes to mind?

It is likely that you thought of blueberries. That's because I primed your mind to think about blueberries by referencing the color of the sky and breakfast foods that often feature blueberries. If the priming worked and you did indeed think of blueberries, you'd be more likely to buy blueberries if you went into the grocery store right now.

Here's another. Imagine that it's the middle of very dark night, but you are able to see someone across the street. The person appears to be wearing a long cape, like something that Dracula or Severus Snape would wear. Now, what's the first color that comes to mind? Probably black, right? Even though I never said the word black, I made many references to it. That primed your mind to think about black.

Our brains are highly associative. We draw on what we already know as we process new information, and we unconsciously seek out connections as we receive stimuli. Thus, when I wrote about darkness and Dracula and then asked a question, your mind naturally looked for the answer that would connect the story and question.

There have been some fascinating experiments on priming. In one, researchers asked undergraduate students to work on a scrambled sentence task. One set of students received words that people tend to associate with elderly people: worried, Florida, old, gray, retired, and wrinkled. Afterward, researchers thanked the students for their participation and excused them. Then the researchers covertly timed how long it took the students to walk down the hall to the exit before they debriefed them on the experiment. Subjects who received the words associated with the elderly walked slower than those who received neutral words. During the debriefing, researchers asked the students if they thought the words had influenced their behavior. None of the participants thought there had been an effect.[165]

Here's another classic example. Researchers had participants hold either hot or iced coffee for twenty seconds. Then they were asked to rate someone's personality. Those who held the hot coffee rated the person as having what we would call "warmer" personality traits, such as generous and caring. Subsequently, the researchers had people hold either a hot or a cold therapeutic pad and then choose whether their reward for participation in the study should be a gift for themselves or a gift for a friend. Fewer than half of the people holding the warm pad kept the gift for themselves, compared with about 75 percent of the people holding the cool pad. In both cases, participants were unaware that the temperature of the object had any impact on their behavior.[166]

Another study exposed subjects to financial information on either green or red backgrounds. The researchers found that people who saw information on the red background overestimated the values and likelihoods of loss events relative to those who saw the same information on the green background.[167]

Implications for the Marketing Mix

The research indicates that you can prime people to change their behavior with just a few words, underscoring the importance of more consequential touchpoints like the website or store environment.

Advertisers tend to be adept at emotional priming. We instinctively show bright colors, happy people, and music with major key tonality preceding a product, when we want the audience to associate happiness with our product. While emotionally engaging promotions are a critical aspect of priming, we can also employ more subtle approaches to priming across the marketing mix.

Consider price. People shopping at discount retailers aren't prepared to pay a premium for a higher-quality product; they're primed to shop for a good price. Similarly, people at high-end retailers are primed to pay more in exchange for superior quality and service. For those reasons, you wouldn't want to launch a luxury brand at a discount retailer, where people would think the price is far too high, regardless of quality.

The physical and digital environments are critical factors as well. If you sell bespoke products, you will undermine your brand value if you mass-produce your goods for Costco. That's because people shopping at Costco are primed for homogenized products and bulk discounts. By comparison, consider a high-end shopping center or an artist's market where people are expecting unique experiences and direct interaction with the creators. Similarly, you shouldn't try to sell your daughter's Girl Scout cookies outside of a convenience store at noon because shoppers at those locations are popping in for a quick lunch or some cigarettes. It would be better to set up a stand outside a grocery store at 5 p.m. to catch busy parents shopping for last-minute dinner ingredients. Shoppers in that context would be primed to think about helping children.

The digital environment is no less important than the physical environment, but far easier to control. Jaguar and Rolex don't use comic sans font—the unofficial typestyle of elementary schools and comic strips—on their websites because it's too casual and cartoonish for their elevated brands. Pixar Animation Studios uses a sans-serif type and features bright, engaging photos on a carefully designed site to demonstrate the casual, fun nature of its brand and its design expertise. Just as you shouldn't try to sell high-end jewelry from a kiosk in a dollar store parking lot, you should not develop an excessively formal website for a children's brand.

You should also think carefully about priming when marketing extensions to product lines or services, ensuring that everything is well-aligned with the brand you're trying to create. Every product should make a good first impression for the brand because, in a world where people can take countless paths to product discovery, you can't control which product they'll see first. You wouldn't want a product that's outside of the optimal brand image to be a new customer's first impression.

Your customer service team may thank you for priming expectations. If customers come to your website to find help and encounter pictures of smiling agents who appear to enjoy helping clients, the subtle reminder that your agents are friendly people will prime customers to treat them with kindness. If, on the other hand, frustrated customers have to endure an excessively long task flow or deal with poorly performing AI before they can talk with a live agent, then you can expect them to be angry. This experience with a less-than-human entity will prime customers to treat your agents as less-than-human.

Our brains function by making associations and so priming, for marketers, should be about activating a category in people's minds, to predispose them to see your brand in a certain light. A credible presentation of a product, within the right context, can prime people to buy. Presenting your product or brand in a sub-optimal context, however, can subtly deter purchases. In addition, customers can be primed to think of things in terms of how similar or different they are from one another, which can lead to different perceptions and choices—due to context effects.[168] [169]

Context Effects

When we encounter new information, we often try to make sense of it by comparing it to other things. Fiction writers use contrasts to illuminate important points and to elucidate our understanding of characters. In *Frankenstein*, Mary Shelley juxtaposes the monster's eloquence with his repulsive appearance and terrifying strength to simultaneously humanize and dehumanize him, drawing us into the complex tragedy of his existence. Elsewhere, the cautious, kind, humble Dr. Watson builds our understanding of Sherlock Holmes' brash, erratic, egotistical nature. (The same could be said of *Toy Story*'s Buzz and Woody.)

These storytellers took advantage of the contrast effect, which leads our perceptions of something to be distorted by comparisons between it and another thing. Suppose instead of the gentle and meticulous Dr. Watson, Doyle had chosen to contrast Sherlock with an even more careless, and even smarter detective. In that case, we might have an entirely different perception of Sherlock Holmes. The contrast effect also explains why restaurants like to select side dishes or recommend wines to accompany courses. An orange would taste sweeter if it followed a bite of grapefruit than if you tried it after ice cream, even though the orange itself wouldn't have changed, only your perception of it.

Further demonstrating that our memories are extremely subjective, experimental researchers have shown that they could influence subjects' reported levels of satisfaction with life by first selectively asking about positive or negative experiences in the past. If you asked someone to recount a horrible time in her life and then asked how she was doing at that moment, the contrast between the two periods would lead her to a more positive evaluation of her current happiness. But if you asked her to tell you about the happiest day of her life and then asked her how she was doing in the present moment, she would more likely offer a tepid review of her current state.

Using contrasts can be helpful in framing a message or positioning a brand, but there is an art to selecting the right attributes for that contrast.

It is common for marketers to leverage contrasts to demonstrate the superiority of a product, but attempts at comparison tend to be absurd in their hyperbole. In the Slap Chop infomercial, Vince Offer points out how boring tuna is before he uses the Slap Chop to mix it with vegetables. "Stop having a boring tuna, stop having a boring life" he promises. Later, after chopping pickle, ham, and hard-boiled egg together, he says, "you're going to have an exciting life now." Such tongue-in-cheek hyperbole is expected in infomercials, but you almost certainly couldn't get away with something so heavy-handed beyond the infomercial format.

Sales professionals who work on commission often employ contrast effects. Imagine you owned an aging, undependable car and had saved up for a new car. You've budgeted $30,000 for the new car, and you know there are a few vehicles on the lot that will fit that budget. After you share your budget, the first thing the salesman does is walk you past a $50,000 car while referring to a few of its bells and whistles. He acknowledges that it's outside of your budget, but he claims that he's merely showing it to you because he's so excited about its new features. After chatting about that car, he shows you a $35,000 option that's almost as cool, thus creating the impression that this car is by comparison a great deal. The salesman has leveraged the contrast effect; compared with the first car, the second seems amazingly affordable. If he had shown you a $25,000 car first, you might've wondered whether the second car was worth that extra $10,000.

The inclusion/exclusion model holds that, when we're trying to evaluate a new option, we're essentially comparing it to a mental reference model to determine which is best. [170] Suppose a man is shopping for a Valentine's Day gift for his fiancée in a mid-market jewelry store at a shopping center. His most recent jewelry purchase was an engagement ring from Tiffany's, where he was thoroughly educated in the 4Cs of diamond quality before making his purchase. If the shopping center store is having a sale and promises great deals, the man will compare the price of a necklace with the thousands he just plunked down at Tiffany's and agree that he's getting a great deal. He might even buy the matching earrings or recommend the sale to friends. If, however, this store tries to claim that a diamond necklace is "of the highest quality" without offering any substantiating information, the man will question whether he's being lied to.

The assimilation effect is essentially the inverse of the contrast effect. This occurs when marketers emphasize the similarities between two products, which can distort perceptions of just how similar they are. If, for instance, you could convince your customers that your store-brand frozen pizza is just as appetizing and delicious as the more expensive Freschetta, and that your pizza's ingredients are just as fresh and natural, then your customers would obviously see that selecting your store-brand pizza is the better option. Weak brands and new entrants sometimes take advantage of the assimilation effect with associative positioning strategies. They intentionally use slogans, campaigns, or packaging that look similar to dominant brands. This is a shortcut to achieving a more prominent position in the market by piggybacking on the work of the established brand, but this approach can backfire if comparisons with the dominant brand aren't favorable.

No matter how new or innovative your brand is, consumers aren't considering it in isolation, they're considering it within the context of the alternatives available to them. Careful selection of which information is presented will influence which information the customer deems applicable to then trigger either assimilation or contrast effects[171][172] thereby influencing the customer's decision.

The point of comparison you establish for your customers should be relevant, important, and credible to ensure that your target audience will adopt it as they make their choice. And, of course, you only want to call the customer's attention to competitions you can win.

Classic Case: Think Small

One classic example of great positioning that always bears repeating is the Think Small campaign that introduced the Volkswagen Beetle.

For readers who aren't car buffs or old enough to remember 1960, let me start with a couple of words on how American companies were advertising cars at that time: land yachts. Buick advertised power and a smooth ride. Chevrolet said its Impala had "room to sprawl and sit tall in." And Chrysler's De Soto ads cut right to the chase, saying its cars "are big for a reason—to give plenty of room, comfort, performance." Another notable example was the ad for the Superba made by Checker Motors. Touting a "sensible, full-size, economy car," the ads showed a woman sitting tall with legs outstretched in the back seat and emphasized room to "stretch out in." Not exactly today's definition of sensible or economy car.

Enter the Think Small campaign for the Volkswagen Beetle. DDB needed to introduce an ugly little car that was manufactured in a plant built by Nazis to an audience that remembered WWII. Consumers, at the time, were buying giant gas guzzlers and ads seemed to indicate that the problem car brands were solving was an acute lack of room to stretch.

Volkswagen didn't try to convince consumers that they didn't need all that room or that they should start thinking more about efficiency. Instead, the ads emphasized how different the cars were from others on the market. One print ad had a picture of the car with the call to "think small." The copy emphasized the economies of the car, such as fuel efficiency, lesser oil needs, and the ability to get more miles out of tires. VW's "Funeral" TV ad showed a funeral procession with the deceased reading his will on voiceover. Viewers learned that the dead man had left little to his spendthrift wife, friends, and business partners. As the camera panned to a teary man, who brought up the rear in a Beetle, the narrator said that he was leaving his entire fortune to his nephew, who "ofttimes said a penny saved is a penny earned and who also ofttimes said, 'Gee, Uncle Max, it sure pays to own a Volkswagen.'"

By presenting the nephew as more relatable than the other relatives, the ad primed the viewers to see themselves in the loving, intelligent nephew, thereby triggering assimilation effects. This positioned the

Beetle as the antidote to conspicuous consumption, a car designed for smarter, more sensible consumers. The ads invited consumers to think: "I'm a conscientious, intelligent person like the nephew, so I should be driving a smarter, more efficient car like the Beetle."

Balancing Cost, Risk, Complexity, and Attention

The core goal of customer experience practices is to figure out how to make the customer's interactions with your brand as frictionless as possible. In less buzzy terms: When people are considering giving you money, you need to make it as easy as possible for them to do that. Easing friction also means taking a hard look at the cost, risk, and complexity of the customer's decision. As you work to present choices to prospective customers, you should minimize their perception of cost, risk, and complexity. You should also consider how much your customer cares about this decision; that is, the decision-making process should not demand more attention from the consumer than she thinks it's worth.

Risky Decisions

Though risk tolerance varies between individuals, people are generally risk-averse when they're making choices. People are also loss-averse; so much so that a loss often causes more pain than an equivalent gain brings pleasure. As we saw earlier in the chapter, people are so loss-averse that they're willing to take on uncharacteristic levels of risk to avoid prospective losses. It follows that to nudge people to choose your brand, you need to minimize perceptions of cost and risk.

Decisions that are permanent or that bear significant consequences will make choices seem riskier. This is problematic because when people become overwhelmed, they can procrastinate or fail to make any decision.[173] [174] To increase your prospect's chances of choosing your business, you must increase his perception of reward and reduce his perception of costs and risks. To do this, you can shield him from decisions that require significant technical knowledge. For example, dishwashers can range from $400 to $1500. Consumers can select different finishes, sizes, and brands, and they can compare models based on criteria such as the machine's quietness, but usually consumers are not shown details about motor types or sprinkler configurations. Those factors matter, but consumers cannot be expected to have the technical knowledge needed for those details to help them make the right choice.

However, sometimes customers want more detailed information to reduce the perception of risk. If that is the case, you can mitigate that risk by providing comprehensive information in a format that makes it easy to consume, and you can offer relevant guidance from credible professionals. For example, financial services firms are on a continual quest to build trust and reassure consumers by offering blog posts, product comparison charts, calculators, and other tools to help people make decisions.

Another way to reduce the feeling of risk is to assure customers that they can change their mind at any time. The knowledge that a choice can be revisited later reduces the risk associated with a choice.

It is crucial for you to consider whether the customer perceives that the risk and reward associated with making the choice is balanced. If your product is inexpensive, the decision shouldn't be complex and shouldn't feel permanent. If you're offering a more expensive product or requiring a long-term contract, then the customer will worry about making the wrong choice. In this case, you need to balance the perceived risk with greater rewards (and greater emphasis on rewards in communications).

Costly Decisions

A leading cost of decision-making is the time lost on research and analysis. The emotional toll of the process is more deeply felt when the task is tedious or doesn't feel worthwhile. When you're considering the number of product lines or levels of service, consider how differentiated they are and whether the benefit of the addition justifies the additional pain for the customer.

Increase the perception of the reward by meeting expectations for your product or service and offering periodic reminders that this was the right choice. This could be membership benefits or merely awareness campaigns that remind him that smart people choose your company.

In discussing the costs associated with choice, economist and behavioral scientist George Loewenstein uses the example of seatbelt mechanisms. Car manufacturers let consumers choose between colors, models, luxury packages, and engine sizes when they're buying cars, but they don't give consumers options of different types of seatbelt mechanisms because consumers don't have the expertise necessary to select the right seatbelt mechanism, wouldn't be interested in taking the time to learn about them, and could be deeply harmed by making the wrong choice.[175]

Complex Decisions

The more complex a decision is, the less likely consumers will be to get it right; that is, to behave in the way that's best for their self-interests. The outcome is dissatisfaction, and a dissatisfied customer is never a good thing for your brand.

Depending on the market segment and consumer profile, the tradeoff between complexity and utility in the decision-making process will vary. A study on mass customization options for personal computers found that users who had less expertise were more intimidated by complex customization options and valued the choices less than expert users.[176] This indicates that sophisticated, complex products and services will be more easily sold to expert audiences, but also more likely to scare away people with less expertise. It follows that you need to know your customers to get the level of complexity right.

People also behave differently when the same decisions are presented as subsequent rather than concurrent. In an experiment involving hypothetical cash gains and losses, most people selected an inferior combination of choices when tasked with choosing two of the four options. By comparison, they made better choices when the same options were combined so that they only needed to make a single choice between two combinations.[177] This indicates that careful combination or disentanglement of options can influence choice. This is particularly important for high-impact, high-complexity decisions like health insurance or financial products.

Attention

People have only so much cognitive power, and the amount you're requiring from the customer should be directly proportional to the amount he cares about the decision you're putting before him. To generate interest in a sector that is not very important to consumers, you should lean on branding work to build awareness. This way your brand will be front-of-mind in the aisle. Despite the frequent criticisms about the cost and effectiveness of "awareness campaigns," the research shows that even incidental ad exposure increases the likelihood that a consumer will include a product in the consideration set, even when the subject doesn't explicitly remember the ad.[178]

Shopper marketing efforts that improve placement in the aisles, attributes that help your product stand out (e.g. scents that make your dish soap more interesting or pleasant), are the efforts that help you beat the competition in low-consideration purchases. If you want these shoppers to know something about your brand, you need to put it on the package or in the ad, because they're probably not coming to your website or social media pages to learn more about you unless you've given them a very compelling reason to do so.

In higher-consideration categories, you can ask for a little more of the consumer's attention because they are more concerned with seeking out brands that align with their identities and aspirations. They will be willing to visit your brand pages to read about your CSR efforts. So, if you have a poor reputation, or if you don't understand your customer's values, you can expect your bottom line to take a hit. People aren't concerned with looking uncool or lacking social awareness when they pick toilet paper, but they absolutely want to signal how fun or socially conscious they are when they choose a car.

Projection Bias

One study about the increase in obesity in the US in recent years found a positive correlation between health insurance and obesity.[179] Because obesity has been linked to a host of other health conditions, and because treating those conditions is more expensive if you're uninsured, a widely used college economics textbook used the study's results as evidence that people are responding to economic incentives. That is, people with insurance are allowing themselves to become obese because they're unconcerned with the costs, while people without insurance stay trim to save money.

But we know that people don't always rationally consider the economic costs of obesity when they lay into a cinnamon roll or a sixpack. People facing caloric temptation aren't thinking about their health insurance; they're thinking about indulging now and working it off at the gym later. Sometimes, they work out longer and harder than planned to offset the calories; but they usually don't go to the gym at all. Projection bias offers one explanation for this mismatch between expectations and actions.

When we make decisions, we implicitly assume that our preferences will remain stable over time, that we'll feel the same way about something in the future as we do now. This leads us to make decisions, often with lasting consequences, based on feelings during the moment of choice. Most of us don't intentionally live in the moment without regard for future consequences, but we can be terrible at predicting how we'll feel about our decisions in the future.

Projection bias could lead a teenager to say she'll never have kids after a rough night of babysitting, without considering that she might feel differently ten years later. This bias can lead you to buy a boat instead of saving that money for retirement, based on the assumption that you'll save more for retirement later. Or it can lead you to buy a bunch of lettuce for lunches, only to throw most of it away a week later because it wilted while you were going out for less-healthy lunches. And it's well-established within crime research that delinquents commit crimes because they're focused on short-term gains, not future consequences.[180]

One issue at play is a lack of empathy for our future selves. Neurologists have shown that when we think about ourselves in the future, we're engaging a part of the brain that is used to think about *other people*, not our current selves.[181] This indicates an emotional disconnect between our present and future selves, as if the future self is a different person. Translation: Thinking about what you'll want in the future is more like thinking about what your neighbor or favorite actor wants than what you want today. This is problematic for brands trying to get people to think about the long term.

Marketing Implications Depend on the Time Frame

Projection bias can lead people to fall victim to momentary temptation at the expense of the future. The implications for the marketing context, therefore, depend on the timeline of your relationship with your customer. If you're selling a product to be consumed in the short-term, your brand can benefit from projection bias, but if you're playing a longer game, you'll have to convince your customers to fight against it.

Long-Term Tactics

People tend to value immediate gains over future gains, which is called "temporal discounting." Economists explain this by showing that we discount rewards as they approach a temporal horizon—either in the future or in the past. Meaning, as rewards recede into the past or are delayed further into the future, they become less valuable to us today. We're hard-wired to prefer instant gratification, so people will need a little nudge if you're trying to get them to invest in a long-term benefit. The following tactics can help you engage prospective customers with brands that require longer relationships.

Feed the Need for Instant Gratification

Studies have shown that people who find a workout they enjoy are more likely to achieve their fitness goals. Likewise, people who focus on the great taste of healthy foods will stick with better eating habits.[182] We're more likely to achieve long-term goals when the journey to achieving them is enjoyable.

People say that they pursue long-term goals (e.g., education or retirement investments) for the delayed rewards, but research shows that they're significantly more likely to persevere toward these goals if they see immediate rewards.[183] By making the investment process fun and joyful, and by including a dose of instant gratification, you will be more likely to adhere to long-term investment goals. Educational institutions could offer fun seminars and inspiring instructors. Gyms could offer trendy classes and energetic music.

If you were to buy a new car today, you would vividly and quickly feel the benefits. At first, the fractional payment each month won't create enough pain to cancel that joy. This potent mix of immediate joy and temporal discounting explains why a long-term financing package can convince customers to buy more car than is fiscally responsible for them. People will overestimate how long they'll continue to enjoy the car, and they'll underestimate the pain of making payments when the car is five or six years old. By continually innovating new features and longer financing packages, car companies are frontloading the joy and amortizing the pain over the life of the purchase, which entices customers to upgrade.

Pre-Commitment

Customers who pre-commit to their investments, such as with automatic deposits to savings accounts or insurance plans, usually have more investing success. It is less painful for people to save more or make payments if they never see the money and don't have to initiate anything. If you can get people to agree to automatic payments or withdrawals straight from their paychecks, you can send them payment confirmation messages reminding them of your brand's value and praising them for their hard work. For instance, an investment company could send monthly updates on how quickly the customer's 401(k) account is growing. An insurance company could send newsletters that remind customers of plan benefits, such as acupuncture, massage, or online education.

Visualizing the Future
Another effective tactic for building equity over the long run is to help people understand the future value of an investment today. For example, the My Fitness Pal app asks dieters to enter their physical activity and food intake. At the end of each day, the app tells them what they would weigh at a specific point in the future if every day were like that day.

Empathizing With the Future Self
Helping people empathize with their future selves can help them prioritize their long-term well-being. A series of studies in 2011 demonstrated that subjects who interacted with their future selves via immersive virtual reality experiences were more likely to plan for the long-term and delay gratification.[184] Apparently, people who looked at their future selves in the [virtual] faces found it easier to connect emotionally and, therefore, were more open to behaving in ways that would benefit them. A separate study found that when consumers see their future selves in a positive light that emphasizes commonalities with the present self, and when this future self is presented in vivid, realistic terms, it increases their willingness to make choices that prioritize that future self.[185]

With this work in mind, Meryl Lynch offered a feature on its website called "Face Retirement" in which photos taken by users' webcams were manipulated to make them look older. This approach encouraged them to think about their needs in the future and to save more for retirement.

Short Term Tactics

Marketers selling products that are bad for you, like chips, often try to fight misconceptions. They look at data points on the proportion of their audience that's trying to lose weight and launch a lower-calorie option. They look at trending health claims and launch a "free from" promise; perhaps they try to reframe the choice set by pointing out that their chips are healthier than pork rinds. Such efforts miss the boat. People *know* that chips are bad for you—they're not substituting them for broccoli because they think they're healthy but because they want something salty and delicious.

Marketers of products that offer instant gratification should signal a hedonic goal frame to encourage the consumer to lean into the delights of sinfulness. Researchers have drawn a conclusion I hope is buried so deeply in this book that my mother will never know I wrote it: Guilt *is* pleasure. While the presence of other negative emotions reduces pleasure, the cognitive association between guilt and pleasure is so strong that experiencing guilt can lead to enhanced feelings of pleasure.[186] This is why alcohol tastes better when you're twenty, and it's why speeding is so much fun. So, when you're selling something that offers more short-term fun than long-term benefits, you should emphasize the pleasure of hedonic consumption.

Personalization and Messaging

Consumers understand that there's a value exchange at play when they access your content. They gain access to free content, and their payment is tolerating ads. But they want us to do better. Consumers increasingly sense that marketers have enough data about them to know which ads are irrelevant and, therefore, annoying. Still, with the glut of data available today, it's important to maintain a balance between personalization and the consumer's comfort.

Even when you've gathered data ethically, with the consumer's knowledge and consent, revealing how much you've learned from that data can backfire. It's not uncommon for people to peruse someone's social media profiles before a date. But if a suitor opened a conversation by commenting on the outfit a woman wore to her junior prom, the relationship probably wouldn't survive past dinner. This is even more true for businesses: Customers are aware that you can track their purchase history, but if your brand uses that information to congratulate a customer on her pregnancy before she has a chance to tell her family, she'll be creeped out.

Consumers don't want to be told that you know more about them than their spouses, but they do want personalized ads. In fact, many consumers want ads to be even more personalized.[187] The goal should be to know your customers well, but to limit the information you reveal about them to only what is needed for them to make a decision. One field experiment on lender advertisements found no difference in the conversion rate when advertisers reduced the amount of information in a message: A message with four examples of how borrowers could use a loan resulted in the same conversion rate as a message with only one example. And the message with just one example had the same effect on conversions as a two-hundred-basis-point reduction in the interest rate.[188]

This is where a working understanding of the Forer Effect can help.

Buzzfeed and The Forer Effect

Many rational people have read a horoscope, read a message in a fortune cookie, or taken a Buzzfeed quiz and thought, "OK, that's pretty accurate." Back in the 1940s, salesmen hawked psychological services akin to today's internet personality tests to business managers. The salesmen promised that managers could hire better employees or make teams more effective with this sort of knowledge in hand. Salesmen would offer to let the managers take the assessments for free, promising to walk away if the results weren't accurate.

Ross Stagner lamented how these so-called psychological services presented "glittering generalities" instead of practical advice from trained professionals, so he conducted an experiment.[189] Stagner went to a conference for personnel managers at the University of Illinois and asked them to take personality tests. Later, he distributed the results and asked each man to keep his report private, and to score its accuracy. Half of the personnel managers described their analyses as "amazingly accurate," and another 40 percent said the results were "rather good."[190]

Here's the best part: The personality analyses were all identical. They comprised statements that psychologist Bertram Forer had pulled from books on dream analysis and astrology. The statements most frequently classified as "amazingly accurate" were:

- You prefer a certain amount of change and variety and become dissatisfied when hemmed in by restrictions and limitations.
- You pride yourself as an independent thinker and do not accept others' statements without satisfactory proof.
- You have a tendency to be critical of yourself.

o   At times you are extroverted, affable, sociable, while at other times you are introverted, wary, reserved.

This issue isn't isolated to HR managers. Before this experiment, Forer had conducted similar experiments on college students, with similar findings.[191] Another experiment found that college students couldn't distinguish analyses of their personalities produced by trained psychologists from fakes produced by Forer's statements even half of the time.[192] Let that sink in: Statistically, these people would've been better off flipping a coin when trying to determine which assessment *of their own personality* was written by a psychologist and which was composed of random phrases from an astrology book.

Implication: Specificity of Messages

The important point here is that the subjects in these experiments weren't uniquely gullible. Study participants found the statements accurate because they were general enough to be true of most people but specific enough to hold some personal meaning. Applications for psychics, grifters, and fortune tellers are clear, but don't assume that all generic affirmations are nefarious. Inspirational quotes on Instagram are liked and reposted because so many people find them valuable and relevant, even if they're relatively general.

The findings are particularly encouraging in an age when many companies have enough data to terrify customers. Like the statements that Forer and others have tested, a great marketing message is general enough that it resonates across the target audience but specific enough that individuals find it personally relevant. Even the smallest business whose 'big data' is largely limited to analytics from the Facebook page probably has some solid demographic and behavioral information to leverage. If you know that your customers are employed, you can appeal to how busy their lives are or to the monotony of dreary commutes in large cities.

The message should be rooted in the data and carefully crafted to convince people that the brand understands them well enough to solve their problem, without making them feel like their privacy has been violated. Similarly, brand claims need to be deep enough to resonate, but commensurate with your actual offerings.

Responding to Backlash … or Not
Sometimes, when an agency executive and a brand manager love their brand onion very, very much, they come to the mistaken conclusion that the rest of the world will be as excited about their brand vision as they are. Subsequently, they can be a little overexuberant about the brand purpose in ads. Such was the case with the Barclaycard spot in 2015 that promised you could "get more out of today with Barclaycard." Criticism was swift from people that didn't care to receive philosophical tidbits from a banking brand, but it didn't seem to matter much to the bank's customers.

If you've done a good job of differentiating your brand, your message is not for everyone. And, in our social media age when every opinion can be shared, you will face some backlash. When this sort of backlash happens, pause to analyze the problem before you respond. Anger really only affects your brand if it's your target audience that's angry.

The brand Always has marketed its products with a campaign that calls users to "have a happy period." A few years ago, the slogan elicited a colorful open letter from one woman. In the rant, she argued that menstruation isn't a happy time and said that she was so offended by the slogan that she would stop buying the products immediately. She concluded by saying, "And though I will certainly miss your Flexi-Wings, I will not for one minute miss your brand of condescending bullshit. And that's a promise I will keep. Always."[193]

Her letter got a fair amount of online attention, but P&G didn't respond or pull back on the campaign. Why not? In an interview, a P&G spokesman noted that the campaign was built on the insight that women who prefer pads to tampons generally have a more positive outlook about their periods. So, while the company recognized that the campaign was a bit polarizing, it noted that most complaints were from women who don't use pads. In this case, Always made the right call by not responding. The overall brand sentiment was unaffected, and market share increased over the life of the campaign.[194]

If you base messages on deeper, human truths to engage emotionally with the target audience, you may build authentic connections. And you may also suffer some backlash. Take a beat to analyze the situation before responding to the haters. Consider whether you've said something hateful or inappropriate. If so, the situation necessitates an immediate, genuine apology. But if you haven't been hateful or offensive, look at how your target audience feels before responding. Otherwise, you might end up walking back a statement that resonates with them, and that could do more harm than good. People that love your brand don't mind it when you're a little overexuberant.

Relatable Marketing & Base Rate Neglect

If you went to a university, you probably encountered stereotypes related to majors: aspiring educators are perky women; an argumentative classmate probably studies law; and the most beautiful, interesting people study economics. (Maybe that last one isn't yet widespread.)

Kahneman and Tversky did an experiment about this idea back in the seventies. They described a graduate student, Tom, as being intelligent, self-centered, introverted, and lacking creativity (among other characteristics). Then they asked subjects to rank a list of nine graduate specializations in the order of likelihood that Tom was enrolled.[195] The most popular predictions of Tom's field of study were computer science and engineering, even though far fewer students enrolled in those programs than in others, making them statistically less likely.

These rankings were assigned by graduate students studying psychology who knew that a personality description wasn't accurate or diagnostic enough to be predictive. Nevertheless, the students were apparently biased by it. Over 95 percent of them said Tom was more likely to be studying computer science than humanities or education. They held this view even though they estimated there were about three times more students enrolled in humanities or education programs. So, why would these subjects ignore the laws of probability and their own knowledge of personality descriptions when predicting Tom's situation?

This is base-rate neglect or the base-rate fallacy. Logically, you should consider the overall likelihood of something—the base rate—when you're making a judgment about a specific case, but most people fail to do so.

Specific and Relevant Content Marketing

Researchers have identified a few factors that contribute to base-rate neglect. One explanation is that we depend on the representativeness heuristic.[196] In other words, Tom seemed to represent the psychology students' mental model of a computer science major. This made them feel confident about making that prediction, even though they knew that a small proportion of students enrolled in that program.

Another factor is that we give outsized attention to the information we deem to be most relevant, and specific information seems more relevant than broader generalities. [197] So, while the survey respondents knew that any individual graduate student was more likely to be studying education, the specific information about Tom made them feel confident that he was probably not.

The impact of designing a campaign that feels relevant and personal is clear. Your customer won't consult statistics about what most people buy, but he will think about his problem and decide whether your product can solve it. If you present customers with a problem that they can relate to and demonstrate how your brand can solve it, you will win. You can identify and communicate the relevant problem in several ways. First, by using in-depth research for persona development, you should be able to understand your customers and their problems well enough to tell a compelling, relatable story. Second, you can use social media analytics—guided by a great qualitative analyst who understands the nuances of social communications—to give you deep insights into how customers see their problems. Third, by appropriately framing the problem, you can help customers understand how your brand solves a problem—even if they hadn't thought of it as a problem before.

After you understand the customer's perception of his problem, it's time to present him with relevant, personalized solutions. This is an important win-win: Relevance keeps the customer from becoming annoyed with your company for showing him things he doesn't care about and the specificity of the information will lead him to view it as even more relevant. All this will predispose him to choose your brand.

Microsoft's example is worth emulating. The company has amassed mountains of quality content, but it never hits people with all the case studies at once. Instead, it shows information that's relevant to the customers' needs and, after the customer has opted into sharing contact information in exchange for assets like white papers, MS peppers clients with relevant information on the site and via email. Prospective customers will never have an inkling of the amount of content Microsoft.com holds because they'll only see the hyper-relevant bits.

Leveraging Loss Aversion to Incentivize Switching

People are illogically averse to loss—so much so that they'll work harder to avoid a loss than they will to experience a gain.

Therefore, an effective way to entice your competitors' customers to switch to you is to emphasize what those customers will lack by not signing up for your service. That is better than simply stating the benefits of your product.

The best way to pull off this type of messaging is to build it from a deep understanding of your existing customers. To leverage loss-aversion in your favor, you need to know:

1. What are the customer expectations for your category?
2. What does the customer want from your company?
3. What are you offering that your competitors aren't?
4. Is there anything surprising or unexpected that your customers value about your brand?

A basic requirement of growing a business is to make it easy for customers to switch to your brand. Unfortunately, it's far easier for your competitors' customers to maintain the status quo than to make a change. So, you need to heavily leverage your strengths and emphasize the competitors' weaknesses. You need to make a case for switching that is so compelling that the customer will feel like he's losing out if he doesn't act. You also need to understand what he loves about your competitor's product so you can reassure him that he won't miss out on that great benefit by switching to your company.

Be careful not to disproportionately scare customers lest you make them feel manipulated. Customers expect you to work to grow your business, but you can do that without being sleazy and without dropping the quality of your brand's discourse. Today's hyperconnected consumers will see through dishonest tactics. On the TV show *Arrested Development*, Gob promises, "A frozen banana that *won't* make you sick and kill you." Funny, but sleazy enough that it's unlikely to land with modern consumers.

Every communication from a brand could be the first impression for a new customer. It could be the only impression for someone reading about your brand in Facebook posts or articles on news sites. Don't be tempted to refer to competitors with petty insults or half-truths. Have more respect for your consumers than that.

The Halo and Horns Effects

The halo effect is the tendency to let a positive impression of someone or something in one domain influence our opinion of them in unrelated areas. Our tendency to judge a book by its cover. For example, we might assume that a handsome man is also kind, even though we know nothing about his personality. Similarly, customers might assume that a great service experience means that the brand is socially conscious, even though they have no knowledge of the company's social responsibility practices.

The halo effect can lead to a great experience that disproportionately benefits a brand, but there's also a dark side. The inverse of the halo effect is the horns effect. A negative impression of a single aspect of a brand can lead us to think less of the brand in other areas, too.

In one study, subjects were asked to review orange juice ads while shopping for orange juice. The ads contained specific wording: "real ingredients," "artificial ingredients," or, in the control, no additional information about the ingredients. Shoppers exposed to the "artificial ingredients" ads viewed the juice as less healthy and higher in calories, which demonstrated how a single negative phrase could influence perceptions of the product's other attributes.[198] Another study found that defiant children were more likely to be rated as inattentive and hyperactive, and more likely to be incorrectly labeled as having ADHD, than compliant children who displayed the same symptoms.[199]

Imagine boarding a plane and finding a seat with filthy upholstery and a broken tray table. Neither issue amounts to more than an annoyance, and fixing them wouldn't have a direct impact on the airline's revenues. But as a passenger, you might look at the filthy seat with discomfort and begin to worry about what disease you might catch in the bathrooms or by breathing the in-flight air. Worse, you may begin to wonder whether the engines are maintained with the same care as the tray tables.

A couple of years ago, I conducted an in-depth website review for an entity that collected a significant amount of personal information. One form on the site required enough personal information—social security number, birth date, address history, mother's maiden name—to recover a password for a bank account. I soon noticed that the site's security certificate had expired. Shocked, I immediately emailed my client rather than make them wait for my full presentation to learn about the issue.

I pressed on with my review, but as I prepared for the presentation days later, I noticed the issue hadn't been fixed. On the day of my presentation, I opened the meeting by asking whether they'd received my message. They had received it, the client's management team assured me. They added that the site's technical team had assured them that renewing the security certificate wasn't a big deal.

The technical team planned to fix the problem within the next week or two.

The people who maintained the site weren't lying; it is, in fact, easy to renew a security certificate. But, with management appeased, they had no reason to rush. They were far more concerned with the looming deadline of another major project, which was logical behavior for them. Managers were also unconcerned because (a) they trusted the technical experts, (b) the brand was a trusted household name, and (c) they didn't think an expired certificate would deter people from filling out the form.

Now, imagine being a visitor to that website. You don't know the URL off the top of your head, so you do a search, click on the top link and, instead of loading the site, your browser throws a scary security warning at you. At that point, you decide to backtrack and make sure that you have the right URL. You confirm that it is correct. Then you face a decision: Should you override the browser warning and visit the site anyway? If you decide to load the site anyway, would you be comfortable surrendering highly private identity information on an unsecured site?

The website form was an important tool for prequalifying leads. I never saw data to prove or disprove this, but I bet that the site failure drove people to use more-expensive channels like phone calls and in-person appointments. The deeper question is this: In today's world, where a good website is essential for major brands, how much would you trust a brand that can't even maintain the security of its website?

The halo and horns effects remind us that an early impression of your brand could affect consumer perceptions of your entire brand. This is further evidence of the importance of ensuring that every effort—from your latest Instagram post to your store bathrooms—is a well-considered, polished representation of your brand.

Adaptation Effects, The Hedonic Treadmill, and Marketing Messages

Can money buy happiness? Marketing can be a bit of a highwire act as we imply that buying from *our* brand will bring consumers some measure of happiness while entertaining the competing hope that our customers know better but will respect our work anyway.

As researchers have broadened our understanding of happiness and well-being, a dichotomy has arisen between momentary happiness and overall satisfaction with life. Happiness, Kahneman and Deaton argue, is fleeting because it is related to a momentary experience. Satisfaction, by contrast, is about your evaluation of your life and whether you've achieved your goals to build a life you admire.[200][201] This is in line with Seligman's work on positive psychology, which finds that positive emotion is one aspect of happiness, but factors like meaning, purpose, achievement, and accomplishment are among the building blocks of well-being and satisfaction with life.[202] So, someone who achieved her goals to finish college and marry for love might be very satisfied with her life, even while working in a low-level retail position. Another person in the same job and in a similarly happy marriage, however, might be very unsatisfied with her life because she could not fulfill her dream of touring internationally with her band.

Poverty makes adverse circumstances worse, and money does buy some comfort, stability, and positive experiences. But after incomes reach a certain point—$75,000 annually, it appears—money plays less of a role in increasing happiness (specifically, emotional well-being).[203] What's more, we seem to have default levels of happiness as individuals. Researchers have observed that people get a temporary lift in happiness from winning the lottery, but they return to their default level of happiness in the long run. Interestingly, the same study found that the decline in happiness suffered by paralyzed accident victims was also temporary.[204][205] Adaptation effects are so strong that, even after becoming unexpectedly paralyzed or winning the lottery, people gradually adjust and return to their previous levels of happiness.

The same happens with purchases. Imagine that your coffeemaker develops a leak, which you discover one morning when you clean up a puddle of coffee that has spilled onto the floor. After work, you head to the home department at your local retailer to buy a better machine. The first few times you use the new coffeemaker, you're excited. It doesn't leak and you appreciate the features your old machine didn't have, like delayed brewing or a built-in grinder. But, over time, the excitement fades, and the fancy, new machine brings no more joy to your morning than its predecessor.

This is called hedonic adaptation, or the hedonic treadmill. People who buy something get only a short-term lift in happiness from the purchase. After they adapt to having it, their happiness returns to its usual level. They must purchase or experience something else to experience that lift again.

What does your audience want from you?

Should your brand strive to deliver more than the temporary lift that Mr. Coffee brought you in the aforementioned hypothetical? It depends on what kind of brand you're managing and what people are seeking from it: happiness or satisfaction.

It's reasonable to assume that people want to be happy. But if happiness were their top priority, people would emphasize spending more time with friends and family and consistently prioritize the pursuit of joy. Thus, a rational choice for maximizing happiness would be to stop working overtime and striving for income beyond the $75,000 happiness index. They would instead focus on experiences that bring more joy than working. Curiously, though, many people don't stop striving to earn more after they reach the happiness-maximizing salary or a certain salary or net worth. Instead, the research finds, people are pursuing more than momentary happiness; striving for satisfaction and to build a life they can admire.[206]

The hedonic reference point isn't just about objective reality; it's also about expectations and social comparisons.[207] People aren't settling for happiness. They want to build admirable lives. They're ambitiously pursuing goals, jumping through hoops to forward their careers, and keeping up with the Joneses. After all, it's difficult to feel good about your life accomplishments if your neighbor drives a new Audi while you wonder if your old car will start each morning.

Your success in creating messages that connect with your customers will be proportional to your understanding of their adaptation levels and aspirations. To make the right promise in marketing messages, you must carefully consider the experience you're offering and the customer's underlying need for that experience.

Happiness

Health and time with loved ones bring happiness, so if you're offering a new drug that mediates suffering or marketing vacation packages, you should by all means promise happiness. In those situations, emphasizing the emotional well-being of consuming the product would be both compelling and accurate.

Similarly, if you're marketing a product that's easily affordable for consumers, your messages can emphasize emotional engagement right up to the point of purchase. After the purchase, the product itself can provide that moment of emotional lift, at least until the consumer's hedonic adaptation runs its course.

Even though that adaptation will inevitably occur in relation to a specific product (e.g., a coffeemaker), the little lifts of happiness provided by the product can support your brand in the long term. For example, Target shoppers are delighted to find a fresh selection of trendy décor options at affordable prices each season. Target doesn't offer customers a path to deep satisfaction with their lives, but its reasonable prices provide customers with an opportunity to regularly update their homes with affordable products that inject some happiness. Target enables them to fight hedonic adaptation effects without breaking customers' budgets. As a result, customers associate the Target brand with those little bumps in happiness.

Satisfaction

The story is a little different if you're marketing a premium brand. We tend to overpay to own premium products relative to the utility that we could get from cheaper alternatives. Even affluent audiences can't regularly replace premium products. It follows that if you try to emphasize happiness to sell a premium product, you're essentially promising the customer that the product will provide ongoing happiness each time it's used. Unfortunately, research about the hedonic treadmill demonstrates that, eventually, buyers will adapt to the luxury item and the happiness it offers will decline. This sets them up for disappointment with your brand. Even people who drop a quarter of a million dollars on a new Bentley won't feel the same excitement the hundredth time they turn the key that they did the first time.

Instead of promising Christmas Morning Excitement each time they use your product, you should center marketing messages on the feeling of life satisfaction. You can emphasize the status associated with owning the premium brand, showing how it's better than what they owned before, and/or that your customers deserve it. You can help people see that your brand can signal their life achievements to themselves and others.

Grabbing a designer tote on the way out the door may not make every Monday morning feel like Christmas, but it can remind the owner that her hard work is paying off and that she should feel proud of her achievements. For this message to be credible, though, your brand must be meaningful to the target customer. Nowadays, conspicuous consumption is likely to be insufficient. Your brand must represent something aspirational, not just offer expensive products. For example, the ultimate tote for the elite businesswoman can be a symbol of her power to overcome sexism. Messages about a luxury car can emphasize environmentally friendly technology that reverses the past generation's damage to the planet. A haute couture brand can demonstrate that it's more ethical than others by offering clothing for a variety of body types or rejecting the use of animal products.

Your brand is only a symbol of achievement for the buyer if she believes it is—only then can it purport to offer satisfaction. By elevating aspirational themes in marketing messages, you can elevate your brand to one that offers true satisfaction.

Go Forth and Slay the Competition

Modern consumers are faced with a constant onslaught of choices: what to click on, what to eat, what to watch, which gum to chew. We want to make the best decisions we can, but we have limited processing capacity and limited desire to give each choice exhaustive consideration. Thus, when people are tasked with making choices, we try to limit our cognitive effort.[208] This leads us to inconsistently apply a variety of decision-making strategies, which depend on the person, task, environment, perceptions, and context.[209] Even when we're doing our best to be logical, our choices are subject to all sorts of biases.

The heuristics, biases, and inattention that consumers bring to purchase decisions leave them open to influence by marketers. The marketer who carefully considers the weight of heuristics, cognitive biases, and environmental factors in consumer decision-making will be more effective at cutting through the noise to sway consumers. And the marketer who considers choice architectures when framing products, messages, anchors, and defaults will have an edge.

The opportunities to influence consumers are vast, but strategies should be carefully planned and methodically executed. You should draw attention to factors that authentically convey the superiority of your brand rather than shamelessly manipulating people into buying snake oil. Carefully consider the role your brand plays in the customer's life and the true aim of your behavioral marketing efforts—including what they would sound like in clips of congressional testimony—to ensure that you're serving both your business and your customer, without acting like a predator.

Loyalty & Retention

Many marketers can relate to the sheer exasperation Tom Cruise's Jerry Maguire felt when he found himself standing in the bathroom, begging his only client, "Help me help you. Help *me* help *you*!!"

If the user of a free product won't upgrade to a subscription that costs less than he spends on his morning latte but complains about having to see ads. When a customer writes a scathing letter to customer service because of a change, without taking a moment to realize that the change is actually better for her.

We've all been there. We've worked so hard to frame our messages, position our brands, and win customers, but we just can't retain and grow our customer base like we should, even though the solutions we offer are solid.

In this chapter, we'll delve into the psychology of why customers either stick with or abandon a brand. We will also look at how you can keep the customers you've worked so hard to win and grow your business. And I'll argue that you should focus more on penetration than loyalty. But first, we look at the foundations of your value to consumers and, therefore, your ability to win, engage, and retain them.

Changes, Expectations, and Retention

Chris Rock once joked that if Bill Gates woke up with Oprah's money, he'd jump out of a window. Wealth, and the perception of what it means to be wealthy, is relative. Even if you grew up in abject poverty, after a few years of high income, you might become accustomed to organic blueberries and microbrews and then have trouble returning to a life of counting pennies at the grocery store.

Logically, people should consider empirical reality as we evaluate a situation, but we're naturally much better at noticing changes than absolute magnitudes.[210] Consider how you would feel if your company announced you were getting a 2 percent pay cut. You would probably be really upset about the change, even though 2 percent is relatively small. You wouldn't care about the fact that your salary was still very good in relation to others in your profession and the cost of living in your city. You'd be livid because the company wanted to pay you less than it had promised.

Customers, similarly, expect the brand to deliver on its promises. Once you've won the customer, your service and its cost become internalized and become the customer's baseline expectation. From that point on, the way he evaluates your company won't be defined by objective reality, but by deviations from that baseline. This means he's apt to become upset if you reduce your offering, even if you're still offering a great deal compared with competitors.

Framing Changes

The customer's focus on change rather than the broader reality makes business difficult when you must cut services or increase costs, because the customer is focused on the feeling that you've taken something away and not your changing business environment. This insight makes a clear case against offering products or services for free or cheap to build your customer base. Once you offer something for free or cheap, customers will forever anchor to that price, and they'll jump ship if you try to ease prices up.

Customers code changes as either gains or losses, then decide whether to proceed with your company accordingly. This presents an opportunity: Because customers think more about net changes than the broader picture, they're vulnerable to framing effects. The way that you present gains and losses can, therefore, impact their perceptions of the situation. To persuade people to view your company in the best light, take a painstaking approach to planning how you'll frame changes and then stick to the plan at all costs.

Analyze the Net Impact to Nail the Communication

A key to successfully framing changes is a deep understanding of how the changes will impact the customer. Strategic separation and integration of changes can have an outsized impact on consumer perceptions,[211] so the first step in planning how you'll frame the change is to consider how positive or negative the change might be for customers.

Positive changes will be well-received, so those should be communicated separately for maximum impact. You should give each major improvement—better design, lower price, more content, more horsepower, improved efficiency, recycled materials, etc.—its own social post, and then let the warm glow of the customer's gratitude wash over you.

It follows that negative changes should be combined. When consumers learn that they will suffer multiple losses, they'll obviously be displeased, so just rip the Band-Aid off and combine the bad news into a single message. On *The West Wing*, White House staff tried to save up all of the stories that painted the president in a bad light, then deliver them to reporters in a single press briefing. They called this "taking out the trash." Combining all of the bad news and then *taking out the trash* results in less disappointment from customers than releasing each news item individually because we don't process loss in a linear, logical fashion. That is, a loss of $10,000 feels about the same as a loss of $10,100, whereas a loss of $1 feels much different than a loss of $101.

To mitigate the negative impact of announcing changes that will feel like losses, offer transparency around the changes, recognize that you understand that this is not positive for the customer, and then emphasize why having a relationship with your company is still great for the customer.

If you have a mixed bag of positive and negative changes, and if they will result in a net gain to the consumer, then you can elicit the best reaction by combining them. Attempting to quantify utility can be a fool's errand because people have difficulty predicting how they'll feel about something until they experience it and, even then, impressions will be subject to presentation and interpretation. Do your best to take a deep, honest look at what the changes will mean for consumers who have adapted to your current offerings. As you present the changes, don't try to snow consumers with lies, but frame the changes in terms of why you believe they add up to a net gain. You might say, "Our prices will be increasing by $1 per month, but this will enable us to deliver thousands more hours of the great content you love, including x, y, and z. We can no longer offer one popular show, but we'll be releasing a dozen new shows this month."

Be careful if you have a potpourri of mixed changes that result in a net loss. In this case, your presentation comes down to the *magnitude* of the gains relative to the losses. You should separate the messages if the gain is small relative to the loss. For example, if a customer's car transmission needs to be replaced for $3,000, a free oil change won't be viewed as a meaningful benefit, so save that news for later. Once the customer has absorbed and accepted the news of the expensive repair, she'll be able to appreciate the free oil change. If the gain is nearly the size of the loss, you should combine the messages, saying something like, "The most recent product launch was a flop that cost us a million dollars, but the gains in other markets nearly offset that loss."

Predicting Customer Reactions to Changes

With the usual caveat that your customer is not a robot and probably won't react to changes with cool indifference, you can predict how customers will respond to changes by understanding what matters to them. If you've been careful in brand management work, your customer cares most about your brand values and little about peripheral changes that don't undermine the essence of your brand.

The classic example of a company underestimating its brand's power is the New Coke launch. But, in recognition of that example's overuse in marketing textbooks, let's balance the discussion with a look at a Pepsi flub. In a 2009 rebrand, Tropicana redesigned its Pure Premium orange juice carton and suffered massive sales losses. The new carton was beautifully designed. It featured an image of a pretty glass of orange juice that wrapped around the corner of the carton to appear three-dimensional. The cap was rounded and orange with leaves at the bottom, so it looked like a little orange. And the brand name was lightened and turned ninety degrees. Altogether, the new packaging lent a cleaner, more modern impression than the old carton.

Unfortunately for Tropicana, customers weren't looking for a sleek, modern brand. They wanted the same freshly squeezed juice that they'd enjoyed for years. The Pure Premium juice was worth the premium price because it's fresh juice, not from concentrate. But now, the company had removed the image of the orange with a straw from the front and dropped the image of the farmer picking oranges from the side. This led some customers to wonder if the formula had also changed. To them, the modern design implied that Tropicana might have added synthetic ingredients to the juice.

Sales plummeted and outcry from customers was so strong that the brand did an about-face and returned to the original packaging within weeks. Ironically, the marketers over at Tropicana didn't understand how iconic that image of the orange with a straw in it was to customers.

If you've done a good job of selling customers on the value of your brand, you can't strip away essential parts of that brand without major blowback. The essence of Tropicana's brand was pure, natural juice straight from oranges, so it was a problem when the brand launched a modern package without pictures of oranges on it. It doesn't matter that the new carton looked nice or that the original logo looks a little like WordArt, because "sleek, modern aesthetic" isn't the reason loyal customers choose Tropicana.

The Role of Expectations

At its core, a positive customer experience is one in which expectations have been exceeded.

A customer whose expectations are not met can become a giant liability. He could drain customer service time, create nightmares for social media managers, make scenes in stores, and write reviews that deter others. The best way to avoid this is to set expectations carefully.

Because customers evaluate change relative to a specific point of reference, you can shift that point of reference to align their satisfaction with your objectives and, therefore, facilitate the retention of customers. By establishing a clear point of reference, you can control expectations from the outset. If you know your prices are going to increase, be sure to frame the current price as an introductory offer, trial period, or beta test. If you aren't certain that you can maintain a feature, or replace it with a better feature, it's best to never offer it in the first place.

Above all, understand what your customers value most and avoid taking it from them at all costs without significant compensation.

Fairness

I once opened a lecture at Oregon State with a question: "Has anyone ever told you that life is unfair?" There was a collective groan as hands shot up. I struggled to get the lecture back on track because students couldn't control their urges to share stories of people who had slighted them. Mothers who *always* let siblings get away with *everything*. Teachers who let bullies roam free after punishing victims who retaliated. Managers who denied vacation requests unreasonably.

Fairness is an incredibly important behavioral driver. A desire for fairness explains why people tip terrible waitstaff in restaurants they'll never visit again and donate money to charities, rather than spending it on themselves. But does fairness matter to a lot of people, or just the most ethically minded?

The Ultimatum Game

I played a version of the Ultimatum game[212] with three of my microeconomics classes. For those who played the game, I offered five points of extra credit on the final exam, but with the caveat that they had to agree on how to allocate the points.

Rules

To play the game, I divided the class into two groups: allocators and recipients. Members of each group drew numbers to match them randomly and anonymously with a member of the other group. Allocators started with five extra credit points each to divide between themselves and their corresponding recipient, with the promise that I would be the only one who would ever know their identity and offer. Each allocator could divide the points between himself and his recipient however he liked (fractional division of points was allowed).

Next, I presented the anonymized offers to the recipients. Each recipient reviewed her offer, then decided whether to accept or reject the point allocation she had been offered, also with the promise that the allocator would never know her identity. If the recipient accepted, points were awarded as the allocator proposed. If the recipient rejected the offer, neither the allocator nor the recipient would get any points.

What should happen?

Before we review results, let's consider what we would *expect* to happen. The final exam was worth a significant portion of the grade, and each point awarded in the game was guaranteed to be worth at least an additional 1 percent on top of the exam grade, so we would expect all students to try to maximize their points in the game.

This implies that a logical recipient would accept any nonzero offer because any offer larger than zero would improve her grade on the final (and her course grade). Knowing this, we would expect a logical allocator to offer only a small amount above zero. Remember, everyone had been promised anonymity, so there were no social repercussions for an allocator who improved her own grade by lowballing a classmate.

Altogether, this means that it would be logical to expect a lot of 4-point/1-point or even 4.5-point/.5-point proposals from allocators. We would also expect recipients to accept all proposals. After all, if an allocator offered a recipient 1 point, that would be 1 point more than she previously had, and far better than nothing.

Results

In the three classes that played the game, allocators offered an average of 2.3 of the five points to recipients—a nearly even split. This implies that the allocators cared about fairness, even though the game incents unfair behavior, and even though they could've gotten away without anyone ever knowing. In the face of incentives to behave selfishly, the students wanted to do what was fair. One student even kept a single point for himself and offered the other student four points because he was confident that he'd ace the exam and wanted to help a random classmate that might need it more than him.

Of course, there were students that played as economists would expect, offering a point or less to their recipients. But it is worth noting that only one student accepted an offer of one point or less. Rather than being glad for the opportunity to leave class with a small amount of extra credit, the recipients of low offers were so vexed that they were willing to punish allocators for their mean-spirited behavior by turning down offers, even though this punishment meant sacrificing points.

Other Experiments

My results are in line with other ultimatum game experiments,[213][214] which generally use cash rather than extra credit. But there's an important question: When an allocator offers a relatively even split, is it because she wants to be kind and fair, or is it because she wants to ensure that she'll get some points?

To explore this question Kahneman, Knetsch, and Thaler iterated on the Ultimatum game.[215] In their experiment, allocators received $20 and only two options for dividing it: They could either keep $18 for themselves and give $2 to the recipient, or they could offer the recipient a fifty-fifty split. This time, though, offers made by allocators were final and could not be rejected by recipients. Of the 161 allocators in the experiment, 122 chose to divide the money evenly. They were willing to sacrifice income to treat strangers fairly, even when there was no fear that an unfair offer could be rejected.

In a subsequent trial, students had two options:

- o Keep $6 for themselves and give $6 to someone who had previously been an unfair allocator (who kept more than she shared with her recipient).

o   Keep $5 for themselves and share $5 with someone who had previously been a fair allocator.

In that scenario, 74 percent opted to take the lower sum, demonstrating that they valued fairness enough to sacrifice their own earnings to reward fair behavior (or punish unfair behavior).[216]

This thinking probably isn't news to anyone who's ever been so displeased with a company that they've been willing to pay more to support its competitor. And it's also consistent with findings that consumers are willing to sacrifice to support issues they care about. An estimated two-thirds of US consumers (and fully 70 percent of millennials) say they're willing to pay more for products that support issues they care about. And most Americans would be willing to earn less if it meant working for a responsible company.[217]

Clearly, it would be unwise to categorize your customers as entirely selfish or wholly self-sacrificing. You can't expect them to be completely loyal to your company to reward your CSR efforts, and you can't expect them to completely abandon you after one poor customer service experience. As Thaler pointed out, "Most people prefer more money to less, like to be treated fairly, and like to treat others fairly. To the extent that these objectives are contradictory, subjects make tradeoffs."[218]

What is Fair?

As you try to assess implications of these studies for marketing, the focus should be on what consumers consider to be fair, which is harder to define than you might imagine.

Fair: Aligning with Expectations, Costs, and Reference Transactions

A fair price for a product or service is based on, among other factors, the consumer's transactional utility, which is the difference between the actual price and the price the consumer expects to pay.[219] If a consumer plans to pick up a slice of cheesecake to eat at home, she'll pay more to pick it up from a fancy restaurant than a grocery store, even if it's the exact same cheesecake. She expects to pay more at the fancy restaurant than at the grocery store, so if the grocery store charged the restaurant's price, it would feel like gouging. Her perception of store's unfairness would lead her to buy the cheesecake at the restaurant, even though the cheesecake is the same price in both locations. Thus, trying to convince your customers that you offer the same product or service as a pricier competitor might not be enough to win their business.

Another factor in a consumer's perception of fairness is his reference transaction. When one of my beginning economics students talked about increases in local rents, he said he'd lived in the same apartment for years and had seen significant increases in rents even though there had been no costly improvements to the apartment complex. He raged about his avaricious landlords and their predatory, profit-maximizing behavior. Another student advised him to take it easy, adding that rising rents had occurred all over town, not only at his complex. The first student was enraged because his reference transaction was the first month's rent some years in the past. He thought the rent increases were unfair because they were disproportionately high compared with the landlord's cost increases. The second student felt the same rent was fair because it was in line with market prices, which weren't set by any individual landlord.

These students' feelings are in line with broader research: Consumers will withstand a price increase with empathy when a firm's costs increase, and they will have some patience if they believe the firm's competitor has led the market in a price increase.[220] That said, you should expect backlash if customers think you're raising prices simply to take advantage of market conditions.[221]

Not Fair: Leveraging Market Conditions for Gain

Concert tickets often sell out quickly, partly because scalpers buy and resell them for well over the purchase price. Artists see what the scalpers get and know they could charge more, and cut the scalpers out of the equation. Why don't musicians raise ticket prices to maximize their earnings? They don't want to be seen as exploiting fans. The artists want fans to continue purchasing and streaming their music long after that concert is over, and they know that increasing ticket prices would prioritize short-term income over long-term gains.

Sony also demonstrates best practices here. After releasing several popular consoles and dozens of successful games, Sony probably expected that its PS5 would sell out quickly, that people would buy up any available consoles in stock, and then resell them on third-party marketplaces for more than the in-store price. So, why wouldn't Sony increase the price of its new console in anticipation of high demand? After all, it would seem wise to split profits between the brand and the retailers rather than share profits with the people who flipped consoles on eBay and Craigslist.

By controlling what retailers could charge, the brand ensured that people would blame unprincipled flippers, not the gaming brand itself, for the higher prices. As people blamed the scalpers, Sony could maintain its good reputation and continue to sell accessories, subscriptions, and games long after the excitement over the PS5 console died down.

Pricing Implications

Some have speculated that, for marketing reasons, Sony intentionally underproduces gaming consoles to create scarcity. After all, a console that is heavily in demand forces consumers to compete to get one, which feels like a coup for the brand. Sony is undoubtedly enjoying the success, but there is a bigger factor at play. Sony knows that raising prices, even in response to strong demand, would lead customers to perceive unfairness. Today's money grab is tomorrow's public relations crisis.

One study found that 82 percent of consumers felt it was unfair for a hardware store to increase the price of shovels from $15 to $20 the morning after a snowstorm.[222] The same research found that if, in response to a shortage, a car dealer sold cars at $200 above list price, consumers would find it unfair. But, if that same dealer simply stopped offering a $200 discount it had been offering, bringing the cars to list price, most people would find that acceptable. These scenarios are mathematically equivalent: The consumer is out $200 either way. The difference is that, when the sale ended and prices returned to the MSRP anchor, customers didn't feel a loss. But a $200 price increase felt like the dealership was behaving unjustly, and with malicious intent.

When a price increase is unavoidable, you've got a couple of options. Since our model suggests that satisfaction is about perceived losses compared with expected losses, you can try to shift expectations by shifting the customer's reference point. You can offer a more luxurious experience, leading her to choose a different reference transaction. In the cheesecake example we discussed, the grocery store could charge more for bakery food if it created an in-store experience reminiscent of a restaurant, perhaps with a cordoned-off cafe area. Another way to get away with price increases is to liken yourself to a higher-end competitor to elicit context effects. Many coffee brands intentionally crib branding techniques from Starbucks, leading customers to expect Starbucks prices. You can also make price comparisons more difficult by offering a totally unique product or combination of products that must be purchased together. Without a cheaper alternative at the ready, the customer is less likely to balk at your prices.

If you can't shift the point of reference, you can carefully frame the change to soften the customer's perception of the magnitude of the loss. In 2020, Netflix framed an increase in subscription prices as a part of a wider update. The email said, "This update will allow us to deliver even more value for your membership — with stories that lift you up, move you or simply make your day a little better." The email also thanked subscribers for choosing Netflix and offered imagery that piqued interest in new and upcoming content.[223] So, Netflix recognized that it was asking customers to pay more, but assured customers that the increase in value outweighed the increase in cost.

Remember, the goal in framing a price increase is to convince the customer that he's still getting a great deal and he need not revisit his decision to buy your brand.

Retention and Intent

People value fairness so much that they're willing to make sacrifices to be fair, to reward others who are fair, and to punish those they view as unfair. The question of how unfair you can be without losing customers depends on your brand equity and the individual customer. But we do know that people will heavily weigh your intent—or their perceptions of your intent—when deciding whether to forgive your bad behavior.

Though economists recognize that Uber is just responding to the market with its "surge pricing," the company has gotten a lot of bad press from consumers who think it's unfair at best (and predatory at worst). They take issue with higher prices because they know Uber's labor and app maintenance costs aren't increasing during surge periods, so they think it's unfair that their prices should increase. The service is so convenient that many people find the higher prices reasonable, but the bad press is undoubtedly deterring some.

The great news is that you don't need to walk on eggshells or fear consumer backlash. If your brand tends to balance profits with consumer experience, one bad call won't sink it. People will make personal sacrifices to punish intentionally mean behavior from brands, but they tend to be more tolerant of inadvertently mean behavior.[224] Context and intentions matter, so your brand will survive an honest mistake or a change that's better for the company than the customer with careful framing. And it helps if you apologize when you're wrong. That's how Beyonce and Lizzo reacted when a disability advocate pointed out how offensive it was to use the term *spaz* on their 2022 albums. Both recognized that they had disrespected people with disabilities, publicly apologized, and updated their lyrics. There was no backlash; instead, many people—including those who had initially called out the issues—celebrated the artists' sensitivity.

Bottom Line on Retention and Fairness

Your reputation and CSR records may have helped you win customers, but your ongoing business practices will determine whether you can keep them. Formal studies—and the lived experiences of social media managers—demonstrate that your customers will punish you for intentional injustices. When you make pricing, customer service, and policy decisions, you should objectively consider your actions and how they might be perceived by customers. The finance department may advise you to take advantage of favorable market conditions without a second thought, and the folks in the legal department might try to parse the true definition of monopoly, but marketers should avoid any strategy that requires your company to pursue gains solely by taking an equivalent amount from customers, without offering them added value.

Adhering to a code of fairness has advantages beyond sound sleep. Firms that have built trust and have demonstrated values that are aligned with their customers can survive in markets plagued by consumer distrust.[225] They will find support even if prices are higher than the prices of competitors.[226] Firms that behave unfairly will lose customers, even when switching brands is inconvenient.[227]

Loyalty

Identity or Reality?

Thought exercise: Think about a friend, coworker, or family member you know well, and then consider how you would describe them to others. Would you describe this person the same way they would describe themselves?

I have a very vocal, opinionated family member who often responds to conversations with unvarnished feedback and comprehensive advice. At best, this can feel like devotion and support; at worst, it can feel like meddling. Once, at dinner, she began a story with, "You know, I would never say anything, but … " Two other family members snorted in amusement, because the comment was so far from their perceptions of her typical behavior that they thought she was kidding. I have another family member who is the most extroverted person I know. She has the high energy of a cartoon character, is extremely talkative, appears to draw energy from being around others, and seems to be happiest on stage or at parties like her enormous, two-day wedding. She's a prolific participant in social media sites, where she has told her hundreds of followers that it's difficult to put herself out there because she's "extremely introverted."

If our perceptions of people differ from how they describe themselves, who is correct about their identities? We can clearly observe the day-to-day behaviors of others, but don't we each know our own minds better than any outsider could? More importantly: If we don't even understand the identities of those closest to us, how can we possibly use identity as a factor in shaping marketing strategies?

Psychologists believe that many factors impact how we identify and portray ourselves. Context and relationships are critical considerations. For instance, you might behave differently in a job interview than around friends. You probably expect to be treated differently by your mother than by a date. And we behave cautiously in high-stakes situations like impressing a date or a prospective employer. When I surveyed my students, only a fifth said their restaurant orders are *never* affected by the people they're with. Many said they avoid meat when dining with a vegetarian, avoid ordering alcohol with particular companions, or otherwise tweak their orders depending on their group.

Because we tend to contextualize our behaviors, we create different impressions of ourselves. A manager might say that you're responsible but lack confidence, whereas friends might describe you as wildly fun, unpredictable, and the life of the party. The people I described as opinionated and extroverted might be viewed as quiet and reserved by others because they present themselves differently in each environment.

Adding to the difficulty of pinpointing identity, our person perception skills—the skills we use to draw conclusions about others—are subject to many biases that can lead to erroneous judgments. Perceptions are heavily influenced by how we categorize people socially,[228] our implicit personality theories,[229] our views on whether they're "like us" and members of our ingroup,[230] and a host of stereotypes. So, the question of the reality—the truth of who people really are—is moot.

Identity is an elastic construct, dependent on context, not an unchanging reality.[231] And our perceptions are biased enough that we can't consistently trust our views about people. Thus, who our customers are matters less to us as marketers than their own self-concepts, which groups they identify with, and who they aspire to be. This means that building loyalty requires that we understand the context of how our brand fits into the customer's life, and how the consumer identifies within that context.

Let's unpack this with an example. Many men who were athletes in high school struggle with their weight later on because they continue eating junk even as their metabolisms slow down and as they spend long hours at sedentary jobs. If you were to plan a campaign for a weightlifting gym, you might be tempted to disregard as irrelevant the fact that a thirty-eight-year-old man played sports in high school twenty years ago. But participation in sports as a teenager tends to become a deep-seated part of someone's identity. This means that the fact that a prospective customer played high school football is very relevant to how he sees himself today and his relationship with a gym. He learned how to use weights with his teammates as a teenager and the sight of free weights and the smell of the mats bring him back to the Friday night lights. This man's identity as an athlete and his longstanding relationship with gyms have more of a bearing on his propensity to choose your gym than today's story that he works in sales, drives a sedan, and has two kids.

Thus, to build loyalty and grow your relationship with this customer, you shouldn't write copy that emphasizes his obesity and desk job. Instead, the messaging should recognize that he *is* an athlete, even though he struggles to carve out the time he once did for the gym. He won't be inspired by a commercial that touts your inclusiveness for every fitness level; he wants to be inspired to release his inner athlete. This guy doesn't want a gym where beginners can be comfortable; he wants to go where the *real* athletes go.

Identity and Loyalty

A customer's general demographic information has limited value for marketers seeking to engender loyalty. The important information isn't who your customer is, but how she sees herself. Consumers prefer brands that are consistent with their self-perceptions and aspirations, and they're loyal to brands that are consistent with their identities.[232][233] They'll also buy brands to signal their group membership and to dissociate with outgroups.[234] And the purchases we make are more about who we are than what we can afford: Recent research has underscored the connection between purchases and identity, noting that materialistic behaviors are about constructing and maintaining one's identity. Sometimes, the researchers assert, a purchase is more about signaling an identity to oneself than to others.[235]

All combined, this means that you need to understand how the customer sees herself—and who she wants to be—to engender loyalty. Customers will choose your brand time and again if it's congruent with their identity and the image they want to project.

Sometimes, brands can become a part of how people define their own identities. Consider the character sketches that come to mind when you hear brand-oriented labels like VSCO girl, Apple loyalist, Marlboro man, PGA Golfer, JP Morgan Chase executive, or Instagram Influencer. People willingly describe themselves with these branded labels because they see the labels as shorthand for their self-identities. Identity loyalty like this is the deepest level of loyalty and brand engagement, but it's only attainable when customers are willing to adopt all of the associations that come with the brand.

It follows that retaining customers is dependent on your ability to remain consistent with the image they want to signal to those around them. The case for research and careful brand management is clear: You must ensure that your brand image is one that your core customers want to portray, which means first understanding the context of their relationship with your brand and how customers wish to appear within that context.

The casual Instagram user might hear an Instagram influencer describe herself as a VSCO girl and roll her eyes. This casual user views the VSCO girl as someone who spends hours applying makeup and playing with filters to create a false image of herself to share online, to the detriment of other women's self-images. But the self-described VSCO girl likes the app for the natural-but-better filters because she thinks they enhance her natural beauty without making her look fake. She wants to be recognized as a natural beauty on Instagram and beyond and the app helps her achieve that goal.

The perception of how "natural" the app filters appear to the casual user doesn't matter—all that matters for the app's marketers is helping the VSCO girl feel like the app is bringing out her natural glow.

Looking to another vertical, people who buy sportscars might want to demonstrate to those around them that they're both successful and fun. The Corvette is a great solution for this consumer because the brand is shorthand for premium, fun, and performance. The car is powerful and impractical, demonstrating that the buyer is fun, and it's expensive, demonstrating his success. If Corvette cut prices in half or marketed increased trunk space for groceries, the brand would find new customers, but it would sacrifice its core audience to do so, because it would no longer allow the core customers to portray themselves as successful and adventurous.

To build loyalty, you must continually prove that your brand is just as relevant to the identity customers want to signal today as it was when they first chose the brand. You should take a multi-pronged approach to this effort: Ongoing research so that you know you're evolving with your key customers and marketplace; aggressive brand management to ensure that equity isn't fading over time; and emotional engagement, to keep your brand front of mind.

We Want to be Optimally Distinct

Demonstrating your relevance to someone's ingroup requires a more nuanced approach than simply pointing out that you're beloved by other members of that group.

Social psychologists posit that individuals have both the need for inclusion and the need for differentiation. These needs are, fundamentally, in competition and need to be balanced for us to feel satisfied. That is, people don't want to be identified by social categorizations that are too inclusive or too differentiating. We want to feel *optimally distinct*.[236] This means that marketers must take a cautious approach to addressing social identities in marketing. We need to demonstrate our relevance to a target's ingroup with relationships with relevant influencers, messaging that addresses their common problems, meaningful brand placements, etc. But we also need to demonstrate that we see our customers as individuals. This could manifest as curated choice sets or personalized experiences. Popular brands can also cash in on this need for differentiation with unique customization options and limited-edition products.

Academic researchers have found that marketers can shift focus between assimilation and differentiation based on the stage of the relationship with the buyer. They noted that you can focus on highlighting the benefits of your differentiated service to demonstrate how the buyer can benefit from your brand early in the relationship. Then, you can emphasize your shared values and goals (assimilation) to expand the relationship. Importantly, you must balance the customer's interest in assimilation and differentiation to remain appealing as the customer lifecycle wears on.[237]

Social Identity and Community

Social identity research has revealed that the way we define ourselves is heavily influenced by the formal and informal groups to which we belong: NRA member, PTA president, lawyer, Volvo driver, cat person, NSYNC fan, bitcoin investor. If loyalty depends on your brand's congruence with identity, it follows that loyalty depends on your brand's congruence with relevant groups.

Some brands take a direct approach to building community. Earlier in the text, we talked about how Harley-Davidson has become a symbol of a community and has supported and grown that community. This has helped to strengthen loyalty, and that loyalty has carried the brand through several macroeconomic challenges.

Building community is also effective for brands that don't feel "cool" or worthy of tattoos. Colgate maintained online communities before the dawn of social media marketing. The secret to that brand's success has been engaging audiences on topics that are important to followers, relevant to the brand, and deeper than toothpaste. We all know that Colgate sells toothpaste and mouthwash. While the brand does remind us of this with celebrity endorsements and coupons, it also adds depth to the conversation with knowledge bases, oral health resources for individuals and professionals, and social media campaigns around things that make people smile. This content offers opportunities for more interesting and valuable discourse than communities could ever have around toothpaste.

Brands have embraced social media because of the opportunity to engage with customers. But it is important to remember that social media can be a time sink with low ROI when not approached strategically. Brands tend to have, proportionally, very few actively engaged social followers. Most of the followers followed the brand when it offered some sort of incentive, such as coupons or product discounts, but then never interacted with the brand. There are many "lurkers" who passively scroll past messages and occasionally react to a post, but without ever communicating directly. Nearly all active engagement—chats, contest entries, comments, etc.—is from a single-digit percentage of followers.

For marketers, this means that you should be cautious about how you spend your time on social media. Social media can be useful for developing customer loyalty and to support your brand identity, but talking to a small fraction of your audience in a public forum isn't a scalable strategy. You can kick complaints to direct messages, thank those who send compliments, and avoid wasting time on aspiring influencers, bots, and conspiracy theorists. You don't want to ignore customers who attempt to engage with you on social media, but you do want to make a strong effort to improve the actual brand experience for most of your customers. That is far more important than spending time on *talking about* the brand experience with a tiny faction of social media warriors.

Harley-Davidson has a product that people want to talk about and build communities around. Colgate has been able to connect its products with concepts like oral health and optimism that are more worthy of conversation than mere toothpaste. But what if you don't have a brand that people want to discuss around the campfire? Social identity theory is still helpful! Drug companies have built online communities for people with specific diseases. These communities require registration and aren't wide open to the world and are more private. Participants give drug companies access to deep insights about the struggles of people living with diseases and connect people who are suffering with others who truly understand what they're going through. The communities also connect the brand with niche audiences and ease recruiting for ongoing research.

If your customers don't want to shout from the rooftop about your brand, and if they don't want to join a group related to your brand, you can still engage with them by finding their existing communities. By forming partnerships with relevant influencers and communities, you can get closer to your audience and garner the kind of insights you need to better support your customers and engender stronger loyalty. You could partner with an Instagram influencer, sponsor a 5k charity run, or donate to a local project that's important to your audience. Sponsorships and partnerships won't give you the ownership and access of a homegrown community, but they will allow you to demonstrate your relevance to the customer's ingroup, and they require far less investment.

Network Effects

Economists use the term network effects to describe situations in which the value of something depends on how many other people are using it. Consider dating apps. If you're single and you've decided to meet someone through a dating app, that app is only valuable to you if people that you want to date are also using the app. The most valuable app is the one that has the greatest number of potential dates—so that app benefits from network effects. Similarly, a social networking platform is only appealing if you know other people using it.

Network effects increase the desirability of your brand—sometimes even more than quality—and they can deter competitors.[238] For many business models, this means that quickly gaining market share is more important than short-term profits. If you can dominate the market, then you can ultimately take advantage of economies of scale and/or raise prices, then allow your network to be your marketing engine. As your brand grows, deepening penetration within your target market will multiply the desirability for your brand as it becomes a symbol of your customer's identity. For this reason, network effects can multiply loyalty. This opens an important question: Should we focus on loyalty or growth?

Growth *versus* Loyalty or Growth *is* Loyalty?

There's an age-old debate amongst marketers about whether brands should focus on penetration or loyalty. The prevailing theory is that it's less costly to grow a customer than to acquire one, and this is repeated so often in meetings that you might assume it's true. *Au contraire!* The claim that loyalty is king isn't without merit—you should be nice to the people who give you money—but the evidence doesn't support conventional wisdom on this issue. The empirical fact is that it's far more effective and profitable to focus on increasing penetration than on increasing loyalty.

The first problem with the loyalty-first logic is that most customers in most categories aren't actually loyal. Rather, people tend to choose from a repertoire of three or four brands within various categories. One brand often serves as a substitute for another. In these cases, buyers of your brand are probably buying other brands more frequently than they buy yours.[239] One analysis of frequently bought grocery products found that only about 10 percent of buyers were completely loyal to a brand over the course of a year.[240] Many dating app users are using multiple apps simultaneously to ensure they don't miss out on a great match. Most buyers rotate between your brand and others, so winning isn't about how loyal your buyers are; it's about how many buyers you have.

Further supporting the argument that you should emphasize penetration over loyalty is the double-jeopardy law of marketing, which says that loyalty and penetration are correlated. Brands with larger market shares attract more buyers who buy more often. Smaller brands have fewer buyers who are less loyal. In other words, increases in loyalty can coincide with increases in penetration. (As an aside, we refer to double jeopardy as a law because research has supported it across cultures and time,[241] and in dozens of categories, ranging from grocery items to retailers to jet fuel.[242] [243])

You should obviously investigate what might be causing customer attrition and then address any problems, but your brand will experience some churn. The best way to combat the negative effects of that churn on revenue is to increase your market share.

But what about the 80/20 rule? We all know that the top 20 percent of customers produce about 80 percent of the sales, right? We've all heard this conventional wisdom, but Pareto's principle doesn't apply here. The proportion of sales contributed by the most loyal customers tends to be much lower. A big study of body sprays and deodorants back in 2007, for example, found that the top 20% of buyers were accountable for about half of sales for major brands.[244] And, in 2019, only about 40% of Starbucks' daily transactions were from customers using the rewards program.[245]

The erroneous assumption that Pareto's principle applies to consumer purchases across verticals leads marketers to focus far more campaigns on loyalty than penetration.[246] But if you don't have hard data that shows that the bulk of your sales really are coming from a small minority of your buyers, focusing on this minority comes at the expense of the larger population of customers who, as the data show, generate more revenue.

Loyal customers are important, but that group's contribution isn't grounds to split the ad budget between the loyalty campaign and a campaign designed to attract new customers. A recent meta-analysis found that campaigns designed to increase loyalty are rarely successful either in terms of business metrics or industry accolades. Even when these campaigns are successful, the success tends to come from attracting new and light buyers from the long tail, not increasing sales amongst loyal buyers or reducing churn. Only about 9% of campaigns designed to increase loyalty do so—a figure rendered even less impressive compared to the 7% of non-loyalty campaigns that increase loyalty.[247] Further, loyalty perks—like so much modern ad work—tend to manifest as campaigns designed to activate customers in the short term at the cost of longer-lasting effectiveness.[248]

This research doesn't suggest ignoring your existing customers as you seek greener pastures; rather, it implies that you should focus on increasing penetration in your market. And you're almost as likely to increase loyalty with a campaign targeting penetration as with a loyalty campaign, making it hard to justify ad budget for loyalty alone. This finding certainly jives with our assertion that brand loyalty is about congruence with identity. Stop trying to offer the fifth item for free and start using the marketing budget to tell your target customers that your brand shares their values and helps them achieve their goals.

What of the loyalty program?

Most companies would benefit from a strategic audit of their loyalty programs. The program is only valuable for your brand if it's making customers more loyal and giving you access to customer insights you can't get elsewhere. If you're simply offering a punch card—or its digital equivalent—you're probably not seeing much return on the program.

Consider recent moves from Starbucks, purveyor of the loyalty program that every major brand includes in their competitive research. The last couple of updates to Starbucks' loyalty program have reduced the rate at which rewards can be earned. At the time of this writing, a customer would need to spend about $75 to get a free drink and about $100 to receive a free sandwich. On the surface, the program appears far better for the company than the consumer. A free drink valued at $4 after spending $75 equates to a 5% loyalty discount for the customer, while Starbucks is getting boatloads of behavioral data in return. And yet participation in the program continues to increase.

How does Starbucks get away with this? Segmentation. The highest-spending customers don't care that returns are only about 5 percent, because Starbucks is a part of their routine. Their demand for Starbucks is probably pretty inelastic at this point, so raising that return to 6 percent or dropping it to 4.5 percent probably wouldn't change their behavior. For these customers, rewards are just a nice little bonus. The app offers many perks beyond reward accumulation that disproportionally benefit top customers—like the ability to order ahead, reorder favorites, and pay quickly. In short, there's no more business to be won from top customers, so they're not the focus of the program's biggest perks.

The true beneficiaries of the Starbucks program are the semi-regular customers. These customers are more frequently targeted with incentives to visit the store, like limited-time offers for free drinks or snacks. This is smart: Regular customers don't need incentives to spend. The program will drive real business growth if it can make the infrequent visitors more loyal to the brand.

Coffee is cheap, and you can only drink so much, so it's possible to reach a point where there's not much more revenue to squeeze from the most loyal customers. In some verticals, however, there's more revenue to be realized from recognizing top customers. In these cases, a more progressive rewards program is in order. Retailer Ulta Beauty offers a broad assortment of cosmetics, fragrances, and self-care products, and many locations have salons. Armed with the knowledge that a good discount can often incentivize top customers to try new products or services, the company offers a tiered loyalty program, in which higher spenders can accumulate rewards more rapidly and earn additional perks.

Similarly, couture reseller Rebag offers a progressive program that offers top customers larger discounts and earlier access to new inventory. The company allows customers to trade purchases in for cash or credit and it allows customers to earn points on purchases and sales. The used couture customer has numerous options beyond Rebag, including indirect competitors like eBay and local consignment shops. By rewarding customers for their purchases and sales, Rebag gives customers a reason to be loyal.

Poor planning makes loyalty programs ineffective. If your program focuses on the wrong customers, you will leave money on the table. Smart marketers get more scientific, designing programs that are focused on customers that could become more loyal, without making loyal customers feel slighted. A freebie will usually not engender loyalty, but you can use perks to get infrequent customers in the door. At that point, the goal of building customer loyalty will depend on your understanding of the customer's identity within the context of your brand.

A Final Word on Loyalty Campaigns

You shouldn't neglect your brand or your customer relationships, but you should remain cognizant of your opportunity cost. By that I mean that you should not focus on loyalty efforts at the expense of expanding the penetration of your brand. Otherwise you could end up in a death spiral of declining revenue and shrinking market share. Instead of throwing your advertising dollars at a loyalty campaign, you should spend them on powerful creative that captures the attention of and resonates with your market. Your goal is to acquire new customers and to remind existing customers that you're still aligned with their identities. Then you can leverage cognitive biases to retain them.

Cognitive Biases That Influence Retention

When *The Office* began, Pam had been engaged to her high school sweetheart, Roy, for three years, but they still hadn't set a wedding date. It was obvious that Roy and Pam weren't a great match. He didn't support her dreams of being an artist and he didn't seem to enjoy her company. Roy once expressed his gratitude for Jim and Pam's friendship (to Jim), explaining that it meant he didn't have to listen to her talk about her day. Comments like that made Roy and Pam seem like a bad match, leaving millions of viewers to think Pam belonged with Jim. And yet Pam stayed with Roy.

Pam didn't stay with Roy because she feared being alone—Jim made it clear that he was available to her. I submit that Pam had fallen victim to status quo bias. This occurs when our natural preference for the status quo supersedes our need to make a change. Status quo bias can be confounded by other biases related to loss aversion, so we'll explore the biases as a group, as early researchers did.[249]

Status Quo Bias and Mere Exposure

Status quo bias occurs when we demonstrate an irrational preference for maintaining the current state of affairs. There are many reasons one might prefer to maintain the status quo, including inertia, a desire to avoid making a decision, and the mere-exposure effect.

Sometimes referred to as the familiarity principle, the mere-exposure effect leads people to develop a preference for something merely because it's familiar. This explains why people prefer foods they've experienced before and it's part of the reason that nostalgic products are purchased in favor of modern alternatives. Mere exposure is also an explanation for why Pam stayed with Roy for so long. She preferred the comfort of a familiar relationship, perhaps more than she actually cared about poor Roy.

Our preference for maintaining the status quo can influence decisions from cereal to business strategy. In 2020, Oregon's government employment department had already known for years that its technology, used since the eighties and nineties, was dangerously outdated. Audits had revealed that the systems couldn't handle an uptick in unemployment or a change in federal policy. The system was a ticking time bomb, but the state did not act.

Lack of funding was no excuse. The federal government had given the state an $80 million grant to upgrade the system in 2009 but, eleven years later, the state still hadn't produced anything other than a plan to upgrade the system by 2025, and even that five-year plan looked overly optimistic.

To the surprise of no one, the system buckled when unemployment surged in 2020, leaving thousands of Oregonians waiting weeks, sometimes months, for needed assistance. Ultimately, the state decided it wouldn't even try to fix the underlying problems until unemployment declined. In the meantime, the state increased staff tenfold to process claims manually, temporarily avoiding the computer system altogether.[250]

Numerous factors contributed to the kerfuffle in Oregon, but it's clear that status quo bias played a major role. The issues with the system were well-documented for years. But the United States had enjoyed an uncharacteristically long economic recovery, so officials saw no need to act urgently, even though they knew that unemployment would increase at some point in the future. It was easier to scrape by than to commence a complicated, time-consuming upgrade process.

It is easy to cast blame for this issue, but most people with work experience can identify the situation as extreme but not unique. Many companies run their businesses on legacy systems that seem to be held together with popsicle sticks and duct tape. They know the systems need to be overhauled or replaced, but they procrastinate because, on any given day, it's easier to maintain the status quo than to face the deluge of decisions and pain involved in making a change.

We humans are biased towards keeping things as they are, so it's natural to expect government officials and executives to keep with old habits rather than re-evaluating, just like Pam. Change is risky, and requires more effort than maintaining the current state. Fortunately, this is far better news for marketers than it was for the unemployed workers of Oregon: If you don't give your customers a reason to leave, they won't look for one.

Endowment Effect

Logically speaking, we should consider our stuff to be worth the price we'd be willing to pay for it. If we would only be willing to pay $2,000 for a particular used car, we shouldn't expect to be able to sell that same car for $3,000. But experimental research has demonstrated what Craigslist users already know to be true: People tend to overvalue things they own. In defiance of logic, we tend to expect more compensation when selling an object than we would be willing to pay to acquire that same object.

In one early experiment, researchers randomly distributed either raffle tickets or $3 to students as they entered a classroom. At the end of class, students who had raffle tickets were told they could stay for the drawing or they could trade their tickets for $3. Similarly, students who had initially gotten $3 were told they could either keep the $3 or trade it for a ticket. (The raffle prize was a gift certificate for the bookstore.) Because the first distribution of prizes was random, we would expect the group of students who first got a ticket and the group who initially got cash to be equally interested in tickets. But 82 percent of students who initially got a ticket chose to keep it, rather than sell it for $3, while only 38 percent who initially got cash were willing to pay $3 to get a ticket. This indicates that the students who were holding tickets valued tickets more than the students with cash.[251]

Later, Kahneman, Knetsch, and Thaler held a series of market simulations, with similar results.[252] In some experiments, they randomly distributed mugs and pens from the university bookstore to students, then asked them to trade for cash. You would logically expect to see many trades, as mugs and pens made their way to whichever students valued them the most. On the contrary, the trading volume was low—about half of what the researchers expected. Students didn't trade because they couldn't agree on price. The median mug owner wasn't willing to sell for less than $5.25, while the median amount people were willing to pay for a mug was under $3.[253] Clearly, the mug owners were over-valuing their possessions relative to the market price.

The Endowment Effect and the Market for Used Couches

You've probably seen the endowment effect play out on Craigslist, classified ads, garage sales, or another local marketplace. Whether it's a beat-up old car, dated furniture, or the world's dustiest collection of eight-track tapes, the sellers often think the old stuff in their garage is worth more than buyers are willing to pay.

A woman in my neighborhood tried for weeks to sell a lumpy old couch on Nextdoor.com. The couch clearly dated to the 1980s and was heavily worn. There was a large, yellow stain on one of the bottom cushions, and there was a lot of stuffing poking through one of the arms. It looked like a pet (or rodent!) had viciously attacked the upholstery. The owner tried to sell the couch for $650. Her ad copy stated that the couch was originally purchased at a high-end store and the upholstery was custom. She also noted that with a slipcover, nobody would ever notice the "wear" to the arm.

I watched that posting with great interest because it was such a fantastic example of the endowment effect. You and I know that this woman would have been lucky to *give* the couch away, and that there was a greater chance that she would have to take it to the dump as Goodwill doesn't take furniture in that condition. But this woman, apparently blind to market conditions and the unappealing prospect of sitting on that yellow stain, believed she had quality furniture that someone else would be lucky to own.

The endowment effect is bad news for people trying to buy used furniture on Craigslist, but it's great for brands. The mere fact that someone has purchased a product from you leads them to overvalue it.

Loss Aversion and Anticipated Regret

Status quo bias and the endowment effect are often observed in concert with—and sometimes explained by—loss aversion. We want to avoid losses even more than we want to reap gains. Essentially, our abhorrence of loss leads us to experience more regret if our actions lead to a negative outcome than if inaction leads to that same negative outcome.

Another factor is regret aversion. The fear of how bad we'll feel if we're wrong can cause us to focus on the potential for shame or guilt instead of the choice at hand. Anticipated regret can lead us to hang on to a bad situation for too long and prevent us from making necessary changes. This is why investment advisors frequently urge customers not to bail when market conditions are poor so that they don't miss out on profits during the recovery.

Apparently, contrary to your mom's advice, it's far *worse* to try and fail than never to have tried at all. It's important to remember that our aversions to loss and regret can leave us overly sensitive to risk, sometimes leading us to bury our heads in the sand or move into CYA mode instead of making a hard choice.

Risk Avoidance Has Costs, Too

In *The Office*, Pam was hesitant to close the door on her relationship with Roy. Perhaps Pam understood that it could be bad to stay in the relationship with Roy. But maybe she feared that it would be even worse if she left Roy, started a relationship with Jim, and then saw that relationship fall apart. If that happened, maybe she would forever wonder what could've been with Roy. As you can see, her aversion to loss and fear of anticipated regret might have led her to avoid risk. But by staying in a failing relationship, Pam compromised her chances of a better relationship with Jim.

Our hatred of losing options isn't just limited to the fictional realm. Consider the overscheduled child whose hyper-engaged parent hates to see the child abandon a single activity for fear that a door will forever be closed. The child, who hates soccer practice, probably won't have the commitment needed to win a sports scholarship, even if he has the raw talent. Nevertheless, the boy's mother requires him to keep playing only because she is so terrified of him losing an opportunity.

A friend once received a cold call from the CEO of a small company who said he wanted to buy her a coffee and discuss his company. She was excited to talk shop with such an experienced professional in her field. After a couple of conversations, he extended an appealing job offer. The title was better than her current position, and she was confident the compensation would at least be equal to what she was already earning, even though the CEO's company had a lower profile. She spent several days agonizing and discussing with friends. She wondered whether the job would improve her resume. She worried the CEO might be too good to be true. She questioned how the job might impact her life in five years. Stuck in these questions, my friend kept delaying her answer. Eventually, the CEO reached out, thanked her for her time, and said, "If it's not a hell yes, then it's not a yes."

The CEO was the company's founder, and he closely protected its culture, so it is understandable that he would be reticent to hire someone who wasn't excited about the job. But my friend wasn't underwhelmed by his company; she was suffering from decision paralysis. She attempted to keep both options open while she agonized over two nearly equivalent options. Her hesitancy to close the door on either option, for fear of making a wrong decision, cost her dearly. This is consistent with MIT research which found that, even in a virtual environment, people would expend resources to keep options open, even when those options weren't being used.[254]

People often underestimate the value of the time and resources they waste while trying to keep options open. My friend lost a great job opportunity as well as her chance to make a choice. An overscheduled child's parents may be depriving him of the opportunity to be truly great at one thing by forcing him to split his time between several activities. And the student who can't commit to a major and shifts between several ends up racking up debt and exhausting himself rather than making real progress toward graduation.

Loss Aversion & Retention

Our preferences to maintain the status quo and avoid losses—even at irrational costs—lead to some quirky consumer behaviors that can work to the marketer's advantage.

The clearest way to nudge customers into action is to highlight the superiority of your products and/or services. But the way you choose to frame this information is critical. The psychological research on the status quo bias, loss aversion, and the endowment effect indicate that consumers are more likely to make a change to avoid a loss than to reap a gain. Demonstrating the benefits of your product or service in a meaningful, credible way is always important. But your messages will be most effective when you can emphasize what prospective customers are losing if they don't stick with your brand.

LinkedIn Emphasizes Losses to Improve Retention

LinkedIn offers premium subscriptions for individuals and businesses who want access to extended features like information on who has viewed a profile or the ability to contact people who aren't closely connected. The company offers free trials, but users must enter credit card information for future charges to take advantage of the offer. With the subscription automatically renewing each month, LinkedIn is betting that a combination of its strong features and status quo bias will retain paying users.

To LinkedIn's credit, the free trial is simple to cancel. But the brand also uses the loss aversion bias to its advantage by reminding users about the many benefits of a premium subscription—and even offering some additional options—before allowing subscribers to cancel. LinkedIn adds a little friction to the cancellation process, like many other brands. But, unlike many companies, LinkedIn does not hit users with an unreasonably long and complicated cancellation process. LinkedIn's barriers to cancellation feel more like additional considerations than annoying blockers.

You shouldn't block cancellations or compromise the user experience to retain customers. That will probably upset them and feed their motivation to sever ties with your company. Instead, you can take a page from LinkedIn's playbook: offer a last-minute incentive and remind users about everything they'll miss if they end their subscriptions.

Gilt Balances Urgency and Credibility

We should expect people to work harder to avoid a loss than to realize a gain, but retailers got this memo long ago, so we have to be clever to leverage this knowledge as marketers. While psychology dictates that calling customers to "buy now, before this amazing sale ends" should drive sales, today's consumer is hit with nearly constant prompts to "act now before it's too late."

The Macy's "one day" sale is nearly always extended across multiple days and repeated every few weeks. Banana Republic has "40 percent off" sales so frequently that email subscribers become immune to the "only hours left!" warning. Black Friday sales are increasingly extended from the Wednesday before Thanksgiving to Cyber Monday and beyond, making consumers skeptical of whether they need to line up for hours to get a discount.

Gilt's marketing team does a great job of leveraging our aversion to loss to create a sense of urgency while maintaining credibility. Because of its history as a flash-sale site, consumers may expect all items on Gilt's site to be in short supply. But that's no longer the case for everything in the inventory. Gilt tells consumers when a product's quantities are severely limited, instilling a sense of urgency. The product listing pages show sold-out items and include countdown timers to show when sale events end. This adds credibility to the claim that product availability is limited. Finally, Gilt includes a prompt to "shop it while it's still here" if you add an item to your cart but fail to check out.

Importantly, Gilt also works to reduce the sense of risk in making a purchase decision. Product information is impeccably produced with high-resolution images and comprehensive details, giving consumers the best possible understanding of what they're purchasing. And the return policy is generous, further reducing the risk of participating in a transaction.

Nordstrom Uses Loss Aversion & Endowment Effect to Speed Checkout

Nordstrom Rack (formerly HauteLook) uses flash sales to drive demand for some items. Like Gilt, NR emphasizes the scarcity that comes with limited inventories and limited sale events to drive decisions. Product pages show sold-out colors and sizes, note when limited quantities remain, and include countdown timers to show the remaining time in a sale event.

Additionally, items can only sit in carts for fifteen minutes. If the shopper hasn't checked out by that point, his reservation to purchase the item expires. If inventory is sufficient, the item can be re-added, but there's always a chance another shopper will snag it. The brand was ostensibly forced to use this tactic to ensure that customers don't hoard items in carts when they don't intend to buy. But this is also an example of the endowment effect in action: When an item is in your cart, you feel as though it's already yours. After all, you opened the app, sorted and filtered the items available, and snapped up the best items before another user could take them. Even though you haven't paid, you've beat the other users to the punch.

Don't Overstate the Urgency of an Offer

Today's consumers are hit with a barrage of marketing messages across media channels. These messages come from traditional retailers trying to survive, startups trying to gain share, local shops trying to fight Walmart and Amazon, casual acquaintances trying to hawk wares from the latest multilevel marketing schemes—the list goes on. Each message's call to action is more urgent than the last.

Bending the truth to create a sense of scarcity isn't a long-term business strategy. That will only undermine your credibility, personifying your brand as the archetypal used car salesman who screams on a local TV commercial while standing between dancing hotdogs.

At best, overselling the urgency of an offer will lead your customers to roll their eyes and ignore your frantic orders to buy. Instead, you should either demonstrate true scarcity—with limited quantities or truly infrequent sales—or skip the threatening messages in favor of a more credible tactic.

Sonos: A Cautionary Tale

Sonos sells wireless speakers that can be managed through an app. The speakers can be connected to your TV or used to listen to music, but Sonos added a smart home component. With the app, you can create groups of speakers on the fly so that you can play the same audio in certain rooms while other speakers play different audio or remain silent. The app integrates with Apple Music, Spotify, Amazon, Google, Pandora, Sirius, and others, which makes it easy to create a seamless music experience in all parts of a home. The brand's most engaged users own multiple Sonos speakers—meaning they've made sizeable investments in Sonos hardware.

In January 2020, Sonos sent the following email out to users with the subject line, "Your system requires attention."

End of software updates

In May the following products in your system will be classified as legacy and no longer receive software updates and new features. This will affect your listening experience.

[Products listed, specific to the customer]

Legacy products were introduced between 2005 and 2011 and, given the age of the technology, do not have enough memory or processing power to sustain future innovation.

Please note that because Sonos is a system, all products operate on the same software. If modern products remain connected to legacy products after May, they also will not receive software updates and new features.

Below the fold, the company added that customers had options, such as continuing to use legacy products or trading up to new products. The trade-up program offered a 30 percent discount to those who traded in older speakers.

Imagine being a user who had invested hundreds or thousands of dollars in a brand's ecosystem and then receiving an email announcing that your products are obsolete and that they'll prevent any new products from working properly!

Predictably, users took to social media to express their displeasure. Using #BoycottSonos and tagging the CEO, the angry Sonos users complained that they felt ripped off. They ranted about the cost and environmental impact of replacing hardware that they expected to last for years.

Part of the issue was expectations. People expect audio equipment to be relatively durable, as the Sonos products had been to that point. In fact, at the time of the announcement, 92 percent of the products the company had shipped since its inception were still in use.[255] The email left users with the impression that their expensive equipment was being bricked. By essentially forcing an upgrade, Sonos made its best customers—people who thought they had years left in their equipment—feel like they were being punished for their commitment to the ecosystem.

Walking It Back

After being pummeled by internet outrage for a couple of days, Sonos relented. The CEO sent an apology in which he acknowledged fault and pledged that the company wouldn't brick older speakers.

> We heard you. We did not get this right from the start. My apologies for that and I wanted to personally assure you of the path forward:
>
> First, rest assured that come May, when we end new software updates for our legacy products, they will continue to work just as they do today. We are not bricking them, we are not forcing them into obsolescence, and we are not taking anything away. Many of you have invested heavily in your Sonos systems, and we intend to honor that investment for as long as possible. While legacy Sonos products won't get new software features, we pledge to keep them updated with bug fixes and security patches for as long as possible. If we run into something core to the experience that can't be addressed, we'll work to offer an alternative solution and let you know about any changes you'll see in your experience.
>
> Secondly, we heard you on the issue of legacy products and modern products not being able to coexist in your home. We are working on a way to split your system so that

modern products work together and get the latest features, while legacy products work together and remain in their current state. We're finalizing details on this plan and will share more in the coming weeks.

While we have a lot of great products and features in the pipeline, we want our customers to upgrade to our latest and greatest products when they're excited by what the new products offer, not because they feel forced to do so. That's the intent of the trade up program we launched for our loyal customers.

Thank you for being a Sonos customer. Thank you for taking the time to give us your feedback. I hope that you'll forgive our misstep, and let us earn back your trust. Without you, Sonos wouldn't exist and we'll work harder than ever to earn your loyalty every single day.

If you have any further questions please don't hesitate to contact us.

Sincerely,

Patrick
Patrick Spence
CEO, Sonos

What's most interesting here is that the CEO's response isn't exactly full of material changes. The initial message warned that older products would stop getting software updates in five months and the follow-up offered a promise that obsolescence wouldn't happen overnight. The initial message said new products couldn't be updated if they were connected with old products, beginning in five months, and the update said they'll work on a way to allow that to happen.

Spence's note is more of a reframing than a strategic shift. The most notable part of the CEO's response to the user revolt was his promise: "We are not taking anything away." The company realized that its initial attempt to minimize the impact of bad news with a brief, transparent message had left loyal customers feeling like something had been taken from them.

The Problem in Context of Biases

The Sonos case is a study in how blindness to status quo bias, the endowment effect, loss aversion, and the consumer's need for fairness can impact a brand. If the company had framed the change as a new product announcement or an opportunity to upgrade to a new experience at a discount, users might've been excited, or at least indifferent. Instead, the first Sonos email:

- offered specifics about what was being taken away, triggering feelings of loss.
- framed its plans for "future innovation" as a loss for current customers, making them long for the status quo.
- made customers feel like the company didn't value older speakers that, thanks to their financial investment and endowment effect, customers valued deeply.
- left customers feeling like Sonos was going to brick equipment they paid for and expected to be a long-term investment, leading to resentment at a perceived injustice.

In the follow-up message, the CEO offered some messages that the marketing team should've written at the outset.

- Sonos values its customers and appreciates their investment in its products.

- o Sonos has some exciting new technology coming up.
- o Sonos is committed to supporting the older products so that users can enjoy the original functionality for years to come, even while adding new equipment to enjoy upcoming features.

Juxtaposing Apple's Approach

Sonos' hardware isn't as pricey as Apple's. Sonos had also supported that hardware for far longer than Apple does before reclassifying hardware as "legacy" and phasing out software updates. But Apple users haven't been outraged when Apple reclassifies its hardware as "legacy" because Apple has been better at framing its updates.

Apple offers compelling reasons to upgrade to new devices.
Sonos marketers were trying to be transparent when they revealed the company's plans to sunset old hardware. And it even offered a discount for upgrading. But instead of offering clear benefits, it only communicated vague promises of innovation. This left users wondering who benefitted from the Sonos software updates. Online chatter speculated that Sonos was forcing an upgrade to make it easier for them to push unwanted updates or to sell more speakers.

In contrast, Apple's messages consistently emphasize new features in terms of tangible benefits to users: better photos, faster performance, easier navigation.

Apple doesn't make users feel like it's taking something away.
Apple leaves users with the impression that older devices can't handle newer features because of the sheer speed of the company's innovation. The old phone can't handle the new map experience because it doesn't have the onboard compass that senses the direction you're pointing or enough memory to handle the mass of local details that Apple has made available.

Sonos told customers what they were losing, but didn't hint at what they might gain. As a result, it didn't feel like a balanced exchange; it felt to customers like the brand was only taking something away from them after they had already paid for products.

Worst-Case Scenario: Status Quo
Even though the Apple updates tend to only support devices for a few years, the worst-case scenario for the user is status quo: Your old device can't support the fancy new features, so you don't get to upgrade, but you can keep your current experience.

When companies invest months of time and thousands of hours in a new product or an update, they naturally assume that everyone will want to throw out the old and embrace the new. But people generally prefer the status quo. Therefore, your brand's update might be important to your employees, but your customers will be perfectly happy to amble along with their outdated products or software until they have a compelling reason to upgrade. As the Sonos saga taught us, customers will be livid if you take away something they value and force them into an "upgrade" they didn't ask for.

Best Practices

People tend to prefer maintaining the status quo. And academic work on loss aversion and the endowment effect teaches us that losing something you have feels much worse than forgoing a potential gain. Further, quantitative studies have also consistently shown that a loss is felt more dramatically than a gain.

For us as marketers, this means that we can safely assume that consumers won't go out of their way to switch away from our brand if it's working, and it won't be easy to get them to switch from their current brand to ours. They will be more willing to take a risk to avoid a loss than they would be to realize a gain. We can use this information when tailoring promotions and other communications with customers.

Use status quo bias to aid retention. Your customers are biased to maintain the status quo, so make it easy for them. Optimize task flows, remove barriers to repurchase, enable subscriptions, and default to auto-renewal as applicable.

Don't depend on the status quo bias to increase loyalty. Some customers will remain loyal to your brand simply because they're averse to change. But you should focus on building the loyalty that comes from deep engagement with a brand that meets the customer's needs, not just his laziness preventing him from switching.

It's better to end a long-running promotion than to increase a base price. Logically, we know that adding $10 to a price is the same as ending a $10 promotion, but consumers have shown that ending a promotion feels fair and that raising prices does not. Make use of promotions for discounting and upgrades but avoid raising prices or taking away features wherever possible.

Boost retention by reminding customers of what they have. You can also remind customers of what they'll lose if they end their subscriptions. Consider giving them additional reasons to stay, with targeted promotions or additional value. Don't try to retain them by making it hard to unsubscribe. That will make them angry.

Position changes in terms of how they will benefit your customers, not your company. Ensure that an update feels like an upgrade *to customers*. Following Apple's model, you should position changes so that customers will *want* to upgrade. You shouldn't force updates on people without offering compelling benefits. Otherwise, customers will feel like you're taking something away from them, as in the Sonos case.

Nudge, but don't lie or cheat. Leveraging our preference for the status quo by setting subscriptions to auto-renew by default and optimizing task flows to repurchase are effective strategies to grow your business. By emphasizing the scarcity of a product, or by displaying the time left in a promotion, you can nudge customers to make a purchase. But don't disrespect your customers with scare tactics or deceptive claims about scarcity. If you do that, they will figure it out and become angry, which will undermine your brand.

Customers Want to Like You

When I was a teenager, a good friend and I whiled away a cool summer night talking about the qualities that made the ideal mate. With all the wisdom typical of the inexperienced, we discussed the requirements and the compromises we could never make. At the time of this writing, she was deeply in love with someone who's wildly out of line with the requirements on her list, but I'm confident that their relationship is going to go the distance. That's because once we're in a relationship, we start to care less about positive traits that are missing and to care more about the positive traits that are present.[256]

The *Dirty Dancing* soundtrack taught us that "love is strange." This applies to brands, too. What if I told you that you could buy a car, but that it would cost more than most, that it would have manufacturing issues, that it would take months to be delivered, and that it would have an incredibly subpar paint job? Repairing the car would require quite a lot more effort than repairing other cars because nobody in your area works on this model. And the company

CEO is constantly in the news for saying something that's out of line with your values, politics, or beliefs. Would you be ecstatic about my offer? Yes.

If you know someone who has a Tesla, they've talked to you about their Tesla. Tesla owners *love* these cars so much that they'll tolerate the repair hassles, long waitlists, and faulty paint jobs. Even if the car owner finds Musk's public persona abhorrent or faces another six months in his clunker before the Tesla arrives, the Tesla owner will tell you that this car was the perfect choice and that the competing options were awful. This is "choice supportive bias" in action.

As the name suggests, choice supportive bias leads you to prefer your choice simply because *you* chose it. Just like we do with romantic partners, we tend to downplay faults and play-up benefits of purchases after we've made them. And we do the inverse with competing options, putting increased emphasis on flaws and paying less attention to benefits.

Also known as "post-purchase rationalization," this bias is great for marketers because it predisposes our customers to loyalty. If your target customer isn't as deeply loyal as a devout member of an American political party or a Tesla customer, you'd do well to avoid testing how far you can push that loyalty. Still, you should rest easier knowing that the people who have already purchased your brand *want* to like you.

Increase Engagement with Ziegarnik

I had a music teacher who told a story about how he once risked arrest to play a piano. He loved Elton John and was thrilled to get a ticket to a concert. The concert did not disappoint. The crowd was excited, the songs were even better live, and the performance was top-notch ... until the last song. As the crowd cheered, Elton played through a popular hit and then, abruptly, stood up, thanked the crowd, and left without playing the final notes.

At first, my teacher was mildly annoyed. But as the night went on, the unfinished song kept playing (grating) in his mind, to the point that he couldn't focus on anything else. Finally, he got out of bed, crossed town, broke into the venue, climbed up onto the platform, sat at the piano, and played the final chord. He knew he was trespassing and risking arrest, but he felt this was the only way he would be able to sleep.

It sounds a little nutty if you're not the type to be vexed by unresolved chords, but we've all struggled with unresolved situations of some kind. A project is close to being done, but a meeting reminder pops up, the phone rings, or a coworker walks in. Suddenly, you're forced to direct your efforts elsewhere, but you struggle to shift focus away from the project. Or, perhaps you've binge-watched several episodes of a suspenseful show with a cliffhanger at bedtime. As you try to go through the next day, you keep thinking about the show, wondering how the characters will find their resolution, and planning when you'll be able to watch.

There's a name for the tendency of incomplete or interrupted tasks to take over our minds: The Ziegarnik Effect. Named for psychologist Bluma Ziegarnik, whose experiments demonstrated that subjects had better recollections of tasks that were interrupted than those that were completed. Specifically, she found that unfinished tasks are remembered twice as well as completed ones.[257] Her explanation was that once we've begun a task, we feel a tension until it is complete, and this tension manifests as improved memory.

Besides testing your sanity, the Ziegarnik effect can drive retention and growth in digital marketing efforts. You can integrate progress indicators to encourage users to complete tasks. Online learning sites can show that twelve of fifteen modules are complete, nudging learners into finishing the course. LinkedIn emails users to show their progress against its measure of a "complete" profile, encouraging them to engage just a little more to get the full benefit of the product. Netflix sends out emails reminding viewers to finish something they've started watching.

Assuming that your brand experience is a positive one, you can leverage the Ziegarnik effect to lead users to engage more with your brand, thereby driving growth and retention. Creating the sense that there's more to the experience can lodge your brand in the customer's mind, the way Elton John's unfinished melody drew my mild-mannered teacher from his comfortable bed into a criminal act.

Temporal Discounting and Subscription Design

If someone offered you the choice of $100 now or $500 in five years, what would you do?

If you were *homo economicus*, the perfectly rational human, the decision would come down to investment options. You'd look at interest rates and compounding schedules to determine whether you could turn $100 into more than $500 over the course of 5 years. *Homo economicus* has time-consistent preferences, meaning that he's indifferent between receiving an amount now or that amount plus the appropriate interest rate after some time, so he'll take whichever deal is most profitable.

While waiting for the $500 is the rational choice if you can't earn 38% annually in returns, most people would take the $100 today. This is because we tend to have time-inconsistent preferences and the temporal discounting we tend to do in our heads looks quite different from the discounting in math textbooks.

People discount costs and rewards as they stretch further into the future in an exaggerated fashion. Our tendency is hyperbolic temporal discounting with particularly strong discounting between the present and the first time period.[258][259][260] That is, for most people, the possibility of $500 in six years is about as appealing as $500 in five years, but neither is quite as attractive as $100 today, even though we're extremely unlikely to be able to turn $100 into $500 in five or six years. Now, in English: People generally prefer to experience the benefits of consumption sooner, even if that means reducing the benefits we'll receive overall.

The opposite is true of costs. We would prefer to delay costs, even when that means we end up paying more in the long run. For instance, an additional $50k on a mortgage loan with a 4% interest rate costs nearly $60k to pay back over the course of 30 years, but many people would opt to finance that extra $50k anyway because they could enjoy a better house now and they payment would only be $239 more this month.

Temporal Discounting and Consumer Behavior

Even when we recognize hyperbolic temporal discounting, we tend to underestimate how much it impacts us. We tend to underestimate our desire for immediate gratification and overestimate our immunity to hyperbolic temporal discounting. We think that the splurge today is a one-off and that we'll be better at saving in the future. And we think that the doughnut in the breakroom is a well-deserved treat, since we'll probably eat a lot of salad in the coming month.

The relevance to marketers is that our customers are impatient. They prefer immediate benefits and delayed costs. This means that loyalty incentives will become less effective at retaining customers as the timeline to receive those rewards stretches on. It also means that costs that are pushed into the future are less of a deterrent to consumption than costs that are paid today.

It follows that a company offering a service that requires up-front effort (or other non-monetary costs) and delayed gratification for the customer would need to defer costs to the customer as much as possible, even if this presents a loss to the company. You see this a lot with financial services firms. They invest heavily in making transferring funds in as easy and painless as possible with great service for new accounts, free transfers, and great web functionality around money transfers. The bank is willing to offer these features at a loss, because switching banks requires so much effort for the customer that a charge to transfer money to a new bank would be one deterrent too many.

Implications for Delayed Gratification Brands

This means that if you're offering a product or service that requires up-front investment and delayed gains for the customer, you can price transactions below marginal (per transaction) costs, on the assumption that customers will over-estimate how frequently they will use your service. The classic example of this type of business is a gym: The customer must forgo more pleasurable activities and exert effort in a workout today to see gains in terms of better health and physical appearance at some point in the future. Because of the immediate effort and deferred benefits, we expect most customers to overestimate how frequently they'll go to the gym. Thus, a gym can price subscriptions so that they cost the customer less than their daily attendance would cost the gym, expecting that most customers won't visit daily.

Indeed, to the delight of behavioral economists, this theory held in a study of Boston gyms. The study found that area gyms charged about $60 per month, which made the per-visit monetary cost to the frequent user well below the marginal cost to the gym. In other words, someone who paid $60/month and visited daily in a thirty-day month would effectively spend $2 per visit. But gyms estimate that each time someone visits, it costs them around $5 for staffing, overhead, equipment, etc. A gym could safely advertise costs of $2 per day, even though it would lose money on customers who visited that frequently, because most customers wouldn't come to the gym that often.

Some gyms offered higher per-visit fees for those who didn't want commit to memberships. The average buyer of the annual or monthly gym membership would save money with such a plan. But few people signed up for those plans because, due to hyperbolic time discounting, they overestimated how frequently they would work out.[261]

Delayed gratification businesses should also minimize costs associated with renewal, lest the customer reconsiders his decision with his past behavior in mind and concludes that the subscription isn't a good deal for him. You can offer discounts for longer subscriptions or simply reduce friction to renew.

Many gyms offer automatic renewals, but this approach risks upsetting some customers. You could mitigate that risk by emailing customers to advise of upcoming renewals, as Evernote does, or by offering discounts on renewals to incentivize low-frequency users.

Slack's Fair Billing Policy promises that the cost of unused seats will be prorated, so there's no risk of overbuying.

For many delayed gratification businesses, low-usage customers are highly profitable, because they're paying higher marginal costs than regular customers. As a result, businesses in this situation can probably afford to offer renewal incentives. Just be careful not to devalue your brand with prices that are too low. Consumers are suspicious that if a deal is too good, it must be because the business is failing (and there must be a reason for that).

Implications for Immediate Gratification Brands

Companies in lines of business that offer immediate gratification have it a little easier because it is our natural tendency to want to have our fun now and delay the costs. These companies can get away with more aggressive pricing, charging customers well above their marginal costs.

As DellaVigna and Malmendier pointed out, credit card companies offer means to instant gratification via free short-term loans, then charge customers that spend beyond what they can pay off within the billing cycle. Similarly, Las Vegas casinos under-charge for the luxury rooms and free buffets that draw customers in, expecting to make it up by over-charging on gambling transactions.[262] In both cases, these businesses take an initial loss to win the customer, but can charge well above their marginal costs because usage is so gratifying. By being totally transparent, these companies effectively diffuse suspicions that they're dishonest or predatory. After all, they aren't forcing anyone into transactions. You could go to Las Vegas for a discounted vacation and choose not to gamble, or you could pay off your credit card each month and never pay interest.

Planning for Temporal Discounting

The human tendency to inaccurate temporal discounting should be your central consideration as you plan initiation costs, subscription models, and the broader customer experience. Careful strategic planning will support retention and growth by making your service feel like a better value for customers. Just be mindful of what you're selling and what you emphasize as you build the model.

If your business offers immediate benefits to customers, you can charge more up-front and set prices above your marginal costs without compromising growth or renewals. If your service requires customers to make upfront investments and defer gains, like a gym, then you should emphasize the long-run in messaging, defer the consumer costs wherever possible, and price below your marginal costs to incentivize subscriptions and renewals. The goal is to make today's customer experience more pleasant without undermining the customer's illusion of perfect long-term orientation. This means reassuring them that they're doing the right thing by investing in the future, while making the day to day as pleasant as possible.

Mental Accounting and Customer Growth

Suppose a friend gives you a lottery ticket for your birthday and you win $1,000. Think for a moment about what you would spend it on. Would you use it the same way you would normally use income or would you treat yourself to something special? Would you allocate the same percentage of the lottery money to your 401(k) that you do your usual income or save the money for a rainy day? If you're like most people, you would jump at the opportunity to treat yourself to something special because you would think of the lottery winnings as a windfall, not ordinary earnings subject to your ordinary budget.

Here's another: Imagine that you had been playing poker in a casino for a few hours and had won $1,000. Would your betting strategy be different than if you were down $1,000? Most people bet more aggressively when they're up because they feel like they're playing with "the house's money," not their own.

One more hypothetical situation: Imagine that you're married and have only joint accounts and your spouse buys you an expensive watch. You love the watch but would never buy it yourself because, even though it wouldn't cause financial hardship to spend this money, you know there are good watches for far less and this is an irresponsible use of household funds. Would you keep the watch? Many people are comfortable with spouses gifting them something they'd never purchase for themselves, even though the accounts are joint so they are, in effect, buying it themselves.

Strictly speaking, this isn't logical behavior. The watch drains the same amount from your joint account whether you swipe the card or your spouse does. Similarly, money you've won gambling is the same as money in your checking account, so you shouldn't think of it—or spend it—differently than any other income. But people irrationally view these transactions differently. An economist would say that mental accounting like the examples above violates the principle of fungibility. That is, money should be completely interchangeable—money you win gambling or find on the sidewalk should be treated the same as the money from your paycheck or your savings account. It's not logical, therefore, to be happy when a joint account holder buys you a gift that you wouldn't buy yourself because of the cost.

We violate the principle of fungibility because our minds like to separate things into categories. We have a mental category for windfall money, which we think gives us permission to spend differently than the money in our account for groceries, transportation, or retirement. A gambler will bet more aggressively when he's ahead because he doesn't really think of the winnings as his money. Mental accounting like this helps us balance our hedonic need for a little fun with our long-term goals, but without having to face the cognitive dissonance of one goal contradicting the other. So, we find ourselves thinking things like: *The kid's college fund isn't quite as healthy as it should be, but that money I lost in Vegas wasn't really mine.* (This is all noted without judgment. In a world run by *homo economicus*, there would be no cupcakes or water slides, only kale and 401(k)s.)

Mental Accounting and Your Brand

There's an opportunity for marketers to leverage mental accounting to grow customer value by enticing customers to allocate a certain budget to your platform or to make a mental account for your brand. This is another aspect of Starbucks' rewards program that shines: Users transfer money into the app in lump sums, then pay for drinks from that account. Once the money is in the app, the customer has mentally allocated it to Starbucks. As long as the account is funded, the customer doesn't have to worry about adding a bagel, an extra latte a week, or a coffee for a friend. It all comes from the "Starbucks budget." Starbucks' strategy in popularizing the app has been all carrot, no stick. Customers who choose not to use the app aren't penalized, and customers who choose to track rewards with the app can still pay with cash or a card. But those who choose to use the app are rewarded with many benefits including discounts, freebies, preordering functionality, and simpler ordering and checkout.

By incentivizing customers to participate with the app, and without penalizing those who don't, Starbucks has avoided the negative sentiment that usually results from major corporations trying to force users into dedicated accounts while building loyalty.

Another company that benefits from mental accounting is Poshmark, an online resale shop that specializes in clothing, shoes, and accessories. (Think eBay, with higher commissions, specialization in fashion, and consistent authentication for high-dollar items.) When you sell an item on the site, the proceeds appear in your Poshmark account. From there, you can transfer the money to your bank account or leave it in your Poshmark account to spend it on the site later.

People sometimes use their Poshmark accounts to purchase items they wouldn't have otherwise purchased. For instance, a woman who has earned $500 reselling items from her closet might use that money to buy a $700 designer bag, even though she's never spent more than $250 on a bag. She could have easily transferred that money into her checking account and allocated it toward her normal budget, but she decides to splurge because she only has to spend $200 out of pocket. And because she earned that money by selling accessories and clothing, she has mentally classified the money as belonging to her fashion account. That makes her more comfortable with spending money on a handbag than if the money had come directly from her family budget.

As for Poshmark, the company experiences the upside of absolving that woman of the guilt she feels for treating herself to something nice. By encouraging the natural tendency of users to keep a separate mental account for earnings, Poshmark drives customer value. By keeping customers' money on the platform, they can increase the number of buyers and generate more commissions.

Rebag does something similar. By offering customers a trade-in credit and loyalty benefits when they sell high-end bags to Rebag, the company strengthens loyalty. Customers can easily transfer proceeds from sales to checking accounts, but Rebag knows that they're more likely to earmark their funds on Rebag for couture, which encourages them to spend more on the site.

Success in getting users to keep money on your platform depends on both your approach and your line of business. Many brands just aren't candidates for this type of play—users don't want to have an app and account for each store they shop—so you'll have to consider if your brand is heavily-used enough that consumers will take the extra step. Follow Starbucks, Poshmark, and Rebag in making separate accounting worth users' time, but not forcing it in any way. If there's one thing guaranteed to sour a relationship, it's the impression that a business is trying to take money it hasn't earned.

Final Notes on Loyalty and Retention

Foundational to customer loyalty is, naturally, winning the customer in the first place. A brand that can tell an emotionally engaging story that resonates with a customer can beat out the competition. While most brands can never enjoy *absolute* loyalty, winning the initial battle affords home field advantage, thanks to cognitive biases that lead us to prefer the status quo and over-value what we already have. After that, a brand that's consistent with a customer's identity and helps her create the image she wants to project will earn her preference.

Remember also that *penetration* campaigns will probably benefit your loyalty efforts more than traditional *loyalty* campaigns. But churn remains a perennial problem for marketers. To address that issue, you should seek to understand why some customers are leaving. If the customer's habits or values have changed, you may need to rethink how your product fits into their lives, or you may only need to offer a new campaign. Reactivation campaigns tend to have fantastic ROI, because they're inexpensive (you already know where to find the customers) and because they tend to have high conversion rates.

If your brand is losing share to a competitor, your instinct may be to insist to general audiences that your brand is superior, but the smarter play would be a penetration campaign that's laser-focused on the audience that will find your identity most compelling.

Research & Planning

Great marketing work is built on great strategy. Insightful research and planning are foundational to great strategy. Problematically, we're plagued by the same biased thinking at work, when we're doing the work of marketing as when we're at home making purchasing decisions.

In this chapter, we'll look at strategies for overcoming our cognitive biases and the logic pitfalls that can undermine strategic work. I'll also offer up some research strategies for times when the budget won't allow you to outsource to a dedicated research firm. First, you might be wondering whether consumer research is a worthwhile endeavor in light of the fact that consumers' own self-perceptions are so biased.

Consumers Don't Know Why: Should we ask?

The easiest way to gather information about consumers is to ask them about their purchase intent or about why they chose a product. The resulting information is clear, quantifiable, and actionable. The catch is that, whether they realize it or not, their after-the-fact explanations are unlikely to be accurate accounts of their own thinking.

Experimental research has demonstrated that people have difficulty explaining their thought processes and, when asked, tend to offer up the reasons that are the easiest to explain and remember, not necessarily the most accurate. The issue isn't that people are intentionally lying. We just have limited insights into our cognitive processes because we're not fully aware of all of the factors that influence our decisions or the level of influence each factor has. As Nisbett and Wilson once noted, "there may be little or no direct introspective access to higher-order cognitive processes."[263]

For that paper, the researchers examined the question of how much we know about our own thinking with a group of experiments. Essentially, they would manipulate factors, then ask subjects to explain their reactions. Most subjects provided explanations for their behaviors without actually noticing the manipulations. The experimenters thus concluded that people tend to "tell more than they can know."

In one of the experiments, consumers in a commercial setting were asked to inspect four identical pairs of nylon stockings, identify which were of the highest quality, and then explain their reasoning. Since all of the nylons were the same, we would expect each pair to be chosen about a quarter of the time. But participants were nearly four times as likely to choose the stockings on the right side of the line as the stockings at the left. Importantly, not a single participant said placement on the table influenced the choice. Even when researchers directly asked about whether the position in the lineup could've affected their perceptions, nearly all participants denied that position mattered.[264]

This research indicates that we don't really understand our own decision-making processes. As researchers, we generally won't have a problem finding consumers that are happy to provide explanations about why they chose products, but we can't be sure those explanations are accurate.

Love & Branding

An expanding body of research demonstrates that we don't have any idea why we make some choices, even when it comes to something as important as love.[265]

Online matchmaking companies have built their businesses on a couple of fundamental ideas: We know ourselves and we know what we want in a mate. So, into the search engines go our self-descriptions and our enumerations of the traits we want in a mate, and out from the algorithms come our "best" matches. Assuming a favorable exchange of messages, a date is arranged. Placing hope in this model, a growing number of online daters are wading through the results and finding marriage material. But these companies would do well to look to the late, great John Hughes for some inspiration as they build out their feature sets.

Andrew McCarthy, with his flowing hair and white tux, may have been the stuff of teen dreams when he played Blane in the 1986 film *Pretty in Pink*, but protagonist Andie's life would've been much easier if she had fallen for her friend Duckie instead of Blane. In the movie, the brooding, dreamy Blane bent to social pressures from his upper-class friends and treated Andie horribly while her friend

Duckie worshipped her. But when they all met at the prom in the final scene, and Blane told Andie he loved her, she followed him into the parking lot where they made out and, presumably, lived happily ever after.

You can refuse to suspend disbelief and poke holes in John Hughes' portrayal of high school life all day long, but the film presents an intriguing question: Why aren't we attracted to the people we'd expect? Which roughly translates to: Do we really know what we want in a mate? Many of us have wondered what a friend sees in the person they're dating, or perhaps we've found ourselves interested in a person who didn't fit our preconceived notion of the ideal match.

For psychological researchers, the question could be worded like this: When we're in a cool, logical state of mind and thinking of hypothetical dates, can we accurately predict who we'll be attracted to when we meet a potential match in person? The research says, quite clearly, no.

In a 2017 study, researchers employed machine learning to predict which speed daters would click. The researchers had singles answer over a hundred questions about themselves and their preferences for a mate. The surveys took respondents about thirty minutes to complete and included questions on personality, relationship goals, values, and traits. Later, subjects participated in speed dating events in which they had a dozen four-minute dates with potential mates. After each date, they filled out a short questionnaire about their interest in the person they'd just met.

Even armed with dozens of data points, the researchers were unable to predict which people would match. They offered a few possible interpretations of the findings, including the suspicion that it may not be *possible* to predict which two people will click before they meet.[266] This conclusion is supported by other recent research that found almost no correlation between what people say they value in an ideal romantic partner and traits of people they're actually attracted to.[267]

In a separate series of studies, researchers created written profiles that corresponded with respondents' most- and least-desired traits in a mate. They asked respondents about their levels of interest in the profiles. Then, actors met with the participants to deliver scripted responses that corresponded (or conflicted) with preferences on "dates." It turned out that stated preferences were good predictors of which *written* profiles people would choose; however, the stated preferences weren't good predictors of whether participants would find dates they'd met *in person* attractive.[268]

Perhaps online dating companies should mix unexpected matches into the search results and encourage users to have an open mind when they enter their preferences into the app. Or, better yet, perhaps the dating sites should encourage people to have in-person meetings rather than online messages. Or not—dating sites make money on subscriptions, after all.

Your romantic partner, for as long as that person is in your life, has an outsized influence on your general happiness. Thus, your choice of mate is one of the most consequential decisions of your life. Even so, the research suggests that gut feelings and sparks have more to do with your interest in someone than practical, preconceived notions of what a good partner should be like. Maybe it all comes down to chemistry, contextual factors, or other cues and biases that are so numerous and difficult to measure that they'll remain elusive.

Regardless, the fact remains that if people are making the critical decision of whether to pursue relationships with others based on gut feelings, there's no reason to believe they'll be any more deliberate in making decisions while shopping for groceries or clothing. Further, if self-reported data isn't a good predictor in the dating market, we should look upon that type of information with great suspicion in any other marketplace. Can we realistically expect people to know more about what they want in an appliance than in a spouse?

The Inherent Problems with Asking Why

People aren't great at predicting what they'll find attractive in a romantic partner, which means they are even less likely to predict which cake mix, laundry detergent, or car seat they'll select at the moment of choice. To further confound the issue for marketers, people can't accurately recall factors that influenced their decisions. And, the mere act of asking why people made a choice will make them feel less satisfied about the decision.

In one experiment, social psychologist Timothy D. Wilson and his team found that when they asked subjects to explain their jam preferences, the subjects ended up changing their minds about which brand they preferred. The new preferences correlated less with expert ratings than those of the control subjects, suggesting that the act of introspection itself led to inferior decisions. The team drew similar conclusions from an experiment that asked subjects to evaluate potential college courses.[269]

In another experiment, researchers analyzed preferences for posters and found that subjects that were asked to consider reasons for their selections made different selections than the control group that didn't have to explain themselves. People that had to explain their preferences were also less satisfied with their choices after the fact.[270]

What's happening here? The dominant theory is that people have an initial preference but, when they're asked to explain their decision-making process, they focus on factors that are easiest to explain. This might force a re-evaluation of their initial impressions, leading to different choices. Later, though, people were less satisfied with the new choices, indicating that their explanations of their own decision-making processes were inaccurate. So, you might explain that you chose the Lady Gaga poster over the Monet poster because of the more empowering message, leading you to realize that, since you care so much about the *message* on your poster, you should've chosen the poster with the philosophy quote. Really, you would've been happier if you'd just gone with the Lady Gaga poster, which brings you joy for reasons that you can't explain to the researchers.

If we assume that people have no reason to lie about their preferences for posters or jam, we can also assume that we simply don't know that much about how our own minds work. And, when we try to force ourselves to behave logically, to systematically make rational decisions according to our own criteria, we end up less satisfied with our choices. Gut Instincts: 1. Logical Mind: 0.

Research Implications of Inaccurate Introspection

The first step in any research project is to establish the research question. Behavioral economics teaches us that a key consideration as we develop this question should be whether we're concerned with snap decisions or the sort of choices people carefully consider.

When we're marketing high-consideration products, for which we know our audience is conducting considerable research, we're looking at slow-thinking mode. These consumers are doing research and approaching the purchasing decision methodically. Thus, we can ask B2B software decision-makers and people comparing vendors for government contracts post-hoc questions about their choices and expect more accurate answers.

We've established, however, that people rely on the fast-thinking mode for most decisions. That is great news for marketers because it means that consumers are open to influence by framing and promotional efforts. The downside for marketers is that fast-thinking decisions can confound research about why consumers made their choices. Measuring post-exposure metrics won't help us understand why these consumers made choices because they're generally unaware of many of the factors influencing their decisions. This type of research might, however, give you some insights into brand equity. Consumers have little idea of why they made the decisions they did at the moment, but asking them to talk about your brand after the fact will give you some information on what they value about it and how to grow your relationship with them.

For insights into how people make choices in the moment, instead of asking them questions, dig deeper with some combination of observational and ethnographic approaches. Look for the patterns in the selections they're making, look at intersections between selections and needs, and get as close to the buying process as possible to draw your own conclusions about their choices.

Methodology Should Depend on Context

Your customers' self-perceptions aren't necessarily equivalent to what the demographic or observational research would imply. Therefore, decisions on which information you need and, by extension, your methodology, should be driven by context.

If you're simply trying to measure your market to win investors or make financial projections, you only need demographics. To get investors excited about your pet bed business, you need to know how many people in your region have pets, how many pets they have, and what kind of pets they own.

As you refine your brand positioning, you need to go deeper and consider actual consumer behaviors, such as purchase patterns and current ownership. For instance, app marketers need to understand which apps their target audience currently uses and how they use those apps. Simple self-reported survey data can often suffice here, but user interviews or observational research may be required depending on your needs. If you want to predict how customers will behave in the future, rather than asking them about intent, consider asking about their attitudes. For instance, people who are very comfortable banking on their smartphones and currently pay for everything with credit cards may not know what the future holds for other payment methods. They might report that they're not comfortable with a new payment method that they haven't yet tried, but the fact that they're very comfortable trusting apps and mobile service providers with that data now indicates an openness to digital technology that's likely a more accurate bellwether of future behavior than their current luddite claims.

Deeper marketing work, like refining your brand image and the work of anthropomorphism, requires an understanding of the customer's self-perception. You need descriptions of the customer's values, preferences, and characteristics directly from the customer. Major research suppliers offer information like this, or you can survey consumers or analyze their social media connections. This information must come directly from the consumer, though, either via self-reported data or analysis of their digital behaviors. The consumer's self-perception may be out of line with your observation—or even objective reality—but the individual's self-perception is the best predictor of what he'll buy because it hints at the types of brands that support his self-image.

Regardless of where the data points us, marketing researchers must be aware that customers are approaching product decisions with complex combinations of emotion and social cognition, not simple logic. The time of day, physical state (hunger, thirst), music, and other contextual factors impact decisions more than consumers realize. Accordingly, researchers must be vigilant in experimentation and observation as we try to isolate causality.

Profiling Customers

To develop marketing work that resonates with consumers, a deep understanding of the customer should be shared across the entire team. As we've established, some aspects of consumers' choices are driven by immediate need-states, like the purchasing environment and goal frame. Other factors are somewhat more stable drivers, like the specific problem that's driving the decision (e.g., I need AP software to send a bill to my company's vendors).

The best way to get internal teams to relate to the customer is to make the data as memorable as possible. You can do this by telling a story and using the data to paint a picture of a customer that is realistic and memorable. A persona is a well-established tool for accomplishing this, with the caveat that every single point of information included in the persona should be based on research. If you don't have comprehensive data on your audience, this isn't the tool for your brand.

A well-produced persona is a research-based archetypal snapshot of a segment of users that's clear and memorable. It must be easy enough to understand and remember that it will stick in team members' minds as they make marketing or user experience decisions.

Personas are deeply respected amongst top marketers as an excellent tool for making information actionable, but they can also elicit strong, negative reactions. I've worked with clients that found personas so useful that they printed them and put them on walls in hallways, so teams would have constant reminders of the customer. And I've been in meetings with clients who referred to personas by name, as though they're real people, as in, "This is a feature Dave and Jessica would both use." But I've also read more than one article that proclaims: "The persona is dead!" Just as it's hard to convince someone that's had a bite of bad seafood to try it again, it's hard to convince someone that's seen poorly designed personas that they can be valuable tools.

If you ladder down with people that don't value personas, you'll generally find that their distaste for personas is rooted in concerns of credibility or budget. Many of us have seen personas that were more creative writing than data storytelling. And if a manager previously saw teams waste time developing personas that were never used to drive critical decisions, she'll view them as a waste of resources. In these cases, the horns effect has led a poor first impression to poison the manager's attitude about what's really a fantastic strategy to bring the customer to life.

Marketers love well-designed personas because they help us get into the heads of consumers, aligning teams and inspiring improvements across the marketing process, from campaign planning to journey optimization. When we all have a clear idea of who our customer is and what she wants from us, we can prioritize accordingly. Clients usually love personas for many of the same reasons. Putting a face on the customer helps teams across functions empathize with his needs and refine marketing messages through the entire funnel.

A set of personas a mentor once delivered led the clients to understand that they were neglecting a key segment. The clients had been focused on marketing to their mostly male fan base, but data on site visitors led my mentor to realize that the heaviest users of the online store were mothers buying merchandise for their sons. The clients were surprised, but because she had painstakingly cited credible data, the work withstood scrutiny. The insight shifted the client's team from viewing mothers as an afterthought to prioritizing them as a critical segment. This shift in focus dramatically impacted the marketing strategy from that point forward.

A well-researched, accurate set of personas will provide actionable insights that can guide marketing and user experience journeys. But if you want your personas to be respected and adopted by the team, you need to optimize your approach to ensure that they are accurate and credible.

Writing Better Personas

My father-in-law, who was a band director for many years, says that the guitar is the easiest instrument to play badly. He means that nearly anyone is a YouTube tutorial from a passable version of the riff from *Smoke on the Water*, without learning fundamentals (e.g. how to read music and proper intonation). Similarly, anyone with enough enthusiasm and a keyboard can produce a persona that *looks* passable, but without deep customer insights, these are *short stories*, not research deliverables that should be driving marketing decisions.

Just like rock stars make playing the guitar look easy, a well-written persona is as fun and easy to read as great fiction. Because great personas can look like creative writing samples, the inexperienced tend to underestimate the research behind them. Novices tend to take a few data points on the audience and then make stuff up based on anecdotal evidence from hallway conversations and Facebook friends. I once saw a high-ranking marketer produce a persona from only personal opinions because, and this is a direct quote, "I *am* the target audience, so we don't need to waste our limited time with more research." Yikes! Hear me when I say the plural of anecdote is not data—you need real customer insights to develop a valuable persona.

Approaches to researching, developing, and writing personas vary between organizations and departments, and that's OK. Ideally, you should merge ethnographic research with relevant digital analytics and secondary research to develop bulletproof profiles that address the team's concerns. In practice, most organizations are forced to balance research with time and cost constraints. I've written personas within exceedingly tight timeframes based only on secondary data. I've also created personas from the transcripts of two dozen in-depth interviews with carefully recruited customers. Neither of these approaches was as comprehensive as academics would prefer, but they both resulted in robust profiles that proved valuable assets for the clients who requested them.

If I could offer only one piece of advice on writing personas, it would be that you should never make anything up. If you don't have enough data, make a less-robust profile, but don't make any assumptions.

Types of Personas

Personas can be created at different points in your project and with different goals. There's a particularly contentious debate in the field about how dramatically the "design persona" should differ from the "marketing persona." Though there are key differences between the two, it's much more important to consider your goals than to adhere to a specific template or worry about semantics.

Design Personas

Design personas should be based on user research and supplemented with relevant information from other sources as relevant. The goal is to help your team build empathy for the consumers by considering how they behave and why. These are all about use cases and specific consumer goals. Demographic information generally isn't important in this work and will probably add clutter or introduce bias. (Introducing age, gender, or income to the persona could lead your team to make assumptions that aren't supported by the research and shouldn't impact the design.)

The information in the following samples was prepared for a B2B company that offers online training on a subscription basis.

> Ben is a data scientist working for our client. He needs to collect and analyze data from our platform so he can report usage details to management. He needs to export raw data and he would prefer to get it all in one, big batch, so he can clean and analyze it using his preferred methods.
>
> Eileen is our client's COO and has ultimate control over the budget. She sees value in offering our tools to her teams, but she's also always looking for ways to trim excess expenses. She will only approve next year's contract if the report her team prepares shows that her employees are taking advantage of the subscription.

While some argue for adding photos and demographics to design personas to make them more relatable, others argue that putting faces on the profiles can introduce bias. For instance, if you put a young face on the persona, experience planners might erroneously assume a higher level of comfort with technology, which could lead to a more complex UX that frustrates users. One great way to avoid introducing bias is to present design personas as graphical descriptions of skills and usage patterns with simple, clear use cases that can be referred to throughout the design process.

Marketing Personas

Marketing personas are more geared towards helping strategists understand key segments for targeting and messaging purposes, so they generally need to provide a more complete profile that's representative of a segment of the market. The best marketing personas pool data from many sources into succinct, believable snapshots that represent key audience segments.

Demographic, attitudinal, and behavioral information are all important here. For example, knowing the number and types of pets a customer owns is important for pet store owners. They wouldn't want to offend a large segment of people who own both cats and dogs by referring to them as "dog people." Knowing that a woman balances professional and parenting responsibilities and therefore feels overwhelmed is important for a company marketing time-saving products.

As with design personas, you'll want to include goals and use cases for your product and the wider market. You'll also need to consider relevant needs and challenges. Depending on the scope of your project, you'll likely also want to consider touchpoints or how the user journey crosses channels as they consider, purchase, and interact with your product or service.

A marketing persona for a car company offering an all-electric model with sophisticated in-dash technology might include this sort of information, depending on the project goals:

Mary drives everywhere she goes, whether she's meeting friends a few blocks away for lunch or driving across town to pick up her grandkids. She considers both bicycles and public transportation hassles that are unsafe and impractical. She cares about the environment and is interested in vehicle efficiency, but safety ratings and interior features have been more important to her purchase decisions in the past. Also, she worries about the dependability of all-electric cars. What if she needs to run an unexpected errand across town and her battery dies?

Mary is pragmatic when it comes to technology adoption. She'll purchase and use devices that have clear benefits, but she won't buy a new phone just because an upgraded model has been released, and she has the same attitude about vehicle technology. She was extremely annoyed by the difficulty of changing the clock in her last car and she never even used the GPS because the interface threw too many errors the first time she tried to use it. But she's very interested in synching her phone so she that can talk while driving without getting a ticket and she is willing to invest some effort into learning how to set that up.

Post-purchase, Mary doesn't want to call an 800-number or go to the website for a live chat when she's having a problem; she expects the people at her local dealership to assist. She likes how the dealership sends her coupons when her car is due for an oil change, but she made multiple requests to be removed from their phone list due to intrusive dinnertime calls. And Mary only logs in to Facebook twice a month. She doesn't follow many brands on social media and she doesn't remember many posts; she's mainly interested in what's new with her extended family.

Marketing personas require significantly more research than design personas. You should combine segmentation studies, ethnographic studies, user research, and secondary data as relevant and available. A research foundation will ensure rich personas that are truly representative. And the research budget pales in comparison to the cost of a failed campaign.

Unfortunately, limitations on time, money, or both generally preclude in-depth research for every project. I've seen very effective marketing personas that were developed on shoestring budgets by researchers who combined institutional knowledge and customer data with data from secondary sources like consumer panels and industry analyses.

The secret to developing the best possible marketing personas with limited research is to recognize what you don't know and steadfastly refuse to make any assumptions. Instead, recognize the hole in your knowledge, so you'll know if additional research is necessary later in the course of the project.

Context Is Everything

Hospitals, charitable organizations, and laws designed to protect people who attempt to help others are often named for the parable of the good Samaritan. The parable begins with a Jewish traveler who was robbed, beaten, and left for dead. The man suffered on the side of the road and was ignored by passersby—including a priest and a fellow Jew—until he was finally helped by a Samaritan, despite the adversarial relationship between Jews and Samaritans at that time.

Perhaps inspired by the detail that one of the passersby was a priest, some psychologists at Princeton ran an experiment with some seminary students.[271] The experimenters told the students that they were studying religious education and vocations. Students were first asked to complete a personality survey that included questions about their relationships with religion. Then the researchers asked the students to deliver a short talk on either the parable of the good Samaritan or the best jobs for seminary students. The subjects were told their comments would be recorded in a nearby building because of space constraints in the current building. Next, the experimenters told some of the subjects that they were running late for this next phase, while others were told they were running on time or a little early. After receiving directions to the next building, the students set off, presumably considering what they would say.

Then things got interesting. The experimenters surreptitiously placed another participant in a doorway along the route. This person pretended to be suffering: coughing, groaning, obviously in need of help. What do you think happened?

Even though the ideas of spirituality, kindness, and service must've been front-of-mind for all the students, fewer than half stopped to help. Remarkably, personality variables did not play a role. The students who stopped to help were the ones who believed they had time. Nearly two-thirds of the students who were running early paused to help, compared with 45 percent of the students who were on time and only 10 percent of the students who were running late.

I'd wager that many of those seminary students—like students in social work, nursing, or even political science—were pursuing their field of study because they wanted to help others. They may have been described by those who knew them as "good people." But these good people who wanted to help were unlikely to help a person in need if they were running late—even as they were about to deliver a lesson about helping others.

Our choices aren't always good, logical, well-considered, or even consistent; rather, our decisions are contextually dependent. Our sense of personal identity and some personality characteristics are relatively stable, but our behavioral choices are heavily influenced by the specifics of each situation.

For marketers, this means that it is insufficient to only know our customers and their needs. We also need to know *the context* in which our customers interact with the product. We need to understand things like:

- Where is she when she's making the decision?
- How does the environment influence his mood?
- Is this a planned purchase in which she's taking advantage of System 2 thinking, and doing some research at home?
- Is this a quick, low-consideration purchase, like grabbing a candy bar in line at the grocery store?
- How does the customer typically feel when she's interacting with the product?

Who the customer is and how he thinks is only part of the picture. Just as important is *where* he is—physically and psychologically—when he's making the purchase.

Profiling Advice Potpourri

I love a well-crafted persona even more than I hate one that's poorly crafted, so I'd like to offer a potpourri of tips for writing strong customer profiles.

Obsessively adhere to the research

Do not include details about her hair color or shoe size if you do not have a reliable data point to back them up. Do not assume that, because they fit the profile, the opinions of your team members can be generalized to the entire population. Even if your mother fits the profile, you cannot assume that your mother's behavior is typical and representative. If you don't have information about your target consumer's behavior, then you should avoid the temptation to fill in the blanks with assumptions based on the behavior of someone you know, even if that person fits the profile. If you ensure that every statement you make in the document has a footnote—a reliable, relevant source—you'll minimize bias.

Only include relevant information

As with any marketing communication, we're building personas for people with limited time, attention, interest, and cognitive capacity. It would be arrogant to assume that they would like to use their limited resources on our research. Because our audience has a limited ability to consume and internalize information, every single piece of information that does not add value is a distraction, detracting from the value of the document.

Personas must be easy to digest and brief enough that they can be read and reread as teams make important choices. Cluttering the document with irrelevant facts obscures critical insights. You can't possibly explore every facet of the target's life and you don't need to. You only need the relevant information, within the context of the marketing problem you're trying to solve.

Keep it actionable

Your colleagues' preferences may vary when it comes to recreational reading, but most of them probably won't select "random consumer profiles" as a favorite genre. So, your persona should offer actionable insights into the problem your readers are trying to solve. You should provide the team with research-based insights into the challenges and problems that customers are trying to solve, and about the way they interact with your product, service, or category.

Pick a point

Many persona templates on the internet offer data like "80% female" or "ages 18-25." This approach preserves precision at the expense of readability and memorability—and that cost is too high. Don't write "78.92% of the target are women and 89.71% are parents." Instead, simply note that the profile is a mom and put the data point and source citation in the footnotes.

Consider which of the following profiles you'll remember 10 minutes from now.

1. 92% are 18-23, 97% are female, they're 385% more likely to be a college student, they're 813% more likely to rent an apartment, 78% of the vertical use public transportation, 68% ride a bike, 91% call or text their moms at least three times a week, 98% own smartphones, 97% text message more often than they talk on their smartphones, 87% use TikTok.
2. Emma is 21 and she's a full-time student at Michigan State. When the weather is nice—and classes aren't too early—she rides her bike from her apartment to campus. Lately, she's been taking the bus because it has been so cold and rainy. She misses the exercise, but the 15-minute ride gives her a chance to text her mom and look at friends' TikToks.

Your writing will be far more memorable if you provide a portrait of the consumer rather than a long list of statistics. Researchers tend to appreciate the accuracy of precise data points, but the goal of this task is to make information relatable and memorable, and Emma is far more memorable than the data-rich #1.

Don't default to demographic segmentation

Personas should represent segments that are delineated by behaviors and preferences as relevant to your service, not on demographics. Sometimes these are heavily correlated, sometimes they are not. If you're profiling listeners who are interested in a professional seminar, or if you are marketing products related to a certain religion, then demographics may have a causal relationship with the consumer's behaviors or needs. In most situations, however, segmenting based on demographics can lead to dangerous assumptions that aren't grounded in research.

Defining personas along demographic lines can also lead to a disproportionate representation of a group. In purchasing plane tickets, a single Gen Xer who travels infrequently may use Kayak to find the cheapest fare that fits her schedule, whereas a millennial and baby boomer who are both frequent business travelers may prioritize loyalty to an airline so that they can use or accumulate frequent flyer miles. In addition to being redundant, these profiles probably overrepresent the influence of business travel for some airlines, and they also fail to represent family vacationers and people with flexible schedules who buy tickets based on fare promotions. A better approach would be to divide people based on their fare selection behaviors and/or purchase triggers (e.g., frequent business traveler, family vacationer, etc.).

In deciding how to delineate personas, consider where the causation lies. Pet ownership and parental status are probably not key predictors of how a B2B purchaser chooses cloud computing technologies, so there's no reason to use those demographic factors to delineate profiles. But because odors from kids and pets are key drivers of air freshener purchases, parents and pet owners would be important segments. Their status as parents or pet owners is important information. You get the picture.

I know one experienced practitioner who recommends the elimination of demographic information and photos from personas—to reduce the risk of conscious and subconscious bias. This person's argument is that the stories—the logic behind decisions, the beliefs that drive relationships with products—could stand alone without photos and demographic details. This is a valid opinion, but in my experience, the stories are more memorable when they're given a face. This helps the story resonate with people, which, in my view, outweighs the risk of introducing some bias. It's your job as the writer to remind the people who use your persona that the profile is merely a composite of a larger, more diverse audience. You will return to the granular data about the audience when it's time to plan media buys or conduct other business that requires comprehensive customer data.

Researching Identity

We've covered the importance of understanding the customer's identity throughout the book, on the assumption that you can get information about how the customer sees himself. But this research can be tricky to conduct. You're not going to find it in a database, and it might not come out during interviews with user-experience or product-development specialists.

Questions will depend on how your brand and how your product fits into your customer's life, but a few of my favorite questions follow.

Can you tell me a little about yourself?
Once you've gotten your customers comfortable—with some small talk or some softball survey questions—you can hit them with this one. The question is generic enough that they probably have a

practiced answer that will tell you a little about their identity and group membership.

Can you tell me a little about your typical day?

I love this question because it's also relatively easy for the interviewee and it gives us marketers lots of information. You need to know how your brand fits into the customer's life, but you should not ask the person to tell you "everything about how you use my brand." This question will yield some specifics of how the customer uses the product and, usually, a little on how the customer views the brand.

Why did you choose our brand?

You and I know that memory is imperfect, thinking is biased, and there are many subconscious factors that impact purchase decisions. But this question isn't about gathering an accurate account of factors that influence the consumer. It's about getting a sense of the post-purchase story that the customer tells herself about why she chose your brand. Answers to this question will tell you how to refine your position and create a story that resonates with your target.

What should we keep/start/stop doing?

This is a little trick I picked up teaching at universities. If you ask students how things are going or what they liked most or least, they'll shrug and give you a half-baked answer. That's not good, because you don't want any surprises at the end of the year when they're filling out instructor reviews. Naturally, the same goes for businesses. Your customers are the best resource for information about how you can improve your services, but you need to prompt them with questions that are easy to answer. I like these:

- What should we keep doing?

- What should we start doing?
- What should we stop doing?

These specific and easy questions might elicit simple, addressable suggestions.

What else should we know?

Customers who have been recruited for a study often come in with feedback to share. Encourage this!

Case Studies Are Not Evidence

After spending a decade working in research for a major advertising agency, I have inside knowledge of the type of information that agency employees reference when creating the world's campaigns. To my endless exasperation, case studies are a favorite resource for strategists. People ask for case studies that deal with the vertical they're marketing, the audience they're targeting, or a channel they're considering, hoping that imitating a better marketer's work will lead to similar success. The practice is defended as "stealing like an artist" and derided as "cargo cult thinking," but the ethical argument is beside our point. Instead, let's look at the behavioral economics of why looking to case studies to increase marketing effectiveness is a terrible idea.

First, The Caveats

Before we delve into the reasons that case studies are not evidence, there are some caveats to accompany the analysis.

1. The case studies that agency folks reference aren't the carefully-researched sort from books and *Harvard Business Review* that marketing professors distribute. These don't

reference experimental research. They're looking at the self-promotional sort that brands and agencies create for their websites and awards submissions.
2. Winning awards is awesome and recognition from a committee that includes your industry's most prominent leaders is career-defining. Clients love hardware, so agencies must have awards to display for clients. At issue here is whether these case studies—the ones written in hopes of winning an award—contain replicable insights that can improve the effectiveness of your campaigns.
3. Examining outcomes that result from various approaches is, of course, a very important part of learning. You should read case studies, including those developed for award submissions. Just don't fall for claims that the writers have established causal links between processes and outcomes.

We See Patterns That Aren't There

As humans, we often learn by trying something, then evaluating the outcome. Scientists call this experimental research. World Series of Poker champion Annie Duke calls it outcome fielding. My dad calls it "f--ing around and finding out." The problem with this approach to learning is that it doesn't establish a causal link between the action and the outcome. If you're writing a case study, the work was considered successful, but was the success the result of smart choices or luck? Which of the ten levers the marketers pulled affected the outcome?

Our brains are built to look for patterns and infer connections. This is great for teaching kids not to touch fire—they only have to make that mistake once—but this aspect of brain function can also lead us to assume that things that are merely correlated are causally linked.

Tyler Vigen found a 99 percent correlation between the divorce rate in Maine and the per capita consumption of margarine. [272] A resident of Maine might, thus, assume that banning margarine would protect the institution of marriage. But without experimental research, we only know that people are getting divorced and that people are eating margarine. We don't know if one is *causing* the other.

When marketers write case studies, they make claims like this one: "Building on the insight that moms love Instagram, we increased our social media investment and saw a three-fold increase in sales vs. the previous quarter!" It might be true that moms over-index for Instagram usage, that social media investment increased, and that sales increased, but this claim presents no evidence that one caused the other. Case studies also conspicuously omit other factors. Was this the first Instagram investment the brand had made? Was the product seasonal? Was the Instagram investment the only part of the marketing mix that changed? Were there other reasons for the creative's success beyond its appearance on Instagram? Were sales already trending up? How bad was the previous marketing strategy?

You're never going to get the comprehensive information you need from a case study, partly because the writers are hoping that presenting only select information will nudge you into inferring a causal link so they can look clever.

It's Hard to Separate Fact from Fiction

One reason that case studies are bunk is that people are generally pretty bad at analyzing the reasons for our own success, in part because of the following biases.

Self-Serving Bias

I was at a party where a neighbor was telling a story about a fender-bender. I listened for several minutes to her chatter about the dearth of stop signs in the neighborhood, the city's unresponsiveness to her complaints, and the shortage of suitable new cars at dealerships. Eventually, I was able to piece together what had happened. She had blown through a stop sign and hit an oncoming car. She didn't feel responsible for the accident; rather, she blamed the inconsistent placement of stop signs at intersections. In her view, this made it difficult to discern where to stop.

This woman was so convinced this accident was caused by a shortage of stop signs—like the one she completely missed—that it didn't occur to her that her listeners would conclude that she was at fault. If you've ever heard a story about a car accident, you're probably thinking that her self-serving bias is typical. Indeed, Professor Maccoun at Stanford Law School found that drivers blamed others in 91 percent of accidents, and 37 percent of drivers even refused to accept blame when their vehicle was the only one involved in the accident.[273]

Self-serving bias refers to our tendency to take credit for positive outcomes and blame external factors beyond our control when things go wrong. This comes up a lot when students explain their grades. In one survey, I asked students to explain the grades they earned on a recent assignment. Students who did well tended to credit themselves. They said they studied hard, understood the concepts, and/or regularly attended class. Students who did poorly tended to blame external factors, such as the difficulty of the concepts, harsh grading, etc.

A self-serving bias can protect our self-esteem, which is critical to survival, but it can also cloud our judgment when performing tasks like writing case studies. If a campaign was successful enough to warrant a case study, the writers will naturally assume that it's a result of their brilliance. They'll fail to note—and maybe fail to notice—the myriad other factors that led to success: luck, a shortage of substitutes, or a competitor's reduced budget.

Actor-Observer Bias

Actor-observer bias is the academic name for a bias we see outside of textbooks all the time. We tend to consider external factors when explaining our own behavior but focus on internal factors when explaining someone else's.

Returning to my student survey, students who did poorly on their most recent assignment tended to blame external factors: the difficulty of the assignment, discipline, or the grading schema. By contrast, when I asked students why others did poorly on that same assignment, they were more likely to blame internal factors: too lazy to study, didn't care about grades, didn't read the instructions, or skipped lectures. In other words, the students who missed points blamed outside factors and, simultaneously, blamed the failures of other students on internal flaws.

There are a couple of lessons here. First, please consider this bias and be kind when you review your professors. Second, and more to our point, it's easy to see how our tendency to blame factors beyond our control for our own failures but blame other people for their failures could color our ability to accurately explain the reasons for our project's success. Often, case studies, presentations, and post-mortems include wildly biased explanations of the competitive landscape. They'll assert that the competitors suffered dull positioning, bland products, or boring content, blaming their weak marketing teams. Then, paradoxically, they'll point out that any weaknesses in their own campaign were due to a difficult macroenvironment.

Confirmation Bias and Memory

Another problem is confirmation bias, which leads us to seek out and remember information that supports our preexisting beliefs. Our brains are primed to see even neutral or irrelevant data points as confirmation of our success, which seriously undermines the value of case studies written by the agencies and brands behind the work.

Psychologists have proposed that our brains function more like diaries than recordings. That is, memory isn't a tool for perfect recollection; it plays a role in forming our personal narratives, the stories we weave to help us understand our current situation and guide our future actions.[274] Therefore, if the writer of a case study believes himself to be a brilliant marketer, as evidenced by his contributions to a successful campaign, he'll be most likely to remember only the information that supports that story.

Hindsight Bias and Memory

Also harming our ability to accurately recall the past is the hindsight bias, which is the belief that you were right from the start. This is the feeling that you *just knew* something would be successful or you could've told someone that something would fail. Sometimes, we're right. Sometimes, the brain is giving itself a little too much credit.

Hindsight bias can be dangerous for marketers because it can stack with other cognitive biases like overconfidence bias—which is exactly what it sounds like—to lead us to hubris. We begin to believe that we're so smart that we can skip important steps like research and user experience analysis. Hindsight bias also calls into question the common case study claim that a campaign's success was based on nothing more than the team's strategic brilliance.

It's not just the uniquely egotistical that believe they knew the campaign would be successful all along: It's how we're wired to reflect on our perceptions. For this reason, we should be careful to consider the role of luck in our success—and in the case studies we read.

Success is Somewhat Random

Another reason case studies shouldn't be mistaken for research is that it's folly to believe in the existence of a surefire formula for success, and random variables play a *huge* role in successful outcomes.

Even experts are mediocre at predicting hits. Top producers have sunk millions into movies that have flopped, like the 2019 film *Cats*. Major publishing houses have rejected books like *Harry Potter*, which ended up becoming bestsellers. In one of my all-time favorite studies, researchers demonstrated that computer-simulated "monkeys" outperformed fund managers in the stock market.[275]

One study, which you should immediately forward to your musician friends, evaluated whether a sample of fourteen thousand participants—divided into nine groups—could predict which of forty-eight songs would become hits. No two groups produced similar top-ten lists, demonstrating that a song's likelihood of becoming a hit is largely random.[276]

Low-quality work built on flawed insights isn't going to be effective. But, every day, brilliant marketers are turning out amazing creative that won't win awards. Expertise and great work are important, but they're table stakes, not guarantees of success. Any case study that fails to mention the role of dumb luck should be considered highly suspect.

Let's Get Smarter

Case studies, like novels, make interesting reading. They can provide inspiration when we're stuck and they can give us great insight into how the competition is framing their successes during pitches. But case studies aren't reliable sources for credible insights on how to make your marketing work more effective. In fact, case studies, as marketers know them, are merely marketing tools for the writer and his agency. And neither one of them wants to help you succeed. Mining incomplete anecdotes written by your competitors in hopes of uncovering a clear path to success is not a good use of your time.

If marketers hope to garner the respect we deserve within the business world—to avoid being viewed as people who play with Instagram all day, or who, as Daniel Cleaver put it, "swan in, in [our] sexy see-through blouse[s] and fanny around with press releases"—we must treat marketing like a science. This means we must look to subject-matter experts and reliable research for information, not to peers who are, however understandably, glossing over details to defend their careers.

It's virtually impossible to separate the clever choices that led to success from the lucky breaks with the limited, biased information available in a case study. There's no recipe for effectiveness here.

You Can't Overestimate the Impact of Culture

The importance of culture to brand choice can't be overstated. The influence of culture underlies every aspect of our identities, how we see ourselves, and what we aspire to. It is the lens through which we view choices as we decide what is necessary, what is desirable, and how we should present ourselves. In this section, I'll discuss how culture impacts perception and how marketers can prepare and respond. Note that many concepts here apply to researching any cross-cultural research, whether that means people united by a national culture or by a subculture (e.g. such as parents, skateboarders, or cat people).

Can You See Blue?

My favorite example of how heavily culture influences our perceptions is a study that demonstrated that vision is impacted by the language you speak. The human eye is *physically* able to sense millions of different colors, so we would expect that if we sampled people without vision impairments from around the world, they would perform similarly on visual tests relating to color. It turns out that this isn't the case.

Seeing color has to do with how our eyes and brains perceive light from a spectrum of wavelengths. We would call a range of wavelengths "orange," not just one specific wavelength. This means that the words you know to describe color—red, orange, yellow— are the names for categories of colors, and different languages handle this color categorization differently. For instance, in English, we refer to "dark blue" and "light blue," but you'll rarely hear a native speaker refer to something as "light red" because pink is a basic color category that native English speakers learn as young children. This is where culture comes in. Scientists have found that these color categories impact which colors you notice.

In one study, researchers tasked people with viewing a series of thirteen shapes, then recalling the orientation of a semicircle and, when present, a triangle. Native speakers of German—which, like

English, does not have separate, dedicated words for light blue and dark blue—were equally likely to notice the triangles that were light blue on a dark blue field (or vice versa) or light green on a dark green field (or vice versa). But native speakers of Greek, which has entirely separate words for light blue and dark blue, were more likely to notice the blue triangles than the green. The experimenters replicated the results with native speakers of Russian, another language with separate words for light blue and dark blue. Like their Greek counterparts, Russian speakers were more likely to notice the blue triangles than the green.[277] The differences were small but significant, and support the hypothesis that language influences our perception of the world around us.

If you're wondering whether learning a new language shifts your perception, it does! One study found that Greek speakers living in the UK, where they're exposed to far more English than Greek, lose some of their ability to distinguish between shades of blue.[278] Speaking English all the time causes their perceptions to be less like the Greeks and more like the English.

The extent to which language shapes our broader perceptual experience is heavily debated in academia. Still, if language alone can impact our visual perception, it's easy to imagine that the culture we live in has a tremendous influence on our brand choices.

Multicultural Research

Dutch social psychologist Geert Hofstede has described culture as "the collective programming of the mind that distinguishes the members of one group or category of people from others."[279] Culture has been demonstrated to affect us at every level: our shared history and perception of our place within the world; our place within our national society; our expectations about marriage and friendship; and our perspectives on signaling wealth. Cultural norms impact the way we experience, perceive, and show emotion. And researchers in the emerging field of cultural neuroscience are even finding connections between culture and the physical structures of our brains.[280] Because of this, culture should be a foundational consideration to marketers, whether your work is multinational, intersectional, or even just local. It should, therefore, be an early consideration in research and planning.

A full exploration of the myriad ways culture impacts our identities and decisions is beyond the scope of this text and, likely, beyond the scope of most marketing projects. Suffice it to say, because culture affects human perceptions at every level, it must be carefully considered within even domestic marketing projects. And an understanding of how to garner insights from multicultural consumers doesn't just benefit international brands: Nielsen estimates that 40 percent of the US population is African American, Asian American, or Hispanic, and that figure is expected to increase in coming years.[281]

Adding visual diversity and language translations to marketing materials is a great first step, but your multicultural marketing efforts can't end there. Next, you need to take a deeper look at how customer journeys differ between segments. Sometimes, cultural identities drive differences in the customer journey that should impact your marketing strategy.

Applying Cross-Cultural Insights

Let's say we're working for a cereal brand in the US. The data indicate that mothers who primarily speak Spanish at home are more interested in delighting their children with treats, and non-Hispanic White moms are more interested in free-from claims (gluten-free, sugar-free, etc.). Both groups are essential audiences that you need to beat the competition.

In this scenario, there is a strong case for exposing paths to coupons for both types of products early on the website. These insights might also affect decisions on which type of cereal should be featured in flyers for different zip codes and which content should be prioritized in the Spanish-language version of the US website. Because the Spanish-speaking mother is less likely to be interested in sugar-free cereal, simply translating the website that her English-speaking counterparts see would lead us to waste valuable homepage real estate on products that aren't relevant to her interests.

Brands are increasingly working to demonstrate respect for diverse audiences, but some marketers are simply employing actors with a range of skin tones, rather than seeking to understand how increasing cultural diversity can require considering a broader range of customer journeys. And if we leave the journeys of some consumers unaddressed or poorly optimized, we will leave money on the table.

Regardless of whether your consumers are in the US or spread across the globe, you can benefit from a basic understanding of cross-cultural research methods, no matter your budget. This, in turn, will help you improve your messages and add depth to your engagement efforts.

A Brief Survey of Cross-Cultural Research Methods

Many marketers outsource international and multicultural research projects to research firms that specialize in the audiences they want to target. Consulting with specialists is never a bad idea but, often, deadlines and budgets can't stretch to accommodate them. In these cases, you shouldn't be afraid to gather your own insights. To that end, in the following pages, I will offer a high-level overview of the benefits and downfalls of various methodologies for gathering cross-cultural insights.

Start With What You Have

Your first step should be to evaluate the data you already have from sources like website analytics, social media sites, and institutional knowledge. From that information you can determine whether large portions of your customers also follow brands that target certain cultures or subcultures. Social media sites are a great source of qualitative insights on the consumer's culture, like challenges that come with the lifestage your customers are in, trends, behavioral norms (what consumers think is normal or cool), and how your customer sees his place within society (and, hopefully, how he sees your brand within his life).

Secondary Research

The value of desktop research is often underestimated. There is a massive amount of information available from skilled analysts and panels around the world. That data and analysis, when used in the early stages of planning, could save time and money.

If a ride-sharing brand wanted to gauge interest in new cities, it could recruit focus groups to discuss problems about commuting, conduct interviews to determine how people decide on a mode of transportation, and do ethnographic research with commuters in each potential market. But this approach would be extremely expensive and time-consuming—just as competitors are racing to market with their services. By leveraging desktop research from subscription sources, social listening tools, and other tactics, the company could learn about consumers' commuting problems (car ownership rates, traffic, average commute times during peak hours) in each market within days. With this background research in hand, the brand could identify the best markets, then focus subsequent research on gathering deeper insights and uncovering subtle differences between markets that may be overlooked by regional strategists.

Qualitative Methods

Qualitative research is often underestimated in our "big data" world, where it's so quick and easy to field a survey. This is a shame, because qualitative methods are truly invaluable when it comes to getting a sense of the cultural drivers influencing consumers. Qualitative has long been prized for its ability to uncover the customer's opinions, knowledge, and needs as related to products, but it can do so much more! These approaches can uncover emotional needs, aspects of the consumer's identity that are relevant to the brand, and the customer's ingroup and its signals.

Qualitative methods allow researchers to improve the depth of their insights, provided they have skilled moderators. Lab environments minimize distractions and enable skilled moderators to probe for the true values and drivers behind opinions. But these benefits can also become costs. Brands are forced to depend on the moderator to ask the right questions. They must hope that the respondent will be able to remember and communicate important information. And they need to be sure that the responses to theoretical questions about situations outside of the lab are accurate.

Focus Groups
Focus groups can enable deeper conversation between participants and allow clients to see users interact with products, creative samples, or ideas. This can be an excellent venue for brainstorming, prototype testing, or evaluating specific aspects of a product, service, or experience. The downside is that moderators can struggle to combat groupthink, and focus groups could be more appropriate in some markets than others. For instance, in a highly collectivist

culture, some respondents may not share a dissenting view.[282] Young people in some cultures might hesitate to express opinions in front of older participants.

To address these concerns, it is critical that the focus group is preceded by desktop research—such as a consideration of Hofstede's cultural dimensions outlined in the upcoming section—and designed with the audience, the purchase process, and the culture in mind.

In Latin America, for example, children have more input into purchasing decisions related to toys and games than most other cultures.[283] So, interviewing a group of parents in Latin America about holiday purchases without including children in the group could lead to inaccurate assumptions.

In-Depth Interviews
Skilled interviewers can use techniques like laddering, hidden-issue questioning, and/or symbolic analysis to probe the underlying factors that contribute to a respondent's purchasing decisions. This is also an appropriate technique for exploring sensitive topics, which may vary by culture. For instance, a company interested in learning more about gay men may be successful in using a focus group in Canada, where homosexuality is generally accepted and gays can speak openly. But IDIs may be more appropriate in Egypt or Russia, where subjects would be less open about being gay.[284]

Dyads and triads are another take on the in-depth interview, in which two or three respondents are involved instead of just one. A benefit is that a wealth of information can be gathered without introducing larger group dynamics, but these types of interviews can be long and costly and require skilled moderators. Cultural and life-circumstance factors can present barriers. For example, Middle Eastern women may be particularly averse to male interviewers and busy moms may require that you allow them to bring their children or provide childcare.

The in-depth interview method isn't ideal for gaining a breadth of information, but it can help you gain a deeper understanding about questions related to how a product is chosen, used, or stored.

Digital Methods
Research methods continue to evolve as we gain more access to technical innovations. These advancements can alter old methods and introduce new research alternatives. Now, for instance, we can use tools like FaceTime, Skype, or Zoom to interview moderators or connect with subjects if they have internet access with any device. We can watch as respondents test live versions of digital experiences or survey them while they're in stores, rather than depending on what they report from memory after the fact. Mobile research panels are increasingly robust and accessible, even when the budget is limited.

In effect, these digital approaches allow us to move a step closer to the consumer experience in context—while they interact with products—so we can learn from consumers in more natural environments where they are more comfortable. But shifting control of the environment from the moderator to the consumer also forces us to fight distractions and technical issues.

Anthropological methods
Qualitative research can also include anthropological methods like ethnographic and observational research. These approaches allow us to capture qualitative insights in the moment, environment, and context that are relevant to the question at hand. They also help us see beyond the consumer's opinion about a product; we can gather broader insights about the society, context, infrastructure, environment, and cultural factors.

Observational methods allow researchers to study consumers either directly, by observing them, or indirectly, by studying reported observations from others. Direct observations allow the researcher to interact with the subject, thereby allowing the researcher to be more certain of his conclusions, even though these interactions may introduce bias. Indirect methods eliminate the researcher's direct bias, but they force the researcher to depend on others for unbiased, accurate reporting. In addition, testing effects are always and everywhere a concern during observational research. There's a bit of a catch-22 involved: People behave differently when they know they're being observed, but it would be unethical to observe people without their knowledge.

Ethnography is an anthropological method designed to help researchers gain a deeper understanding of how people live. This method involves observing people in their natural environments—homes, offices, etc.—without directing them. It can be inefficient and time-consuming compared with straightforward methods like survey research, but it allows us to gather deep and important insights into behaviors that can't be observed in a lab environment.

In the 1990's, Intel took an ethnographic approach to researching a consumer market and found the method to be so advantageous that the company decided to create a new business unit dedicated to targeting home users. In an article, principal researcher Ken Anderson said, "By understanding how people live, researchers discover otherwise elusive trends that inform the company's future strategies."[285]

The in-home studies by Febreze led researchers to the successful "nose blind" campaigns. As a part of that study, researchers interviewed a woman with nine cats. They wanted to know about her cleaning routine. Her home reportedly smelled so awful that one researcher became ill. When they asked her how she dealt with the smell, she said it wasn't a problem because her cats didn't smell.[286] If the researchers had not been able to observe the woman in her home, Febreze researchers wouldn't have delivered the golden insight that people are "nose blind" to the smells in their own homes.

Selecting a Method

There is no clear-cut approach—or mix of approaches—that should be considered the ideal solution for an international or multicultural research project. The first consideration when designing a study should not be the preferred methodology, but the business questions and markets that are most relevant. Once the scope is defined, we can move on to designing a methodology that is relevant and balances research goals with timing and budget constraints.

In an international study, comparison is made simpler if the same methods are applied to respondents in each country studied, but this may not make sense from a cultural perspective. Returning to the toy example, research has shown that children play a greater role in this decision in some countries than others, so interviewing children is crucial in some markets and may be less relevant—even a waste of budget—in others. When the decision-makers differ between countries, the methods for obtaining information should differ. While group interviews of families may make the most sense for learning about the toy purchasing market in Latin America, a focus group that includes only parents may be a better path to learning about purchasers in other cultures. Thus, conducting the same kind of research on the same kind of buyers could yield insights of mixed value in an international study.

With the caveat that the method for data collection should depend on the business questions and markets, it is clear that there should be an anthropological component to any international or multicultural study wherever possible. To truly understand the consumer's context and considerations, we much conduct observational and ethnographic research to understand factors that impact purchase decisions beyond simple correlations of product purchases with demographics.

Quantifying Cultural Differences

To translate cultural differences into actionable insights, it helps if we can compare cultures. To do that, we need to quantify differences or, at the very least, enumerate qualitative differences that might drive differences in perceptions. This need has intimidated marketers around the world since the dawn of globalization, and it has inspired countless academic studies.

To gain a truly comprehensive understanding of how cross-cultural differences can influence the diverse ways that consumers relate to your brand, you'll need to bring in professionals. But don't fret if timelines and budgets don't allow. There are approaches and resources that you can leverage on your own. Desktop research and digital methods may never yield the depth of insights that professional international and cross-cultural researchers can uncover, but they will allow you to better understand your customers and incrementally improve your marketing efforts.

The Hofstede Model

Geert Hofstede's cultural dimension research offers a six-dimensional framework within which cultures can be described. This framework helps people to communicate about and understand cultural differences. Dimensions include power-distance, individualism, motivation towards achievement and success, uncertainty-avoidance, long-term orientation, and indulgence.[287]

The power-distance dimension essentially measures how egalitarian a society is. People who live in cultures that score high on the power-distance dimension generally accept that those in superior positions will have more power and privileges. People who live in cultures that score low on the power-distance dimension prefer and expect more equality. Understanding the power-distance dimension is critical to identifying the audiences you research. If you are researching a B2B market within a high power-distance culture, such as China or Saudi Arabia, you could assume that managers would not delegate decision-making authority or seek buy-in from subordinates. Thus, it might be sufficient to research only the manager in charge of a purchase.[288] In a country that scores lower on the power-distance dimension, such as the UK or Finland, B2B managers would be more likely to consider themselves part of a team and to seek input from subordinates. In this case, you would probably want to explore the opinions of both decision-makers and influencers.

The individualism dimension frames whether the culture is primarily concerned with individual achievements and supporting immediate family, or oriented toward the prioritization of collective needs and group belonging. In collectivist cultures, people will hesitate to share dissenting views.[289] This indicates that a diverse focus group may not be the best choice in a collectivist culture, like those of Japan and China. It would, however, be natural to interview a family group in a highly collectivist culture, because multiple generations might influence the purchase decision.

Societies with high motivation towards achievement and success tend to be more competitively oriented. These types of cultures value achievement and material rewards for success, in contrast to the emphasis placed on consensus, cooperation, and quality of life in others. In a high MAS society, we can expect better outcomes when products are positioned as offering "high performance" or "dominance." (The Corvette comes to mind.) In a society with lower MAS scores, we can expect more success from positioning strategies that emphasize quality of life and/or the environment. (The Chevrolet Volt comes to mind now.) Within the same product family, we can emphasize different attributes to appeal to different audiences.

The uncertainty-avoidance dimension frames the degree to which people avoid unknown situations. Cultures that score high on the uncertainty-avoidance dimension tend to frown on deviation from cultural norms, and they are more likely to trust experts. Those cultures that score low on the uncertainty-avoidance dimension are more willing to take chances. They place more trust in common sense than in experts. Researchers have attributed Japan's willingness to trade with Europe and the US to the country's lower score on the uncertainty-avoidance dimension. By comparison, companies in India and the Middle East would probably be more hesitant to jump into relationships with international companies. When conducting research or building relationships with companies in countries that have scored high on the uncertainty-avoidance dimension, you would be wise to seek assistance from local advocates.

Long-term-oriented cultures look to the future and are concerned with patience and pragmatism. By contrast, Western cultures operate with a short-term orientation, placing more emphasis on immediate gratification. For this reason, we shouldn't expect modeling of perks that drive purchases for Americans to effectively predict the behaviors of Japanese consumers.

Finally, *the indulgence* dimension helps us frame cultures that place more emphasis on the free fulfillment of desires and fun. The opposite would be restraint-oriented societies that tend to regulate self-gratification with stricter social conventions or norms. The US and UK score much higher on the indulgence dimension than China and Japan. Accordingly, we might expect messaging that normalizes instant gratification to be more engaging in the US or UK than in China.

At the time of writing, Hofstede Insights offered a country comparison tool for free on its website. You can use it to compare up to four countries across the six dimensions. The tool is based on years of research from Hofstede and his team.

Applying Cross-Cultural Insights

As you apply cultural comparison insights, like those offered by Hofstede's model, remember that the insights aren't actionable in a vacuum. Measures of power-distance or individualism in a culture don't apply to every single member of a population, and they aren't necessarily actionable in isolation. But they help you compare cultural differences, broaden your understanding, and add depth to your strategy.

You should also consider the interaction effects between Hofstede's dimensions. The US scores relatively high on the individualism and MAS dimensions. This indicates that the US culture generally values individual achievement and self-sufficiency, and so people value displays of individual success. By contrast, the Swedish culture emphasizes cooperation and quality of life. A company in the US might lure employees by offering high pay and perks, but the same company might recruit employees in Sweden by emphasizing its positive impacts on the community and quality of life.

Using Customer Journey Research to Refine Messages

A recent Geometry Global project highlights how marketers could use multicultural research to better understand divergences and convergences between consumer groups.[290] Geometry combined Hofstede's insights with findings from ethnographic research to create journey maps. Its "culturally optimized" journey maps provide actionable information for marketing teams.

For this research, samples of Hispanics, Asian Americans, African Americans, and non-Hispanic Whites were given an online survey designed to score them in relation to Hofstede's six cultural dimensions. Each group also answered an additional ten to fifteen questions about shopping behaviors and attitudes. These answers were framed according to Hofstede's cultural dimensions. Next, ethnographic research was employed to observe shopping behaviors and attitudes in relation to purchases of mobile phones and snacks. Participants answered questions, drew diagrams to illustrate desired product attributes, and visited stores where they made purchases. Activities were then added to video diaries for researchers to review. The researchers used the insights to create journey maps to show how purchase triggers and need states differ between consumers.

The first-phase data showed that multicultural samples tended to fall between US and country of origin scores on Hofstede's scales. For instance, Hofstede's research shows that the US tends to be a highly individualistic society (it scored 91 on the individualism dimension) while China tends to be a highly collectivist society (scoring 20 on the same scale). Non-Hispanic Whites on Hofstede's scale scored 88, as one might expect, while Chinese Americans scored 19. Mexican Americans, however, scored 67—just between the US score of 91 and Mexico's score of 30. These findings could show that, at least in terms of collectivist ideals, Chinese Americans are retaining their cultural values while Mexican Americans are assimilating into American culture.

Data was combined with the research on shopping behaviors and attitudes to draw conclusions about how Hofstede dimensions like individualism correlate with behaviors like involving the family in purchase decisions. The analysts concluded that culture—and status as a multicultural consumer—directly impact consumer behaviors at certain points in the journey. Also, importantly, they concluded that these consumers are "ambicultural," meaning that they move between ethnic and American identities as they live and shop.

The resulting journey maps aligned behavioral profiles and cultural value dimensions to demonstrate how culture influences the path to purchase. For instance, when shopping for mobile phones, consumers across the board were most likely to be triggered to make a purchase by having a broken phone and about half browsed phones online before coming to a store. Culture didn't seem to affect those behaviors, but it heavily influenced in-store behaviors. Hispanics, who tend to score lower on the individualism dimension than the broader population, were the most likely group to visit with family and friends. By comparison, African Americans, who score higher on the individualism dimension, were most likely to visit stores alone.

The analysts noted that marketers who only try to identify differences between multicultural consumers and others operate on an outdated assumption: that members of ethnic minorities view themselves as separate from the wider population. However, this methodology helped the marketers find both the behavioral commonalities among multicultural consumers and the wider population and the places in the purchase journey where unique cultural factors played a role. For instance, research found that Chinese consumers had anxiety about choosing the right cell phone, whereas African American consumers were less likely to trust sales associates. These findings present clear insights for designing messages that reassure consumers and build trust.

Don't Underestimate Cross-Cultural Insights

In today's globalized world, we are influenced by a variety of cultures. Even within small geographical regions, our identities as immigrant parents, third-culture children, adoptees, or students can impact the way we see ourselves and the world around us. These factors undoubtedly impact our relationships with brands.

Most Londoners speak English, but there are strong cultural differences between the heavily Asian Newham borough and the predominantly White Havering borough, and between the city's Muslim and Bengali subcultures. History colors the way Irish people view themselves and other UK residents today. The Brexit vote made clear that people in Scotland and Wales don't share the same views about EU membership as other UK citizens. And urban residents, regardless of which city they live in, tend to vote more similarly to one another than to their rural countrymen. These factors could affect sales at a chain of ethnic groceries, hold implications for holiday promotions that reference cultural traditions, or have general implications for how to represent diversity or reference the identities of people within these markets.

Understanding cultural norms in a market enables us to understand the decision-making processes that affect purchase decisions. Cultural awareness is critical to accurately interpreting behavioral thinking and contextual factors that affect choice. Even lower-budget efforts to understand how the preferences of multicultural consumers differ from those of the wider population can prove helpful as you segment, refine your message, and work to forge deeper connections with consumers.

Multinational brands can employ vastly different strategies across borders, but multicultural campaigns *within geographical regions* require more finesse. No consumer lives or shops in a vacuum. We're all subject to numerous influences and many people engage in code-switching between groups. This means that consumers sometimes behave like the wider population and sometimes in alignment with their distinct cultural identities. A nuanced approach to marketing that considers which differences will matter during the purchase process will pay dividends.

Better Brainstorming

Brainstorming is in the DNA of many marketing operations. It is often the first step in planning and the go-to solution to roadblocks. Brainstorming was first proposed by ad executive Alex Osborn. If you're an advertising history wonk, you may recognize him as the O in BBDO. Osborn saw BBDO through the Great Depression—no small feat—before writing several books on creativity.

Sadly, brainstorming hasn't changed much since Osborn's day. We still gather our team around a conference table and ask everyone to throw out as many ideas as they can, with no regard to feasibility. You can build on ideas, but criticism is strictly *verboten*.

Osborn proposed brainstorming as a way to improve the quality and quantity of ideas produced by groups. That proposition aligns with conventional wisdom: A group of brainstormers will inspire synergy and yield more ideas than isolated individuals. But years of studies have demonstrated the opposite: People ideating independently are more productive than brainstorming groups, in terms of both quality and quantity.[291] As the authors of one research paper on this topic said:

> *"It appears to be particularly difficult to justify brainstorming techniques in terms of any performance outcomes, and the long-lived popularity of brainstorming techniques is unequivocally and substantively misguided."*
> -Productivity Loss in Brainstorming Groups: A Meta-Analytic Integration[292]

We've all been in brainstorming sessions that feel less like a meeting of the minds, and more like fodder for a sitcom script. (The town forums on *Parks and Recreation* come to mind.) It would be logical to assume that unproductive brainstorming sessions are caused by economic factors, such as employees who take advantage of an opportunity to laze about and contribute nothing. But researchers have found that the inefficiency of brainstorming is more related to quirks of the human mind, and these meetings can be productive, if done right.

Preserving Diversity of Thought

Group brainstorming is unproductive because of how our memories work. Cognitive psychologists believe that our brains store information in conceptual networks, where closely related ideas have stronger connections than less-related concepts. This grouping of memories means that when one concept comes to mind, closely related ideas become more accessible.[293] [294] It also means that when someone brings up an idea in a brainstorming session, the others in the group can't help but think along similar lines. This undermines the goal of producing a diverse array of ideas.

The tendency to combine related ideas is harmful during the initial phase of ideation, but, paradoxically, it's an asset later in the process. Research found that as engineers in a group built on each other's ideas, the quality of product solutions improved significantly.[295]

Your team will be more creative and produce better solutions if participants first work alone to come up with new ideas and then come together to share their thoughts. Don't skip meetings; just encourage people to take some time to think and do a little homework first.

Thinking Inside the Box

Brainstorming sessions traditionally welcome wild ideas and encourage people to think outside the box. But this process can feel contrived. We can't sit in the same conference room where we've been trained on billable hours, sexual harassment, and expense-report policies and then pretend to live in a world without constraints. Moreover, we've all been living with constraints since we were children, so we've had plenty of time to get used to a world where our time, budgets, and other resources are limited.

Truth be told, we don't need wild ideas to generate good, creative, and practical solutions. In fact, research on Nobel Prize winners found that their ideas started to flow when they were able to focus on the right question. Based on this insight, McKinsey strategists recommend that we formulate specific questions based on careful consideration of constraints (budget, staffing, timeline, etc.) before we start any ideation session.[296]

Asking the right questions can prime a group for success, leading to ideas that have real impact. If we merely ask, "How can we increase sales?" the resulting ideas will vary widely in terms of quality and feasibility. But if we ask a series of specific, constrained questions like, "Are there any new markets that we haven't explored for our existing services," we will produce more actionable ideas.

Considering the Group Makeup

Smaller groups tend to be more productive because they spend more time ideating and less time waiting to share. This means that large teams should be broken into smaller brainstorming groups, working in parallel. When dividing the groups, consider how the employees like to work and share.

During one college semester, I had a particularly high rate of complaints about group projects. So, for the next project, rather than the usual random grouping, I surreptitiously created groups based on the order in which students turned in assignments. (E.g. People who had consistently turned in assignments early were grouped, as were people who tended to wait until the last minute.)

Complaints plummeted. And, to my surprise, most of the procrastinator groups did well, even without the leadership of a go-getter. I asked one procrastination-prone student how the project went. He said it was the best group project he'd ever had because he had time to really consider his approach, without a bossy student taking over and edging him out. Students were happier with people who shared their approach to getting the work done.

In most workplaces, a handful of people will dominate meetings. Introverts see them as rude because they interrupt and overshadow everyone else, even when they have little to say. Fellow dominant personalities recognize this as "thinking out loud," or as enthusiastic support of their own ideas. McKinsey strategists therefore recommend putting pushy folks in one group so they can build off of each other's ideas without silencing everyone else.[297]

Spurring Innovation with Dissent

Groupthink happens when a group of individuals all agree to an idea without critical consideration of whether it's actually good. Problematically, this logical folly is incentivized by the traditional brainstorming process and our very biology, which makes social conformity more comfortable than conflict.[298]

The idea behind prohibiting criticism during brainstorming sessions was that limiting negativity would reduce the fear of sharing, thereby spurring more ideas and innovation. Researchers disagree.

Experimental research has demonstrated that when brainstorming teams were encouraged to debate and critique ideas, they produced about 20 percent more ideas than teams whose ability to debate was discouraged.[299] The authors noted that debate encourages diverse ideas and stimulates creativity. One theory is that hearing an answer you disagree with forces you to revisit your initial assumptions. It requires you to think about a different perspective which, in turn, spurs new ideas.

Nobody likes the hater that quashes every idea that's not her own, but most of your teammates are probably mature enough to discuss and debate ideas without driving one another to tears. Giving the group permission to debate ideas will enable them to refine their ideas and come up with creative solutions to problems as they emerge.

Knowing When to Start Planning

Imagine that you're attending a concert. You decide to park in a garage near the venue. You arrive early, so you expect to find open spots. You see a spot as you're entering the garage, but you drive past because it might be hard to exit if everyone leaves the concert at the same time. You immediately come upon another spot, but you again decide to drive on because it's all the way across the lot from the elevators. As you come upon the next spot, you notice it's adjacent to one just taken by a teenager. As his friends exit the car, you notice that they don't look very conscientious, so you worry they might ding your doors. You pass a couple of other spots for equally inane reasons but your standards drop as your quest continues. Eventually, as you near the top of the garage and worry that options are running out, you get to a point where you're willing to wedge into any spot you can find, even if it's narrow or far from the elevator.

Homo Economicus, that perfectly logical person who exists only in theory, would either select the first available spot that fit his preferences, or compare all available spots before selecting the best one. But mere humans are more likely to experience a shift in preferences as we go along. We worry that settling too soon could lead us to miss out on a better opportunity in the future. *Then*, we worry that time is running out, and if we don't settle quickly, we won't have any choices at all.

Researchers in Zurich observed behavior like this in simulated appliance and airline purchase scenarios. Early during the tests, consumers wanted to hold out for a good deal, but their willingness to pay increased as the deadline to make a decision approached.[300] (This finding is not out of line with my grandmother's taunt that someone who is too picky in her choice of mate will run out of time and have to settle for "whatever other pathetic, lonely soul is left.")

Of course, the same applies to planning. We want to hold out until there is enough information to make the right plan. Unfortunately, in the context of marketing, that is almost impossible. The team will never have all the insights necessary to make a perfect, failsafe plan. There's an endless amount of information to explore, and the speed of business requires us to make a plan long before we can have confidence that it will succeed.

Unfortunately, the longer we wait to finalize a plan, the higher the cost. If we don't act, competitors will beat us to market, options will be fewer or more costly, and opportunities will pass us by.

Freewill and Opportunity Cost

Accountants think of cost in terms of dollars and cents, but economists think of cost as being relative to the next-best alternative. The question isn't how many dollars, but what you sacrifice if you choose one option over another. If you choose to read for an hour, you sacrifice the opportunity to watch two episodes of your favorite sitcom. If you work full-time, the cost of attending a full-time graduate program isn't only the tuition; it's also the annual salary you'll sacrifice if you quit your job.

One of the biggest mistakes in decision-making is the failure to consider these *opportunity costs*. We see this most often in the workplace when decision-makers fail to recognize that not making a decision is still a decision. (One of my favorite professors explained this idea with lyrics from Rush's *Freewill*.)

Making a choice carries risk, but not making a choice is also a choice. And that can be very costly.

Zero-Sum Bias in Planning

In a zero-sum game, one player's gain is the other's loss, which means that the mathematical sum of benefits is zero. Most sports competitions are zero-sum. When one player or team wins, the other loses. Naturally, this concept applies outside of games. In politics, only one candidate can win an election. Sharing popcorn at the movies is also a zero-sum scenario because each handful I take is a handful you can't have.

Because one player's victory is, by definition, the other player's loss, zero-sum games incentivize competitive behavior. If you're at a party and there's a limited amount of your favorite pizza, your incentive is to grab a slice quickly, lest others take it and leave you hungry. Similarly, if a professor grades tests on a curve, only the best test scores will garner top grades. This means that students will shift their goal from achieving a "good" test score to "beating the curve" (i.e., outperforming their classmates). That's why students who know grades will be curved usually refuse to share notes or otherwise help classmates during group review sessions.

Most Situations Aren't Zero-Sum

Most situations we face are not zero-sum. For example, most professors don't give tests, normalize the scores, and then assign an A to only the top two scores. Usually, professors divide the number of correct answers by the total possible points and then give everyone that earns 90 percent or more an A. In those scenarios, it's possible for every student in the class to earn an A, so all students could benefit from cooperative behaviors. Still, many bright students withhold answers in group review sessions, as though the test is a zero-sum game and as if classmates are competitors. This is the essence of zero-sum bias. Anyone who's spent time in the workplace can confirm that the bias isn't limited to students.

People can be irrationally biased towards zero-sum thinking, behaving as though a situation is zero-sum when it's not. This is a problem. If everyone approaches a situation like it's a zero-sum game, behavior will become excessively competitive or even toxic. That will undermine both group and individual success.

If course grades are assigned according to a curve, and there can be only two As in a given class, then competitive behaviors are appropriate. A student who cares about her grades and finds herself in this situation would logically choose not to participate in a group study session. She would know that her insights might help a classmate outperform her, at the expense of her own GPA. But if grades are assigned according to the percentage of correct answers, a refusal to participate in a group review or otherwise share information would be illogical and asocial. Such behavior would undermine overall learning and would lead others to view the student as rude or excessively competitive, harming both the group and the student.

Similarly, Southwest Airlines used to sell tickets without seat assignments, forcing customers to find a seat on a first-come, first-served basis, like a bus. The infamous "cattle call" created a zero-sum game in which customers had to compete for seats. This led to competitive behaviors, such as line-cutting, spot-saving, and a crush of passengers simultaneously rushing the gate during the boarding announcement. Asocial behaviors such as cutting in front of slower elders or pushing past mothers with toddlers were generally accepted as the norm. Everyone wanted to get the best seat possible. But these same behaviors are less acceptable—even punished—by passengers at any other airline's gate. On flights where people all have seat assignments, a person who didn't assist a grandmother who dropped her purse or elbowed past a mother wrestling a stroller would be subject to harsh judgment. After all, the plane won't take off until everyone in the boarding area is seated--it isn't a zero-sum situation.

Overcoming the Zero-Sum Bias

Many plans are made by committees. Discord in those planning meetings can have consequences that last for longer than they should. In my experience, conflict usually occurs for one of two reasons.

> *First, is the failure to recognize opportunity cost.* In most cases, limited time and resources force us to make decisions before we have enough research to feel confident that a plan will succeed. In the face of uncertainty, we have to make the best call we can, given our knowledge. But some people drag their feet, refusing to recognize that refusal to make a choice *is a choice*, one that carries its own costs.
>
> *Second is zero-sum thinking.* A researcher on the team has spent hours or days with the information, but he believes his insights are being ignored. Someone else in the meeting has a decade of experience in the industry and believes that the plan should be built on the instincts she's developed. Another person, for reasons that remain unclear, is completely confident that his course of action will be the most successful. Each passionately defends his or her stance, acting as though choosing the path forward is a zero-sum game and, if one coworker wins, everyone else loses.

You can't change the reality that people will always debate the merits of a plan, but it's almost always illogical to assume that a situation is zero-sum. Sure, choosing one option means the other options "lose," but it usually doesn't mean the project will certainly fail, or that your department will be eliminated, or that your professional nemesis will be immediately promoted after the boss lays you off.

During a discussion about the challenge of quickly making good decisions when stakeholders can't reach consensus, Amazon CEO Jeff Bezos recommended that they should say, "Look, I know we disagree on this, but will you gamble with me on it? Disagree and commit?"[301] The "disagree and commit" principle is a part of the "leadership principles"[302] that guide all employees at Amazon.

Have Backbone; Disagree and Commit

> Leaders are obligated to respectfully challenge decisions when they disagree, even when doing so is uncomfortable or exhausting. Leaders have conviction and are tenacious. They do not compromise for the sake of social cohesion. Once a decision is determined, they commit wholly.

In other words, you have an obligation to speak up when you disagree. Debate and dissent are valuable during a decision-making process. But once the decision is made, everyone needs to get on board and commit to the project's success.

Zero-sum thinking can lead us to believe that if a coworker's plan wins favor then we've lost and/or the company will fail. An employee with this mindset can sink a team. I've seen this a lot with immature practitioners who sometimes become so passionate about an idea that they become devastated if management doesn't adopt their solution. Then they see every setback along the way as evidence that the management's decision was a mistake. (Note that "immature" here means low emotional intelligence and/or poor business acumen, weaknesses that are not necessarily correlated with age.) The sad irony is that the most knowledgeable and engaged employees tend to be the most passionate about defending their visions. Those employees are true assets when they're happy, but they can be utter liabilities if they refuse to disagree and commit. Their inability to move past zero-sum thinking can lead to endless grousing that undermines managers and kills efficiency.

It Doesn't Matter that Much

Here's the thing about losing The Battle of the Plans: It probably doesn't matter much. Most decisions in marketing planning aren't zero-sum; they just feel that way in the conference room. Some affirmations might help you forge ahead.

- You can't know for certain that one choice is correct.
- A choice today doesn't preclude you from correcting course in six months.
- A lack of budget to execute a new plan doesn't preclude improvements to an existing plan.
- If a client vetoes your favorite idea, it doesn't mean that you won't run any campaign.
- If your worst coworker wins the battle, it doesn't mean that he'll become your manager.

Take the loss with grace and then pivot to helping the team succeed. That will be better for the company and you'll win the respect of your coworkers. Your illogical brain may tell you that the winners take all, but by calmly disagreeing and then committing to being helpful, you will improve your company and, by extension, your career.

When to Get Out

Bad managers sometimes leverage our natural tendency to see everything as a zero-sum situation. They foster competition, rather than encouraging collaboration, because they think it will increase productivity. They are, of course, wrong. Competition tends to undermine productivity, and much ink has been spilled on how the resulting dog-eat-dog culture deters women[303] and contributes to employee burnout.[304]

Because workplaces can be competitive, it's easy to give in to our tendency to think that everything is zero-sum. It's important to rise above that instinct. If your workplace really is zero-sum, and only the winning idea or person is rewarded, then you should get out before you burn out.

No, We Didn't Already Know This: Hindsight Bias in Research and Planning

I briefly mentioned hindsight bias, also known as creeping determinism, earlier in the book. It is the feeling that you were right from the start. After the fact, you believe that you "saw this coming" or "knew it all along." Like the Monday Morning Quarterback who boasts with confidence that he knew that play call wouldn't work, hindsight bias leads you to look back and think, *I knew this would happen* or *I was right all along*. Sometimes, we're right. Sometimes, the brain is giving itself a little too much credit.

There are several levels of this bias. First is memory distortion. This occurs when you inaccurately remember an earlier prediction, leading you to claim, "I told you this would happen!" The second level, inevitability, occurs when, in retrospect, we believe that we thought something was inevitable. At the third level, foreseeability, we believe we could've foreseen an event, leading us to say, "I knew this would happen." Roese and Vohs proposed that key factors of hindsight bias can stack, making us susceptible to hindsight bias on multiple levels at the same time.[305]

Hindsight bias can be a great protector of egos within a marketing organization. The nature of the field can sometimes lead a business to make heavy investments in a single project and, if that project fails, we must face the fact that several leaders signed off on a bad idea. That can shake teams and undermine their confidence in future endeavors. Hindsight bias can protect individuals on a team by protecting egos and, by extension, building confidence and offering comfort in the face of setbacks. (E.g. It's healthier if the team thinks, "We knew the client would mess this great idea up, but we just had to try anyway" than when the team thinks, "We're not very good at marketing.")

Even when no one in the organization is at fault for a flopped campaign, considering the impact of hindsight bias can create valuable learning opportunities that improve processes and outcomes. And failing to recognize hindsight bias can also lead you to skip important steps like research and usability testing.

Experiments

Numerous experiments have explored hindsight bias in a variety of contexts.

Geopolitics

In early experiments on the bias, researchers required participants to predict the likelihood of several outcomes ahead of President Nixon's visit to China. After Nixon's trip, they were asked to reconstruct their predictions. In recalling their initial predictions, participants reported assigning greater likelihood to the events that occurred; that is, they remembered being better at predicting events than they were.[306]

Subjects weren't compensated for accurate predictions, and they knew that the researchers had records of their initial predictions, so there was no reason to lie. Subjects simply thought they were better at predicting events than they were.

The Market

More recently, researchers tested how hindsight bias might play out in a market context. Participants were asked to make predictions about events that had been heavily reported in the media: the weather, sports scores, and the popularity of new movies. Then they were compensated for some of the accurate predictions. The researchers found that participants who earned higher profits from accurate predictions exhibited greater hindsight bias,[307] meaning that they overestimated their performance, even though it was easily measured by outcomes and payments.

Sports Scores

In another study, one group of people was asked to predict the score of a football game before the game while another was asked what they expected the score to be after the game was over. Even after controlling for ego involvement in an individual's knowledge of football, researchers found that the hindsight predictions were more accurate.[308]

The implication is that hindsight bias wasn't related to a desire to seem knowledgeable about football; rather, it reflected information processing biases. The problem wasn't egos. The problem was the human brain!

Celebrity Photos

In experiments on *visual* hindsight bias, researchers presented degraded images of celebrities and asked subjects to identify the celebrities as the images slowly resolved to full clarity. Observers were then surprised with memory tests, which asked them to recall the point at which they could recognize a celebrity.

Other experiments asked observers to begin by looking at normal-resolution images and then look at degraded images. As the degraded images gradually became clear, the participants were asked to stop the resolution process at the point where they thought someone outside the study would be able to identify the faces.

Across these experiments, observers overestimated their abilities and those of their peers once they had knowledge of the images. This occurred even after they received education on how to avoid being biased, and even though there was no incentive to be the first to identify an image.[309] Once they had seen the image, it seems that subjects couldn't ignore their knowledge of what it contained. They couldn't unsee the identity of the celebrity.

These experiments are merely the tip of the iceberg. Researchers from a range of disciplines have considered myriad topics to pinpoint the sources of hindsight bias. There's even one study that correlates situational hindsight bias with handedness.[310]

The common thread across the studies is that we don't realize how biased we are. In processing information, our brains introduce biases that convince us that we're better at predicting outcomes than we are. They make us think that we knew something all along when we didn't.

Application: Improving Insights Operations

There's a delicate balance to managing hindsight bias in a marketing organization. Fragile egos must be protected to maintain the confidence teams need to come up with original ideas. But egos and hindsight bias can be a potent mix that undermines the team's ability to learn from mistakes and produce better work going forward.

To fight hindsight bias, you should force yourself to document expectations before the project begins and then return and review those assumptions when the project is completed. This could mean formally building question identification, hypothesis formulation, and review steps into your research process. This doesn't need to be a time-consuming affair. You can take a few minutes to note the information during a kickoff meeting and then spend a few more minutes to evaluate results after the project. This could lead to behavioral changes that make teams smarter and more effective.

Identify the Real Questions

The scientific method requires that we begin by identifying questions. Applying the method to the early stages of marketing strategy development lays the foundation for productive communications and actionable insights, ultimately improving outcomes. Careful problem identification will help you allocate resources more efficiently and, thus, reduce the time that you must wait for answers.

"A problem well-stated is half-solved."
-Charles Kettering, head of research at GM

Research projects should generally begin with two questions: (1) What information do you need? (2) How will the information be used?

Be sure you have answers to both questions before you dedicate time or resources to the project. If you can't identify how the information you'll gather will contribute to outcomes, you'll end up amassing clutter that will obscure the actionable insights.

Formulate a Hypothesis

In science, a hypothesis is a theory that is formulated and then proven or disproven by research. In statistics, it tends to be a statement describing a population, which analysis of a sample proves or disproves. In this context, the hypothesis only needs to answer a single question: "What do we think the research will tell us?"

Your hypotheses will depend on your research question(s), but it could sound like these:

- We think the most important customer segment is baby boomers who have diabetes.
- This customer is frequently on Instagram, but she never watches TV.
- Our customers are switching to competitors because they believe our customer service is poor.
- Green juice drinkers care more about heart health than looking slim.

For marketing projects, we don't need to worry about the level of formality that would be required in scientific research. But forcing your team to consider their expectations and assumptions as they begin the research will lead them to refine and rethink their questions. It will spark conversations about how potential outcomes may lead to different actions. Furthermore, this process will foster a culture of deep thinking that can only benefit your business and customers.

The After-Action Review

After the launch, champagne, and numbers, make time for an honest postmortem review, or after-action review. This is a structured debriefing of what went well, what didn't, and why.

There's always something more urgent, but this is important. A thirty-minute meeting should give you time to think about the following:

1. What were our expectations going in?
    - What did we know about the customer or client?
    - What did we expect to learn?
    - What strategy did we expect to work?
2. Were we right?
    - What were we right about?
    - What were we wrong about?
3. Did we learn things along the way that changed our strategy?

The first two questions help us overcome hindsight bias. The final question helps us to turn the pain of facing our shortcomings into an investment in the future of our organization.

Don't get drawn into lazy postmortems
How many times have you heard one of these statements after the project finally shipped?

- We knew where this needed to go from the beginning, but we had to get the client on board.
- We all understood the target from day one, but we had to work through the process to appease the project managers and clients.
- We knew what we were doing from the start, but we got into the weeds and needed to circle back to our true north.

This is such a great story! Maybe it's true, but in my experience, that type of tale is more often a raging case of hindsight bias that discounts a lot of learning along the way.

Agencies also tend to dedicate staff to specific accounts, which enables those teams to build strong expertise, much like the expertise people build after working for the same brand for a number of years. Experienced marketers often have deep understandings of their audiences. Still, when boastful higher-ups try to build up their teams with claims that they were "right all along," everyone is already biased to believe them. That's incredibly dangerous because it supports the belief that research is a mere formality, not an essential part of marketing planning.

As agencies struggle to meet twenty-first-century needs, research is continually a target of budget cuts. Subscriptions and skilled researchers are expensive so they're tempting to cut, especially if companies think they instinctively understand the customer and therefore don't need research anyway.

Perhaps this combination of bias and necessity has fueled a viral spread of the idea that we can rely on instinct rather than research. I know of one top-tier agency that routinely sent account planners to intercept people on the street and in the grocery store to strike up conversations about products. They refer to this as a legitimate, standalone research methodology. This approach has a name, that name appears on slide decks in client presentations, and findings have been the sole drivers behind strategies for campaigns. This is the stuff of nightmares for trained researchers the world over. If these practices are not stopped, we will continue to see weak marketing strategies.

Taking the time to thoroughly evaluate how goals, assumptions, and strategies might have shifted over the course of a project will help you overcome your hindsight bias, making your marketing organization smarter and more effective. Don't be afraid to admit that you didn't know all along; it's a hit to the ego, but it will make you more successful in the future. And don't be the manager who claims that your team knew all along; that will undermine the quality of future work, and it will inflate some egos at the expense of the vigilant truth-seekers that could grow your business.

Anticipating the Future: Why We're Just Awful at It.

Our forecasts about the future are heavily, irrationally influenced by our perceptions of the present. This can be described as an empathy gap because, in the current moment, it's hard to imagine feeling differently in the future. To become better at planning for the future and reacting to changes, we must recognize that our minds tend to be prisoners of the moment and plan accordingly.

Projection Bias and New Year's Resolutions

Imagine that it's January. Your pants are too tight, and you think you might be sick if you see another holiday cookie. You join the millions of optimists who decide to drop the holiday weight and, within days, you've purchased five pounds of lettuce and boxes of protein bars from the local warehouse store. After the first week of what feels like utter starvation, you've lost a couple of pounds.

Fast forward to February. You've inched closer to your goal weight, but motivation is waning and you're feeling increasingly open to the idea of trading your soul for a slice of cake. What's more, if you see another salad or protein bar, you might break down in tears.

Back in January, as you stood before shelves of protein bars while painfully aware of the waistband digging into your stomach, you planned to clean up your diet for at least a couple of months. Maybe even long enough to get back to your high school weight. But your

January self had experienced what behavioral economists call an "empathy gap" with your February self. In January, you had been projecting your feelings onto your future self, expecting that you'd always feel the way you did in January. Motivated to lose weight, you had been happy to trade your usual culinary pleasures for salad and protein bars. It didn't occur to you that by February, at the very least, you might be ready for a new flavor.

Maybe you haven't turned to protein bars or to New Year's resolution diets, but you've probably experienced a problem with projection bias before. Perhaps you've gone to the grocery store hungry and wound up with more food than you should have because, in your hungry state, you overestimated how much food you'd need later. Or maybe you've overspent on an item of clothing that you expected to frequently wear. Maybe you loved the 2020 edition of a game so much that you bought the 2021 game the day it released, only to find that you hadn't played that 2021 game when preorders opened for the 2022 release. In each case, the issue is that we tend to project our current state of being as we try to anticipate the future, and this can undermine our ability to make good plans.

Projection Bias: Not Only for the Small Stuff

You may expect people to buy more snacks when they're hungry or visualize a life of healthy eating when they're feeling bloated and overdosed on cookies. But projection bias doesn't just sneak in on low-consideration purchases. Vehicles are major expenses for most people, so we would expect them to be the sort of high-consideration purchase that's shielded from emotions and impulses. But researchers have found that abnormally sunny days during the winter lead to increases in convertible sales, and purchases of four-wheel-drive vehicles are higher during snowstorms.[311]

Projection bias can have big impacts on a business' bottom line because it leads us to expect that both the business and the macroenvironment will continue unchanged, which is not a reasonable expectation. Consider some of these infamous predictions:

- o The President of the Michigan Savings Bank told Henry Ford's lawyer not to invest in the Ford Motor Company because, "The horse is here to stay but the automobile is only a novelty – a fad."[312]
- o Oxford professor Erasmus Wilson said, "When the Paris Exhibition [of 1878] closes, electric light will close with it and no more will be heard of it."[313]
- o Darryl Zanuck, a studio executive at Twentieth Century Fox once said, "Television won't be able to hold on to any market it captures after the first six months. People will soon get tired of staring at a plywood box every night."[314]
- o The chairman of IBM said in 1943, "I think there is a world market for maybe five computers."[315]

These people weren't uniquely ignorant or out of touch with trends. To the contrary, their positions alone indicate that they were all deeply knowledgeable about their fields. They were looking at markets and projecting their current views onto the future, without complete information about what the future would bring.

Adding Optimism Bias to the Mix

Optimism bias is precisely what it sounds like: people tend to be irrationally optimistic about the future and think we're less likely to have negative experiences than we are. This has been shown to impact expectations in every area of our lives. People expect to live longer than is probable; we underestimate our likelihood of getting divorced; we overestimate the career success we'll see; and we believe our children are more talented than average.[316] Don't feel bad, though; optimism bias has even been observed in birds and mice.[317]

Optimism bias can lead us to overestimate the likelihood that our projects will succeed and underestimate the likelihood of failure. This bias, combined with projection bias, results in irrationally positive expectations for the future. You probably see this at work all the time: A company has a couple of huge wins in January and the CEO announces that you'll shatter revenue goals. Or, a project manager oversees the flawless completion of the first phase of a project and proclaims, "At this rate, we should deliver two months ahead of schedule!" Your CEO and PM might not be wrong, but their observations about the current state and their optimism that this good fortune will continue are heavily influencing their expectations for the future.

This doesn't mean you should become a pessimist. Scientists believe that optimism is vital to mental and physical health.[318] But you should wield it carefully. Use it to build morale or justify bonuses, but don't let it guide you as you set deadlines and future expectations. A little too much optimism can become a big problem if fortune turns against you.

Application: Making Better Plans

Good planning is predicated on our ability to break free of our tendency to be prisoners of the moment. Overcoming the obstacles of projection bias and optimism bias in planning requires us to recognize that they could be impacting your teams without their knowledge. Our brains are wired to project today's state onto expectations for the future and healthy brains err on the side of optimism. Optimism isn't an attitude you want to train away, but a good plan will take this wiring into account from the outset.

To overcome innate biases and make better plans:

1. Recognize that cognitive biases are natural and be mindful of their effects as you begin planning.
2. Conduct an honest evaluation of your current situation.
3. Create plans for multiple contingencies.

Recognize the Biases

Making inferences based on our experiences is critical to survival. This was as true when we were cave dwellers as it is in the modern office. Our brains help us with that, but there's a cost. It's not possible to imagine the future without using the past as a frame of reference. In fact, neuroscientists have demonstrated that when we visualize the future, we access the same part of our brains that handles memories. So, the first step to being prepared for the future is to recognize that we don't live in a vacuum, and that we can't be completely objective when making plans.

Think about the current factors that might be coloring your outlook.

- Is the team feeling optimistic because it has experienced a big win? If so, do you have reason to expect another win?
- Are you feeling productive because you've completed a lot of small tasks? If so, are upcoming tasks equally straightforward?
- Is the team feeling overwhelmed by a large project, but failing to realize that the subsequent tasks will be easier?
- Is the company benefitting from macroeconomic factors beyond your control that may change in the coming months?

Great managers know how to leverage the high of a big win to motivate a team. But great planners can recognize that productivity ebbs and flows, and factors beyond our immediate control can impact long-term plans. The goal should be to temper expectations without undermining morale.

Merits of the Painfully Honest Analysis

Next, take an objective look at your current situation. What macroeconomic factors are impacting your business? How are your customers changing? How does your planning process fit within the company's broader plans?

For smaller projects and weekly planning, it will probably suffice to informally consider factors within the company and the macroenvironment. But for projects with lasting impacts, I prefer a more formal approach, like the 5Cs and/or the SWOT.

Note on 5C Analysis

If you went to business school, you probably wrote a few 5C analyses, and for good reason. This is the gold standard for analyzing the market environment. It can serve as a part of a marketing plan or as a standalone effort. Either way, working through each section forces you to think through internal, micro, and macroenvironmental factors that are impacting your business.

As you conduct the analysis, be mindful of both irrational exuberance and the instinct to project today's status forward. People tasked with these analyses often feel compelled to balance positive and negative observations or, worse, they try to say only positive things about their brand and only negative things about competitors. The pats on the back may feel nice, but this isn't valuable information.

To add value, you need to take an honest look at where competitors are shining and where you're weak. It will hurt, and telling executives that their baby is ugly is a delicate situation that requires nuance. But an honest, analytical approach will help you enumerate the threats to your brand and the advantages that you can leverage to fight them.

Note on SWOT Analysis
Another example from the Business School Greatest Hits album is the SWOT analysis. This approach asks you to consider current strengths and weaknesses alongside opportunities and threats that could impact the future of your business. SWOT analysis can be a part of a marketing plan, or part of a larger situation analysis, or it can stand alone. A quick SWOT is always a solid gut check when you're planning a midsize project, one that requires some formal consideration but isn't big enough to justify a larger analysis.

Note that for a SWOT analysis to be valuable, it must be actionable—we need the "so what." To refine the analysis into organizational implications that are truly actionable:

- o Combine strengths and opportunities to identify key leverage points that your company can use to win in the marketplace. For example: To win, we must engage consumers at major life stages such as moving or becoming parents.
- o Combine weaknesses and threats to identify the external threats that you're not ready to face. Something like, "to avoid loss of share, we must improve customer satisfaction and improve our product's efficiency."

Final Word on Formal Analyses
The 5C and SWOT frameworks are valuable tools because they guide you through the consideration of a situation from multiple angles. More importantly, familiar frameworks like these enable you to get right into the content of your reviews without having to justify the approach.

These are comfortable, time-tested approaches that are a good default when you have time, but this level of analysis can be overkill for some projects. By adhering to a formal framework, you force yourself to cover each bullet point even if it's not directly relevant to the project, which can cause you to sacrifice time that could be spent on critical issues.

Whatever approach you choose to conduct the analysis, bring it full circle by connecting conclusions with recommendations to ensure that you deliver actionable information, not just inbox fodder. Many analysts stop short of making recommendations because they prefer to stick with concrete, provable data. But nobody is better positioned to make recommendations than the analyst who has spent twenty hours analyzing a situation. The recommendations are the "so what" that makes your report useful to others, so don't skip them!

Case: Shell Plans for Anything

After considering how today's point of view may be creating bias as you look ahead, and then completing an appropriately in-depth analysis of the current state, you should go through the exercise of planning for a variety of scenarios.

Since the early 1970s, Shell has made a practice of asking "what if?" Then the company develops possible visions for the future to help executives prepare. These "Shell Scenarios" are essentially predictions of various futures that force leaders to think through how they should act in different situations. This ensures that executives are better prepared to adapt as different situations arise. And the company says the approach works.

> *"The sheer breadth and depth of perspective gained from our scenarios continues to inspire many successful partnerships and initiatives around the world, on individual country levels as well as regional and global."*[319]

In each scenario, Shell begins by analyzing macroenvironmental factors like demographic changes and changes in technology. It then considers how these changes could impact behaviors and attitudes. Next, analysts think through how these factors could impact economies and verticals as they develop models of specific situations that the company may need to respond to. Scenarios become business plans, publications on the website, and most importantly, tools to help key decision-makers prepare for the future.

In one set of scenarios, Shell looked at the 2015 Paris Agreement, demographics, politics, the economy, and other factors in Germany to map out two scenarios that could unfold as the country transitioned to more efficient, greener energy.[320] In another scenario, Shell worked with UNAIDS to build predictions of how AIDS could spread through Africa, and how the company could assist the UN and others in optimizing responses.[321]

By forcing itself to think through "what ifs," Shell forces strategists out of the comfort of projection biases and into the challenge of agile planning.

Framing for Internal Decision-Making

Frames are one of the many ways our minds seek to make sense of the glut of information we take in but, by distorting our perceptions of information, the frameworks we choose can distort our decisions. This is advantageous for the marketer who's able to get prospective customers to view his products in the proper light, but you also need to be careful to remain conscious of how you're framing the information you consume.

Sometimes, marketers can get so wrapped up in our own narratives that it's easy to slip into justifying sub-optimal behaviors. For example, we can become so accustomed to the same frame of reference and competitive set that we can lose objectivity and miss opportunities for strategic realignment. Or, just as an employee can justify stealing supplies from the office because he feels he's a hard worker, marketers can come to believe in the brand to the point that they can feel justified in employing deceptive practices, thinking the business deserves it.

We must remain vigilant about questioning our practices and biases, making sure that we consider how they might impact others and whether others might perceive our messages and actions to be unethical.

Reframing and the Challenger Launch

Framing can seem to be self-evident, even easy to ignore. As children, we intuitively offer only the best points to a teacher or parent when trying to win permission or privileges. We've seen a lifetime of ads that show only the upsides of products. We emphasize benefits over costs to win raises and budget increases. But framing effects can be incredibly subtle—and incredibly pervasive. Functional MRI studies demonstrate that our brains are highly susceptible to framing effects. I submit that framing errors can lead to egregious decision errors, even by intelligent people. The disastrous end to the *Challenger* space shuttle is a good case in point.

364 | Science, Not Sorcery

Once they heard how cold it would be on the morning of January 28, 1986, engineers at Morton Thiokol Incorporated (MTI) were unanimously opposed to launching the shuttle. They hadn't tested their O-rings at temperatures that low and so they didn't know if the rings would perform properly. After intense pushback from NASA, which was under immense pressure from the government, the head of engineering at MTI was asked by his manager to revisit the engineers' recommendation to postpone the launch. More specifically, he was asked to "take off his engineering hat and put on his management hat."[322][323] In doing so, the lead engineer ended up changing his mind and signing off. NASA went ahead with the launch, and the Challenger exploded just over a minute after liftoff, killing everyone on board.

Later that year, as he testified before the Senate subcommittee, the engineer was asked, "How do you explain the fact that you seemed to change your mind when you changed your hat?" He explained that, in retrospect, he had always been in the position of proving that the components were ready for space flight. That day, he had to prove that they weren't ... and he couldn't.[324]

As the head of engineering, his job had been to prove MTI was ready for launch. When he and his team couldn't prove they were ready because they didn't have data to show the O-rings could stand up, they wouldn't sign off. When the engineer's manager forced him to change perspectives, the manager reframed the task from proving they *were* ready to proving they *were not* ready. In the absence of data, the engineers couldn't prove the O-rings *wouldn't* hold up, so they were unable to definitively prove that they were not ready.

Many held this engineering VP to be partly responsible for the disaster. But it should also be argued that when, under pressure from NASA and the government, his manager reframed the question, it all but forced the engineer manager to sign off.

This story means that when you encourage employees to think like managers, you will reduce the diversity of thought behind decisions, which is never good. Put another way, we should consider both how we can increase revenue, and how our efforts might look when presented by an angry blogger or before a Senate subcommittee.

Planning Opportunity: Form a Red Team

As marketers, we don't find ourselves in a lot of life-or-death situations at work. But we should be aware that the way we frame information can have a profound effect on how our customers and teams behave. Sometimes we can get swept up in the excitement of our campaigns, becoming so emotionally attached to our messages and proud of our creative work that we can become blind to errors in execution or judgment.

To combat biases towards our work, we must make conscious efforts to flip questions and identify potential downsides of our strategies. To accomplish this, we can establish a "red team," a team of people who are not involved with the work and whose purpose is to identify holes in our logic. Branches of the US military use red teams in wargaming. These teams emulate adversaries to help leaders identify holes in defenses or tactical executions. The Department of Defense, Microsoft, IBM, and others employ cyber red teams to identify security vulnerabilities. In pop culture, HBO's *The Newsroom* portrayed a group of reporters presenting a big story to a red team of colleagues who were intentionally left out of the loop so they could objectively identify holes in a story or problems with sources.

Internal red teams can be extremely valuable. They share goals and culture of the company, but by remaining out of the project loop, they retain objectivity. Pitching major campaigns internally will add an extra gut check, which can reduce the odds of embarrassment or soothe nerves when campaigns are edgy or unique. These double-checks can be good investments when marketing efforts are expensive, rushed, or involve a difficult client.

Management Imperative: Align Incentives by Reframing

Sometimes small companies want to hire employees at startup wages and, in exchange, they ask for around-the-clock commitment. When they can't find anyone qualified who's willing to work seventy hours a week for peanuts, they lament the "poor work ethic" of an entire generation. These business owners don't seem to realize that they're asking employees to suffer all the downsides of startup life (long hours, low pay) without any upside (strategic control, a significant ownership share, payday if it sells).

You see the same thing at occur at large companies. The leadership hopes to incentivize managers to behave in the company's best interest with perks like stock options that tie compensation to the company's performance. But, when stock incentives are tiny relative to salaries, the possibility of a fractional increase in stock value isn't enough to deter the manager from expensing overpriced lunches and upgrading his seats on flights.

If you want employees to behave in the company's best interests, it will be more effective to tweak incentives than to micromanage. Counterintuitively, you can't expect people to always respond to the right incentives, even when it's in their own best interests. This means that, to tweak behavior, you need to understand the employee's frame of mind.

Goal Framing at Work

If you consider the workplace from a goal framing perspective, you can see how employees are simultaneously balancing multiple goals. Normative framing encourages people to think of the company's good first, then to behave in a manner that's optimal for the company or workgroup. This could mean reducing waste, increasing profitability, or generally doing their best to create a more pleasant and collaborative workplace environment. Gain framing for most employees involves keeping a job, getting a raise, or winning a promotion. Hedonic goals, all about feeling good, will likely lead to reducing effort, having fun, and expensing a nice lunch out.

Employers generally approach employees with a carrot and a stick, believing that stock incentives and the looming threat of being fired should align employee behavior with company goals. Problematically, employees often have a murky view of why someone else was fired, and incentives tend to be weak. The promise of a Christmas ham or a small allotment of stock options is not going to motivate employees to inconvenience themselves for the good of the company or fully deter delinquent behavior, such as ordering the steak instead of the pasta at a company-sponsored luncheon.

At the other end of the spectrum are companies with laid-back cultures that pay above-market wages, offer perks like catered lunches and onsite arcades, and encourage employees to work when they feel inspired. These companies hope that these kindnesses will lead employees to care more about the good of the company. But, thanks to hedonic- and gains-oriented goal framing and hedonic adaptation, employees become used to the incentives and still want more. Worse, these environments can attract immature types and demotivate productive employees who become frustrated when the company rewards slackers. This explains why companies tend to outgrow this carrot-only approach to motivation.

Identity and Goal Frames Outweigh Incentives and Deterrents

Guilt trips and threats of firing won't be effective deterrents to bad behavior, for a few reasons. First, people can commit dishonest acts, like time theft or unethical expensing, and still see themselves as honest, good employees.[325] They won't be concerned with the threat that thieves will be fired, as they'll view that as a punishment for the bad employees with whom they don't identify.

Adding to that problem, people are constantly balancing a mix of goals and conflicting priorities. They may be fully aware that it's in their long-term best interest to keep the company afloat, but the hedonic drivers to slack off and have fun are stronger drivers of behavior in the moment. Further, hedonic adaptation to stagnant salaries and the pressure to show forward momentum on resumes can lead intelligent employees to prioritize gains-oriented goals over the long-term health of the company. After all, the company's fortune isn't relevant to an employee who has been downsized, and American employees are well aware of how abruptly they can be cut loose. They know it's smarter to focus on continued employability than to put all of their efforts into building a single company.

This presents a challenge for top managers. Employee satisfaction is tied to autonomy and respect for management, both of which would be undermined by micromanagement that attempts to quash efforts towards hedonic goals (e.g., perusing Facebook or playing Minesweeper on the clock). Even more importantly, the paths to achieving gains goals, like raises and promotions, are often more about appeasing the immediate manager than aiding the broader company mission. Few people outside of movies have been promoted for doing what's best for the company if it makes their immediate manager look stupid or incompetent. You're far more likely to see a raise for *appeasing* your manager, even if you know his goals run counter to the long-term health of the company. Even the highest-level executives can face far heavier incentives to achieve quarterly KPIs than to think about the five-year health of the company or shareholder gains. (Executive compensation packages comprise far more value in salary and bonuses than stock allocations, so meeting short-term KPIs is a stronger behavioral driver than focusing on long-term value for shareholders.)

Aligning Incentives

A more effective way to convince employees to behave in the company's best interest would be to align normative, gain, and hedonic goals so that the goal at the forefront of the employee's mind is also the company's priority.[326] The leader who understands the conflicting goals faced by his employees, and who works to align individual incentives around what's also best for the company, will see lasting benefits.

First, ensure that the normative goals are clear and well-supported by executives. After all, when employees see others disregarding the greater good, they're more apt to ignore the rules themselves.[327]

Next, provide hedonic and gain rewards for achievements in service of normative goals. To do this, you must understand your employees well enough to know what motivates them. For instance, if your employees are not a bunch of high school-age friends, then you can assume that they're not motivated by the prospect of a pizza party or company retreat with "fun teambuilding opportunities." They want money, promotions, and time for personal pursuits, not more time with coworkers. More effective hedonic rewards could include a better working environment, upgraded workspaces, or additional PTO. Gain-oriented rewards could include promotions, bonuses, or other opportunities. Importantly, though, messaging should emphasize that these perks are designed to show your appreciation for employees' commitment to the greater good; they are not goals in and of themselves. To nudge people to behave normatively, the emphasis must be on the greater good and the shared benefit for all at the company, not individual gain. Talk of individual gain will shift the employee's goal frame and, therefore, his behavior.

Similarly, when rules and sanctions have relatively low levels of punishment but seem like they're for the good of the group, people will comply. If those same rules and punishments seem like they're more related to private gain, people will be less willing to cooperate.[328] One of my employers asked employees to enter the company's frequent flyer account numbers instead of our personal numbers when we booked flights. The idea was that the company would amass those rewards to give executives more comfortable flights and/or additional opportunities to manage us in person. Based on the chatter I heard around the office after that announcement, I don't think *anyone* complied. A far more effective approach would've been to ask for something that mattered (e.g., nearly anything but seat upgrades for executives that could afford to upgrade themselves) and then emphasize that, if we all complied, it would benefit the company in a tangible way. For instance, the company could've asked that choose less-expensive lunches or trade conference attendance for online learning for one year, to reduce expenses and stave off layoffs.

Your task as a manager is to figure out how to align divergent goals while framing the greater good in a manner that appeals to employees. The approach should vary with the goal, but there are many scenarios when goals can be aligned. Training opportunities serve the employee's goal of advancement and benefit the company. Bonuses for achieving specific KPIs ensure everyone is working towards the same priorities. Fostering a more comfortable environment where praise is shared and employees feel like they matter will encourage collaboration and increase productivity compared with a competitive environment which will hinder long-term workplace efficiency.

Cutting Your Losses

If we ever hope to get anything done, we need to stick with what we've started. Fortunately, our brains come equipped with a few ways to help us stay committed. But these assets can become liabilities when circumstances change.

When we're heavily invested in something—financially, emotionally, or otherwise—it's hard to cut our losses and walk away. But sometimes the information, situation, or marketplace changes mean that the path we've been on no longer makes sense. Several cognitive biases and logical fallacies lead us to believe we should see our ideas through, but that instinct isn't always one we should follow.

The Sunk Cost Effect

In economics, a sunk cost is one that has already been incurred and can't be recovered. Once the money is spent, it's illogical to include that cost as a factor in making decisions about the future. But people tend to give sunk costs heavy consideration when making decisions.

Let's say you paid $100 for a ticket to an outdoor concert. At the time of purchase, you were excited about spending a summer night at a concert with friends. But, on the day of the concert, the weather became so bad that your friends decide not to go. It's too late to sell the ticket. What should you do? Some might say that you'd be wasting the $100 if you didn't go. But an economist would remind you that you've already spent the $100, there's nothing you can do to get it back, and so that expenditure shouldn't have any bearing on your decision. The choice is whether you'd prefer to attend the concert in bad weather or stay home.

This seems straightforward enough, but people fail to consider sunk costs all the time. In a 2017 blog post, online clothing reseller ThredUp wrote:

In the age of [fast] fashion and retailers who restock racks with new trends every week, the biggest issue we face isn't fashion fomo—it's #throwmo, the fear of throwing out.[329]

The company's research found that, on average, women only wear 20 percent of the items in their closets, but they're hesitant to get rid of the other 80 percent. Clearly, these women are holding onto items they don't really like, but they still don't want to donate the clothing because they had spent so much to acquire it. It feels painful to resell the clothing because they know the resale value will be far lower than the purchase price. But holding on to clothing you don't want because you couldn't recover the purchase price is irrational. The initial purchase price cannot be recovered and therefore shouldn't influence the decision of what to do with the clothing. The real decision is whether to keep the jeans, donate them, or sell them for a few dollars.

Here's another example. Imagine that you had taken out $90,000 in loans to get a BS and MBA and then spent ten years in the workforce. At that point, you were promoted to Marketing Director at a prominent company. Soon after the promotion, a friend introduces you to Steven Spielberg. You really hit it off and, based on your deep knowledge of obscure Celtic archaeology, he offers you a job as a consultant on a new series he's producing. Should you take the job?

That was a trick question. I gave you a bunch of sunk costs—time and money that are already gone—but none of the information you need to make the decision. For this decision, you don't need to tally up the sunk costs, you need to know which job has the higher salary, which job you would enjoy more, where each job is located, etc.

Arnold Kim has a story like this. He spent hundreds of thousands of dollars and years becoming a surgeon, but he ended up quitting surgery to focus on his blog, Mac Rumors. When he made that decision, he ignored the time and money he had put into becoming a surgeon and, logically, considered which of the two careers would be best for his needs going forward.

The sunk cost effect leads people to continue working toward a goal even when it's no longer the right choice. New experimental research finds that there's also an interpersonal effect at play, too: People illogically take sunk costs into account when making decisions, even when the costs were incurred by someone else, and even when the costs were incurred by someone who wasn't a close friend or relative.[330]

Adding Loss Aversion, Endowment Effect, and Ziegarnik Effect

In addition to struggles with the sunk-cost effect, another trio of biases makes it even more difficult to abandon a task. Loss-aversion effects mean we're hardwired to hate loss, even to the point of taking irrational steps to avoid it. The endowment effect leads us to value something more than it's worth; that is, to think something is worth more just because it's ours. This can lead managers to feel a strong sense of ownership of projects when those projects should be delegated to others. It can lead intelligent workers to overcommit to projects that have become obsolete. And the Ziegarnik effect means that incomplete tasks will stick in our minds more than tasks we've completed. All combined, this trio of cognitive biases might explain why you find it so hard to switch directions before a project is complete.

Without these biases, we'd never get anything done. We'd abandon projects easily or lose our commitment to seeing them through, so they're not wholly destructive. But they do lead us to hold onto plans and projects longer than we should. It can be incredibly difficult to walk away from a project you've invested time and effort in and, problematically, the more engaged an employee is, the more difficult it will be to pry him away from a project if priorities change.[331] This can lead valuable team members to toil endlessly on low-priorities and obsolete tasks instead of forging ahead.

Overcoming Bias and Leaving the Past Behind

The key to overcoming these biases is to recognize that what's done is done. You can't recover what you've already invested in a project, but you can decide to move forward with the best possible option. Anticipating these biases will serve you well as you plan.

Set Performance "Trip Wires"

When guides take climbers up Everest, they often set a hard deadline in advance. If the group fails to reach the specified point by the set time, the group will head back down. No matter how close the summit is, no matter the extenuating circumstances, the group agrees that they will reverse course if the goal isn't met by the specified time.

A marketing organization should do the same thing. Fair or otherwise, we're all subject to KPIs. Opening the project with an enumeration of KPIs and a hard date on which you'll review performance and kill the project if they're not met will ensure that everyone is committed to the review from the outset.

When that date comes, if you haven't met your objectives, you should take an honest look at what could be holding you back. There could've been an external force that prevented the work from progressing and a simple extension will ensure progress. Or maybe it's time to start considering alternatives.

A/B, A/B, A/B

A great way to test a hypothesis in isolation is an A/B test. This is a test in which some consumers are shown one version of the creative and others are shown a second version. Then you can compare how they perform. Ideally, you would only use this sort of testing for individual changes, so that you're sure that you can attribute performance differences to the individual attribute in question.

The process is straightforward:

1. Develop a hypothesis, such as, "The new placement of the 'buy' button will increase conversions."
2. Test the hypothesis by exposing some of a sample to the new or "test" experience and some to the original or "control" experience. For example, half of the website's visitors could randomly be served a version of the product page with the new 'buy' button placement, while the other half sees the original page.
3. Compare and conclude.

The Netflix TechBlog has some articles about the company's practice of A/B testing everything from minor tweaks to artwork for movies.[332] In one test, Netflix randomly exposed members to one of three images (the original and two alternates). They found that they could increase engagement with the title by changing the image. But that begged the question: Did they simply draw more attention to that individual title, or was the better artwork increasing streaming hours? [333]

The team ran similar tests on more titles, with the hypothesis that they could increase overall streaming hours with improved artwork. The team tested multiple versions of "box" art for the selected movies and TV shows. Then they displayed the most successful artwork. The details of the experiments are on the blog, but the major takeaway is that Netflix was able to significantly increase engagement with tested titles *and* overall streaming hours by changing the artwork.

Simple, clear experiments tend to yield simple, clear answers. And definitive proof is often what we need to break the hold that our biases have on us so that we can move forward with clear eyes.

Test Early

In the previous example, Netflix tested artwork on customers, so the product under scrutiny had to be complete and polished. Wherever possible, though, we should test early. Because teams struggle to ignore sunk costs and become irrationally attached to their projects, we should expect it to become increasingly challenging to abandon projects as the time put into them increases. We can't completely prevent a team's disappointment and continued discussion of an abandoned project, but the earlier we can cut ties with a project, the easier it will be for the people involved.

Test early and often. It's usually cheaper to pause, assess, and abandon a weak prototype than to continue sinking resources into a product that's going to flop.

Emphasize the Shiny and New

Often, a project needs to be abandoned because something has changed. Research or experimentation can produce new insights that change the customer's view. Top management's priorities might change. The macroenvironment could change and, with it, consumer preferences.

Regardless of the reasons, when a project becomes obsolete, you should help the team to avoid thinking that their time was wasted. You should remind them about the reasons for the change and help them to focus on the new information that forced you to revise the plan. That will help you and your team shift gears without feeling ineffectual.

As you plan for the path forward, allow yourself (or your team) the freedom to fall down the rabbit hole a bit in initial conversations. The more discussion you have around the new idea, the more mentally engaged the team will become with it, leading the very biases that made it hard to abandon the old plan to strengthen the team's commitment to the new plan.

Focus on What You Can Change

Many obstacles to research and planning are beyond our control: oppressively tight budgets, slow approvals processes, insufficient staff. Still, whether you're trying to wade through the murky waters of a giant bureaucracy or building a marketing plan from scratch on your own, many of the biggest challenges are the result of biased thinking. This is a great place to focus your efforts because it's addressable. What's more, your closest competitors are probably held back by the same challenges that are plaguing you, so overcoming biased thinking to create better plans will give you an edge.

In Closing

With knowledge of biases that lead to irrational thinking, we can move forward with a heightened awareness that will, ultimately, debias our brains and lead us to lives of rational, unbiased thinking, right? Sorry ... the research indicates that awareness of bias isn't enough to fully debias your decisions.[334] Awareness is a great first step, but you'll be better served by accepting cognitive bias as a part of human life and then planning for it. Try to take advantage of it where you can, finding comfort in the upsides of overconfidence, perhaps. Then, build checks and balances into your process. Research, conceptualize, launch, analyze, rinse, repeat.

In one of his fantastic Ted Talks, behavioral economist Dan Ariely uses optical illusions as a metaphor for cognitive bias.[335] He points out that we use our eyes more than any other sense, so they're theoretically trustworthy. Still, our eyes deceive us in consistent and predictable ways. Ariely points to classic optical illusions, like the Rubik's Cube-meets-Mondrian image. Two blocks of color look different until the rest of the image is removed. Then it becomes obvious that the blocks are the same color. But even after you've seen the two blocks and registered that they're the same color, the moment the full image is restored, your brain goes back to telling you the colors are different.

Unfortunately, our cognitive processes aren't much more dependable than our vision. Why should they be? As Ariely points out, a huge part of our brain is dedicated to vision, which we use all the time. Why would we expect to be any better at things we're less practiced at, like planning a campaign or choosing a peanut butter?

Still, awareness is a critical first step. With an awareness of classic reasoning failures, you can build safeguards into your processes and enjoy an improved understanding of your customers. These will, in turn, yield more effective marketing strategies that edge out competitors and grow your business.

Applying behavioral science to marketing means considering the incentives, deterrents, and biases that are impacting behaviors and then considering how you could change the choice architecture to achieve your desired outcome. Framing your customer's behaviors as reactions to your choice architecture is critical for business growth. When you step back from your own experiences and consider why people are behaving the way that they are (without judgment), it can lead to insights that impact every facet of your business.

Integrating behavioral economics into marketing work can look like sorcery from afar, but like any other science, it only looks like magic until you study it. And, like any other science, it requires a scientific approach that includes careful problem definition, research, experimentation, and an unbiased critique of outcomes.

You could, theoretically, exploit the biases in this book to market unethical or damaging products, but it's my assumption that the intellectual sort who reads about behavioral economics recreationally will not try to "nudge for evil." You folks have a world of employment opportunities available to you that don't require you to engage in unethical behavior. And one upside of our connected culture is that bad actors—practitioners of dark magic, if you will—tend to be discovered and punished.

References

Aaker, J. (1997). Dimensions of Brand Personality. Journal of Marketing Research, 347-356.

Aarons, W. (2007, February 6). An Open Letter to Mr. James Thatcher, Brand Manager, Procter & Gamble. Retrieved from McSWEENEY'S: https://www.mcsweeneys.net/articles/an-open-letter-to-mr-james-thatcher-brand-manager-procter-amp-gamble

Accident, P. C. (1986). Report of the Presidential Commission on the Space Shuttle Challenger Accident. Washington, D.C.

Administration, U. G. (2019). Top 100 Contractors Report. Retrieved from US Federal Government Procurement: https://www.fpds.gov/fpdsng_cms/index.php/en/reports/62-top-100-contractors-report3.html

Aggarwal, P., & McGill, A. L. (2012). When Brands Seem Human, Do Humans Act Like Brands? Automatic Behavioral Priming. Journal of Consumer Research, 307-323.

Ahmed, M., Ullah, S., & Alam, A. (2014). Importance of Culture in Success of International Marketing. European Academic Research, 3802-3816.

Amazon Staff. (2011, April 17). 2016 Letter to Shareholders. Retrieved from Amazon:

https://www.aboutamazon.com/news/company-news/2016-letter-to-shareholders

Amazon. (2022, July 12). Leadership Principles. Retrieved from Amazon Jobs: https://www.amazon.jobs/en/principles

Anderson, K. (2009, March). Ethnographic Research: A Key to Strategy. Retrieved from Harvard Business Review: https://hbr.org/2009/03/ethnographic-research-a-key-to-strategy

Ariely, D. (2008). Are we in control of our own decisions? Retrieved April 21, 2022, from https://www.ted.com/talks/dan_ariely_are_we_in_control_of_our_own_decisions/transcript

Ariely, D. (2009). Predictably Irrational Revised and Expanded Edition. New York: Harper Collins.

Ariely, D. (2010). The Cost of Social Norms. In D. Ariely, Predictably Irrational (pp. 75-102). New York: Harper Collins.

Arlich, D., Guttman, I., Schonbach, P., & Mills, J. (1957). Postdecision Exposure to Relevant Information. Journal of Abnormal and Social Psychology, 98-102.

Arrow, K. (1973). Social Responsibility and Economic Efficiency. Public Policy, 303-317.

Athanasopoulos, P., Dering, B., Wiggett, A., Kuipers, J.-R., & Thierry, G. (2010). Perceptual shift in bilingualism: Brain potentials reveal plasticity in pre-attentive colour perception. Cognition, 437-443.

Atkinson, J. (1953). The achievement motive and recall of interrupted and completed tasks. Journal of Experimental Psychology, 381-390.

Austen, I. (2017, August 11). Canada Letter: Ice Cream Revival and Cross-Border Trade Anxiety. Retrieved from The New York Times: https://www.nytimes.com/2017/08/11/world/canada/canada-letter-ice-cream-revival-and-cross-border-trade-anxiety.html

Bahns, A. J., Crandall, C. S., Gillath, O., & Preacher, K. J. (2017). Similarity in relationships as niche construction: Choice, stability, and influence within dyads in a free choice environment. Journal of Personality and Social Psychology, 329-355.

Bar-Hillel, M. (1977). The Base-Rate Fallacy in Probability Judgments. Arlington, VA: Defense Advanced Research Projects Agency.

Bargh, J. A., Chen, M., & & Burrows, L. (1996). Automaticity of social behavior: Direct effects of trait construct and stereotype activation on action. Journal of Personality and Social Psychology, 230-244.

Bargh, J. A., Gollwitzer, P. M., Lee-Chai, A., Barndollar, K., & Trötschel, R. (2001). The automated will: Nonconscious activation and pursuit of behavioral goals. ournal of Personality and Social Psychology, 1014-1027.

Batley, R. P., & Daly, A. J. (2006). On the equivalence between elimination-byaspects and generalised extreme value models of choice behaviour. Journal of Mathematical Psychology, 456-467.

Baumann, C., Signman, H., Gershman, S. J., & von Helversen, B. (2020). A linear threshold model for optimal stopping behavior. Psychological and Cognitive Science, 117-140.

Benson, K. (2022, April 20). The Magic Relationship Ratio, According to Science. Retrieved from The Gottman Institute: https://www.gottman.com/blog/the-magic-relationship-ratio-according-science/

Berns, G. S.-S. (2005). Neurobiological correlates of social conformity and independence during mental rotation. Biological Psychiatry, 245-253.

Bertrand, M., Karlan, D. S., Mullainathan, S., Shafir, E., & Zinman, J. (2010). What's advertising content worth? Evidence from a consumer credit marketing field experiment. The Quarterly Journal of Economics, 263-306.

Bhattacharya, C. &. (2018). Degree of handedness: A unique individual differences factor for predicting and understanding hindsight bias. Personality and Individual Differences, 97-101.

Bhattacharya, J., Bundorf, K., Pace, N., & Sood, N. (2009). Does Health Insurance Make You Fat. Cambridge, MA: NBER Working Paper Series.

Binet, L., & Field, P. (2007). Marketing in the Era of Accountability: Identifying the Marketing Practices and Metrics that Truly Increase Profitability. World Advertising Research Center Ltd.

Bishop, B. (2009). *The Big Sort.* New York: Houghton Mifflin Harcourt Publishing Company.

Bless, H., & Burger, A. M. (2016). Assimilation and contrast in social priming. Current Opinion in Psychology, 26-31.

Boatwright, P., & Nunes, J. C. (2001). Reducing Assortment: An Attribute-Based Approach. Journal of Marketing, 50-63.

Botti, S., & Iyengar, S. S. (2004). The Psychological Pleasure and Pain of Choosing: When People Prefer Choosing at the Cost of Subsequent Outcome Satisfaction. Journal of Personality and Social Psychology, 312-326.

Brandom, R. (2018, June 28). Using the internet without the Amazon Cloud. Retrieved from The Verge: https://www.theverge.com/2018/7/28/17622792/plugin-use-the-internet-without-the-amazon-cloud

Brewer, M. B. (2011). Optimal distinctiveness theory: Its history and development. *Handbook of theories of social psychology, 2,* 81-98.

Brickman, P., Coates, D., & Janoff-Bulman, R. (1978). Lottery winners and accident victims: is happiness relative? Journal of Personality and Social Psychology, 917-927.

Briesch, R. A., Chintagunta, P. K., & Fox, E. J. (2009). How Does Assortment Affect Grocery Store Choice? Journal of Marketing Research, 176-189.

Brown, J. R., Farrell, A. M., & Weisbenner, S. J. (2015). Decision-Making Approaches and The Propensity to Default: Evidence And Implications. National Bureau of Economic Research Workding Paper Series, Working Paper 20949.

Bullmore, J. (2013). Why it's Time to Say Goodbye to IKTHTMISOAIW*. Retrieved from WPP 2013 Annual Report: https://reports.wpp.com/annualreports/2013/what-we-think/why-its-time-to-say-goodbye-to-ikthtmisoaiw/

Busse, M. R., Pope, D. G., Pope, J. C., & Silva-Risso, J. (2015). The psychological effect of weather on car purchase. Quarterly Journal of Economics, 130, 371-414.

Caillaud, B., & Jullien, B. (2000). Modelling Time-Inconsistent Preferences. European Economic Review, 1116-1124.

Camerer, C., & Thaler, R. H. (1995). Anomalies: Ultimatums, Dictators and Manners. Journal of Economic Perspectives, 209-219.

Camerer, C., Babcock, L., Loewenstein, G., & Thaler, R. (1997, May 1). Labor Supply of New York City Cabdrivers: One Day at a Time. The Quarterly Journal of Economics, 112(2), 407-441.

Carmon, Z., Wertenbroch, K., & Zeelenberg, M. (2003). Option Attachment: When Deliberating Makes Choosing Feel like Losing. Journal of Consumer Research, 15-29.

Chandler, J., & Schwarz, N. (2010). Use does not wear ragged the fabric of friendship: Thinking of objects as alive makes people less willing to replace them. Journal of Consumer Psychology, 138-145.

Chelley-Steeley, P. L., Kluger, B. D., & Steeley, J. M. (2015, September). Earnings and hindsight bias: An experimental study. Economics Letters, 134, 130-132.

Chick-fil-A Foundation. (2019, November 18). Chick-fil-A Foundation. Retrieved from Chick-fil-A | News: https://thechickenwire.chick-fil-a.com/news/chick-fil-a-foundation-announces-2020-priorities

Clare, A., Thomas, S., & Motson, N. (2013, April 03). Monkeys vs Fund managers - An evaluation of alternative equity indices. Retrieved from Bayes Business School: https://www.bayes.city.ac.uk/faculties-and-research/research/bayes-knowledge/2013/april/monkeys-vs-fund-managers-an-evaluation-of-alternative-equity-indices

Cone Communications. (2015, September 23). New Cone Communications Research Confirms Millennials as America's Most Ardent CSR Supporters. Cone Communications Press Release.

Cone. (2014, May 28). Perceptions, Millennials and CSR: How to Engage the New Leaders of Tomorrow. Retrieved from Cone: https://www.conecomm.com/insights-blog/csr-and-millennials

Cordova, D. I., & Lepper, M. R. (1996). Intrinsic Motivation and the Process of Learning: Beneficial Effects of Contextualization, Personalization, and Choice. Journal of Educational Psychology, 715-730.

Cova, B., & Cova, V. (2001). Tribal Marketing: The tribilisation of society and its impact on the conduct of marketing. European Journal of Marketing | Special Issue: Societal Marketing in 2002 and Beyond.

Coyne, K., Clifford, P. G., & Dye, R. (2007, December). Breakthrough Thinking from Inside the Box. Retrieved from Harvard Business Review: https://hbr.org/2007/12/breakthrough-thinking-from-inside-the-box

CRM, M., & JD, N. (2003). What a speaker's choice of frame reveals: reference points, frame selection,. Psychonomic Bulletin & Review, 596-602.

Dahlström, A. (2019). Storytelling in Design. Sabastopol: O'Reilly Media, Inc.

Damasio, A. (1994). Descartes' Error. London: Penguin.

Daniel L. Wann, F. G. (2008). Motivational Profiles of Sport Fans. Sport Marketing Quarterly, 6-19.

Dar-Nimrod, I., Rawn, C. D., Lehman, D. R., & Schwartz, B. (2009). The Maximization Paradox: The costs of seeking alternatives. Personality and Individual Differences, 631-635.

Darley, J. M., & Batson, D. C. (1973). "From Jerusalem to Jericho": A Study of Situational and Dispositional Variables in Helping Behavior. Journal of Personality and Social Psychology, 191-214.

Davis, M. (1991). Thinking Like an Engineer. Retrieved from Center for the Study of Ethics in the Professions at Illinois Institute of Technology.

Davis, T. R., & Young, R. B. (2002). International Marketing Research: A Management Briefing. Business Horizons, 31-38.

De Martino, B., Kumaran, D., Seymour, B., & Dolan, R. J. (2006). Frames, Biases, and Rational Decision-Making in the Human Brain. Science, 684-687.

Dehdashti Shahrokh, Z., Kenari, J., & Bakhshizadeh, A. (2012). The impact of social identity of brand on brand loyalty development. Management Science Letters.

Delbaere, E. F., & Phillips, B. J. (2011). Personification in advertising: using a visual metaphor to trigger anthropomorphism. Journal of Advertising.

Delgado-Ballester, E., Palazón, M., & Peláez, J. (2020). Anthropomorphized vs objectified brands: which brand version is more loved? European Journal of Management and Business Economics, 150-165.

Dellaert, B. G., & Stremersch, S. (2005). Marketing Mass-Customized Products: Striking a Balance Between Utility and Complexity. Journal of Marketing Research, 219-227.

DellaVigna, S., & Malmendier, U. (2004). Contract Design and Self-Control: Theory and Evidence. The Quarterly Journal of Economics, 353-402.

Dember, W. N., Galinsky, T. L., & Warm, J. S. (1992). The role of choice in vigilance performance. Bulletin of the Psychonomic Society, 201-204.

Dhiraj, A. B. (2017, July 2). Some of the Absolute Worst Tech Predictions of All Time. Retrieved from CEOWorld Magazine: https://ceoworld.biz/2017/07/02/some-of-the-absolute-worst-tech-predictions-of-all-time/

Dickson, P. R., & Sawyer, A. G. (1990, July 1). The Price Knowledge and Search of Supermarket Shoppers. Journal of Marketing, 54(3), 42-53.

Dittmar, H. (1994). Material Posessions as Stereotypes: Material images of different socio-economic groups. Journal of Economic Psychology, 561-585.

Dittmar, H. (1994). To have is to be: Materialism and person perception in working-class and middle-class British adolescents. Journal of Economic Psychology, 233-251.

Dove. (2020, August 27). Welcome to Dove. Retrieved from Dove USA: https://www.dove.com/us/en/home.html

Duck, S., & McMahan, D. T. (2020). Identities, Perceptions, and Communication. In S. Duck, & D. T. McMahan, Communication in Everyday Life: A Survey of Communication (pp. 20-37). Los Angeles: SAGE Publications, Inc.

Duhigg, C. (2012, February 16). How Companies Learn Your Secrets. Retrieved from The New York Times Magazine: https://www.nytimes.com/2012/02/19/magazine/shopping-habits.html

Eastwick, P. W., & Finkel, E. J. (2008). Sex Differences in Mate Preferences Revisited: Do People Know What They Initially Desire in a Romantic Partner? Journal of Personality and Social Psychology, 245-264.

Eastwick, P. W., Finkel, E. J., & Eagly, A. H. (2011). When and why do ideal partner preferences affect the process of initiating and maintaining romantic relationships? Journal of Personality and Social Psychology, 1012-1032.

Eastwick, P. W., Finkel, E. J., Luchies, L. B., & Hunt, L. L. (2014). The predictive validity of ideal partner preferences: A review and meta-analysis. Psychological Bulletin, 623-655.

Eckersley, R. M. (2005, March). 'Cultural fraud': the role of culture in drug abuse. Drug and Alcohol Review, 157-163.

Edgar, Lisa; Bunker, David; BBC. (2012). It's all in the mind: Changing the way we think about age. London: Market Research Society, Annual Conference, 2012.

Ehrenberg, A. S. (2000). Repetitive Advertising and the Consumer. Journal of Advertising Research, Published Online.

Ehrenberg, A. S., Goodhardt, G. J., & Barwise, P. (1990). Double Jeopardy Revisited. Journal of Marketing, 82-91.

Ehrenberg, A. S., Uncles, M. D., & Goodhardt, G. G. (2004). Understanding Brand Performance Measures: Using Dirichlet Benchmarks. Journal of Business Research, 1307-1325.

Ellemers, N., Spears, R., & Doosje, B. (1997). Sticking Together or Falling Apart: In-Group Identification as a Psychological Determinant of Group Commitment Versus Individual Mobility. Journal of Personality and Social Psychology, 72(3), 617-626.

eMarketer. (2017, April 5). Personalized Ads? Consumers Tell Marketers to Up Their Game. Retrieved from eMarketer.com:

https://www.emarketer.com/Article/Personalized-Ads-Consumers-Tell-Marketers-Up-Their-Game/1015572

Esch, F.-R., Moll, T., Schmitt, B., Elger, C. E., Neuhaus, C., & Weber, B. (2012). Brands on the brain: Do consumers use declarative information or experienced emotions to evaluate brands? Brand Insights from Psychological and Neurophysiological Perspectives, 75-85.

Ethier, K. A., & Deaux, K. (1994). Negotiating Social Identity When Contexts Change: Maintaining Identification and Responding to Threat. Journal of Personality and Social Psychology, 67(2), 243-251.

Fehr, E., & Gächter, S. (2000). Cooperation and Punishment in Public Good Experiments. American Economic Review, 980-994.

Field, P. (2016, July 26). Selling Creativity Short | Creativity and Effectiveness Under Threat. London: IPA In Association WIth ThinkBox. Retrieved from https://www.youtube.com/watch?v=ivrmhpsyNvM

Fischer, G. W., Carmon, Z., Ariely, D., & Zauberman, G. (1999). Goal-based construction of preferences: task goals and the prominence effect. Management Science, 1057-1075.

Fischhoff, B., & Beyth, R. (1975). 'I knew it would happen': Remembered probabilities of once-future things. Organizational Behavior and Human Performance, 13, 1-16.

Fletcher, G. J., Simpson, J. A., & Thomas, G. (2000). Ideals, Perceptions, and Evaluations in Early Relationship

Development. Journal of Personality and Social Psychology, 79(6), 933.

Flory, J. A., Leibbrandt, A., & List, J. A. (2015). Do Competitive Workplaces Deter Female Workers? A Large-Scale Natural Field Experiment on Job Entry Decisions. The Review of Economic Studies, 122-155.

Forer, B. R. (1949, January). The fallacy of personal validation; a classroom demonstration of gullibility. Journal of Abnormal Psychology, 44(1), 118-123.

Foxall, G. R., Oliveira-Castro, J. M., James, V. K., & Schrezenmaier, T. C. (2007). Brand Choice in Behavioral Perpective. In G. R. Foxall, J. M. Oliveira-Castro, V. K. James, & T. C. Schrezenmaier, The Behavioral Economics of Brand Choice (pp. 1-24). New York: Palgrave Macmillan.

Frederick, S., & Loewenstein, G. (1999). Hedonic Adaptation. In D. Kahneman, Wellbeing: The Foundations of Hedonic Psychology (pp. 302-329). New York: Russel Sage Foundation.

Geometry Global, Shopper Marketing, Path to Purchase Institute. (2015, July 22). Ethnic Marketing Research. Retrieved from Shopper Marketing: https://shoppermarketingmag.com/ethnic-marketing-research-part-1-where-culture-meets-shoppers

Goldsmith, K., Cho, E. K., & Dhar, R. (2012). When Guilt Begets Pleasure: The Positive Effect of a Negative Emotion. Journal of Marketing Research, 872-881.

Gonzalez, C., Dana, J., Koshino, H., & Just, M. (2005). The framing effect and risky decisions: Examining cognitive functions with fMRI. Journal of Economic Psychology, 1-20.

Greenberg, D. M., Matz, S. C., Schwartz, H. A., & Fricke, K. R. (2021). The self-congruity effect of music. Journal of Personality and Social Psychology, 137-150.

Gretz, R. T., & Basuroy, S. (2013). Why quality may not always win: The impact of product generation life cycles on quality and network effects in high-tech markets. Journal of Retailing, 89(3), 281-300.

Güth, W., & Schmittberger, R. S. (1982). An Experimental Analysis of Ultimatum Bargaining. Journal of Economic Behavior and Organization, 367-388.

Haidt, J. (2011, October 20). The Moral Foundations of Occupy Wall Street. Retrieved from Reason: https://reason.com/2011/10/20/the-moral-foundations-of-occup/

Harley, E. M., Carlsen, K. A., & Loftus, G. (2004, October). The "Saw-It-All-Along" Effect: Demonstrations of Visual Hindsight Bias. Journal of Experimental Psychology: Learning, Memory, and Cognition.

Hart, P. M., Jones, S. R., & Royne, M. B. (2013). The human lens: How anthropomorphic reasoning varies by product complexity and enhances personal value. Journal of Marketing Management, 105-121.

Hartung, C., Lefler, E., Tempel, A., Armendariz, M., Sigel, B., & Little, C. (2010). Halo Effects in Ratings of ADHD and

ODD: Identification of Susceptible Symptoms. Journal of Psychopathology and Behavioral Assessment, 128-137.

Haslam, S. A., Oakes, P. J., McGarty, C., Turner, J. C., Reynolds, K. J., & Eggins, R. A. (1996). Stereotyping and social influence: The mediation of stereotype applicability and sharedness by the views of in‐group and out‐group members. British Journal of Social Psychology, 35, 369-397.

Hershfield, H. E. (2011). Future self-continuity: how conceptions of the future self transform intertemporal choice. Annals of the New York Academy of Sciences, 30-43.

Hershfield, H. E., Goldstein, D. G., Sharpe, W. F., Fox, J., Yeykelis, L., Carstensen, L. L., & & Bailenson, J. N. (2011). Increasing Saving Behavior Through Age-Progressed Renderings of the Future Self. Journal of Marketing Research, S23-S37.

Hoch, S. J., & Ha, Y.-W. (1986). Consumer Learning: Advertising and the Ambiguity of Product Experience. Journal of Consumer Research, 221-233.

Hofstede Insights. (n.d.). National Culture. Retrieved April 23, 2019, from Hofstede Insights: https://www.hofstede-insights.com/models/national-culture/

Hofstede, G. (2011). Dimensionalizing Cultures: The Hofstede Model in Context. Online Readings in Psychology and Culture.

Hogg, M. A., & Reid, S. A. (2006). Social Identity, Self-Categorization, and the Communication of Group Norms. Communication Theory, 16(1), 7-30.

Hogg, M. A., Terry, D. J., & White, K. M. (1995). A Tale of Two Theories: A Critical Comparison of Identity Theory With Social Identity Theory. Social Psychology Quarterly, 58(4), 255-269.

Huber, J., Payne, J., & Puto, C. (1982). Adding Asymmetrically Dominated Alternatives: Violations of Regularity and the Similarity Hypothesis. Journal of Consumer Research.

Huber, J., Payne, J., & Puto, C. (1982). Adding Asymmetrically Dominated Alternatives: Violations of Regularity and the Similarity Hypothesis. Journal of Consumer Research.

Iyengar, S. S., & Lepper, M. R. (2000). When Choice is Demotivating: Can One Desire Too Much of a Good Thing. Journal of Personality and Social Psychology, 995-1006.

Iyengar, S. S., Jiang, W., & Huberman, G. (2003). How Much Choice is Too Much?: Contributions to 401(k) Retirement Plans. Philadelphia, PA: Pension Research Council Working Paper | Pension Research Council | The Wharton School, University of Pennsylvania.

Jarden, A. (2010). An Interview with Daniel Kahneman | Princeton University. International Journal of Wellbeing, 186-188.

Joel, S., Eastwick, P. W., & Finkel, E. J. (2017). Is Romantic Desire Predictable? Machine Learning Applied to Initial Romantic Attraction. Psychological Science.

Johnson, E. J., & Goldstein, D. (2003). Do Defaults Save Lives? Science, 1338-1339.

Kahneman, D. (2011). Thinking, Fast and Slow. New York: Farrar, Straus and Giroux.

Kahneman, D., & Deaton, A. (2010). High income improves evaluation of life but not emotional well-being. PNAS, 16489-16493.

Kahneman, D., & Tversky, A. (1972). Subjective probability: a Judgment of Representativeness. Cognitive Psychology, 430-454.

Kahneman, D., & Tversky, A. (1973). On The Psychology of Prediction. Psychological Review, 237-251.

Kahneman, D., & Tversky, A. (1983). Choices, Values, and Frames. APA Award Addresses.

Kahneman, D., & Tversky, A. (2004). Prospect Theory: An Analysis of Decision Under Risk. In A. Tversky, Preference, Belief, and Similarity (pp. 549-581). Cambridge, Massachusetts; London, England: The MIT Press.

Kahneman, D., Fredrickson, B. L., Schreiber, C. A., & Redelmeier, D. A. (1993, November). WHEN MORE PAIN IS PREFERRED TO LESS: Adding a Better End. American Psychological Society, 4(6), 401-405.

Kahneman, D., Knetsch, J. L., & Thaler, R. (1986). Fairness as a Constraint on Profit Seeking: Entitlements in the Market. The American Economic Review, 728-741.

Kahneman, D., Knetsch, J. L., & Thaler, R. (1990). Experimental Tests of the Endowment Effect and the Coase Theorem. Journal of Political Economy, 1325-1348.

Kahneman, D., Knetsch, J. L., & Thaler, R. H. (1986). Fairness and the Assumptions of Economics. Journal of Business, S285-S300.

Kahneman, D., Knetsch, J. L., & Thealer, R. H. (1991). Anomalies: The Endowment Effect, Loss Aversion, and Status Quo Bias. American Economic Association, 193-206. Retrieved from https://www.jstor.org/stable/1942711

Kang, S. (2015, June 17). Abercrombie & Fitch Tries To Be Less Haughty, More Nice. Retrieved from The Wall Street Journal: https://www.wsj.com/articles/SB111895784668361882

Keizer, K., Lindenberg, S., & Steg, L. (2008). The Spreading of Disorder. Science, 1681-1685.

Kim, S. &. (2011). Gaming with Mr. Slot or gaming the slot machine? Power, anthropomorphism, and risk perception. Journal of Consumer Research, 94-107.

Kim, S. &. (2011). Gaming with Mr. Slot or gaming the slot machine? Power, anthropomorphism, and risk perception. Journal of Consumer Research, 94-107.

Kim, W. C., & Mauborgne, R. (2015). Blue Ocean Strategy, Expanded Edition: How to Create Uncontested Market Space and Make the Competition Irrelevant. Boston: Harvard Business Review Press.

Kitayama, S., & Uskul, A. K. (2011). Culture, Mind, and the Brain: Current Evidence and Future Directions. Annual Review of Psychology, 419-449.

Kleine III, R. K. (1993). Mundane consumption and the self: A social identity perspective. Journal of Consumer Psychology, 209-235.

Kleinman, Z. (2020, January 22). Sonos speaker update sparks anger. Retrieved from BBC News: https://www.bbc.com/news/technology-51206604

Kliger, D., & Gilad, D. (2012). Red Light, Green Light: Color Priming in Financial Decisions. Journal of Socio-Economics, 738-745.

Knetsch, J. L., & Sinden, J. A. (1984). Willingness to Pay and Compensation Demanded: Experimental Evidence of an Unexpected Disparity in Measures of Value. The Quarterly Journal of Economics, 507-521.

Kristal, A. S., & Santos, L. R. (2021). G.I. Joe Phenomena: Understanding the Limits of Metacognitive Awareness on Debiasing. Harvard Business School Working Paper.

Langer, E. J., & Rodin, J. (1976). The Effects of Choice and Enhanced Personal Responsibility for the Aged: A Field Experiment in an Institutional Setting. Journal of Personality and Social Psychology, 191-198.

Lazarus, G. (1995, May 17). GOODBY'S NORWEGIAN AD CAMPAIGN SAILS HIGH SEAS. Retrieved from Chicago Tribune: https://www.chicagotribune.com/news/ct-xpm-1995-05-17-9505170200-story.html

Leander, P., Chartrand, T. L., & Bargh, J. A. (2012). You Give Me the Chills: Embodied Reactions to Inappropriate Amounts of Behavioral Mimicry. Psychological Science, 772-779.

Leary, M. R. (1981). The Distorted Nature of Hindsight. The Journal of Social Psychology, 25-29.

Lee, C. (2015, April 9). The stranger within: Connecting with our future selves. Retrieved from UCLA Newsroom: https://newsroom.ucla.edu/stories/the-stranger-within-connecting-with-our-future-selves

Lefcourt, H. M. (1973). The function of the illusions of control and freedom. American Psychologist, 417-425.

Levin, I. P. (1987). Associative effects of information framing. Bulletin of the Psychonomic Society, 85-86.

Levin, I. P., & Gaeth, G. J. (1988). How Consumers Are Affected by the Framing of Attribute Information Before and After Consuming the Product. Journal of Consumer Research, 374-378.

Levin, I. P., Johnson, R. D., Deldin, P. J., Carstens, L. M., Cressey, J. J., & Davis, C. R. (1986). Framing effects in decisions with completely and incompletely described alternatives. Organizational Behavior and Human Decision Processes, 46-64.

Levin, I. P., Wall, L. L., Dolezal, J. M., & Norman, K. L. (1973). Differential weighting of positive and negative traits in impression formation as a function of prior exposure. Journal of Experimental Psychology, 114-115.

Li, X. (2008). The Effects of Appetitive Stimuli on Out-of-Domain Consumption Impatience. Journal of Consumer Research, 649-656.

Liberman, V., Samuels, S. M., & Ross, L. (2004). The Name of the Game: Predictive Power of Reputations Versus Situational

Labels in Determining Prisoner's Dilemma Game Moves. Personality and Social Psychology Bulletin, 1175-1185.

Lindenberg, S. (2016). Social rationality, semi-modularity and goal-framing: What is it all about? Analyse & Kritik, 670-687.

Lindenberg, S., & Foss, N. J. (2011). Managing Joint Production Motivation: The Role of Goal Framing and Governance Mechanisms. The Academy of Management Review, 500-525.

Lindenberg, S., & Steg, L. (2013). Goal-framing Theory and Norm-Guided Environmental Behavior. In H. C. van Trijp, Encouraging Sustainable Behavior: Psychology and the Environment (pp. 37-54). New York: Psychology Press.

Linsey, J. S., Clauss, E. F., Kurtoglu, T., Murphy, J. T., & Wood, K. L. (2011). An Experimental Study of Group Idea Generation Techniques: Understanding the Roles of Idea Representation and Viewing Methods. Journal of Mechanical Design.

Livni, E. (2018, December 21). Quartz. Retrieved from A Nobel Prize-winning psychologist says most people don't really want to be happy: https://qz.com/1503207/a-nobel-prize-winning-psychologist-defines-happiness-versus-satisfaction/

Lockheed Martin. (2020, August 22). Who We Are. Retrieved from Lockheed Martin: https://www.lockheedmartin.com/en-us/who-we-are.html

Lockheed Martin. (2020, August 31). Sikorsky Black Hawk Helicopter. Retrieved from Lockheed Martin:

https://www.lockheedmartin.com/en-us/products/sikorsky-black-hawk-helicopter.html

Loewenstein, G. (2000). Is More Choice Always Better? Retrieved November 11, 2020, from Carnegie Mellon University: http://www.contrib.andrew.cmu.edu/~gl20/GeorgeLoewenstein/Papers_files/pdf/too_much_choice.pdf

Lowenstein, G., & Prelec, D. (1992). Anomalies in intertemporal choice: Evidence and an interpretation. Quarterly Journal of Economics, 573-597.

Lucas, A. (2019, March 29). When customers do the math on Starbucks' new rewards program, they may not like what they see, Bernstein says. Retrieved from CNBC: https://www.cnbc.com/2019/03/29/starbucks-rewards-program-changes-could-alienate-customers-bernstein.html

Maccoun, R. (1993). Blaming Others to a Fault? Chance, 31-49.

Madrian, B. C., & Shea, D. F. (2000). THE POWER OF SUGGESTION: INERTIA IN 401(K) PARTICIPATION AND SAVINGS BEHAVIOR. National Bureau of Economic Research Working Paper Series, Working Paper 7682.

Maier, M., & Rahman, R. A. (2018). Native Language Promotes Access to Visual Consciousness. Psychological Science, 1757-1772.

Maric, D. (2016, April 12). Consumers in Training: How Children in the Americas are Influencing the Purchasing Decisions of their Parents. Retrieved from LinkedIn: https://www.linkedin.com/pulse/consumers-training-how-children-americas-influencing-purchasing?articleId=8740076856070420445

Mangus, S. M., & Ruvio, A. (2019). Do opposites attract? Assimilation and differentiation as relationship-building strategies. *Journal of Personal Selling & Sales Management*, 39(1), 60–80. https://doi-org.proxy2.cl.msu.edu/10.1080/08853134.2018.1471696

Mazar, N., Amir, O., & Ariely, D. (2008). The Dishonesty of Honest People: A Theory of Self-Concept Maintenance. Journal of Marketing Research, 633-644.

McNulty, J. (1938, April 16). The Sizzle. Retrieved from The New Yorker: https://www.newyorker.com/magazine/1938/04/16/the-sizzle

McRobbie, L. R. (2015, October 29). On the Science of Creepiness. Retrieved from Smithsonian Magazine: https://www.smithsonianmag.com/science-nature/science-creepiness-180957093/

Meg Farren, C. K. (2018, June 28). How KFC became FCK to Say Sorry in The U.K And Ireland. (Adweek, Interviewer) https://www.youtube.com/watch?time_continue=122&v=V6cEM0RvT9Y&feature=emb_logo

Merchant, A., Latour, K., Ford, J. B., & Latour, M. S. (2013, June). How Strong is the Pull of the Past? Measuring Personal Nostalgia Evoked by Advertising. Journal of Advertising Research, 150-165.

Meyersohn, N. (2020, March 06). Taking a stand on social issues is risky. The world's largest advertiser did it anyway. Retrieved from CNN: https://www.cnn.com/2020/03/06/business/procter-gamble-carolyn-tastad-risk-takers/index.html

Mitchell, T. R., Thompson, L., Peterson, E., & Cronk, R. (1997, July). Temporal Adjustments in the Evaluation of Events: The "Rosy View". Journal of Experimental Social Psychology, 33(4), 421-448.

Molenberghs, P., & Louis, W. R. (2018). Insights From fMRI Studies Into Ingroup Bias. Frontiers in Psychology, 9, 1868. Retrieved from https://www.frontiersin.org/articles/10.3389/fpsyg.2018.01868/full

MoralFoundations.org. (2019, October). Home. Retrieved from MoralFoundations.org: https://moralfoundations.org/

Mullainathan, S., Schwartzstein, J., & Shleifer, A. (2006). Coarse Thinking and Persuasion. Cambridge, MA: NBER Working Paper Series | Working Paper 12720.

Mullen, B., Johnson, C., & Salas, E. (1991). Productivity loss in brainstroming groups: A meta-analytic integration. Basic and applied social psychology, 3-23.

Mussweiler, T., Rüter, K., & Epstude, K. (2004). The ups and downs of social comparison: mechanisms of assimilation and contrast. Journal of Personality and Social Psychology, 832-844.

Neff, J. (2009, September 07). WHAT TO DO WHEN SOCIAL MEDIA SPREADS MARKETING MYTH. Retrieved from AdAge: https://adage.com/article/digital/social-media-spreads-marketing-myth/138845

Nemeth, C. J., Personnaz, B., Personnaz, M., & Goncalo, J. A. (2004). The liberating role of conflict in group creativity: A study in two countries. European Journal of Social Psychology, 365-374.

Netflix Technology Blog. (2016, April 29). It's All A/Bout Testing: The Netflix Experimentation Platform. Retrieved from Medium | The Netflix Tech Blog: https://medium.com/netflix-techblog/its-all-a-bout-testing-the-netflix-experimentation-platform-4e1ca458c15

Netflix Technology Blog. (2016, May 3). Selecting the best artwork for videos through A/B testing. Retrieved from Medium | The Netflix Technology Blog: https://medium.com/netflix-techblog/selecting-the-best-artwork-for-videos-through-a-b-testing-f6155c4595f6

Netflix. (2020, December 2). We're updating our prices — here's why. Los Gatos, CA, USA.

Nguyen, T. (2019, September 5). Uber wants to redeem itself. Does the public even care? Retrieved from Vox | The Goods: https://www.vox.com/the-goods/2019/9/5/20849632/uber-public-relations-crisis-qanda

Nielsen. (2012, April 4). Consumer Trust in Online, Social and Mobile Advertising Grows. Retrieved from Nielsen.com: https://www.nielsen.com/us/en/insights/article/2012/consumer-trust-in-online-social-and-mobile-advertising-grows/

Nielsen. (2018, July 10). The Database: Meeting Today's Multicultural Consumers. Retrieved from Nielsen: https://www.nielsen.com/us/en/insights/news/2018/the-database-meeting-todays-multicultural-consumers.html

Nisbett, R. E., & Wilson, T. D. (1977, May). Telling More Than We Can Know: Verbal Reports on Mental Processes. Psychological Review, 84(3), 231-259.

Norwood, F. B., & Lusk, J. L. (2007). The Dual Nature of Choice: When Consumers Prefer Less to More. Conference Paper/Presentation Southern Agricultural Economics Association 2007 Annual Meeting, February 4-7, 2007, Mobile, Alabama.

NPR OPB. (2010, May 15). Bet You Didn't Notice 'The Invisible Gorilla'. Retrieved from NPR: https://www.npr.org/templates/story/story.php?storyId=126977945

Ogilvy, D. (1983). Ogilvy on Advertising. New York, NY, USA: Crown Publishers, Inc.

Olivola, C. Y. (2018). The Interpersonal Sunk-Cost Effect. Pscyhological Science, 11072-11083.

OpenX and The Harris Poll. (2018). 2018 Consumer Holiday Shopping Report. Retrieved from OpenX.com: www.openx.com

Outside. (2015, January 20). 'Wild' Movie Boosts Number of PCT Hikers. Retrieved from Outside: https://www.outsideonline.com/1806896/wild-movie-boosts-number-pct-hikers

P&G. (2020, August 23). Brands. Retrieved from P&G: https://us.pg.com/brands/

P&G. (2020, August 23). Who We Are. Retrieved from P&G: https://us.pg.com/who-we-are/

P&G. (2020, August 26). About P&G. Retrieved from Facebook: https://www.facebook.com/proctergamble/about/?ref=page_internal

Paris, W. (2017, July 4). Why We Want Who We Want. Psychology Today, pp. https://www.psychologytoday.com/us/articles/201707/why-we-want-who-we-want .

Paul, A. M. (2012, March 17). Your Brain on Fiction. Retrieved from The New York Times: https://www.nytimes.com/2012/03/18/opinion/sunday/the-neuroscience-of-your-brain-on-fiction.html

Payne, J. W., Bettman, J. R., & Johnson, E. J. (1993). The Adaptive Decision Maker. Cambridge: Cambridge University Press.

Pew Research Center. (2013, June 4). The Global Divide on Homosexuality. Retrieved from Pew Research Center: https://www.pewglobal.org/2013/06/04/the-global-divide-on-homosexuality/

Pham, M. T., Hung, I. W., & Gorn, G. J. (2011). Relaxation Increases Monetary Valuations. Advances in Consumer Research, 38. Retrieved from https://www.acrwebsite.org/volumes/15838/volumes/v38/NA-38

Priester, J. R., Dholakia, U. M., & Fleming, M. A. (2004). When and Why the Background Contrast Effect Emerges: Thought Engenders Meaning by Influencing the Perception of Applicability. The Journal of Consumer Research, 491-501.

Puzakova, M., Kwak, H., & Rocereto, J. F. (2009). Pushing the Envelope of Brand and Personality: Antecedents and Moderators of Anthropomorphized Brands. Advances in Consumer Research, 413-418.

Puzakova, M., Kwak, H., & Rocereto, J. F. (2013). When Humanizing Brands Goes Wrong: The Detrimental Effect of Brand Anthropomorphization amid Product Wrongdoings. Journal of Marketing.

Quesenberry, K. A., & Coolsen, M. K. (2019, November). Drama Goes Viral: Effects of Story Development on Shares and Views of Online Advertising Videos. Journal of Interactive Marketing, 1-16.

Rabin, M. (1993). Incorporating Fairness Into Game Theory. American Economic Review, 1281-1302.

Raimondo, M. A., Cardamone, E., Miceli, G. N., & Bagozzi, R. P. (2022). Consumers' identity signaling towards social groups: The effects of dissociative desire on brand prominence preferences. *Psychology & Marketing*, 39(10), 1964-1978.

Roese, N. J., & Vohs, K. D. (2012). Hindsight Bias. Perspectives on Psychological Science, 7(5).

Rogoway, M. (2020, August 5). Oregon leaders squandered years on jobless benefits computer upgrade. Now the project's future is again in doubt. Retrieved from Oregon Live | The Oregonian: https://www.oregonlive.com/news/2020/08/oregon-leaders-squandered-years-on-jobless-benefits-computer-upgrade-now-the-projects-future-is-again-in-doubt.html

Rousseau, D. M. (1998). Why workers still identify with organizations. Journal of Organizational Behavior, 19, 217-233.

Royal Dutch Shell plc. (2017, April 28). Shell Energy Scenarios Germany. Retrieved from Shell: https://www.shell.com/energy-and-innovation/the-energy-future/scenarios/what-are-scenarios/_jcr_content/par/tabbedcontent/tab/textimage_2 5172244.stream/1504104048141/87b2684f712f1da82ef32d0 7b19555920412d451/shell-energy-scenarios-germany.pdf

Ruvio, A., Bagozzi, R. P., Hult, G. T. M., & Spreng, R. (2020). Consumer arrogance and word-of-mouth. Journal of the Academy of Marketing Science, 48(6), 1116–1137. https://doi-org.proxy2.cl.msu.edu/10.1007/s11747-020-00725-3

Salganik, M. J., Dodds, P. S., & Watts, D. J. (2006). Experimental Study of Inequality and Unpredictability in an Artificial Cultural Market. Science, 854-856.

Santos, J. P., Moutinho, L., Seixas, D., & Brandao, S. (2012). Neural Correlates of the Emotional and Symbolic Content of Brands: A Neuroimaging Study. Journal of Customer Behaviour, 11(1), 69-93.

Schwartz, B. (2000). Self-Determination The Tyranny of Freedom. American Psychologist, 79-88.

Schwartz, B. (2004, April). The Tyranny of Choice. Scientific American, pp. 70-75.

Schwartz, B. (2016). The Paradox of Choice. Manhattan: EccoPress.

Schwarz, N., & Bless, H. (2007). Mental Construal Processes: The Inclusion/Exclusion Model. In D. Stapel, & J. Suls, Assimilation and Contrast in Social Psychology (pp. 119-141). Philadelphia, PA: Psychology Press.

Seligman, M. E., Railton, P., & al., e. (2016). Homo Prospectus. Oxford: Oxford University Press.

Shah, J. Y., & Kruglanski, A. W. (2001). Priming against your will: How accessible alternatives affect goal pursuit. Journal of Experimental Social Psychology, 368-383.

Shapiro, S. M., & Heckler, S. E. (1997). The Effects of Incidental Ad Exposure on the Formation of Consideration Sets. Journal of Consumer Research, 94-104.

Sharot, T. (2011). The Optimism Bias: A Tour of the Irrationally Postiive Brain. New York: Pantheon.

Sharp, B. (2010). How Brands Grow. Oxford: Oxford University Press.

Shell. What are Shell Scenarios? Retrieved April 25, 2019, from Shell: https://www.shell.com/energy-and-innovation/the-energy-future/scenarios/what-are-scenarios.html

Sherif, M., & Taub, D. (1958). Assimilation and Contrast Effects of Anchoring Stimuli on Judgments. Journal of Experimental Psychology, 150-155.

Shrum, L. J., Wong, N., Arif, F., Chugani, S. K., Gunz, A., Lowrey, T. M., Nairn, A., Pandelaere, M., Ross, S. M., Ruvio, A., Scott, K., & Sundie, J. (2013). Reconceptualizing materialism as identity goal pursuits: Functions, processes, and consequences. Journal of Business Research, 66(8), 1179–1185. https://doi-org.proxy2.cl.msu.edu/10.1016/j.jbusres.2012.08.010

Sijbom, R. B. (2018). Leaders' achievement goals predict employee burnout above and beyond employees' own achievement goals. Journal of Personality, 702-714.

Simon, H. A. (1955). A Behavioral Model of Rational Choice. Quarterly Journal of Economics, 99-118.

Smithsonian National Air and Space Museum. (2020, August 22). Model, Static, Lockheed Electra, Amelia Earhart. Retrieved from Smithsonian National Air and Space Museum: https://airandspace.si.edu/collection-objects/model-static-lockheed-electra-amelia-earhart/nasm_A19600213000

Snapper, K. J., & Peterson, C. R. (1971). Information Seeking and Data Diagnosticity. Journal of Experimental Psychology, 429-433.

Spreng, R. A., Shi, L. H., & Page, T. J. (2009). Service quality and satisfaction in business-to-business services. *Journal of Business & Industrial Marketing*.

Stagner, R. (1958, September). The Gullibility of Personnel Managers. Personnel Psychology, 11(3), 347-352.

Stets, J. E., & Burke, P. J. (2000). Identity Theory and Social Identity. Social Psychology Quarterly, 63(3), 224-237.

Stillman, J. (2018, April 27). 12 Hilariously Wrong Tech Predictions. Retrieved from Inc.: https://www.inc.com/jessica-stillman/12-hilariously-wrong-tech-predictions.html

Stolier, R. M., & Freeman, J. B. (2017). A Neural Mechanism of Social Categorization. Journal of Neuroscience, https://www.jneurosci.org/content/37/23/5711.

Strotz, R. H. (1955-1956). Myopia and Inconsistency in Dynamic Utility Maximization. The Review of Economic Studies, 165-180.

Sundar, A., Kardes, F., & Noseworthy, T. (2017). Inferences on Negative Labels and the Horns Effect. Advances in Consumer Research Volume 42, 377-380.

Sundberg, N. D. (1955). The Acceptability of "Fake" Versus "Bona Fide" Personality Test Interpretations. The Journal of Abnormal and SOcial Psychology, 50(1), 145-147.

Szafarz, A. (2007). Hiring People like Yourself. A Representation of Discrimination on the Job Market. Economic Perspectives on Employment & Labor Law eJournal.

Szczerba, R. J. (2015, January 5). 15 Worst Tech Predictions of All Time. Retrieved from Forbes: https://www.forbes.com/sites/robertszczerba/2015/01/05/15-worst-tech-predictions-of-all-time/#4e74256e1299

Szczerba, R. J. (2015, January 5). 15 Worst Tech Predictions of All Time. Retrieved from Forbes: https://www.forbes.com/sites/robertszczerba/2015/01/05/15-worst-tech-predictions-of-all-time/#4e74256e1299

Szubin, A., Jensen, III, C. J., & Gregg, R. (2000, September). Interacting with "Cults". The FBI Law Enforcement Bulletin, 69(9).

Tajfel, H., & Turner, J. (2004). An integrative theory of intergroup conflict. In M. Schultz, & M. J. Hatch (Eds.), Organizational Identity | A Reader (pp. 33-47). Oxford: Oxford University Press.

Thaler, R. (1985). Mental Accounting and Consumer Choice. Marketing Science, 199-214.

Thaler, R. H. (1988). Anomalies: The ultimatum game. Journal of Economic Perspectives.

thredUP. (2017, April 11). Thredit. Retrieved from ThredUp: https://www.thredup.com/bg/p/how-to-clean-out-your-closet-wear-only-what-you-love

Tversky, A. K. (1974). Judgment under Uncertainty: Heuristics and Biases. Science, 1124-1131.

Tversky, A., & Griffin, D. (2004). Endowment and Contrast in Judgments of Well-Being. In A. Tversky, Preference, Belief, and Similarity (pp. 917-926). Cambridge, Massachusetts: The MIT Press.

Tversky, A., & Kahneman, D. (1981). The Framing of Decisions and the Psychology of Choice. Science, 453-458.

Tversky, A., & Kahneman, D. (1992). Advances in Prospect Theory: Cumulative Representation of Uncertainty. Journal of Risk and Uncertainty, 297-323.

Tversky, A., & Shafir, E. (1992). Choice under Conflict: The Dynamics of Deferred Decision. Psychological Science, 358-361.

Twomey, S. (2010, January). Phineas Gage: Neuroscience's Most Famous Patient. Retrieved from Smithsonian Magazine: https://www.smithsonianmag.com/history/phineas-gage-neurosciences-most-famous-patient-11390067/

Uber. (n.d.). Community | Fostering diversity and inclusion. Retrieved October 23, 2020, from Uber: https://www.uber.com/us/en/community/diversity-and-inclusion/

UNAIDS. (2005, January). Aids in Africa: Three scenarios to 2025. Retrieved from UNAIDS: http://data.unaids.org/publications/irc-pub07/jc1058-aidsinafrica_en.pdf

University of Pennsylvania | Penn Arts & Sciences. (n.d.). The PERMA Model: Your Scientific Theory of Happiness. Retrieved October 24, 2020, from University of Pennsylvania | Penn Arts & Sciences: https://ppc.sas.upenn.edu/learn-more/perma-theory-well-being-and-perma-workshops

Van Gelder, J.-L., Hershfield, H. E., & Nordgren, L. F. (2013). Vividness of the Future Self Predicts. Psychological Science, 974-980.

Vanhuele, M., & Drèze, X. (2002). Measuring the Price Knowledge Shoppers Bring to the Store. Journal of Marketing, 66(4), 72-85.

Vigen, T. (2022, July 13). Divorce Rate in Maine. Retrieved from Spurious Correlations: https://tylervigen.com/view_correlation?id=1703

Wallaert, M. (2019). Start at the End. Portfolio/Penguin.

Waytz, A., Cacioppo, J., & Epley, N. (2014). Who Sees Human? The Stability and Importance of Individual Differences in Anthropomorphism. Perspectives on Psychological Science, 219-232.

Williams, L. E., & Bargh, J. A. (2008). Experiencing Physical Warmth Promotes Interpersonal Warmth. Science, 606-607. Retrieved from https://www.ncbi.nlm.nih.gov/pmc/articles/PMC2737341/?mod=article_inline

Wilson, T. D., & Schooler, J. W. (1991). Thinking Too Much: Introspection Can Reduce the Quality of Preferences and Decisions. Journal of Personality and Social Psychology, 181-192.

Wohl, J. (2019, February 03). Why Burger King Showed Andy Warhol Eating a Burger In Its Super Bowl Commercial. Retrieved from AdAge: https://adage.com/article/cmo-strategy/burger-king-andy-warhol-super-bowl-ad/

Woolley, K., & Fishbach, A. (2016). For the Fun of It: Harnessing Immediate Rewards to Increase Persistence in Long-Term Goals. Journal of Consumer Research, 952-966.

Woolley, K., & Fishbach, A. (2017). Immediate Rewards Predict Adherence to Long-Term Goals. Personality and Social Psychology Bulletin, 151-162.

Zajonc, R. B. (1968, June). Attitudinal Effects of Mere Exposure. Journal of Personality and Social Psychology, 9(2 Part 2).

Ziegarnik, B. (1927). On finished tasks and unfinished tasks. Pschologische Forschung.

Zimbardo, P. (1997, May). What Messages Are Behind Today's Cults? Retrieved from International Cultic Studies Association: http://www.csj.org/studyindex/studycult/study_zimbar.htm

Endnotes

[1] McNulty, J. (1938, April 16). The Sizzle. Retrieved from The New Yorker: https://www.newyorker.com/magazine/1938/04/16/the-sizzle

[2] Outside. (2015, January 20). 'Wild' Movie Boosts Number of PCT Hikers. Retrieved from Outside: https://www.outsideonline.com/1806896/wild-movie-boosts-number-pct-hikers

[3] Paul, A. M. (2012, March 17). Your Brain on Fiction. Retrieved from The New York Times: https://www.nytimes.com/2012/03/18/opinion/sunday/the-neuroscience-of-your-brain-on-fiction.html

[4] Kahneman, D. (2011). Thinking, Fast and Slow. New York: Farrar, Straus and Giroux.

[5] Kahneman, D. (2011). Thinking, Fast and Slow. New York: Farrar, Straus and Giroux.

[6] Seligman, M. E., Railton, P., & al., e. (2016). Homo Prospectus. Oxford: Oxford University Press.

[7] Lazarus, G. (1995, May 17). GOODBY'S NORWEGIAN AD CAMPAIGN SAILS HIGH SEAS. Retrieved from Chicago Tribune: https://www.chicagotribune.com/news/ct-xpm-1995-05-17-9505170200-story.html

[8] Administration, U. G. (2019). Top 100 Contractors Report. Retrieved from US Federal Government Procurement: https://www.fpds.gov/fpdsng_cms/index.php/en/reports/62-top-100-contractors-report3.html

[9] Smithsonian National Air and Space Museum. (2020, August 22). Model, Static, Lockheed Electra, Amelia Earhart. Retrieved from Smithsonian National Air and Space Museum: https://airandspace.si.edu/collection-objects/model-static-lockheed-electra-amelia-earhart/nasm_A19600213000

[10]Lockheed Martin. (2020, August 22). Who We Are. Retrieved from Lockheed Martin: https://www.lockheedmartin.com/en-us/who-we-are.html

[11] Lockheed Martin. (2020, August 31). Sikorsky Black Hawk Helicopter. Retrieved from Lockheed Martin: https://www.lockheedmartin.com/en-us/products/sikorsky-black-hawk-helicopter.html

[12]NPR OPB. (2010, May 15). Bet You Didn't Notice 'The Invisible Gorilla'. Retrieved from NPR: https://www.npr.org/templates/story/story.php?storyId=126977945

[13] Wohl, J. (2019, February 03). WHY BURGER KING SHOWED ANDY WARHOL EATING A BURGER IN ITS SUPER BOWL COMMERCIAL. Retrieved from AdAge: https://adage.com/article/cmo-strategy/burger-king-andy-warhol-super-bowl-ad/

[14]Ogilvy, D. (1983). Ogilvy on Advertising. New York, NY, USA: Crown Publishers, Inc.

[15] Dahlström, A. (2019). Storytelling in Design. Sabastopol: O'Reilly Media, Inc.

[16] Meyersohn, N. (2020, March 06). Taking a stand on social issues is risky. The world's largest advertiser did it anyway. Retrieved from CNN: https://www.cnn.com/2020/03/06/business/procter-gamble-carolyn-tastad-risk-takers/index.html

[17] P&G. (2020, August 26). About P&G. Retrieved from Facebook: https://www.facebook.com/proctergamble/about/?ref=page_internal

[18] P&G. (2020, August 23). Brands. Retrieved from P&G: https://us.pg.com/brands/

[19] P&G. (2020, August 23). Who We Are. Retrieved from P&G: https://us.pg.com/who-we-are/

[20]Bishop, B. (2009). The Big Sort. New York: Houghton Mifflin Harcourt Publishing Company.

[21]Meg Farren, C. K. (2018, June 28). How KFC became FCK to Say Sorry in The U.K And Ireland. (Adweek, Interviewer) https://www.youtube.com/watch?time_continue=122&v=V6cEM0RvT9Y&feature=emb_logo

[22] Quesenberry, K. A., & Coolsen, M. K. (2019, November). Drama Goes Viral: Effects of Story Development on Shares and Views of Online Advertising Videos. Journal of Interactive Marketing, 1-16.

[23] Hogg, M. A., Terry, D. J., & White, K. M. (1995). A Tale of Two Theories: A Critical Comparison of Identity Theory With Social Identity Theory. Social Psychology Quarterly, 58(4), 255-269.

[24] Stets, J. E., & Burke, P. J. (2000). Identity Theory and Social Identity. Social Psychology Quarterly, 63(3), 224-237.

[25] Hogg, M. A., & Reid, S. A. (2006). Social Identity, Self-Categorization, and the Communication of Group Norms. Communication Theory, 16(1), 7-30.

[26] Ellemers, N., Spears, R., & Doosje, B. (1997). Sticking Together or Falling Apart: In-Group Identification as a Psychological Determinant of Group Commitment Versus Individual Mobility. Journal of Personality and Social Psychology, 72(3), 617-626.

[27] Haslam, S. A., Oakes, P. J., McGarty, C., Turner, J. C., Reynolds, K. J., & Eggins, R. A. (1996). Stereotyping and social influence: The mediation of stereotype applicability and sharedness by the views of in-group and out-group members. British Journal of Social Psychology, 35, 369-397.

[28] Ethier, K. A., & Deaux, K. (1994). Negotiating Social Identity When Contexts Change: Maintaining Identification and Responding to Threat. Journal of Personality and Social Psychology, 67(2), 243-251.

[29] Rousseau, D. M. (1998). Why workers still identify with organizations. Journal of Organizational Behavior, 19, 217-233.

[30] Daniel L. Wann, F. G. (2008). Motivational Profiles of Sport Fans. Sport Marketing Quarterly, 6-19.

[31] Eckersley, R. M. (2005, March). 'Cultural fraud': the role of culture in drug abuse. Drug and Alcohol Review, 157-163.

[32] Szubin, A., Jensen, III, C. J., & Gregg, R. (2000, September). Interacting with "Cults". The FBI Law Enforcement Bulletin, 69(9).

[33] Zimbardo, P. (1997, May). What Messages Are Behind Today's Cults? Retrieved from International Cultic Studies Association: http://www.csj.org/studyindex/studycult/study_zimbar.htm

[34] Molenberghs, P., & Louis, W. R. (2018). Insights From fMRI Studies Into Ingroup Bias. Frontiers in Psychology, 9, 1868. Retrieved from https://www.frontiersin.org/articles/10.3389/fpsyg.2018.01868/full

[35] Greenberg, D. M., Matz, S. C., Schwartz, H. A., & Fricke, K. R. (2021). The self-congruity effect of music. Journal of Personality and Social Psychology, 137-150.

[36] Molenberghs, P., & Louis, W. R. (2018). Insights From fMRI Studies Into Ingroup Bias. Frontiers in Psychology, 9, 1868. Retrieved from https://www.frontiersin.org/articles/10.3389/fpsyg.2018.01868/full

[37] Nielsen. (2012, April 4). Consumer Trust in Online, Social and Mobile Advertising Grows. Retrieved from Nielsen.com: https://www.nielsen.com/us/en/insights/article/2012/consumer-trust-in-online-social-and-mobile-advertising-grows/

[38] Kahneman, D., Fredrickson, B. L., Schreiber, C. A., & Redelmeier, D. A. (1993, November). WHEN MORE PAIN IS PREFERRED TO LESS: Adding a Better End. American Psychological Society, 4(6), 401-405.

[39] Brandom, R. (2018, June 28). Using the internet without the Amazon Cloud. Retrieved from The Verge: https://www.theverge.com/2018/7/28/17622792/plugin-use-the-internet-without-the-amazon-cloud

[40] Dove. (2020, August 27). Welcome to Dove ... Retrieved from Dove USA: https://www.dove.com/us/en/home.html

[41] Twomey, S. (2010, January). Phineas Gage: Neuroscience's Most Famous Patient. Retrieved from Smithsonian Magazine: https://www.smithsonianmag.com/history/phineas-gage-neurosciences-most-famous-patient-11390067/

[42] Damasio, A. (1994). Descartes' Error. London: Penguin.

[43] Leander, P., Chartrand, T. L., & Bargh, J. A. (2012). You Give Me the Chills: Embodied Reactions to Inappropriate Amounts of Behavioral Mimicry. Psychological Science, 772-779.

[44] Damasio, A. (1994). Descartes' Error. London: Penguin.

[45] Spreng, R. A., Shi, L. H., & Page, T. J. (2009). Service quality and satisfaction in business-to-business services. *Journal of Business & Industrial Marketing*.

[46] Benson, K. (2022, April 20). The Magic Relationship Ratio, According to Science. Retrieved from The Gottman Institute: https://www.gottman.com/blog/the-magic-relationship-ratio-according-science/

[47] Merchant, A., Latour, K., Ford, J. B., & Latour, M. S. (2013, June). How Strong is the Pull of the Past? Measuring Personal Nostalgia Evoked by Advertising. Journal of Advertising Research, 150-165.

[48] Ibid.

[49] Mitchell, T. R., Thompson, L., Peterson, E., & Cronk, R. (1997, July). Temporal Adjustments in the Evaluation of Events: The "Rosy View". Journal of Experimental Social Psychology, 33(4), 421-448.

[50] Edgar, Lisa; Bunker, David; BBC. (2012). It's all in the mind: Changing the way we think about. London: Market Research Society, Annual Conference, 2012.

[51] Tversky, A., & Griffin, D. (2004). Endowment and Contrast in Judgments of Well-Being. In A. Tversky, Preference, Belief, and Similarity (pp. 917-926). Cambridge, Massachusetts: The MIT Press.

[52] Kang, S. (2015, June 17). Abercrombie & Fitch Tries To Be Less Haughty, More Nice. Retrieved from The Wall Street Journal: https://www.wsj.com/articles/SB111895784668361882

[53] Hart, P. M., Jones, S. R., & Royne, M. B. (2013). The human lens: How anthropomorphic reasoning varies by product complexity and enhances personal value. Journal of Marketing Management, 105-121.

[54] Delbaere, E. F., & Phillips, B. J. (2011). Personification in advertising: using a visual metaphor to trigger anthropomorphism. Journal of Advertising.

[55] Aaker, J. (1997). Dimensions of Brand Personality. Journal of Marketing Research, 347-356.

[56] Waytz, A., Cacioppo, J., & Epley, N. (2014). Who Sees Human? The Stability and Importance of Individual Differences in Anthropomorphism. Perspectives on Psychological Science, 219-232.

[57] Kim, S. &. (2011). Gaming with Mr. Slot or gaming the slot machine? Power, anthropomorphism, and risk perception. Journal of Consumer Research, 94-107.

[58] Hart, P. M., Jones, S. R., & Royne, M. B. (2013). The human lens: How anthropomorphic reasoning varies by product complexity and enhances personal value. Journal of Marketing Management, 105-121.

[59] Chandler, J., & Schwarz, N. (2010). Use does not wear ragged the fabric of friendship: Thinking of objects as alive makes people less willing to replace them. Journal of Consumer Psychology, 138-145.

[60] Aggarwal, P., & McGill, A. L. (2012). When Brands Seem Human, Do Humans Act Like Brands? Automatic Behavioral Priming. Journal of Consumer Research, 307-323.

[61] Cova, B., & Cova, V. (2001). Tribal Marketing: The tribilisation of society and its impact on the conduct of marketing. European Journal of Marketing | Special Issue: Societal Marketing in 2002 and Beyond.

[62] Kleine III, R. K. (1993). Mundane consumption and the self: A social identity perspective. Journal of Consumer Psychology, 209-235.

[63] Dittmar, H. (1994). Material Posessions as Stereotypes: Material images of different socio-economic groups. Journal of Economic Psychology, 561-585.

[64] Dittmar, H. (1994). To have is to be: Materialism and person perception in working-class and middle-class British adolescents. Journal of Economic Psychology, 233-251.

[65] Puzakova, M., Kwak, H., & Rocereto, J. F. (2013). When Humanizing Brands Goes Wrong: The Detrimental Effect of Brand Anthropomorphization amid Product Wrongdoings. Journal of Marketing.

[66] Szafarz, A. (2007). Hiring People like Yourself. A Representation of Discrimination on the Job Market. Economic Perspectives on Employment & Labor Law eJournal.

[67] Paris, W. (2017, July 4). Why We Want Who We Want. Psychology Today, pp. https://www.psychologytoday.com/us/articles/201707/why-we-want-who-we-want .

[68] Bahns, A. J., Crandall, C. S., Gillath, O., & Preacher, K. J. (2017). Similarity in relationships as niche construction: Choice, stability, and influence within dyads in a free choice environment. Journal of Personality and Social Psychology, 329-355.

[69] Aggarwal, P., & McGill, A. L. (2012). When Brands Seem Human, Do Humans Act Like Brands? Automatic Behavioral Priming. Journal of Consumer Research, 307-323.

[70] Mullainathan, S., Schwartzstein, J., & Shleifer, A. (2006). Coarse Thinking and Persuasion. Cambridge, MA: NBER Working Paper Series | Working Paper 12720.

[71] McRobbie, L. R. (2015, October 29). On the Science of Creepiness. Retrieved from Smithsonian Magazine: https://www.smithsonianmag.com/science-nature/science-creepiness-180957093/

[72] Pham, M. T., Hung, I. W., & Gorn, G. J. (2011). Relaxation Increases Monetary Valuations. Advances in Consumer Research, 38. Retrieved from https://www.acrwebsite.org/volumes/15838/volumes/v38/NA-38

[73] Delgado-Ballester, E., Palazón, M., & Peláez, J. (2020). Anthropomorphized vs objectified brands: which brand version is more loved? European Journal of Management and Business Economics, 150-165.

[74] Waytz, A., Cacioppo, J., & Epley, N. (2014). Who Sees Human? The Stability and Importance of Individual Differences in Anthropomorphism. Perspectives on Psychological Science, 219-232.

[75] Puzakova, M., Kwak, H., & Rocereto, J. F. (2013). When Humanizing Brands Goes Wrong: The Detrimental Effect of Brand Anthropomorphization amid Product Wrongdoings. Journal of Marketing.

[76] Chandler, J., & Schwarz, N. (2010). Use does not wear ragged the fabric of friendship: Thinking of objects as alive makes people less willing to replace them. Journal of Consumer Psychology, 138-145.

[77] Chandler, J., & Schwarz, N. (2010). Use does not wear ragged the fabric of friendship: Thinking of objects as alive makes people less willing to replace them. Journal of Consumer Psychology, 138-145.

[78] Delgado-Ballester, E., Palazón, M., & Peláez, J. (2020). Anthropomorphized vs objectified brands: which brand version is more loved? European Journal of Management and Business Economics, 150-165.

[79] Kahneman, D. (2011). Thinking, Fast and Slow. New York: Farrar, Straus and Giroux.

[80] Damasio, A. (1994). Descartes' Error. London: Penguin.

[81] Santos, J. P., Moutinho, L., Seixas, D., & Brandao, S. (2012). Neural Correlates of the Emotional and Symbolic Content of Brands: A Neuroimaging Study. Journal of Customer Behaviour, 11(1), 69-93.

[82] Esch, F.-R., Moll, T., Schmitt, B., Elger, C. E., Neuhaus, C., & Weber, B. (2012). Brands on the brain: Do consumers use declarative information or experienced emotions to evaluate brands? Brand Insights from Psychological and Neurophysiological Perspectives, 75-85.

[83] Zajonc, R. B. (1968, June). Attitudinal Effects of Mere Exposure. Journal of Personality and Social Psychology, 9(2 Part 2).

[84] Kahneman, D. (2011). Thinking, Fast and Slow. New York: Farrar, Straus and Giroux.

[85] Ruvio, A., Bagozzi, R. P., Hult, G. T. M., & Spreng, R. (2020). Consumer arrogance and word-of-mouth. *Journal of the Academy of Marketing Science*, 48(6), 1116–1137. https://doi-org.proxy2.cl.msu.edu/10.1007/s11747-020-00725-3

[86] Kahneman, D. (2011). Thinking, Fast and Slow. New York: Farrar, Straus and Giroux.

[87] Pham, M. T., Hung, I. W., & Gorn, G. J. (2011). Relaxation Increases Monetary Valuations. Advances in Consumer Research, 38. Retrieved from https://www.acrwebsite.org/volumes/15838/volumes/v38/NA-38

[88] Cone. (2014, May 28). Perceptions, Millennials and CSR: How to Engage the New Leaders of Tomorrow. Retrieved from Cone: https://www.conecomm.com/insights-blog/csr-and-millennials

[89] MoralFoundations.org. (2019, October). Home. Retrieved from MoralFoundations.org: https://moralfoundations.org/

[90] Haidt, J. (2011, October 20). The Moral Foundations of Occupy Wall Street. Retrieved from Reason: https://reason.com/2011/10/20/the-moral-foundations-of-occup/

[91] Nguyen, T. (2019, September 5). Uber wants to redeem itself. Does the public even care? Retrieved from Vox | The Goods:

https://www.vox.com/the-goods/2019/9/5/20849632/uber-public-relations-crisis-qanda

[92] Uber. (n.d.). Community | Fostering diversity and inclusion. Retrieved October 23, 2020, from Uber: https://www.uber.com/us/en/community/diversity-and-inclusion/

[93] Chick-fil-A Foundation. (2019, November 18). Chick-fil-A Foundation. Retrieved from Chick-fil-A | News: https://thechickenwire.chick-fil-a.com/news/chick-fil-a-foundation-announces-2020-priorities

[94] Bullmore, J. (2013). Why it's Time to Say Goodbye to IKTHTMISOAIW*. Retrieved from WPP 2013 Annual Report: https://reports.wpp.com/annualreports/2013/what-we-think/why-its-time-to-say-goodbye-to-ikthtmisoaiw/

[95] Wallaert, M. (2019). *Start at the End.* Portfolio/Penguin.

[96] Norwood, F. B., & Lusk, J. L. (2007). The Dual Nature of Choice: When Consumers Prefer Less to More. Conference Paper/Presentation Southern Agricultural Economics Association 2007 Annual Meeting, February 4-7, 2007, Mobile, Alabama.

[97] Lefcourt, H. M. (1973). The function of the illusions of control and freedom. American Psychologist, 417-425.

[98] Langer, E. J., & Rodin, J. (1976). The Effects of Choice and Enhanced Personal Responsibility for the Aged: A Field Experiment in an Institutional Setting. Journal of Personality and Social Psychology, 191-198.

[99] Dember, W. N., Galinsky, T. L., & Warm, J. S. (1992). The role of choice in vigilance performance. Bulletin of the Psychonomic Society, 201-204.

[100] Iyengar, S. S., & Lepper, M. R. (2000). When Choice is Demotivating: Can One Desire Too Much of a Good Thing. Journal of Personality and Social Psychology, 995-1006.

[101] Schwartz, B. (2004, April). The Tyranny of Choice. Scientific American, pp. 70-75.

[102] Cordova, D. I., & Lepper, M. R. (1996). Intrinsic Motivation and the Process of Learning: Beneficial Effects of Contextualization, Personalization, and Choice. Journal of Educational Psychology, 715-730.

[103] Langer, E. J., & Rodin, J. (1976). The Effects of Choice and Enhanced Personal Responsibility for the Aged: A Field Experiment in an Institutional Setting. Journal of Personality and Social Psychology, 191-198.

[104] Briesch, R. A., Chintagunta, P. K., & Fox, E. J. (2009). How Does Assortment Affect Grocery Store Choice? Journal of Marketing Research, 176-189.

[105] Iyengar, S. S., & Lepper, M. R. (2000). When Choice is Demotivating: Can One Desire Too Much of a Good Thing. Journal of Personality and Social Psychology, 995-1006.

[106] Iyengar, S. S., & Lepper, M. R. (2000). When Choice is Demotivating: Can One Desire Too Much of a Good Thing. Journal of Personality and Social Psychology, 995-1006.

[107] Boatwright, P., & Nunes, J. C. (2001). Reducing Assortment: An Attribute-Based Approach. Journal of Marketing, 50-63.

[108] Schwartz, B. (2016). The Paradox of Choice. Manhattan: EccoPress.

[109] Schwartz, B. (2000). Self-Determination The Tyranny of Freedom. American Psychologist, 79-88.

[110] Iyengar, S. S., Jiang, W., & Huberman, G. (2003). How Much Choice is Too Much?: Contributions to 401(k) Retirement Plans. Philadelphia, PA: Pension Research Council Working Paper | Pension Research Council | The Wharton School, University of Pennsylvania.

[111] Iyengar, S. S., & Lepper, M. R. (2000). When Choice is Demotivating: Can One Desire Too Much of a Good Thing. Journal of Personality and Social Psychology, 995-1006.

[112] Iyengar, S. S., & Lepper, M. R. (2000). When Choice is Demotivating: Can One Desire Too Much of a Good Thing. Journal of Personality and Social Psychology, 995-1006.

[113] Snapper, K. J., & Peterson, C. R. (1971). Information Seeking and Data Diagnosticity. Journal of Experimental Psychology, 429-433.

[114] Iyengar, S. S., & Lepper, M. R. (2000). When Choice is Demotivating: Can One Desire Too Much of a Good Thing. Journal of Personality and Social Psychology, 995-1006.

[115] Loewenstein, G. (2000). Is More Choice Always Better? Retrieved November 11, 2020, from Carnegie Mellon University: http://www.contrib.andrew.cmu.edu/~gl20/GeorgeLoewenstein/Papers_files/pdf/too_much_choice.pdf

[116] Batley, R. P., & Daly, A. J. (2006). On the equivalence between elimination-byaspects and generalised extreme value models of choice behaviour. Journal of Mathematical Psychology, 456-467.

[117] Carmon, Z., Wertenbroch, K., & Zeelenberg, M. (2003). Option Attachment: When Deliberating Makes Choosing Feel like Losing. Journal of Consumer Research, 15-29.

[118] Schwartz, B. (2004, April). The Tyranny of Choice. Scientific American, pp. 70-75.

[119] Dar-Nimrod, I., Rawn, C. D., Lehman, D. R., & Schwartz, B. (2009). The Maximization Paradox: The costs of seeking alternatives. Personality and Individual Differences, 631-635.

[120] Botti, S., & Iyengar, S. S. (2004). The Psychological Pleasure and Pain of Choosing: When People Prefer Choosing at the Cost of Subsequent Outcome Satisfaction. Journal of Personality and Social Psychology, 312-326.

[121] Huber, J., Payne, J., & Puto, C. (1982). Adding Asymmetrically Dominated Alternatives: Violations of Regularity and the Similarity Hypothesis. Journal of Consumer Research.
Iyengar, S. S., & Lepper, M. R. (2000). When Choice is Demotivating: Can One Desire Too Much of a Good Thing. Journal of Personality and Social Psychology, 995-1006.

[122] Huber, J., Payne, J., & Puto, C. (1982). Adding Asymmetrically Dominated Alternatives: Violations of Regularity and the Similarity Hypothesis. Journal of Consumer Research.
Iyengar, S. S., & Lepper, M. R. (2000). When Choice is Demotivating: Can One Desire Too Much of a Good Thing. Journal of Personality and Social Psychology, 995-1006.

[123] Ariely, D. (2008). Are we in control of our own decisions? Retrieved April 21, 2022, from

https://www.ted.com/talks/dan_ariely_are_we_in_control_of_our_own_decisions/transcript

[124] Tversky, A., & Kahneman, D. (1992). Advances in Prospect Theory: Cumulative Representation of Uncertainty. Journal of Risk and Uncertainty, 297-323.

[125] Tversky, A., & Kahneman, D. (1981). The Framing of Decisions and the Psychology of Choice. Science, 453-458.

[126] Tversky, A., & Kahneman, D. (1981). The Framing of Decisions and the Psychology of Choice. Science, 453-458.

[127] De Martino, B., Kumaran, D., Seymour, B., & Dolan, R. J. (2006). Frames, Biases, and Rational Decision-Making in the Human Brain. Science, 684-687.

[128] Gonzalez, C., Dana, J., Koshino, H., & Just, M. (2005). The framing effect and risky decisions: Examining cognitive functions with fMRI. Journal of Economic Psychology, 1-20.

[129] Camerer, C., Babcock, L., Loewenstein, G., & Thaler, R. (1997, May 1). Labor Supply of New York City Cabdrivers: One Day at a Time. The Quarterly Journal of Economics, 112(2), 407-441.

[130] Levin, I. P. (1987). Associative effects of information framing. Bulletin of the Psychonomic Society, 85-86.

[131] Levin, I. P., & Gaeth, G. J. (1988). How Consumers Are Affected by the Framing of Attribute Information Before and After Consuming the Product. Journal of Consumer Research, 374-378.

[132] Levin, I. P., Johnson, R. D., Deldin, P. J., Carstens, L. M., Cressey, J. J., & Davis, C. R. (1986). Framing effects in decisions with completely and incompletely described alternatives. Organizational Behavior and Human Decision Processes, 46-64.

[133] CRM, M., & JD, N. (2003). What a speaker's choice of frame reveals: reference points, frame selection,. Psychonomic Bulletin & Review, 596-602.

[134] Fischer, G. W., Carmon, Z., Ariely, D., & Zauberman, G. (1999). Goal-based construction of preferences: task goals and the prominence effect. Management Science, 1057-1075.

[135] Gonzalez, C., Dana, J., Koshino, H., & Just, M. (2005). The framing effect and risky decisions: Examining cognitive functions with fMRI. Journal of Economic Psychology, 1-20.

[136] Hoch, S. J., & Ha, Y.-W. (1986). Consumer Learning: Advertising and the Ambiguity of Product Experience. Journal of Consumer Research, 221-233.

[137] Arlich, D., Guttman, I., Schonbach, P., & Mills, J. (1957). Postdecision Exposure to Relevant Information. *Journal of Abnormal and Social Psychology*, 98-102.

[138] Levin, I. P., & Gaeth, G. J. (1988). How Consumers Are Affected by the Framing of Attribute Information Before and After Consuming the Product. Journal of Consumer Research, 374-378.

[139] Hoch, S. J., & Ha, Y.-W. (1986). Consumer Learning: Advertising and the Ambiguity of Product Experience. Journal of Consumer Research, 221-233.

[140] Hoch, S. J., & Ha, Y.-W. (1986). Consumer Learning: Advertising and the Ambiguity of Product Experience. Journal of Consumer Research, 221-233.

[141] Levin, I. P., Wall, L. L., Dolezal, J. M., & Norman, K. L. (1973). Differential weighting of positive and negative traits in impression formation as a function of prior exposure. Journal of Experimental Psychology, 114-115.

[142] Levin, I. P., & Gaeth, G. J. (1988). How Consumers Are Affected by the Framing of Attribute Information Before and After Consuming the Product. Journal of Consumer Research, 374-378.

[143] Lindenberg, S. (2016). Social rationality, semi-modularity and goal-framing: What is it all about? Analyse & Kritik, 670-687.

[144] Lindenberg, S., & Steg, L. (2013). Goal-framing Theory and Norm-Guided Environmental Behavior. In H. C. van Trijp, Encouraging Sustainable Behavior: Psychology and the Environment (pp. 37-54). New York: Psychology Press.

[145] Bargh, J. A., Gollwitzer, P. M., Lee-Chai, A., Barndollar, K., & Trötschel, R. (2001). The automated will: Nonconscious activation and

pursuit of behavioral goals. ournal of Personality and Social Psychology, 1014-1027.
[146] Shah, J. Y., & Kruglanski, A. W. (2001). Priming against your will: How accessible alternatives affect goal pursuit. Journal of Experimental Social Psychology, 368-383.
Shapiro, S. M., & Heckler, S. E. (1997). The Effects of Incidental Ad Exposure on the Formation of Consideration Sets. Journal of Consumer Research, 94-104.
[147] Lindenberg, S. (2016). Social rationality, semi-modularity and goal-framing: What is it all about? Analyse & Kritik, 670-687.
[148] Li, X. (2008). The Effects of Appetitive Stimuli on Out-of-Domain Consumption Impatience. Journal of Consumer Research, 649-656.
[149] Lindenberg, S. (2016). Social rationality, semi-modularity and goal-framing: What is it all about? Analyse & Kritik, 670-687.
[150] Liberman, V., Samuels, S. M., & Ross, L. (2004). The Name of the Game: Predictive Power of Reputations Versus Situational Labels in Determining Prisoner's Dilemma Game Moves. Personality and Social Psychology Bulletin, 1175-1185.
[151] Lindenberg, S. (2016). Social rationality, semi-modularity and goal-framing: What is it all about? Analyse & Kritik, 670-687.
[152] Ariely, D. (2010). The Cost of Social Norms. In D. Ariely, Predictably Irrational (pp. 75-102). New York: Harper Collins.
[153] Keizer, K., Lindenberg, S., & Steg, L. (2008). The Spreading of Disorder. Science, 1681-1685.
[154] Kim, W. C., & Mauborgne, R. (2015). Blue Ocean Strategy, Expanded Edition: How to Create Uncontested Market Space and Make the Competition Irrelevant. Boston: Harvard Business Review Press.
[155] Austen, I. (2017, August 11). Canada Letter: Ice Cream Revival and Cross-Border Trade Anxiety. Retrieved from The New York Times: https://www.nytimes.com/2017/08/11/world/canada/canada-letter-ice-cream-revival-and-cross-border-trade-anxiety.html
[156] Dickson, P. R., & Sawyer, A. G. (1990, July 1). The Price Knowledge and Search of Supermarket Shoppers. Journal of Marketing, 54(3), 42-53.

[157] Vanhuele, M., & Drèze, X. (2002). Measuring the Price Knowledge Shoppers Bring to the Store. Journal of Marketing, 66(4), 72-85.
[158] Tversky, A. K. (1974). Judgment under Uncertainty: Heuristics and Biases. Science, 1124-1131.
[159] Tversky, A. K. (1974). Judgment under Uncertainty: Heuristics and Biases. Science, 1124-1131.
[160] Sherif, M., & Taub, D. (1958). Assimilation and Contrast Effects of Anchoring Stimuli on Judgments. Journal of Experimental Psychology, 150-155.
[161] Kahneman, D., & Tversky, A. (2004). Prospect Theory: An Analysis of Decision Under Risk. In A. Tversky, Preference, Belief, and Similarity (pp. 549-581). Cambridge, Massachusetts; London, England: The MIT Press.
[162] Madrian, B. C., & Shea, D. F. (2000). THE POWER OF SUGGESTION: INERTIA IN 401(K) PARTICIPATION AND SAVINGS BEHAVIOR. National Bureau of Economic Research Working Paper Series, Working Paper 7682.
[163] Johnson, E. J., & Goldstein, D. (2003). Do Defaults Save Lives? Science, 1338-1339.
[164] Brown, J. R., Farrell, A. M., & Weisbenner, S. J. (2015). DECISION-MAKING APPROACHES AND THE PROPENSITY TO DEFAULT: EVIDENCE AND IMPLICATIONS. National Bureau of Economic Research Workding Paper Series, Working Paper 20949.
[165] Bargh, J. A., Chen, M., & Burrows, L. (1996). Automaticity of Social Behavior: Direct Effects of Trait Construct and Stereotype Activation on Action. Journal of Personality and Social Psychology, 230-244.
[166] Williams, L. E., & Bargh, J. A. (2008). Experiencing Physical Warmth Promotes Interpersonal Warmth. Science, 606-607. Retrieved from https://www.ncbi.nlm.nih.gov/pmc/articles/PMC2737341/?mod=article_inline
[167] Kliger, D., & Gilad, D. (2012). Red Light, Green Light: Color Priming in Financial Decisions. Journal of Socio-Economics, 738-745.

[168] Mussweiler, T., Rüter, K., & Epstude, K. (2004). The ups and downs of social comparison: mechanisms of assimilation and contrast. Journal of Personality and Social Psychology, 832-844.

[169] Bless, H., & Burger, A. M. (2016). Assimilation and contrast in social priming. Current Opinion in Psychology, 26-31.

[170] Schwarz, N., & Bless, H. (2007). Mental Construal Processes: The Inclusion/Exclusion Model. In D. Stapel, & J. Suls, Assimilation and Contrast in Social Psychology (pp. 119-141). Philadelphia, PA: Psychology Press.

[171] Bless, H., & Burger, A. M. (2016). Assimilation and contrast in social priming. Current Opinion in Psychology, 26-31.

[172] Priester, J. R., Dholakia, U. M., & Fleming, M. A. (2004). When and Why the Background Contrast Effect Emerges: Thought Engenders Meaning by Influencing the Perception of Applicability. The Journal of Consumer Research, 491-501.

[173] Tversky, A., & Shafir, E. (1992). Choice under Conflict: The Dynamics of Deferred Decision. Psychological Science, 358-361.

[174] Brown, J. R., Farrell, A. M., & Weisbenner, S. J. (2015). DECISION-MAKING APPROACHES AND THE PROPENSITY TO DEFAULT: EVIDENCE AND IMPLICATIONS. National Bureau of Economic Research Workding Paper Series, Working Paper 20949.

[175] Loewenstein, G. (2000). Is More Choice Always Better? Retrieved November 11, 2020, from Carnegie Mellon University: http://www.contrib.andrew.cmu.edu/~gl20/GeorgeLoewenstein/Papers_files/pdf/too_much_choice.pdf

[176] Dellaert, B. G., & Stremersch, S. (2005). Marketing Mass-Customized Products: Striking a Balance Between Utility and Complexity. Journal of Marketing Research, 219-227.

[177] Tversky, A., & Kahneman, D. (1981). The Framing of Decisions and the Psychology of Choice. Science, 453-458.

[178] Shapiro, S. M., & Heckler, S. E. (1997). The Effects of Incidental Ad Exposure on the Formation of Consideration Sets. Journal of Consumer Research, 94-104.

[179] Bhattacharya, J., Bundorf, K., Pace, N., & Sood, N. (2009). Does Health Insurance Make You Fat. Cambridge, MA: NBER Working Paper Series.

[180] Van Gelder, J.-L., Hershfield, H. E., & Nordgren, L. F. (2013). Vividness of the Future Self Predicts. Psychological Science, 974-980.

[181] Lee, C. (2015, April 9). The stranger within: Connecting with our future selves. Retrieved from UCLA Newsroom: https://newsroom.ucla.edu/stories/the-stranger-within-connecting-with-our-future-selves

[182] Woolley, K., & Fishbach, A. (2016). For the Fun of It: Harnessing Immediate Rewards to Increase Persistence in Long-Term Goals. Journal of Consumer Research, 952-966.

[183] Woolley, K., & Fishbach, A. (2017). Immediate Rewards Predict Adherence to Long-Term Goals. Personality and Social Psychology Bulletin, 151-162.

[184] Hershfield, H. E., Goldstein, D. G., Sharpe, W. F., Fox, J., Yeykelis, L., Carstensen, L. L., & & Bailenson, J. N. (2011). Increasing Saving Behavior Through Age-Progressed Renderings of the Future Self. Journal of Marketing Research, S23-S37. Retrieved from INCREASING SAVING BEHAVIOR THROUGH AGE-PROGRESSED RENDERINGS OF THE FUTURE SELF.

[185] Hershfield, H. E. (2011). Future self-continuity: how conceptions of the future self transform intertemporal choice. Annals of the New York Academy of Sciences, 30-43.

[186] Goldsmith, K., Cho, E. K., & Dhar, R. (2012). When Guilt Begets Pleasure: The Positive Effect of a Negative Emotion. Journal of Marketing Research, 872-881.

[187] eMarketer. (2017, April 5). Personalized Ads? Consumers Tell Marketers to Up Their Game. Retrieved from eMarketer.com: https://www.emarketer.com/Article/Personalized-Ads-Consumers-Tell-Marketers-Up-Their-Game/1015572

[188] Bertrand, M., Karlan, D. S., Mullainathan, S., Shafir, E., & Zinman, J. (2010). What's advertising content worth? Evidence from a consumer

credit marketing field experiment. The Quarterly Journal of Economics, 263-306.

[189] Stagner, R. (1958, September). The Gullibility of Personnel Managers. Personnel Psychology, 11(3), 347-352.

[190] Stagner, R. (1958, September). The Gullibility of Personnel Managers. Personnel Psychology, 11(3), 347-352.

[191] Forer, B. R. (1949, January). The fallacy of personal validation; a classroom demonstration of gullibility. Journal of Abnormal Psychology, 44(1), 118-123.

[192] Sundberg, N. D. (1955). The Acceptability of "Fake" Versus "Bona Fide" Personality Test Interpretations. The Journal of Abnormal and SOcial Psychology, 50(1), 145-147.

[193] Aarons, W. (2007, February 6). AN OPEN LETTER TO MR. JAMES THATCHER, BRAND MANAGER, PROCTER & GAMBLE. Retrieved from McSWEENEY'S: https://www.mcsweeneys.net/articles/an-open-letter-to-mr-james-thatcher-brand-manager-procter-amp-gamble

[194] Neff, J. (2009, September 07). WHAT TO DO WHEN SOCIAL MEDIA SPREADS MARKETING MYTH. Retrieved from AdAge: https://adage.com/article/digital/social-media-spreads-marketing-myth/138845

[195] Kahneman, D., & Tversky, A. (1973). On The Psychology of Prediction. Psychological Review, 237-251.

[196] Kahneman, D., & Tversky, A. (1972). Subjective probability: a Judgment of Representativeness. Cognitive Psychology, 430-454.

[197] Bar-Hillel, M. (1977). The Base-Rate Fallacy in Probability Judgments. Arlington, VA: Defense Advanced Research Projects Agency.

[198] Sundar, A., Kardes, F., & Noseworthy, T. (2017). Inferences on Negative Labels and the Horns Effect. Advances in Consumer Research Volume 42, 377-380.

[199] Hartung, C., Lefler, E., Tempel, A., Armendariz, M., Sigel, B., & Little, C. (2010). Halo Effects in Ratings of ADHD and ODD: Identification of Susceptible Symptoms. Journal of Psychopathology and Behavioral Assessment, 128-137.

[200] Jarden, A. (2010). An Interview with Daniel Kahneman | Princeton University. International Journal of Wellbeing, 186-188.
[201] Kahneman, D., & Deaton, A. (2010). High income improves evaluation of life but not emotional well-being. PNAS, 16489-16493.
[202] University of Pennsylvania | Penn Arts & Sciences. (n.d.). The PERMA Model: Your Scientific Theory of Happiness. Retrieved October 24, 2020, from University of Pennsylvania | Penn Arts & Sciences: https://ppc.sas.upenn.edu/learn-more/perma-theory-well-being-and-perma-workshops
[203] Kahneman, D., & Deaton, A. (2010). High income improves evaluation of life but not emotional well-being. PNAS, 16489-16493.
[204] Brickman, P., Coates, D., & Janoff-Bulman, R. (1978). Lottery winners and accident victims: is happiness relative? Journal of Personality and Social Psychology, 917-927.
[205] Frederick, S., & Loewenstein, G. (1999). Hedonic Adaptation. In D. Kahneman, Wellbeing: The Foundations of Hedonic Psychology (pp. 302-329). New York: Russel Sage Foundation.
[206] Livni, E. (2018, December 21). Quartz. Retrieved from A Nobel Prize-winning psychologist says most people don't really want to be happy: https://qz.com/1503207/a-nobel-prize-winning-psychologist-defines-happiness-versus-satisfaction/
[207] Kahneman, D., & Tversky, A. (1983). Choices, Values, and Frames. APA Award Addresses.
[208] Simon, H. A. (1955). A Behavioral Model of Rational Choice. Quarterly Journal of Economics, 99-118.
[209] Payne, J. W., Bettman, J. R., & Johnson, E. J. (1993). The Adaptive Decision Maker. Cambridge: Cambridge University Press.
[210] Kahneman, D., & Tversky, A. (2004). Prospect Theory: An Analysis of Decision Under Risk. In A. Tversky, & E. (. Shafir, Preference, Belief, and Similarity (pp. 549-581). Cambridge, Massachusetts: The MIT Press.
[211] Thaler, R. (1985). Mental Accounting and Consumer Choice. Marketing Science, 199-214.

[212] Güth, W., & Schmittberger, R. S. (1982). An Experimental Analysis of Ultimatum Bargaining. Journal of Economic Behavior and Organization, 367-388.
[213] Thaler, R. H. (1988). Anomalies: The ultimatum game. Journal of Economic Perspectives, 195-206.
[214] Camerer, C., & Thaler, R. H. (1995). Anomalies: Ultimatums, Dictators and Manners. Journal of Economic Perspectives, 209-219.
[215] Ibid.
[216] Thaler, R. H. (1988). Anomalies: The ultimatum game. Journal of Economic Perspectives, 195-206.
[217] Cone Communications. (2015, September 23). New Cone Communications Research Confirms Millennials as America's Most Ardent CSR Supporters. Cone Communications Press Release.
[218] Thaler, R. H. (1988). Anomalies: The ultimatum game. Journal of Economic Perspectives.
[219] Thaler, R. (1985). Mental Accounting and Consumer Choice. Marketing Science, 199-214.
[220] Kahneman, D., Knetsch, J. L., & Thaler, R. (1986). Fairness as a Constraint on Profit Seeking: Entitlements in the Market. The American Economic Review, 728-741.
[221] Kahneman, D., Knetsch, J. L., & Thaler, R. H. (1986). Fairness and the Assumptions of Economics. Journal of Business, S285-S300.
[222] Kahneman, D., Knetsch, J. L., & Thaler, R. (1986). Fairness as a Constraint on Profit Seeking: Entitlements in the Market. The American Economic Review, 728-741.
[223] Netflix. (2020, December 2). We're updating our prices — here's why. Los Gatos, CA, USA.
[224] Rabin, M. (1993). Incorporating Fairness Into Game Theory. American Economic Review, 1281-1302.
[225] Arrow, K. (1973). Social Responsibility and Economic Efficiency. Public Policy, 303-317.
[226] Cone Communications. (2015, September 23). New Cone Communications Research Confirms Millennials as America's Most Ardent CSR Supporters. Cone Communications Press Release.

[227] Kahneman, D., Knetsch, J. L., & Thaler, R. (1986). Fairness as a Constraint on Profit Seeking: Entitlements in the Market. The American Economic Review, 728-741.

[228] Stolier, R. M., & Freeman, J. B. (2017). A Neural Mechanism of Social Categorization. Journal of Neuroscience, https://www.jneurosci.org/content/37/23/5711.

[229] Bargh, J. A., Chen, M., & & Burrows, L. (1996). Automaticity of social behavior: Direct effects of trait construct and stereotype activation on action. Journal of Personality and Social Psychology, 230-244.

[230] Tajfel, H., & Turner, J. (2004). An integrative theory of intergroup conflict. In M. Schultz, & M. J. Hatch (Eds.), Organizational Identity | A Reader (pp. 33-47). Oxford: Oxford University Press.

[231] Duck, S., & McMahan, D. T. (2020). Identities, Perceptions, and Communication. In S. Duck, & D. T. McMahan, Communication in Everyday Life: A Survey of Communication (pp. 20-37). Los Angeles: SAGE Publications, Inc.

[232] Puzakova, M., Kwak, H., & Rocereto, J. F. (2009). Pushing the Envelope of Brand and Personality: Antecedents and Moderators of Anthropomorphized Brands. Advances in Consumer Research, 413-418.

[233] Dehdashti Shahrokh, Z., Kenari, J., & Bakhshizadeh, A. (2012). The impact of social identity of brand on brand loyalty development. Management Science Letters.

[234] Raimondo, M. A., Cardamone, E., Miceli, G. N., & Bagozzi, R. P. (2022). Consumers' identity signaling towards social groups: The effects of dissociative desire on brand prominence preferences. *Psychology & Marketing*, 39(10), 1964-1978.

[235] Shrum, L. J., Wong, N., Arif, F., Chugani, S. K., Gunz, A., Lowrey, T. M., Nairn, A., Pandelaere, M., Ross, S. M., Ruvio, A., Scott, K., & Sundie, J. (2013). Reconceptualizing materialism as identity goal pursuits: Functions, processes, and consequences. Journal of Business Research, 66(8), 1179–1185. https://doi-org.proxy2.cl.msu.edu/10.1016/j.jbusres.2012.08.010

[236] Brewer, M. B. (2011). Optimal distinctiveness theory: Its history and development. *Handbook of theories of social psychology*, 2, 81-98.

[237] Mangus, S. M., & Ruvio, A. (2019). Do opposites attract? Assimilation and differentiation as relationship-building strategies. *Journal of Personal Selling & Sales Management, 39*(1), 60–80. https://doi-org.proxy2.cl.msu.edu/10.1080/08853134.2018.1471696

[238] Gretz, R. T., & Basuroy, S. (2013). Why quality may not always win: The impact of product generation life cycles on quality and network effects in high-tech markets. *Journal of Retailing, 89*(3), 281-300.

[239] Foxall, G. R., Oliveira-Castro, J. M., James, V. K., & Schrezenmaier, T. C. (2007). Brand Choice in Behavioral Perpective. In G. R. Foxall, J. M. Oliveira-Castro, V. K. James, & T. C. Schrezenmaier, The Behavioral Economics of Brand Choice (pp. 1-24). New York: Palgrave Macmillan.

[240] Ehrenberg, A. S. (2000). Repetitive Advertising and the Consumer. Journal of Advertising Research, Published Online.

[241] Ehrenberg, A. S., Uncles, M. D., & Goodhardt, G. G. (2004). Understanding Brand Performance Measures: Using Dirichlet Benchmarks. Journal of Business Research, 1307-1325.

[242] Ehrenberg, A. S., Goodhardt, G. J., & Barwise, P. (1990). Double Jeopardy Revisited. Journal of Marketing, 82-91.

[243] Binet, L., & Field, P. (2007). Marketing in the Era of Accountability: Identifying the Marketing Practices and Metrics that Truly Increase Profitability. World Advertising Research Center Ltd.

[244] Sharp, B. (2010). How Brands Grow. Oxford: Oxford University Press.

[245] Lucas, A. (2019, March 29). When customers do the math on Starbucks' new rewards program, they may not like what they see, Bernstein says. Retrieved from CNBC: https://www.cnbc.com/2019/03/29/starbucks-rewards-program-changes-could-alienate-customers-bernstein.html

[246] Binet, L., & Field, P. (2007). Marketing in the Era of Accountability: Identifying the Marketing Practices and Metrics that Truly Increase Profitability. World Advertising Research Center Ltd.

[247] Binet, L., & Field, P. (2007). Marketing in the Era of Accountability: Identifying the Marketing Practices and Metrics that Truly Increase Profitability. World Advertising Research Center Ltd.

248 Field, P. (2016, July 26). Selling Creativity Short | Creativity and Effectiveness Under Threat. London: IPA In Association WIth ThinkBox. Retrieved from https://www.youtube.com/watch?v=ivrmhpsyNvM

249 Kahneman, D., Knetsch, J. L., & Thealer, R. H. (1991). Anomalies: The Endowment Effect, Loss Aversion, and Status Quo Bias. American Economic Association, 193-206. Retrieved from https://www.jstor.org/stable/1942711

250 Rogoway, M. (2020, August 5). Oregon leaders squandered years on jobless benefits computer upgrade. Now the project's future is again in doubt. Retrieved from Oregon Live | The Oregonian: https://www.oregonlive.com/news/2020/08/oregon-leaders-squandered-years-on-jobless-benefits-computer-upgrade-now-the-projects-future-is-again-in-doubt.html

251 Knetsch, J. L., & Sinden, J. A. (1984). Willingness to Pay and Compensation Demanded: Experimental Evidence of an Unexpected Disparity in Measures of Value. The Quarterly Journal of Economics, 507-521.

252 Kahneman, D., Knetsch, J. L., & Thaler, R. (1990). Experimental Tests of the Endowment Effect and the Coase Theorem. Journal of Political Economy, 1325-1348.

253 Kahneman, D., Knetsch, J. L., & Thealer, R. H. (1991). Anomalies: The Endowment Effect, Loss Aversion, and Status Quo Bias. American Economic Association, 193-206. Retrieved from https://www.jstor.org/stable/1942711

254 Ariely, D. (2009). Predictably Irrational Revised and Expanded Edition. New York: Harper Collins.

255 Kleinman, Z. (2020, January 22). Sonos speaker update sparks anger. Retrieved from BBC News: https://www.bbc.com/news/technology-51206604

256 Fletcher, G. J., Simpson, J. A., & Thomas, G. (2000). Ideals, Perceptions, and Evaluations in Early Relationship Development. *Journal of Personality and Social Psychology, 79*(6), 933.

257 Ziegarnik, B. (1927). On finished tasks and unfinished tasks. Pschologische Forschung.

[258] Strotz, R. H. (1955-1956). Myopia and Inconsistency in Dynamic Utility Maximization. The Review of Economic Studies, 165-180.

[259] Lowenstein, G., & Prelec, D. (1992). Anomalies in intertemporal choice: Evidence and an interpretation. Quarterly Journal of Economics, 573-597.

[260] Caillaud, B., & Jullien, B. (2000). Modelling Time-Inconsistent Preferences. European Economic Review, 1116-1124.

[261] DellaVigna, S., & Malmendier, U. (2004). Contract Design and Self-Control: Theory and Evidence. The Quarterly Journal of Economics, 353-402.

[262] DellaVigna, S., & Malmendier, U. (2004). Contract Design and Self-Control: Theory and Evidence. The Quarterly Journal of Economics, 353-402.

[263] Nisbett, R. E., & Wilson, T. D. (1977, May). Telling More Than We Can Know: Verbal Reports on Mental Processes. Psychological Review, 84(3), 231-259.

[264] Nisbett, R. E., & Wilson, T. D. (1977, May). Telling More Than We Can Know: Verbal Reports on Mental Processes. Psychological Review, 84(3), 231-259.

[265] Eastwick, P. W., & Finkel, E. J. (2008). Sex Differences in Mate Preferences Revisited: Do People Know What They Initially Desire in a Romantic Partner? Journal of Personality and Social Psychology, 245-264.

[266] Joel, S., Eastwick, P. W., & Finkel, E. J. (2017). Is Romantic Desire Predictable? Machine Learning Applied to Initial Romantic Attraction. Psychological Science.

[267] Eastwick, P. W., Finkel, E. J., Luchies, L. B., & Hunt, L. L. (2014). The predictive validity of ideal partner preferences: A review and meta-analysis. Psychological Bulletin, 623-655.

[268] Eastwick, P. W., Finkel, E. J., & Eagly, A. H. (2011). When and why do ideal partner preferences affect the process of initiating and maintaining romantic relationships? Journal of Personality and Social Psychology, 1012-1032.

[269] Wilson, T. D., & Schooler, J. W. (1991). Thinking Too Much: Introspection Can Reduce the Quality of Preferences and Decisions. Journal of Personality and Social Psychology, 181-192.
[270] Wilson, T. D., & Schooler, J. W. (1991). Thinking Too Much: Introspection Can Reduce the Quality of Preferences and Decisions. Journal of Personality and Social Psychology, 181-192.
[271] Darley, J. M., & Batson, D. C. (1973). "From Jerusalem to Jericho": A Study of Situational and Dispositional Variables in Helping Behavior. *Journal of Personality and Social Psychology*, 191-214.

[272] Vigen, T. (2022, July 13). Divorce Rate in Maine. Retrieved from Spurious Correlations: https://tylervigen.com/view_correlation?id=1703
[273] Maccoun, R. (1993). Blaming Others to a Fault? Chance, 31-49.
[274] Seligman, M. E., Railton, P., & al., e. (2016). Homo Prospectus. Oxford: Oxford University Press.
[275] Clare, A., Thomas, S., & Motson, N. (2013, April 03). Monkeys vs Fund managers - An evaluation of alternative equity indices. Retrieved from Bayes Business School: https://www.bayes.city.ac.uk/faculties-and-research/research/bayes-knowledge/2013/april/monkeys-vs-fund-managers-an-evaluation-of-alternative-equity-indices
[276] Salganik, M. J., Dodds, P. S., & Watts, D. J. (2006). Experimental Study of Inequality and Unpredictability in an Artificial Cultural Market. Science, 854-856.
[277] Maier, M., & Rahman, R. A. (2018). Native Language Promotes Access to Visual Consciousness. *Psychological Science*, 1757-1772.
[278] Athanasopoulos, P., Dering, B., Wiggett, A., Kuipers, J.-R., & Thierry, G. (2010). Perceptual shift in bilingualism: Brain potentials reveal plasticity in pre-attentive colour perception. *Cognition*, 437-443.
[279] Hofstede, G. (2011). Dimensionalizing Cultures: The Hofstede Model in Context. Online Readings in Psychology and Culture.
[280] Kitayama, S., & Uskul, A. K. (2011). Culture, Mind, and the Brain: Current Evidence and Future Directions. Annual Review of Psychology, 419-449.

[281] Nielsen. (2018, July 10). The Database: Meeting Today's Multicultural Consumers. Retrieved from Nielsen: https://www.nielsen.com/us/en/insights/news/2018/the-database-meeting-todays-multicultural-consumers.html

[282] Davis, T. R., & Young, R. B. (2002). International Marketing Research: A Management Briefing. Business Horizons, 31-38.

[283] Maric, D. (2016, April 12). Consumers in Training: How Children in the Americas are Influencing the Purchasing Decisions of their Parents. Retrieved from LinkedIn: https://www.linkedin.com/pulse/consumers-training-how-children-americas-influencing-purchasing?articleId=8740076856070420445

[284] Pew Research Center. (2013, June 4). The Global Divide on Homosexuality. Retrieved from Pew Research Center: https://www.pewglobal.org/2013/06/04/the-global-divide-on-homosexuality/

[285] Anderson, K. (2009, March). Ethnographic Research: A Key to Strategy. Retrieved from Harvard Business Review: https://hbr.org/2009/03/ethnographic-research-a-key-to-strategy

[286] Duhigg, C. (2012, February 16). How Companies Learn Your Secrets. Retrieved from The New York Times Magazine: https://www.nytimes.com/2012/02/19/magazine/shopping-habits.html
Eastwick, P. W., & Finkel, E. J. (2008). Sex Differences in Mate Preferences Revisited: Do People Know What They Initially Desire in a Romantic Partner? Journal of Personality and Social Psychology, 245-264.

[287] Hofstede Insights. (n.d.). National Culture. Retrieved April 23, 2019, from Hofstede Insights: https://www.hofstede-insights.com/models/national-culture/

[288] Ahmed, M., Ullah, S., & Alam, A. (2014). Importance of Culture in Success of International Marketing. European Academic Research, 3802-3816.

[289] Davis, T. R., & Young, R. B. (2002). International Marketing Research: A Management Briefing. Business Horizons, 31-38.

[290] Geometry Global, Shopper Marketing, Path to Purchase Institute. (2015, July 22). Ethnic Marketing Research. Retrieved from Shopper

Marketing: https://shoppermarketingmag.com/ethnic-marketing-research-part-1-where-culture-meets-shoppers

[291] Mullen, B., Johnson, C., & Salas, E. (1991). Productivity loss in brainstroming groups: A meta-analytic integration. Basic and applied social psychology, 3-23.

[292] Mullen, B., Johnson, C., & Salas, E. (1991). Productivity loss in brainstroming groups: A meta-analytic integration. Basic and applied social psychology, 3-23.

[293] Linsey, J. S., Clauss, E. F., Kurtoglu, T., Murphy, J. T., & Wood, K. L. (2011). An Experimental Study of Group Idea Generation Techniques: Understanding the Roles of Idea Representation and Viewing Methods. *Journal of Mechanical Design*.

[294] Mullen, B., Johnson, C., & Salas, E. (1991). Productivity loss in brainstroming groups: A meta-analytic integration. Basic and applied social psychology, 3-23.

[295] Linsey, J. S., Clauss, E. F., Kurtoglu, T., Murphy, J. T., & Wood, K. L. (2011). An Experimental Study of Group Idea Generation Techniques: Understanding the Roles of Idea Representation and Viewing Methods. *Journal of Mechanical Design*.

[296] Coyne, K., Clifford, P. G., & Dye, R. (2007, December). *Breakthrough Thinking from Inside the Box*. Retrieved from Harvard Business Review: https://hbr.org/2007/12/breakthrough-thinking-from-inside-the-box

[297] Coyne, K., Clifford, P. G., & Dye, R. (2007, December). *Breakthrough Thinking from Inside the Box*. Retrieved from Harvard Business Review: https://hbr.org/2007/12/breakthrough-thinking-from-inside-the-box

[298] Berns, G. S.-S. (2005). Neurobiological correlates of social conformity and independence during mental rotation. *Biological Psychiatry*, 245-253.

[299] Nemeth, C. J., Personnaz, B., Personnaz, M., & Goncalo, J. A. (2004). The liberating role of conflict in group creativity: A study in two countries. *European Journal of Social Psychology*, 365-374.

[300] Baumann, C., Signman, H., Gershman, S. J., & von Helversen, B. (2020). A linear threshold model for optimal stopping behavior. Psychological and Cognitive Science, 117-140.

[301] Amazon Staff. (2011, April 17). 2016 Letter to Shareholders. Retrieved from Amazon: https://www.aboutamazon.com/news/company-news/2016-letter-to-shareholders

[302] Amazon. (2022, July 12). Leadership Principles. Retrieved from Amazon Jobs: https://www.amazon.jobs/en/principles

[303] Flory, J. A., Leibbrandt, A., & List, J. A. (2015). Do Competitive Workplaces Deter Female Workers? A Large-Scale Natural Field Experiment on Job Entry Decisions. The Review of Economic Studies, 122-155.

[304] Sijbom, R. B. (2018). Leaders' achievement goals predict employee burnout above and beyond employees' own achievement goals. Journal of Personality, 702-714.

[305] Roese, N. J., & Vohs, K. D. (2012). Hindsight Bias. Perspectives on Psychological Science, 7(5).

[306] Fischhoff, B., & Beyth, R. (1975). 'I knew it would happen': Remembered probabilities of once-future things. Organizational Behavior and Human Performance, 13, 1-16.

[307] Chelley-Steeley, P. L., Kluger, B. D., & Steeley, J. M. (2015, September). Earnings and hindsight bias: An experimental study. Economics Letters, 134, 130-132.

Chick-fil-A Foundation. (2019, November 18). Chick-fil-A Foundation. Retrieved from Chick-fil-A | News: https://thechickenwire.chick-fil-a.com/news/chick-fil-a-foundation-announces-2020-priorities

[308] Leary, M. R. (1981). The Distorted Nature of Hindsight. The Journal of Social Psychology, 25-29.

[309] Harley, E. M., Carlsen, K. A., & Loftus, G. (2004, October). The "Saw-It-All-Along" Effect: Demonstrations of Visual Hindsight Bias. Journal of Experimental Psychology: Learning, Memory, and Cognition.

[310] Bhattacharya, C. &. (2018). Degree of handedness: A unique individual differences factor for predicting and understanding hindsight bias. Personality and Individual Differences, 97-101.

[311] Busse, M. R., Pope, D. G., Pope, J. C., & Silva-Risso, J. (2015). The psychological effect of weather on car purchase. Quarterly Journal of Economics, 130, 371-414.

[312] Szczerba, R. J. (2015, January 5). 15 Worst Tech Predictions of All Time. Retrieved from Forbes: https://www.forbes.com/sites/robertszczerba/2015/01/05/15-worst-tech-predictions-of-all-time/#4e74256e1299

[313] Stillman, J. (2018, April 27). 12 Hilariously Wrong Tech Predictions. Retrieved from Inc.: https://www.inc.com/jessica-stillman/12-hilariously-wrong-tech-predictions.html

[314] Szczerba, R. J. (2015, January 5). 15 Worst Tech Predictions of All Time. Retrieved from Forbes: https://www.forbes.com/sites/robertszczerba/2015/01/05/15-worst-tech-predictions-of-all-time/#4e74256e1299

[315] Dhiraj, A. B. (2017, July 2). Some of the Absolute Worst Tech Predictions of All Time. Retrieved from CEOWorld Magazine: https://ceoworld.biz/2017/07/02/some-of-the-absolute-worst-tech-predictions-of-all-time/

[316] Sharot, T. (2011). The Optimism Bias: A Tour of the Irrationally Postiive Brain. New York: Pantheon.

[317] Sharot, T. (2011). The Optimism Bias: A Tour of the Irrationally Postiive Brain. New York: Pantheon.

[318] Sharot, T. (2011). The Optimism Bias: A Tour of the Irrationally Postiive Brain. New York: Pantheon.

[319] Shell. (n.d.). What are Shell Scenarios? Retrieved April 25, 2019, from Shell: https://www.shell.com/energy-and-innovation/the-energy-future/scenarios/what-are-scenarios.html

[320] Royal Dutch Shell plc. (2017, April 28). Shell Energy Scenarios Germany. Retrieved from Shell: https://www.shell.com/energy-and-innovation/the-energy-future/scenarios/what-are-scenarios/_jcr_content/par/tabbedcontent/tab/textimage_25172244.stream/1504104048141/87b2684f712f1da82ef32d07b19555920412d451/shell-energy-scenarios-germany.pdf

[321] UNAIDS. (2005, January). Aids in Africa: Three scenarios to 2025. Retrieved from UNAIDS: http://data.unaids.org/publications/irc-pub07/jc1058-aidsinafrica_en.pdf

[322] Accident, P. C. (1986). Report of the Presidential Commission on the Space Shuttle Challenger Accident. Washington, D.C. .

[323] Davis, M. (1991). Thinking Like an Engineer. Retrieved from Center for the Study of Ethics in the Professions at Illinois Institute of Technology: http://ethics.iit.edu/publication/md_te.html#:~:text=Mason%20asked%20him%20to%20think,%2Doff%2C%20killing%20all%20aboard.

[324] Accident, P. C. (1986). Report of the Presidential Commission on the Space Shuttle Challenger Accident. Washington, D.C. .

[325] Mazar, N., Amir, O., & Ariely, D. (2008). The Dishonesty of Honest People: A Theory of Self-Concept Maintenance. Journal of Marketing Research, 633-644.

[326] Lindenberg, S., & Foss, N. J. (2011). Managing Joint Production Motivation: The Role of Goal Framing and Governance Mechanisms. The Academy of Management Review, 500-525.

[327] Keizer, K., Lindenberg, S., & Steg, L. (2008). The Spreading of Disorder. Science, 1681-1685.

Kim, S. &. (2011). Gaming with Mr. Slot or gaming the slot machine? Power, anthropomorphism, and risk perception. Journal of Consumer Research, 94-107.

[328] Fehr, E., & Gächter, S. (2000). Cooperation and Punishment in Public Good Experiments. American Economic Review, 980-994.

[329] thredUP. (2017, April 11). Thredit. Retrieved from ThredUp: https://www.thredup.com/bg/p/how-to-clean-out-your-closet-wear-only-what-you-love

[330] Olivola, C. Y. (2018). The Interpersonal Sunk-Cost Effect. Pscyhological Science, 11072-11083.

OpenX and The Harris Poll. (2018). 2018 Consumer Holiday Shopping Report. Retrieved from OpenX.com: www.openx.com

[331] Atkinson, J. (1953). The achievement motive and recall of interrupted and completed tasks. Journal of Experimental Psychology, 381-390.

[332] Netflix Technology Blog. (2016, April 29). It's All A/Bout Testing: The Netflix Experimentation Platform. Retrieved from Medium | The Netflix Tech Blog: https://medium.com/netflix-techblog/its-all-a-bout-testing-the-netflix-experimentation-platform-4e1ca458c15

[333] Netflix Technology Blog. (2016, May 3). Selecting the best artwork for videos through A/B testing. Retrieved from Medium | The Netflix Technology Blog: https://medium.com/netflix-techblog/selecting-the-best-artwork-for-videos-through-a-b-testing-f6155c4595f6

[334] Kristal, A. S., & Santos, L. R. (2021). G.I. Joe Phenomena: Understanding the Limits of Metacognitive Awareness on Debiasing. Harvard Business School Working Paper.

[335] Ariely, D. (2008). Are we in control of our own decisions? Retrieved April 21, 2022, from https://www.ted.com/talks/dan_ariely_are_we_in_control_of_our_own_decisions/transcript

Acknowledgments

As I come to the end of my first book, I'm filled with gratitude for the many people who have helped me along the way. My life without any one of you would be immeasurably worse.

First, I would like to thank the people who made me love writing. Mom and Dad, who taught me to read, and who made me believe that Ramona, Socks, and Pickles the Fire Cat were as fascinating to them as they were to me. Mrs. Rowan, a born educator whose unbridled passion convinced hundreds of students to love literature. I can still see her jumping up and down, begging us to "answer the question," and I think often of the positive impact she's had on our world. Mr. Case never misses an opportunity to engage with students and, in the course of these casual conversations, he opened my eyes to so much. He introduced me to several concepts that directly influenced my studies, career, and this book, including the law of demand and The *High Fidelity* Question. And Mr. Lorenzen, who opened a world of thought by introducing me to philosophers from Homer and Nietzsche to The Clash that challenged my view of the world around me. He also introduced ideas that directly contributed to this work, including the questions of whether "goodness" is contextual and why he loved that Norwegian commercial so much. (I didn't get it then, I do now.)

Mentoring others is an act of true selflessness that requires time and sacrifice with no hope of repayment. I've been so lucky to have had some truly great mentors in the course of my career. I think often about how fortunate I've been that such kind and brilliant people have taken an interest in me ... and, also, about how difficult it must've been for these people to not laugh at my inexperience. I can only hope to pay forward the mentorship I've received from you.

Perhaps no one in the world is as generous with their time and knowledge as Loré Sampson, who has given me decades of support, education, perspective, and meals. I'll never be able to thank her enough for her selfless advocacy and encouragement. Rusty Neff's unique mix of humanity and wisdom has a way of lifting up everyone around him. He advocated for me tirelessly and I'll never stop working to become as good as he thinks I am. I also have deep gratitude for Paul Hauser, who was already an executive when I became his intern, but has never once let on that he has anyone more interesting or important to talk to than me. Thanks also to Chris and Susan Wallen, who took me in and gave me support and family when I was so young and so alone in a new place. I would also like to thank Rich Spreng and the faculty at Michigan State who first trained me, and then welcomed me into their ranks with such warmth. There's nothing quite as intimidating as working alongside people that were once your professors, and your kindness has *almost* convinced me that I belong in your midst.

Finally, my thanks to Sean, Kate, Amanda, and Rob, for always believing in me, beyond reason.

Index

5C analysis, 359

8 Mile, 20

A Beautiful Mind, 40
Abercrombie & Fitch, 94
Accenture, 109
Actor-Observer Bias, 313
Adaptation Effects, 215
Adobe, 143
Affiliation Motivation, 56
After-Action Review. *See* Postmortem Review
airlines, 35
Always, 206
Amazon, 21, 56
Amazon Web Services, 66
American Eagle, 63, 68
American Library Association, 44
amygdala, 159
Anchoring, 174
anecdotal fallacy, 65
Angelou, Maya, 85
Anthropologie, 153
anthropomorphism, 101
Anticipated Regret, 256
Apple, 72, 100, 267
Aristotle, 49
assimilation effect, 190
AT&T, 109
athlete sponsorship, 108
attribute framing, 161
authenticity, 122
Authenticity, 34
Availability bias, 23

Backlash, 206
bad press, 47
bad publicity, 118
Base Rate Neglect, 207
BBC, 90
behavior modification. *See* nudging, systematic
Bell, Kristen, 68
Bieber, Justin, 60
Big Data, 138
Black Keys, 51
bounded rationality, 15
Brainstorming, 334
brand equity, 33, 45, 121
brand experience, 125, 130
brand identity, 128
Brand Storytelling, 21
Brands as People. *See* Anthropomorphism
Breakfast at Tiffany's, 75
Buick, 109, 191
Burberry, 75
Burger King, 36

Case Studies: Are Not Evidence!, 309
Cash, Johnny, 49
causality, 310

cause marketing. *See* corporate social responsibility
Celebrities, 109
Chanel, 115
Chaucer, G., 122
Checker Motors, 192
Cheesecake Factory, 147
Chevrolet, 191
Chick-fil-A, 133
choice architecture, 145
choice overload, 146
choice, paradox of, 146, 148
Christie, Agatha, 48
Cinnamon Toast Crunch, 100
Clarity, 36
Clustering Illusion, 47
cognitive dissonance, 43
Columbia Sportswear, 109
confirmation bias, 74
Confirmation Bias, 42, 314
constraints, 336
Context, 292, 301
Context Effects, 188
contrast effects, 91
Coors, 88
corporate social responsibility, 131
Corvette, 242
cost-benefit analysis, 144
Count Chocula, 91
Coursera, 154
credibility, 120
CSR, 236
cult, 57
Culture, 316; impact on perception, 317; Multicultural Research, 318; Researching, 320
customer experience, 83, 112, 227
Customer Journey Research, 331
customer service, 117, 147

Damasio, Antonio, 76, 120
DDB, 192
Decoy Effect, 155
Default Effect, 181
Delayed Gratification, 275
Descartes, René, 73
DiGiorno, 173
Dirty Dancing, 270
disagree and commit, 344
Disney, 125, 180
Dittmar, Helga, 103
Diversity of Thought: preserving, 335
Dixon Ticonderoga, 82
Dove, 63, 68
Droga5, 21
Dunkin Donuts, 115

EA, 109
Elton John, 31
emotional engagement, 71
Emotional Engagement, 30
emotions, eliciting, 127
Endowment Effect, 254, 255, 373
Energizer, 53
enjoyment curve, 90
exaggerated emotional coherence. *See* Halo Effect
Expectations, 227, 232

Fairness, 227
familiarity, 122
Farmers Insurance, 47
Fitzgerald, F. Scott, 49
Folger's, 46
Forer Effect, 204
Founders, 109
framing, 173; changes, 223; gain, 167; hedonic, 166; normative, 167
Framing, 157, 362; Gain, 369; Goal, 367; Hedonic, 369; Normative, 369
Franken Berry, 91
Frankenstein, 188
Frankenstein, Dr., 119
Freschetta, 191
Freytag, Gustav, 49
Friends (TV), 46

Gage, Phineas, 76
Game of Thrones, 20
Geico, 147
General Mills, 91
Genie in a Bottle, 24
Gilt, 260
GMC, 53
Godiva, 20
Good Samaritan, 301
Goodby Silverstein & Partners, 27
Grant, Hugh, 74
green-washing, 35
Grey's Anatomy, 20
Group Dynamics, 337

halo effect, 212
Halo Effect, 22
happiness, 216
Harley-Davidson, 113
hedonic adaptation, 216
Hedonic Treadmill, 215
Heinz, 36
Hermès, 105
Hewlett-Packard, 55
High Fidelity, 60
Hindsight Bias, 314, 346
Hofstede Model, 327
Hollis, Rachel, 33, 56, 63
Holmes, Sherlock, 188
Hornby, Nick, 60
Horns Effect, 212
How I Met Your Mother, 46
Hughes, John, 168, 287
Hume, David, 137

identity, 25
Identity, 237, 240, 368; Researching, 307
Inaccurate Introspection, 291
influencers, 68, 110
ingroup, 113
ingroup bias, 56, 57, 59
innovation, 266, 267
Innovation, 338
Instagram, 92
Instant Gratification, 200, 277
Invincible, 20
iRobot, 99

Jenner, Kendall, 35

Jerry Maguire, 221
Jobs, Steve, 72
John Lewis, 31

Kahneman, Daniel, 22, 65, 120
Kentucky Fried Chicken, 47
Kodak, 87, 92
Kool-Aid, 100
Kroger, 147
Krug, Steve, 124

launching a brand, 146
Leno, Jay, 74
LinkedIn, 259
Lockheed Martin, 28
Loss Aversion, 211, 256, 258, 373
Louis Vuitton, 32
loyalty, 45
Loyalty Campaigns, 251
loyalty programs, 249
luxury marketing, 32, 33, 114, 218

Mad Men, 24, 92
magic ratio, 86
Matilda, 40
Maximization Paradox, 150
McDonald's, 34
memory, 43
Memory, 25, 30, 314
Mental Accounting, 278, 280
Mere Exposure, 252
micro-influencers, 110
Microsoft, 210
Monopoly, 91
Monster, 115

Moral Foundations Theory, 131
Mr. Clean, 107

Network Effects, 246
Nike, 31, 109, 130
Nintendo, 88
Nordstrom, 154, 261
Norwegian Cruise Lines, 27
nostalgia, 88
Nudging for Evil, 16
nudging, systematic, 142

Ogilvy, David, 38
Olay, 51
omnichannel, 128
Opportunity Cost, 340
Optimal Distinction, 242
Optimism Bias, 356
Orange Theory Fitness, 42
Oregon, 58
Oreo, 133
Outlander, 21

pallidum, 120
Parent Trap, 34
Pareto's principle, 248
partner brand, 106
peak-end, 64
Pepsi, 35, 93
personal narrative, 25
personalization, 93
Personalization, 202
Personas. *See* Profiling Customers
pharmaceuticals, 124
Pioneer Woman, 67

planning by committee, 36
Polaroid, 92
politics, 131, 132
Poshmark, 281
Positioning, 173, 269
postmortem review, 351
pressure mapping. *See* nudging, systematic
Pretty in Pink, 287
Pricing, 177, 179, 234, 269, 277; value-based, 179
Pride and Prejudice, 40
Priming, 184
Procter & Gamble, 41
Profiling Customers, 294; Personas, Design, 298; Personas, Marketing, 299; Personas, writing, 296
Projection Bias, 197, 354
promotional budget, 162
promotional messaging, 121
Proust, Marcel, 90
purchase decisions, 75

Randomness, 315
Rebag, 281
Red Team, 365
Red Thread, 39
reference point, 217, 227
Relevance, 32
representativeness heuristic, 208
reviews, 123
risk aversion, 193
Risk Avoidance, 257
rosy retrospection, 88

Saks Fifth Avenue, 104
sales, 122
Sales, 189
Samsung, 68
satisficing, 15
Schwartz, Barry, 149
Segmentation, 249, 306
Seinfeld, 64
Selective Search, 107
Self-Serving Bias, 312
SEO, 36
servant brand, 106
Shakespeare, 65
Shell, 361
Shopper marketing, 197
signalling, 106
Skype, 87
Smith, Adam, 137
Snickers, 47
social categorization, 56
Social Identity, 243
social identity theory, 57
social media, 115
somatic marker hypothesis, 72, 77, 120
songwriting, 50, 51
Sony, 233
Spears, Britney, 59
spokespeople, 108
Star Wars, 48
Starbucks, 248, 249, 280
status quo bias, 269
Status Quo Bias, 252
Storytelling, 19
Subscriptions, 273

Suggestion, Power of, 46
Sunk Cost Effect, 371
Super Bowl, 37, 92, 112
SWOT analysis, 360
System 1, 15, 123
System 2, 123

TAG Heuer, 110
Target, 218
Temporal Discounting, 273, 278
testimonials, 66
The Breakfast Club, 168
The Odyssey, 24
The Office, 251, 257
The West Wing, 224
ThirdLove, 63, 68
ThredUp, 372
Thriller, 91
Toy Story, 188
transparency, 122
Trunk Club, 153
Tversky, Amos, 120
Twilight, 44

U2, 51
Uber, 133
Uber Eats, 92

Ultimatum Game, 228
upgrades, incentivizing, 118
Urgency, 261
usability, 124
user experience, 145

Valley Girl, 112
vanity metrics, 34, 116
Ventromedial Prefrontal Cortex, 76
Vikings, 21
Volkswagen Beetle, 191
VSCO, 241

Walmart, 104
Warhol, Andy, 36
Washington Post, 38
Wayne's World, 92
Wild (book), 20
woke-washing, 35
Woods, Tiger, 109
word-of-mouth, 123

Zappos, 147
Zero-Sum Bias, 341
Ziegarnik Effect, 271, 373

www.ingramcontent.com/pod-product-compliance
Lightning Source LLC
Chambersburg PA
CBHW020530030426
42337CB00013B/790